D1549434

Contents

The illustrations are between pages 154 and 155

Preface

Writing does not come easily to me. Finding the right words to express my thoughts can sometimes be an arduous task, but by persevering, or more often just putting down my pencil, standing by the window and gazing at the Thames, the elusive words can be found.

Some people have said that I am a 'talented writer'. An 'aspiring writer' would be a description more acceptable to me.

Fortunately, I have been blessed with a good memory, which is a tremendous asset when writing about one's distant past: incidents, conversations, facial expressions and voice tone are vividly remembered today, even though they occurred half a century ago when, as a fourteen-year-old boy, I first held a bodkin in an East End clothing factory. Of course, it is impossible to quote verbatim the various conversations and arguments mentioned in this book, but I have attempted, to the best of my ability, to record the passages as accurately as I can.

Acknowledgments

I am deeply grateful to the kind friends and acquaintances named below who have never failed to offer me advice and assistance whenever I approached them. Without their valuable contributions it would have been extremely difficult for me to publish this book.

Christopher Lloyd, Tower Hamlets local history librarian; Malcolm Bar-Hamilton, archivist at Tower Hamlets local history library; Canon Tony Williamson, Gary Haines MA, East London historian; Roger Mills of Eastside Writers' Group, James Page-Roberts, Doreen Upchurch née Kemp, Clare Moore, the late much-loved Margaret Ahearn and, finally, my special thanks to Merlin Press for giving me this opportunity to publish my book.

Alfred Gardner
Isle of Dogs
September 2011

'It's the boy's first suit'

What the teenagers hunger for is a sense of dedication, and they have a way of reaching out for it, even in the most unlikely places, with the same gusto with which they will raid the icebox.
Max Lerner (The Unfinished Country)

Like many fourteen-year-old East End schoolboys during the late summer of 1955, I was becoming increasingly interested in girls. Having noticed that the boys who had pretty girls by their side were always smartly dressed, I imagined that if I stepped out of my old jeans, Sloppy Joes and sandals and wore a new suit, I too could have a girlfriend. But there were obstacles that had to be overcome before acquiring this suit.

I had no idea where I could find a suitable tailor and the cost involved. My parents were too poor to buy me new clothes, so I would be left with no alternative but to try and raise the money myself and, lastly and most importantly, decide what style would be appropriate for me. The neo-Edwardian look that was fashionable at the time did not appeal to me at all. I thought that the teddy boys who favoured this style looked ridiculous with their skinny drainpipe trousers, suede shoes and long jackets with velvet collars, and I argued fervently with a vain girl in my class. She had made the silly remark that a boy could not be 'much cop' if he did not have a DA (duck's arse) hairstyle. Eventually, after much thought, I made the decision that a made-to-measure, single-breasted, navy blue serge suit would be ideal for me.

My tall brother-in-law, Jim Attwell, also known as 'Longboat', having been told, probably by my mother, that I was determined to obtain a new suit for Christmas, offered to accompany me to Minamax, a well known Hackney tailoring firm which had a reputation for producing finely cut suits for men and boys, but he warned me that I would have to find a staggering £16.

As a resourceful young boy a year or two earlier I could always have earned a little cash by collecting and selling rags, newspapers and even firewood, but those days were in the past. Fortunately, my friend Camilleri, a Maltese boy who lived in Rampart Street close to my home in Jane Street, told me that the two partners of Standard Tailors, a small jacket factory located at the bottom of his street, were keen to employ a boy to work for two hours every evening at their factory. Not wanting to let this opportunity pass by, I made an appointment and went to see the partners.

The meeting was less formal than I expected. Jack, the taller of the two men, was a Christian; Stanley, shorter and darker, was Jewish. After asking me several questions, Stanley lost interest in me and sat down at his sewing machine. Jack outlined my duties. I would be expected to work for two hours every evening from 5 p.m. to 7 p.m., Monday to Friday. My main work would be soaping the canvas collars, revers and fronts of the jackets and removing basting stitches with a bodkin. Occasionally, I would be asked to run errands and once a week I would have to deliver and collect first and second fitted jackets from shops in Rotherhithe and Shoreditch. My wages would be £1 a week. I agreed to the conditions and would start the following evening. I ran home excited, knowing that in four months time I would have saved the £16 and have my suit made and ready to be worn over the Christmas holidays.

I settled into the routine of the factory quite well and soon became adept with a bodkin. I was given a small corner of a table to stand at and enough jackets to be kept occupied for the two hours. There were about a dozen workers in the factory, which was situated on the upper floors of a large terrace house that had no fire escape. The ground floor was a private dwelling.

Jack and Stanley were highly skilled tailors. I never saw them argue or disagree and they quickly made decisions with the minimum of fuss. All the male staff members were Jewish with the exception of Jack and me. The three female workers were Christian.

I enjoyed the factory atmosphere. Most of my co-workers were friendly and helpful and I was spoken to as if I were an adult rather than a fourteen-year-old. Only Maud, an elderly finisher, seemed to dislike me; her habit of calling me 'boy', was provocative. I reminded her that my name was Alfred. She responded sarcastically to my 'insolence' by remarking that 'little boys should be seen and not heard'.

My weekly visits to the shops in Shoreditch and Rotherhithe were, at first, welcome excursions, but as the weeks went by these trips proved irksome. The sack that I carried had become increasingly heavy, sometimes it rained and twice I was stopped and searched by the police. In late September, I complained to Jack that the sack was now so heavy I was unable to carry it. He responded to my complaint by opening the sack, emptying the jackets onto the floor and divided them into two smaller sacks. Moments later, Jack put on his coat, grabbed one of the sacks and ordered me to pick up the other sack. After I did so he said, 'let's go together to Shoreditch; I could do with some fresh air'. As we walked along the Whitechapel Road, I told Jack that my headmaster, A. A. Bloom, had collapsed in his office that afternoon and had been taken to the London

Hospital. I was startled by his callous answer, 'for all you know he might be dead'. When I arrived at school the following morning, I was told the sad news that our revered headmaster had indeed died.

Working so close to many of the staff I could often hear their conversations. The women mostly spoke of their families and shopping. The men's topics seemed to be restricted to sport, gambling and telling rude jokes, which constantly annoyed the women.

Shortly after I began working at Standard Tailors I became aware that Jack was a womaniser. Although married with two children he was persistently and discreetly trying to fondle Beth, an attractive redheaded sewing hand. She usually pushed his hands away. I wondered whether, if Beth were alone with him, she would have acted differently. If I had witnessed his antics, so must the rest of the staff.

It was during the early evening, when several of the workers had gone home, Jack called Beth over to his workbench on some pretext. Concealed by a heavily-laden clothing rail, he attempted to feel her body. I pretended not to notice but could not resist a quick glance. As I did so, Maud threw a reel of cotton, which struck my shoulder. She obviously saw me having a peep; when I looked in her direction, she wagged her finger at me, indicating that I should mind my own business.

In due course I became quite friendly with Joe, a dark-haired machiner who was in his early twenties. As a former national serviceman, he had seen action in Korea. Joe hated living in the Aldgate area where he was born and having to machine jackets, which he considered to be a lowly profession. It seemed to me that his aim in life was to win the football pools as he spoke of little else. His dream or obsession was to collect the £75,000 jackpot and emigrate to America. I had no idea how much of his wages he spent each week on the pools, but it must have been considerable. Joe seemed to be perpetually without money. He once made me a promise, and I believed him, that if ever he won the big prize he would immediately buy me a new pushbike. Ten years later, I saw a glum-looking Joe coming out of a local betting shop. I had the impression that he was still wearing the same clothes that he had worn in 1955.

Sam, a 50-year-old Hoffman presser, was short, fat, quite bald and very freckled; what ginger hair remained stuck out sideways, giving him an eccentric look. He appeared to be permanently engulfed by steam.

Sam was a bachelor, though not by choice. He had long ago resigned himself to the fact that no women could ever find him attractive. It was common knowledge amongst the staff in the factory that he had never 'been with a woman'. Apparently, several years before, as a birthday treat, his workmates had hired a prostitute to visit him at his home. Sam, either too embarrassed or nervous, was unable to rise to the occasion. The prostitute, it seems, was both honest and compassionate. She returned her fee to Sam's workmates and scolded them, mistakenly believing that they had tried to humiliate their friend.

The staff were having a tea break when Sam explained to the machiners sitting close by that 'during a moment of weakness', while sunbathing in a park, he could not resist positioning himself on the grass so that he could look up a scantily-dressed woman's skirt. Maud overheard his confession and became outraged. She spoke vehemently: 'You are nothing but a disgusting, dirty old man and you should be ashamed of yourself, talking like that in front of a young boy.' I looked over to her, surprised by the viciousness of her tongue. Sam was furious; his freckled face turned completely red. I silently cheered when he retaliated. 'Did it ever occur to you, madam that the woman might have just wanted men to look up her skirt?'

Maud snarled at Sam when she replied, 'Only a whore would do that.'

I listened spellbound; witnessing adults arguing was a new experience for me. The fracas ended as quickly as it had begun when Stanley stood up and called for order.

As I carried on with my soaping, Sam's words echoed in my ears. I asked myself a question: was looking up females' skirts really that disgusting? I was unsure. I had known many schoolboys, who, while larking about in Victoria Park during the summer, had attempted to look up girls' skirts and ogle their breasts; even I was a willing participant. To us boys it was just natural curiosity and no more. I dreaded the thought of what Maud would have said to me had she known my little secret.

Poor Sam! Throughout his life, this harmless and childlike man had been denied physical contact with women and now, in late middle age, he was being accused of being a pervert. It seemed unfair. Although I was young and inexperienced about most things in life, I was capable of recognising that Maud's judgement of Sam was clearly flawed. Perhaps the truth was that she simply did not like him and, on hearing his confession took the opportunity to attack him. If Maud was so puritanical, why did she remain silent and ignore the real disgusting, dirty old man in her midst, her employer, the licentious Jack, or alternatively, call Beth aside, and warn her that she should forcibly discourage Jack's bad behaviour? I suspected that Maud was probably afraid that if she did make a formal complaint it might result in her instant dismissal, but this should not have been a problem for her. It was the mid 1950s and there were ample vacancies for skilled clothing workers in most East End factories. She could have walked out of the workshop in Rampart Street and, within an hour, found a new position in one of the numerous factories in nearby Commercial Road.

When I arrived at the factory the following afternoon, the atmosphere was peaceful. I could detect no sign of the unpleasant scene which had occurred the day before; it was as if the incident had never happened. Sam seemed happy enough; despite the hiss of steam I could hear him singing along to the music on the radio.

As I began soaping the jackets, I could hear Sam exchanging a few words with Maud. I found this odd. I had hoped that he would have snubbed this obnoxious woman. Though I did not realise it at the time, I had just witnessed a Jewish trait: a trait that I would come to recognise in future years. Sam, like so many Jewish people whom I came into contact with in the clothing factories, rarely held a grudge.

In early December my brother–in-law, Jim Attwell, kept his promise and took me to Minamax to be measured for my suit. While the tailor wrote down the measurements, Jim asked him if he would make a special effort to make a good fitting, 'as it is the boy's first suit'. Always hating being referred to as a boy, I glanced upwards and gave Jim a look of disapproval. The tailor assured him that the suit would be made for 'a prince'.

When Jim repeated the words, 'As it is the boy's first suit' a second and third time I began to feel very embarrassed. I certainly did not feel or look like a prince, more like a waif from Dr Barnardo's Home, who had been brought to this place to be clothed and then instantly dispatched to work on some farm in Canada.

I told big Jim that he need not accompany me to Minamax for the next two fittings; I was more than capable of standing on my own two feet. He disagreed, but I insisted that I would come alone or not come at all. Realising that he may have upset me, but not knowing why, he said no more. I thanked him for his time but remained annoyed that he had caused me to be so embarrassed.

On the day that the workshop closed down for the Christmas break, and at the end of my two hour shift I placed my bodkin in a small tin, took off my apron and was about to speak to Jack at his workbench. Earlier he had indicated that he had something to say to me before I went home. Turning round, I was confronted by a smiling Joe, who handed me five one pound notes. I thought that he had won the pools. Alas no, the cash was my 'Christmas box'. Joe had collected the money from the rest of the staff 'for errands run'. I was most grateful and thanked everyone personally, including Maud, although it was unlikely that she had made a contribution.

Jack looked serious when he beckoned to me and sounded genuinely concerned when he spoke. 'Alfred, I am sorry to say that because there will be so few orders until Easter, we have no alternative but to reduce your wages temporarily from £1 to fifteen shillings.'

I was not unduly surprised by the prospect of earning less money. Joe had already warned me that the trade always 'slackened off' for a short period after Christmas. I did a quick calculation. By accepting the fifteen shillings a week for the remaining 12 weeks until I left school in late March, I would lose about £3 in total, but I had just received an unexpected £5 windfall. This amount would more than compensate for the loss.

I accepted Jack's new offer with a silent nod.

He continued, but spoke more quietly, 'It's not me who decided to reduce your wages.'

He paused for a moment and with his eyes he indicated Stanley, who was machining just a few feet away.

'You know how greedy these Jews are.'

I remained silent and expressionless; I thought that I had misheard him. How could he have the audacity to say that Jews were greedy? It was a ridiculous remark, especially coming from someone who had the reputation for being a skinflint. My family and I had always found our Jewish neighbours to be kind and totally unselfish. Who could have been more generous than my late Jewish headmaster A. A. Bloom when two years earlier he had bought me new shoes with money from his own pocket?

My opinion of Jack had always been low. It was even lower now. When I left the workshop, I never returned. I had achieved my goal and had bought a new suit. I could now compete with other teenagers, even the teddy boys. The vain girl in my class proved not to be so vain after all; her advice that I should wear black brogue shoes to go with my navy blue suit rather than the brown ones that I had chosen seemed to make sense.

My new suit was worn with pride over the Christmas holiday, but within six months I had grown so tall and thin that the suit no longer fitted me; the cuffs just covered my forearms and the trouser turnups which had been altered and lowered twice by my sister, barely reached my ankles.

'You resemble a bean-pole,' said one of my friends sarcastically.

Smelling of mothballs, the costly suit was stored in a cupboard ready for the day when it could be worn by Brian my nine year old brother.

Bethnal Green

Finding employment after I left school on Friday March 27, 1956 would not be that difficult. There was a wide variety of light industrial work available in the East End. The local furniture, handbag and clothing factories were all recruiting school-leavers. Most of my classmates found immediate employment. Sitting at a school desk one day and standing in front of a workbench a few days later seemed a natural progression for us boys; we adapted to the change of environment with ease. We had attended metalwork and woodwork classes at school, so we were reasonably knowledgeable of what a factory atmosphere would be like. I also had the advantage of having worked for four months in the jacket factory.

A second change of environment that my friends and I were due to experience would take place in 1959, when we reached our late teens: National Service. This time the change might not be so smooth. Having been an army cadet the previous year and stayed at a big military camp at Colchester, where I had learnt how to handle small arms, had been on manoeuvres and was familiar with the discipline of a parade ground, I knew what would be expected from me if I became a National Serviceman, but I had reservations about some of my friends' ability to adapt to military life. Probably the tougher boys would relish the experience.It was also likely that a few of the same boys might rebel and react violently to the slightest provocation by the NCOs. For the weaker and sensitive boys, it would be a testing time. National Service might have dire consequences for them. I was somewhere in the middle, not tough, certainly not weak, perhaps like the majority of recruits, who would grudgingly conform to service life, accepting the fact that you had no choice but to wear a uniform for the next two years. But National Service was three years in the future. There was also speculation in the press at the time that National Service would be abolished in 1959/60. Although my friends and I would have come of age, there was a strong possibility that we might just be exempt.

During my last week at school, I had been making enquiries about finding employment in the local clothing factories. A career in the Merchant Navy appealed to me, but I knew that my mother would never allow me to go to sea at 15. For the time being I had to consider finding work ashore.

My friend George Hurley, the son of a skilled furniture maker and French polisher, had been offered a job as a wood machinist at the Glendale Cabinet Company in Westport Street, Stepney. George advised me to apply there, but I showed no interest. Two other friends were trainee garment cutters; their company at Whitechapel had several vacancies for school leavers. I visited the factory, which was large and modern with perhaps a hundred employees. The shop floor appeared to be run on wartime lines. Its conveyor belt section-work looked too tedious. Each worker seemed to be part of a giant cog that continually turned, enabling the factory's production to be streamlined. It would be impossible for me to work there; the atmosphere was too rigid and depressing. What would have suited me would have been a small workshop, less noisy, with fewer staff, similar to the jacket factory in Rampart Street.

I had noticed that a large Second World War air raid shelter located in a yard at the rear of some houses in Canon Street Road, just a few minutes walk from my home, had been converted into a children's dressmaking factory called L & J Juveniles. Their notice board had several vacancies, including one for a junior to learn cutting.

'You are too late, lad,' said the sympathetic proprietor when I enquired about the vacancy. 'I have just taken on a boy.'

As I walked away, he called out to me.

'Just a moment lad, if you are prepared to work in Bethnal Green, I have friends who could offer you a job.'

I immediately replied, 'yes please'.

He wrote down his friend's name and address: A. & B. Hyams Ltd, 8 Blythe Street, E2, and gave me directions how to get there.

'Go along and see them now. Meanwhile, I will phone Barney and tell him you are on your way.'

Jumping onto my pushbike, I cycled at great speed to Bethnal Green.

The Blythe Street factory was situated on the upper floors of a large terrace house. There was no means of escaping if a fire broke out. The ground floor was a private dwelling occupied by a Turkish Cypriot family.

A & B Hyams Limited was owned by two Jewish brothers, Alfie and Barney Hyams, who were both in their late thirties.

We sat on wooden stools in the cutting room, where I listened carefully as the brothers outlined the nature of their business. They were subcontractors who manufactured about a thousand cheap-to-medium priced dresses a week. There was no slack period; overtime was available, including Saturday mornings. For some time they had been keen to employ a boy to learn cutting. Barney explained that he did all the cutting himself, while his brother was in charge of the machining room on the floor above.

Alfie produced a button-through dress on a hanger that included its patterns.

Feeling quite confident I remarked, 'I like the colour lavender.'

Alfie smiled, 'Call it lilac, it sounds much better'.

Before replacing the dress on the rail he added, 'This particular dress is typical of the type of garments that we specialise in. Button-throughs are our bread-and-butter lines; they pay the wages.'

Barney got up from his stool, pointed to several rolls of fabric which were under the cutting table and said 'The width of material can vary from 36 to 54 inches, sometimes even wider.'

I helped him lift a heavy roll of fabric onto the cloth-unwinding rail, followed by an equally heavy roll of white marking paper. Having got his breath back, Barney spoke slowly and emphasized every word.

'The first stage of multiple cutting is to check the width of your material. In this case, it's 48 inches wide.' He handed me a yardstick and suggested that I should confirm the width. After he unwound the white marking paper, he began to spread out the patterns and proceeded to interlock them.

I noticed how carefully and methodically Barney worked. After a few minutes, the patterns were fitted tightly together. Satisfied that there was no wastage, he gave me the yardstick a second time.

'Now tell me, Alfie, what is the costin?'

Having worked in the jacket factory, I was familiar with the term costin. It was the amount of fabric allowed for a garment. I quickly and accurately measured the length of the marker.

'It takes two and three eighths yards.'

'Very good,' said Barney, 'Actually we have been given a costin of two and a half yards, so we have saved four and a half inches per dress. It is very important that we are always economical and try to save as much material as we can.'

I was well aware of the necessity to save fabric. Joe, the machiner at Standard Tailors, had already explained to me that most subcontractors depended on saving fabric. They would then use this surplus to make up their own garments. These garments, known as 'Cabbage' were sold to market traders for cash.

Barney asked me if I would like to help him mark in the patterns using pencils. I welcomed this opportunity to show my interest. As we carefully marked around the patterns, I noticed large tattoos on both of his forearms. One clearly read, 'Burma 1944, hot as hell, never again'.

In due course, I was to learn that Barney served in General Slim's 14th Army in the Far East. Being exposed to jungle diseases for long periods, he contracted malaria. Even in the mid-1950s he would still suffer from the recurring effects of the illness.

After we had finished the marking in, he hung up the pattern on a rail, rolled up the marker and proceeded to unwind sand coloured, underlay paper.

'Right,' he said, 'The next stage is to pull the material along the table and lay it perfectly straight on top of the underlay. It is essential that it is laid one hundred per cent straight; I can't emphasise that enough.'

I tried to absorb all that I was being told.

After we placed a flat piece of iron approximately 5 foot long, 4 inches wide and 1 inch thick on top of the fabric to keep it taut he said, 'Now we lay our marker on top of the material, with half an inch added at each end for allowance'.

He picked up an enormous, heavy pair of scissors almost the length of my elbow to my fingertips and proceeded to cut through the fabric and underlay. I removed the marking paper and underlay from the table, while Barney rolled up the marker.

'Now,' he beamed, 'We are ready to lay up the required amount of material, which could be anything from twenty to two hundred high.'

I was becoming more and more fascinated by what was being explained to me. There were several questions I wanted to ask him but I thought I should wait and not interrupt.

Barney continued 'When we have finished laying up the material, we place the marker very accurately on top of the finished laid-up material.' He then produced a box of two-inch steel T-pins.

'We use these T-pins to secure the marker to the material. Under no circumstances would you place a T-pin in a marked in pattern, always in the surplus, otherwise it might leave a tiny hole in the garment.'

I nodded, indicating that I understood.

An Eastman cutting machine was within arm's reach; Barney gripped its handle, switched it on and said, 'With this cutting machine' I was unable to hear him complete the sentence; the roar of the Eastman's engine had startled me. He quickly switched it off. I glanced at the machine's fearsome looking blade; it was about ten inches long.

Using his pencil as a pointer he said 'We cut along the pencilled in pattern of the marker. This, of course, is where the real skill is, a skill which you develop in time. After the lay is cut out, the next stage is to cut the interfacing that is required for the garment.'

We were suddenly interrupted by Alfie, who brought over cups of tea; he grinned at me before remarking. 'I hope we are not confusing you by trying to explain too much too soon, but my brother is an excellent cutter. If you decide to work here, you will have no finer teacher.'

Barney explained that the cut lay is separated into small bundles of about ten garments. Interfacing, zips and labels would be placed inside the bundles. The bundles would be later collected by the overlockers and machinists who work in the machining room on the floor above.

Barney and I sat back down on the old wooden stools; he took a sip of tea, lit up a cigarette and said, 'What do you think about what I have explained; would you like to learn cutting?'

I replied enthusiastically, 'Yes I would'.

Responding to my enthusiasm, he replied, 'Good, of course there is much more to cutting than what I have outlined. First you would help me lay up the material, make bundles and in time I will let you cut out simple lays of interfacing. Eventually, if all goes well, you can assist me to cut out a complete dress lay and if you prove capable, I will let you cut a lay by yourself.'

Alfie, who was drinking tea at the table, intervened, 'Cutting is not my department. I am responsible for the machining room upstairs and the delivering of the finished garments and collecting the matcrial. We would expect you to help unload and load the van. I hope you are strong; the material can be quite heavy.'

I was so keen to be employed there that I quickly answered 'very strong'.

The brothers seemed satisfied that I was suitable for the job. We discussed wages and hours worked. My pay would be three pounds, five shillings for 40 hours; overtime would be time and a half. To avoid confusion, I would be known as little Alfie and Barney's brother would be called big Alfie, but I was growing taller by the day. Within six months, big Alfie was shorter than me. To avoid confusion yet again, I would now be called young Alfie, a title more acceptable than my previous one.

Sensing that I was genuinely interested in learning the trade, Barney suggested that I could start work immediately after I left school. A date was set for early April. To confirm my appointment both Barney and Alfie shook my hand.

Cycling home, I felt that the interview had gone well, believing that I had made a good impression. My one concern was the cutting table; it stretched from wall to wall. To get to the other side, you either had to clamber over the top or crawl underneath, but the table was well constructed and looked enormous compared to the tiny corner of a table that I had been given to work at in the jacket factory.

Arriving home in a slightly excited state, I told my mother that I had just found a job and would be taught dress cutting. I was in no doubt that with Barney's guidance I would in time become a skilled cutter. Although my ultimate dream was to join the Merchant Navy, I thought it wise that I should still learn a trade that I could put to good use whenever I worked ashore.

The following weekend, I was knocked off my bicycle by a car that failed to stop. Apart from shock and a strained wrist, I was unhurt, but the rear wheel of my bike was badly buckled. My mother became worried that I might be involved in a more serious accident if I cycled each day to Bethnal Green. To allay her fears I kept my bicycle at home.

Because Blythe Street was difficult to reach by public transport from Jane Street, I had no alternative but to walk to Bethnal Green. The enjoyable half hour walk that I made six days a week was to continue until June 1960. While walking from Stepney to Bethnal Green during this period I was to witness many familiar streets being demolished as part of the local council's 'Slum clearance' programme.

I found the council's policy baffling. Many of those fine looking terraces, especially in Bethnal Green, seemed to me to be well maintained, but, sadly, the terraces were shown no mercy by the bulldozers. Even the remaining old Artisan and Huguenot weavers' houses that were part of Bethnal Green's heritage and should have been preserved were ruthlessly swept away.

I was so impatient to start work at A. & B. Hyams that when I arrived at Blythe Street on the Monday morning I was too early. The factory had not yet opened. Eventually, the brothers arrived. A smiling Alfie remarked 'Well done, cocker, I can see that we will have to give you the keys to open up.'

The morning went surprisingly quickly. Much of my time was spent helping Barney to lay up 48 inch wide fabric. He was, as I had expected, very patient with my initial clumsiness. Throughout the morning, as we worked, he encouraged me to ask questions and he continued to emphasise the importance of laying the fabric perfectly straight. I was to make a note if the fabric was damaged, shaded or had become narrow. We finished the lay of approximately 150 runs, which seemed to be about eight inches high, just before the 1 p.m. lunch break. I was now free for one hour, ample time to buy food and maybe explore the nearby market.

Growing up quickly, I seemed to be permanently hungry. A hot, cheap meal at 'Tony's', the spotlessly clean Lithuanian café on the corner of Blythe Street, was delicious. With time to spare, I wandered around the area. An old lady, who looked thin and ill, stood nervously on a crossing, She held my arm and we slowly crossed the busy Bethnal Green road. Her words are still vivid today as they were in 1956.

'Thank you, sonny, don't ever get old, it's a crime to get old.'

As I made my way along the market, the aroma of fresh baked bread and the delightful smells of fruit and vegetables filled my nostrils. Outside Ma Hooker's café, an elderly Jewish man sold bagels from a huge sack on the pavement.

I was to learn from Florrie, who was the Hyams overlocker, that two years earlier the 'Bagel man's' son Zala Lenechitsky, a 42-year-old factory hand, had strangled little Wendy Ridgwell who was just five years of age and lived in Blythe Street. He had placed her body in a wooden fruit box and left it at the rear of his home in adjacent Teesdale Street.

The murder of the little girl outraged the local community. During the four years that I worked at A. & B. Hyams, the women workers would periodically mention, sometimes with watery eyes, this horrendous crime. At his trial, Lenechitsky was found guilty of murder and sentenced to hang, but shortly afterwards he was reprieved and subsequently committed to Broadmoor, the prison hospital for the criminally insane.

When I returned to the factory after lunch, Barney had already cut out the lay of dresses; he rarely took a lunch break longer then fifteen minutes. Later that afternoon, while he was cutting soft sanforised interfacing (thin fusible canvas) I prepared labels and zips for the cut lay. I soon learnt how to make bundles efficiently. Barney had emphatically warned me that if I mistakenly put the wrong size labels into the bundles, it would cause total havoc and prove costly to rectify. I heeded his warning and would always take particular care whenever I made bundles.

For the next few months my daily work was repetitious. I would assist Barney to lay wide fabric and if the fabric's width was 36 or 45 inches I could manage to lay it on my own. Bundling I found to be relaxing, but I disliked the loading and unloading of the van, particularly the carrying of heavy rolls of fabric up the stairs. It could be strenuous work for a slightly built 15-year-old boy.

Forever impatient to learn cutting, I asked Barney if I could use the Eastman cutting machine. He cautioned me and gave a stark warning that at fifteen I was too young to use a powerful cutting machine and that my impatience might cause me to be careless, which could result in an accident involving my fingers. However, he did make a promise that when he felt that the time was right, I would be allowed to use the cutting machine for a short period.

After a few weeks, I made a second attempt at trying to persuade him to let me 'Have a go.' This time Barney agreed; I could cut a simple lay of sanforised interfacing, on condition that I 'Watched the fingers.'

Barney hovered over me like a hawk throughout my initiation.

Suddenly, he ordered me to switch off the cutting machine; speaking sternly, he said, 'Alfie, you must listen to me carefully; please watch your fingers, particularly your forefinger; it is too close to the blade.'

Moments later he seemed a little impatient when he repeated his warning. 'You must concentrate at all times and watch your fingers or you will have a nasty cut.'

I switched the machine back on and continued to cut out the interfacing; this time I made sure that my fingers were not too close to the machine's lethal blade.

After I had finished the cutting, I stood by the table while Barney thoroughly checked my work; as he did so, I began to sense that his comments might be favourable.

Turning around to face me, he said 'Not bad Alfie, not bad at all.' However there was yet another note of caution. He again reminded me of the absolute necessity of positioning my left hand correctly in front of the cutting machine's guard.

I felt so proud that I had actually managed to cut the interfacing without making a single mistake.

At 5.30 p.m., just as I was leaving to go home, a buoyant big Alfie remarked 'Keep up the good work cocker.'

A few weeks after I began cutting interfacing for the dockets, I found myself becoming anxious to prove to my employers that not only could I cut accurately and efficiently, but I was quite fast too.

This naïve attitude was to teach me an important lesson: that trying to cut too quickly with a cloth cutting machine was potentially dangerous and that you risk serious injury.

Barney, with his ever watchful eyes, noticed my carelessness. He warned me that I was starting to ignore the 'Number one rule,' of always having the cutting machine guard completely lowered. I heeded his warning, but was still inclined to take the occasional risk.

Inevitably, my risk taking caused me to cut my thumb quite badly.

The look of shock on Barney's face when he saw the blood caused me more pain than the sliced, throbbing thumb. We quickly got into his car and within minutes arrived at the casualty department at Bethnal Green Hospital, where my thumb received four stitches.

When we returned to the factory, I began to feel a little guilty. My accident had alarmed Barney and Alfie. I could hear them in the adjacent, small stockroom arguing and blaming each other for allowing me to use the cutting machine too soon. I did not agree. They were blameless; I should have taken more care.

As expected, my brief cutting career was now over for the foreseeable future. Under no circumstances would I have Barney's permission to resume cutting. It would be several months before he allowed me to clean and oil the cutting machine, and then only after he first removed the ten-inch blade.

My everyday duties were now restricted to laying up the fabric and bundling, but as compensation for being banned from cutting interfacing, I was given the opportunity to learn marker making, which I enjoyed immensely.

Not long after I had my accident, Barney found himself taking another casualty to Bethnal Green Hospital. This time it was Moisha, a little Yiddisher man.

Moisha would arrive at the factory once a week with his ancient barrow to collect our sacks of cuttings. After he had finished piling the sacks on board and leaving us half a dozen empty sacks for the following week's collection, he would set off and push his heavy load to a Hackney rag warehouse. He probably received a few shillings a sack. Because he wore patched-up old clothes and seemed to be permanently in need of a bath, it was impossible to determine his age. I thought he was about fifty. Alfie believed he was nearer seventy.

Moisha was very shy and an introvert; he would never look you in the eye or speak unless spoken to. It was with great difficulty that Barney managed to get him to speak just a few words. When he did respond he would merely say 'right-ho'. If we wished him good morning, asked how he was, or mentioned how cold it was outside, his inevitable answer was 'right-ho,' in fact, before we found out that his name was Moisha, both Barney and Alfie would refer to him as 'Mr Right-Ho.' It was pitiful to see this little man carrying big heavy sacks of cuttings on his shoulders and struggling perilously down the stairs, especially during the summer when he would sweat profusely. We tried to make his work less arduous. Alfie suggested that he should leave us smaller sacks to ease the strenuous humping. Although he gave his customary 'Right-ho,' he still continued to bring us large sacks. The occupants of the flat on the ground floor refused to allow us to place the sacks in the hall because of the fire risk. We tried leaving the sacks on the pavement outside the factory, but Barney received a complaint from an irate neighbour.

One morning Moisha was busy tying up the sacks on the first floor landing. Unknown to him, there were two policemen on the premises. Barney had earlier phoned Bethnal Green Police Station after being told by several of his machinists that for the past few days they had noticed a taxi driver sitting in his cab directly outside the factory, urinating into a bottle.

The two policemen were observing the taxi from the cutting room windows. The moment the driver produced a bottle and undid his trouser-buttons, the policemen rushed out of the cutting room and ran down the stairs to make the arrest. Unfortunately, one of the policemen bumped into Moisha on the landing. The little man fell backwards and crashed bottom first into a wooden tea chest half filled with coal. As he struggled to get out, he received splinters to his hands and legs. One splinter went up the full length of his fingernail. The pain must have been excruciating, but Moisha did not complain; all he wanted to do was to finish loading his barrow and be on his way.

Alfie refused to let him leave the premises, insisting that Barney should take him to Bethnal Green Hospital to have the splinters removed. Eventually, Moisha agreed. I sat next to him inside the car. His body odour was awful. Throughout the short journey, he gazed around the car. It was unlikely that he had ever been inside a vehicle before. When we arrived at the casualty department, Moisha was promptly examined by a doctor. Though shielded by a screen, we could hear the doctor and a nurse attending him. To their questions, he gave his usual

'Right-ho,' suddenly; the doctor poked his head around the screen and made a facial expression which I interpreted as saying 'What a pong.' He told us that he would have to remove much of Moisha's fingernail to extract the splinter. Upon our return to Blythe Street, we found that Irish Mary, a local vagrant, had climbed on top of Moisha's barrow and was fast asleep.

Barney was a skilled marker maker. His work was neat and tidy, the patterns were always marked correctly, compact and on grain. Years of experience had taught him the importance of making markers at least one inch less than the width of the fabric. This allowance was necessary in case the fabric became narrow. He was also a cautious man; an absolute requirement when it came to managing a busy cutting room. His perennial fear of what the effects of costly and irreparable cutting mistakes would have on his business caused him to be exceptionally careful. 'If a machinist damages a dress, we only lose a single garment, but if there is a mistake in the cutting, we could lose hundreds of garments.'

To minimise the possibility of accidents occurring during the cutting process, he laid down certain relevant guidelines which had to be strictly observed. He insisted that before we started work on a new style it was essential that we first measured the exact width of the rolls of fabric that had to be used. Secondly and equally important, we should examine all patterned, floral or striped fabric to see if it was printed 'one way', if so, we must make markers accordingly.

I asked him if he would clarify the meaning of 'one way'.

Fortunately for me, Barney was a patient teacher who never tired of explaining any intricacies that I failed to understand.

'Better still,' he said, as he rummaged through a rail of samples; he soon found what he was looking for, a long-sleeved, floral dress.

'Have a look at this garment, Alfie. You notice how all of the stems of the flowers point downwards.'

I examined the front and back of the dress.

'Now, just try and visualise what this garment would look like if the flower stems on the right front bodice were pointing downwards and the stems on the left bodice were pointing upwards – would not the garment look ridiculous?'

'It certainly would,' I replied, trying to sound more mature than a fifteen-year-old.

Satisfied that I understood what he was explaining Barney continued, 'To avoid our finished garments looking ridiculous, we have to be extremely careful when a marker is made for material that is printed one way. We must never interlock the patterns. Always check your sample thoroughly and then, as I said before, mark in your patterns accordingly.'

After he had placed the dress sample back on the rail he asked me if I had any questions.

As always, I welcomed the opportunity to impress and show that I was keen to learn, yet aware that there was a slight risk of sounding cocky or even arrogant, I stated what I thought might be the obvious.

'Surely if we mark in the patterns the same way rather than interlock them, we can't achieve a tight economical costing.'

'Exactly,' he boomed, 'And that means no cabbage. Unfortunately, we cannot afford to turn away business. If we can't make cabbage on certain dockets, what we lose on the swings we gain on the roundabouts, that's our policy.'

After several months of making sanforised interfacing markers and assisting Barney with single and multiple dress markers, I thought I had gained enough experience to be able to make a dress marker on my own. Barney thought so, too.

On the last Friday of July 1956, the day the factory was to close for the two week summer break, I had his approval to see if I could make a treble dress marker unaided.

I was very grateful at being given this opportunity. Following the strict cutting and marker making guidelines that I was now familiar with, I examined the dress sample thoroughly before checking its patterns to see that none was missing. I also measured the fabric's width, which was 54 inches, and I spent several minutes scrutinising the docket making sure that I fully understood the costing and cutting ratio.

Now that I was in a position to proceed, I set about interlocking the patterns.

To my delight, they all fitted perfectly. Slowly and carefully I marked in the patterns. When I had finished, Barney began to check my work. Thankfully, I had remembered the most important rule of all; to mark in the patterns one inch less than the width of the fabric. Moreover, I had actually saved a few inches on the costin. My only mistake, a small front neck facing, was slightly off grain; but with the use of an eraser it was easily rectified.

Barney was so pleased with my efforts that he invited Alfie to have a look at my marker. After examining the marker, Alfie turned to me and said, 'Well done, cocker'.

The brothers disappeared into the stockroom. Barney emerged a few moments later. There was a smile on his face when he spoke. 'Now that you are a qualified marker maker, Alfie, we have decided to increase your wages by ten shillings a week.'

Before I could thank him, he continued, 'We are also going to pay you two weeks holiday money.'

I gasped at this generous offer. In 1956, new employees usually had to work a whole year before they were entitled to holiday pay.

When I left the factory at 5.30 p.m., I could not believe that I actually had three weeks wages in my trouser pocket, totalling £13. As I walked home, I hastened my pace, impatient to tell my mother the good news of my progress at work, of the increase in wages and the unexpected holiday pay. I felt happy and proud.

Now that I was earning more, I could give her extra money each week. Fearing that I might lose my thick wage packet before I reached home, I grasped it tightly in my pocket, double-checking that there were no holes inside; sometimes there were. I could ill afford to lose so much money. My imagination seemed to be taking over. I became aware of passing strangers, wondering if they might be potential thieves or pickpockets. Of course, none were and I arrived home safely with my wages intact.

The two-week holiday break seemed to be over before it began. I spent most of my time in the East End, apart from a miserable weekend at Paddock Wood in Kent. Two days of eating pilchards from a tin and two nights sleeping in a flea infested, deserted hop-pickers hut was enough for me. I packed my knapsack and returned to the East End, where I knew I could enjoy myself. Also on holiday in early August were my three close friends Brian Miah, Alfie Debono and Sylvio Lomiglio. We kept ourselves fully occupied. Pursuing girls was our priority. When none were available we rowed canoes on the lake at Victoria Park and swam in the Lido. Cycling to Southend was popular but extremely strenuous.

Our many days in Hungerford Street were happy. This narrow, quiet turning where Alfie lived was almost flattened during the Blitz, and with cleared bombsites, few houses and no cars we could play cricket in the street undisturbed. Using tin cans as a wicket and a home-made bat, we amused ourselves for hours. Wandering around docklands, especially Wapping and Shadwell, during the warm evenings was a favourite pastime. We sat on the riverside benches at Shadwell Park and discussed our future plans. Brian and Alfie, who were garment cutters, wanted to leave the trade. They disliked their employers, rarely spoke to other employees and complained about poor pay. Like me, they dreamt of joining the Merchant Navy one day.

I suggested that they should be patient and become experienced cutters before they went to sea, just as I intended to do, but they disagreed. Not only our future aspirations were discussed – we would express our thoughts on many subjects.

As a junior debating society restricted to just a few members, we often spent hours at weekends seated on park benches or just roaming around Stepney's streets airing our views on a variety of topics. I thoroughly enjoyed this activity. High on our list of discussions was always girls, followed by music, cinema and even hypnotism. World news did not escape our young minds; each of us had opinions on the unfolding crisis over the Suez Canal, Eoka terrorism in Cyprus and the unrest in Hungary. The situation in Hungary was of particular interest. Within a few months, hundreds of refugees fleeing from the uprising in Budapest were staying at the recently closed St. George's Hospital at Wapping. Many of these handsome but sad people could be seen roaming aimlessly around the area, easily recognisable by their shabby raincoats and berets. One couple from their community appeared in Shadwell Park and sat on the bench next to us. We tried to make conversation with them but failed; their English was just too limited.

Religion was a subject best avoided. Whenever religion was mentioned in our coterie, it caused arguments.

Alfie was a passionate Roman Catholic, who regularly worshipped at the local St. Mary and St. Michael Church. His arrogance sometimes irritated me. Apart from insisting that the Roman Catholic Church was the only true Christian faith, he believed that all other churches, including the Anglicans, the Methodists, the Baptists and even the Salvation Army, should be closed down and their members converted to Catholicism. I disagreed and pointed out that members of these churches would not convert.

'And why not?' demanded Alfie, who had clearly forgotten that he was again repeating the same dogma that he had expressed in the past.

'The reason is obvious;' I argued, 'Protestants would never revere the Virgin Mary, like Catholics do, or regard Pope Pius XII as God's spokesman on earth.'

Alfie seemed offended, 'That's ignorance, you are implying that we Catholics only worship the Virgin Mary and the Pope.'

'Well you certainly don't seem to place any importance on Jesus Christ,' I asserted.

If ever our arguments became too heated, Brian and Sylvio would interrupt us and try to change the subject.

One afternoon the four of us were loitering on a corner when I unwittingly provoked Alfie by suggesting that if Catholics felt the need to confess their sins to God, they should do so in their prayers and not to a priest sitting in a confession box.

Stupidly, I added 'For all you know, Alf, that same priest might well be a sinner himself.'

Alfie mistook my comment as sarcasm and he reacted furiously by blurting 'Maybe you should go into the confession box, too, because you are a sinner like the rest of us.'

Our disagreement came to a sudden end, as a lone policeman on the other side of the street saw us arguing. He came over and ordered us to 'be quiet and don't obstruct the pavement'.

Another serious exchange of words between Alfie and me occurred outside Gussy's grocery shop in Bigland Street, Stepney. Sylvio and Brian avoided becoming involved in the discussion.

I explained to Alfie that I had recently visited a friend who was a patient at the London Hospital. This friend, a Jamaican Baptist, had complained to me that whenever the Catholic priest came into the ward he would seek out only Catholic patients and ignore those patients of other faiths, but when a Church of England padre or a Rabbi appeared in the ward, they would spend a few minutes with every patient, irrespective of their religious beliefs.

Alfie reacted angrily 'Catholic priests do not operate like that: it would be original sin if they ignored non Catholic patients.' Not deterred, I gave another example of what I perceived to be the Catholic Church's preferences for their own flock.

I asked Alfie to recall a few months earlier when two tragedies occurred that involved young Stepney boys.

Six-year-old John Pitman had been killed not too far from where we stood. The little boy was standing on the pavement in Cable Street when a fifty-foot steel escape ladder fell off a passing fire tender and struck him. He was killed instantly.

This horrific accident was reported in the local press and it may have been mentioned in some of the national newspapers. It was unlikely to have been reported in the foreign press or brought to the attention of Pope Pius XII; but the death of ten-year-old Tony Murphy, a Stepney boy who was killed by a lion, made worldwide news.

Cub master Father Ronald Aylward had taken a party of Catholic wolf cubs and scouts from St. Mary and St. Michael's Church to Whipsnade Zoo.

Somehow, Tony and another cub became separated from the group. They made their way to the lion's cages. Wanting to get closer to the lions, the two boys foolishly climbed over the five-foot safety fence. As they ran along the enclosed path, one of the lions poked his paw through the bars and managed to grip Tony by his foot. The boy was pulled up against the cage and badly mauled. Father Aylward and a member of the public jumped over the fence and managed to beat off the lion, first with their bare hands and then with an iron rod.

Tony was taken to hospital, where surgeons amputated both his arms. He was then placed in an iron lung. News of the incident reverberated around the world. Messages of sympathy and support were sent to Tony's family from all over the country and beyond. Even the Pope sent his blessing. But sadly the little boy's injuries were so severe that he died a few days later.

'Then what are you suggesting?' said a puzzled Alfie, 'Should the Pope have sent his blessings to John Pitman's family, too?'

'No, I am not suggesting that at all' I replied.

'Then what are you implying?' he said impatiently.

Realising that I had struck a winning point, I said 'Do you honestly believe that the Pope would have sent his blessing if Tony Murphy had not been a Catholic?'

Alfie's answer was not convincing, 'Of course he would. I am sure of it.'

Meanwhile Sylvio and Brian had become bored with having to listen to our petty argument. Sylvio insisted that we change the subject. He was supported by Gussy the grocer who stood at his shop doorway.

Gussy, whose real name was Gershon, had known us boys since we were infants, he spoke firmly but politely.

'Do me a favour, boys; if you want to fight, go on to the bombsite; can't you see I am struggling to earn a few bob here.'

Gussy, was indeed struggling. With three other grocery shops in Bigland Street and Watney Street Market close by, it was a wonder that he managed to stay in business at all. He probably survived because he was prepared to infringe the strict retailing laws that existed at the time, but he had to pay a price.

After being 'shopped' by, it was rumoured, other traders in Bigland Street, Gussy was hauled yet again in front of the local magistrate and fined ten pounds for selling just half a bar of soap on a Sunday.

As Alfie grew older, his devotion to Catholicism began to wane. Within a few years he was to become totally disillusioned and even highly critical of the Catholic faith. Finally, he decided to abandon Catholicism altogether and, to my surprise, he eventually became a devout member of the Church of England. Ten years later, he married a New Zealand missionary and settled in Australia.

I felt very happy when I returned to work after my holiday, believing that in just four months I had achieved a great deal. I could make bundles efficiently and was particularly good at laying up fabric by myself. Interfacing markers were simple to make and, most importantly, I was now a qualified marker maker. But I was yet to start cutting the dresses; that ambition would remain unfulfilled until March 1957.

Laying up wide fabric with Barney was always an enjoyable experience. Often it would take us hours to complete the lay. Because the process did not require intense concentration, unlike cutting, and bundling, it was an ideal opportunity to chat. During these laying up periods, I learnt a great deal about my employers and their families. Both brothers were married with young children. They came from a liberal Jewish background and grew up near Petticoat Lane. In 1939 they were called up for military service. Barney was accepted; he joined the Army and spent several years in the Far East. Alfie, much to his regret, was rejected on medical grounds. As a boy, he had contracted rheumatic fever which had left him with a defective heart valve; also his kidneys were not functioning properly. Each week he would collect huge bottles of water from the London Hospital at Whitechapel, to be consumed on a daily basis. Unlike Barney, who had a serious nature, Alfie despite his health problems, was a jovial character who had the habit of calling friends and strangers 'cocker'.

In 1951, the brothers opened their dress factory in Bethnal Green. They chose not to expand their business during the post-war boom, preferring to remain a small company, believing it was easily manageable and 'less of a headache'.

Barney's mother-in-law, who lived in Brighton, was an excellent cook, small and plump with swinging hips. Barney, who found her 'interfering at times', would occasionally imitate her walk. Once a month she would travel up to London to visit her two daughters and grandchildren. Informed that I was fond of Jewish food, she never failed to bring me a small bag of her delicious home made gefilte fish (boiled or fried fish cakes). My employer's father, widowed and retired, may have been in his mid-seventies. Genial and contented, he was always smartly dressed, with impeccable manners. Though usually circumspect, Hyams senior would ignore any of the staff who happened to be in the cutting room and chide Barney over his daily habit of using a matchstick to remove the wax from his ears. Now very frail, he would still regularly visit the factory. Sitting on a stool in the cutting room with both hands resting on his walking stick, he wanted to chat, as the elderly often do. When told of my accident, he became very concerned. Having absolutely no knowledge of cutting himself, he still insisted on given me endless advice and tips on how to avoid future accidents. I listened carefully; I respected him too much to do otherwise. Before the year was out, this charming man had passed away.

During one of our marathon laying up sessions, Barney felt it was necessary for me to be informed of an ongoing dispute that had existed in cutting rooms for decades. Suddenly, he was interrupted by the phone ringing. He picked up the receiver and spent several minutes chatting to his wife. While I waited for him to finish his conversation, I began to wonder what this dispute could be all about. The longer he chattered the more curious I became. When he replaced the receiver, he seemed distracted. Speaking with my now customary mannerism of trying to sound older than I was, I said, 'Barney, you were mentioning some dispute.'

He regained his thoughts and spoke slowly, 'Oh yes, as I was saying, this dispute involves a marker maker and a cutter who each blame the other for a mistake which could quite easily have been avoided.'

He paused for a moment to light up a cigarette. Rather than put the spent matchstick in the ashtray, he used it to poke around the inside of his ear. When he spoke again, his tone was slightly businesslike.

'Let me try and explain the dispute to you Alfie and then I would like you to tell me where you think the blame lies.' Barney must have noticed my bewildered expression because he modified his tone.

'Alfie, it does not matter if you are not sure who was to blame, but I would still like you to give me your opinion.' I answered him with a nod.

After placing his cigarette on the ashtray Barney said 'Let's start from the beginning. After a lay of garments is cut out, it is discovered that a part of the garment is missing.'

'Missing?' I replied.

'Yes, missing, a part has been left out of the marker; for example, it could be a collar, perhaps a cuff, possibly even a sleeve.'

Alfie, who was standing close by, put his hand on my shoulder and remarked 'Take your time, cocker.'

'Thank you, Alfie,' said Barney, who seemed slightly agitated by his brother's interference.

'As I was about to say.' He waited until Alfie turned his back on us.

'Let's take this scenario to its extreme. It's been established that a sleeve is missing from a cut-out lay; perhaps several hundred garments are involved. To the cutter's horror, there is no more material left to recut the missing sleeve. Alternatively, with what material there is in stock, the colours do not match up.'

Blimey, I thought, does it never end. Barney obviously felt that what he was trying to illustrate was of the utmost importance.

After laying his shears on the table, he stubbed out the cigarette and said, 'Now I am not trying to confuse you here and in most cases the mistake can not be rectified, but what I would like you to tell me, if you can, who is responsible for causing this major error and how would you prevent it from happening again? Do you believe that the cutter was to blame, who, of course, will invariably criticise the marker maker for his carelessness in leaving the sleeve out of the marker, or would you say that the marker maker was at fault, who in all probability will accuse the cutter of negligence, because he did not check the marker to see if it was correctly made before he started laying up the material? '

Although at first I felt that I needed a little time to analyse the scenario I came to a conclusion quite quickly. It was obvious that the marker maker was to blame; after all, it was he who made the original mistake.

Just before Barney replaced the receiver, Alfie, who had been discreetly listening, went into the stockroom, but not before whispering in my ear as he passed me, 'The answer is not always what it seems, cocker.'

His remark left me slightly baffled. What was he trying to tell me? Surely the marker maker was the culprit, or was he? Within seconds I had changed my mind, having decided that it was the cutter's fault for taking it for granted that the marker was correct. After convincing myself it was the cutter who was to blame, I changed my mind yet again, wondering if I should still opt for the marker maker. Even then, I still had doubts. I now felt totally confused. Perhaps I should just rely on guesswork; at least my answer would either be right or wrong.

Meanwhile Barney had replaced the receiver and lit up another cigarette. As he did so, my mind suddenly became clearer, you could not blame the marker maker without blaming the cutter; they were both careless.

Now that I had a plausible answer, I could give him my opinion. Speaking positively, which on reflection could have been mistaken for impudence, I said 'It is obvious to me that both the marker maker and the cutter were at fault for not checking their work thoroughly. If they had, at least one of them would have noticed the missing sleeve. So therefore the blame for the mistake must be shared. The way to avoid this kind of problem occurring again would be for the marker maker and the cutter to examine the marker together, not once, but twice. That way, any errors should be spotted. I am sure of it.'

Barney listened carefully as I gave my self-assured answer. When I had finished, he smiled broadly and said 'Good boy, I knew that you were capable of working it out.'

I was having a quiet tea break with Barney and Alfie when we suddenly heard screaming coming from the machining room on the floor above. We raced up the stairs, each dreading what terrible scene might confront us. On entering the machining room, we stopped in our tracks. The women, numbering about twelve, with the exception of Violet, the diminutive presser, were standing on their chairs with their dresses and skirts pulled up high revealing a cross-section of fat and thin legs, knobbly knees, varicose veins and laddered stockings, a disturbing and disappointing sight for a healthy fifteen-year-old boy. Suddenly, Violet bent down and grabbed a large, torpid mouse; dangling it by its tail, she proceeded to swing it from side to side. The sight of the mouse caused the terrified women to scream louder than before.

'It won't hurt you, its half dead,' shouted Violet.

The little intruder must have heard her, because it revived itself, leant upwards and nipped her finger. She shrieked in pain and dropped the mouse, which promptly disappeared down a hole in the old fireplace hearth. After the women had calmed down, I was sent out to the nearby market to buy mousetraps.

During the lunch break a few days later, my growing and burning interest in the female form that had been unexpectedly dampened by the sight of thoser unshapely legs, was now fully restored, thanks to the actress Belinda Lee.

While eating my fish and chips as I crossed a large bombsite at Old Bethnal Green Road, I saw a film being made. The clapperboard read 'A Secret Place' and it featured Belinda Lee, Ronald Lewis and David McCallum. I joined other spectators and managed to get all three stars' autographs. Ronald Lewis proved exceptionally friendly. This fine actor, who showed early promise, never achieved the stardom he deserved. Sadly, in 1982, at the age of 54 and living in reduced circumstances in a working men's hostel at Westminster, he collapsed and died.

Belinda Lee was a beautiful blonde, tall, slim and with a sensational figure. How I envied the teenage boy actor who played one of the central characters in the film.

I was fifteen and madly in love with her. I saw all of her subsequent films over and over again, but her British film career was short-lived. A few years later she left her husband, the celebrity photographer Cornelius Lucan, and went abroad to make continental films, none of which proved memorable.

On March 14 1961 she was a front-seat passenger in a car driven by her boyfriend, the Italian film director Gualtiero Jacopetti. Suddenly a tyre burst, causing the car, which was travelling at high speed, to skid and crash upside down. The accident at San Bernando, California resulted in Jacopetti and two other passengers being injured; tragically, twenty-six-year-old Belinda Lee was catapulted sixty-three feet into the air and killed.

In early March, 1957, Barney appeared unwell. His illness may have been the effects of the recurring malaria. With great effort on his part, we managed to finish laying up a docket of approximately 400 garments just before the factory closed at 5.30 p.m.

The next morning there was no sign of Barney. When Alfie arrived, I could see by the expression on his face that something was wrong. As he unlocked the factory, he told me that his brother was very poorly. Apparently, as Barney drove home to Edgware the previous evening, he was involved in a minor collision with a small van. The occupants, two West Indians, jumped out of the vehicle and physically attacked him, leaving his face badly bruised.

At midday, Alfie had a long conversation with Barney on the telephone. The good news was that Barney felt slightly better, but would remain at home for a few days. After Alfie had replaced the receiver, he went over to the cutting table and stood staring at the huge lay. He seemed a very worried man. Shaking his head and sighing heavily, he turned to face me and said, 'We have a problem cocker; the machinists will need this work tomorrow'.

He picked up the telephone and made a number of calls to business associates, in a vain effort to see whether they could spare one of their cutters for a few hours to come to Blythe Street and cut out the lay. He was not successful.

Sensing the moment to prove my worth, I asked Alfie if I could try and cut out the lay. His reply was disappointing. 'Absolutely not, it's too dangerous for you Alfie, we can't allow it.'

Determined not to let this opportunity pass by, I persisted, 'I can do it, Alfie. It's not that difficult to cut out.' Before he answered me, he made another frantic phone call, but to no avail; turning to me he took a deep breath and said 'Are you sure cocker, would you like to give it a try?'

I replied positively 'Very sure'.

Gripping the Eastman cutting machine's handle, I waited for his permission to start. Alfie glanced at the lay and pondered for a moment before rubbing his forehead in frustration, turning to face me, he spoke slowly, 'Okay, cocker, you can go ahead, but you must, as Barney always reminds you, watch your fingers. If it's too much for you, don't worry, stop work immediately. We will just have to wait until Barney recovers.'

It took me at least three hours to cut out the lay. I worked carefully and at a slow rate; thankfully, over the past year I had learnt a great deal by studying Barney's cutting technique. Being aware of my previous accident, I took extra care not to cut my fingers. I did not want to create a mini-crisis for my employers. If I did have another accident, and with Barney being ill, Alfie may not have been able to cope single handed.

I encountered no problems as I cut out the lay, apart from the cutting machine slightly overheating. A short break was now necessary; the machine needed to cool down so that it could be cleaned, oiled and the blade changed.

By lunch time I had finished cutting the lay. Leaving the factory quickly I bought sandwiches at Tony's Café and fruit from the market. Within fifteen minutes, I was sitting on a bench in Bethnal Green Gardens.

The gardens were often referred to by the older generation as 'Barmy Park'. Apparently, the park was built on the site of a former Victorian hospital for the mentally ill.

Besides my enjoyable lunch, I was also enjoying the view directly opposite to where I sat. Two teams of local nurses had arrived to play netball. Just before I left the park to return to work, about twenty men of various ages and known as the 'dirty raincoat brigade' by local women, had positioned themselves around the pitch. These harmless voyeurs were well-behaved and posed no threat to the nurses.

As I left the park, I checked to see if a short, fat, bald character was among the spectators, but no, Sam, Standard Tailors' Hoffman presser, was nowhere to be seen.

During the afternoon, I made a soft sanforised interfacing marker. With minutes to spare before the factory was to close for the evening, the sanforize had been layed up, its marker pinned down and it was ready to be cut out. Alfie was extremely satisfied with my efforts. After he phoned Barney to tell him the news of what I had accomplished that day he handed me the phone; I was thrilled when Barney congratulated me on becoming 'a fully-fledged cutter'.

The next day, Alfie opened the factory an hour earlier at my request. I needed the extra time to cut out the soft sanforize, sort out the relevant labels, tickets and zips and have bundles made by mid morning.

When we stopped for tea at 10 a.m., the first bundles were ready to be collected by the overlockers and machinist.

At 1 p.m. a grateful Alfie insisted on buying me lunch at Tony's Café.

When Barney returned to work a few days later, he presented me with a large bag of his mother-in-law's gefilte fish. Also, my wages were to be increased by one pound a week and, to my surprise, my employers had decided that every time they sold their cabbage to the market traders, I would receive a one pound bonus. I felt very pleased. At just sixteen I was earning good wages but, most importantly, I could now call myself a qualified cutter, albeit a young one.

The extra money that I was now receiving from my bonus was useful. The amount varied from two to three pounds a week. Market traders would regularly visit the factory to buy the cabbage; they always paid cash, which meant that I would receive my bonus the moment the traders left the premises.

In the cutting room, Barney had a special cabbage rail fitted high up near the ceiling. To reach the garments a small step ladder was needed. Because the cutting room was on the first floor at the front of the building, the rail was clearly visible from the street.

Curious as ever, I wanted to know who actually owned the cabbage. Did the company Barney subcontracted for own it or did it belong to A.& B. Hyams? It seemed to me to be a grey area.

Discussing the cabbage one day with Barney as we layed up a multiple docket, he explained that 'the cabbage question is a bone of contention; for example, let's take this docket which we are working on at the moment; there are a thousand garments to make. We have been given a costin of two and three-quarter yards, but by our ingenuity we have saved a quarter of a yard per garment, which will reduce the costin to two and a half yards, so we have gained about 250 yards of surplus material. If we decide to cut this material in the same style, we would have approximately a hundred garments for ourselves. However, by doing so, we could be creating problems. If the company who gave us this docket became aware that we had made extra garments, they might try and claim ownership. So it is always sensible to use the surplus material on our own styles, but sometimes we do use company styles and this can be risky.'

I asked Barney if the company had found out that he had saved a quarter of a yard of fabric on their costin, would they reduce the costin on follow-up dockets.

'They might, cocker,' said Alfie, who was standing close by preparing a delivery. 'But, as yet, we have not encountered that problem. They probably are aware that we make some cabbage, but only small amounts, just enough to cover any garments that are too damaged to repair.'

A few weeks later, when the cabbage rail was heavily-laden with garments, Barney happened to look out of the window and saw a car being parked opposite. He recognised the driver, who immediately got out. It was six foot six inches tall Harold Smith, a director of one of the companies A. & B. Hyams subcontracted for. Smith was making one of his rare visits.

'Quickly,' shouted Barney to me, 'Get the cabbage down from the rail and take it upstairs.'

Standing precariously on the stepladder, I grabbed armfuls of garments and handed them to Alfie, who dashed upstairs; with the remainder, I followed suit.

Meanwhile, Smith, lean and agile like a gazelle, ran across the road and leapt up the stairs, shouting in the process 'Hiding the cabbage.'

He caught a glimpse of me disappearing from view. Waving his finger and laughing, he shouted louder than before, 'you're collared'.

Barney and Alfie need not have worried about being collared. Mr Smith was an old friend who appreciated the high quality of A. & B. Hyams's work.

With tongue in cheek, Smith said to Barney, 'just be careful'.

Smith obviously knew that the brothers were making some cabbage. Providing they were not too greedy, he was prepared to tolerate their gain.

Other small contractors were not always in the same situation as A. & B. Hyams. Some manufacturers deeply resented their sub-contractors obtaining cabbage. They would stipulate that if the contractors saved fabric on a particular docket, the surplus fabric must be returned to them. However, several manufacturers allowed their contractors to keep the fabric but insisted that under no circumstances must they use the fabric to make up the same style. Sometimes the opposite was encouraged; contractors could make the same style from the surplus cabbage and deliver the extra garments to the showroom as part of the docket. Usually, a double making price was offered for any extra garments received, but these were not favoured options by sub-contractors, who in most cases preferred to use the manufacturers' styles for their cabbage and then sell the garments to market stallholders.

This practice of selling cabbage to stallholders caused a great deal of animosity in the trade. Woe betide a sub-contractor and a market stallholder who were discovered by a manufacturer trading in this way. The contractor and the stallholder could be accused of theft by the manufacturer and sometimes they were.

In the summer of 1953, Albert and Maisy Swanson were the proprietors of a small Stepney clothing workshop trading as Divina Gowns. For some time the couple had been contracted to make girls' skirts for David Conway who was the managing director of Fairie Fashions, a well known East End children's clothing manufacturer. During the previous six-month period, the Swansons had received 4,217 yards of corduroy and 1,159 yards of wool from Conway to make up young girls' skirts at two shillings a piece. When it was brought to Conway's attention that dozens of children's skirts identical to the ones which were being made for him by the Swansons were being sold from a stall at a local street market, he immediately embarked on an internal investigation. Unwilling or unable to accept the fact that the skirts sold at the stall were cabbage, he assumed that the skirts had been stolen from his warehouse. He began to suspect that the Swansons and his own manager, David Leslie, were the culprits.

Leslie was responsible for overseeing deliveries from the subcontractors.

Believing that the trio were conspiring to cheat him, Conway contacted the police.

Jack Hillman, the market trader who sold the skirts, was the first to be interviewed by the police at his stall. He explained that he bought the skirts from the Swansons for cash. He had had no idea that the skirts might be stolen and was unable to show any proof of his purchase although, on a second visit by the police, he did produce a receipt.

The police interviewed the Swansons at their home. The couple denied that they had been involved in any wrongdoing. Mrs Swanson added 'There is nothing stolen here.'

When the police began to search the premises they found several hundred girls' skirts stored there.

Mr Swanson admitted that the skirts were made from Conway's fabric.

'But they are mine, as we used our brains to cut the cloth and get more skirts from it than Conway required; it is known as cabbage; that is how we make a few bob.'

Mrs Swanson said that 'making cabbage was a recognised thing in the trade'.

Her husband continued; 'Yes, you can call it stealing, but it is legitimate stealing.'

The police then questioned David Leslie who, unknown to his employers, had formed a partnership with the Swansons using an assumed name, Joseph Shaw.

Leslie rejected the allegation that as Conway's manager he, rather than his staff, had personally checked deliveries from the Swansons and that he had signed for skirts which had not been delivered.

Eventually the Swansons, David Leslie and Jack Hillman were arrested and put on trial at the Old Bailey.

Hillman was soon found not guilty of receiving 311 skirts valued at £210 knowing that they were stolen. He was discharged.

Mr James Burge, prosecuting, stated that part of the agreement between Conway and the Swansons was that any surplus fabric that was not used for dockets would be returned and that a subsequent stock check at Conway's premises discovered that 157 woollen skirts and 1,036 corduroy skirts were missing and that the Swansons had kept 121yards of corduroy and 147 yards of wool, which they had made up into skirts and sold to Hillman. Mr Burge alleged that it was not a case of making cabbage, but of theft and in order to conceal the theft of the fabric the Swansons had worked in collusion with Leslie, who pretended to check deliveries from them and signed for skirts which had never been received.

When Leslie stood in the witness box he flatly denied that he had ever conspired with the Swansons to cheat his employer.

Mr C. Salmon, Q.C. defending, explained to the jury that according to Conway's skirt costins, the Swansons had delivered all the garments which were required; therefore no fabric was due to be returned. By economical marker making and careful cutting, the Swansons had saved on the costins, which resulted in cabbage being obtained. In due course, from this cabbage, 371 skirts were made up.

Mr Salmon argued that the whole case rested on what was the original agreement between the parties.

Albert Swanson was the last defendant to appear in the dock; he explained to the court that it was generally accepted in the clothing trade, by suppliers and outworkers alike, that cabbage was the property of the outworker. He had been contracted to make skirts for David Conway since the beginning of 1953. On a previous occasion, when he was asked by Conway to return the balance of certain fabric, he did so. He was never asked to return any fabric concerned in the present charges.

At this stage of the trial, the Commissioner, Sir Ernest Goodman Roberts, Q.C. advised the jury that if they had heard enough of the evidence, they were at liberty to stop the case at any time.

The jury immediately retired to consider their verdict. After a short period, they returned to the court, having found the three defendants not guilty.

No doubt this trial could easily have been avoided. If David Conway had had a written, rather than an oral agreement with his sub-contractors that they must return all surplus fabric, and if he had given them prepared markers and not just the skirt patterns, the amount of cabbage obtained would have been minimal. Albert Swanson, who bragged to the police that he and his wife 'had used our brains to cut the cloth and get more skirts from it than Conway required' had obviously failed to use his brain when it came to utilising the cabbage. The Swansons had been foolish to make use of Conway's styles. They should either have sold the surplus fabric to a cloth merchant or alternatively found a style that was not part of Fairie Fashions range. Perhaps both parties had learnt from their mistakes.

In 1958 I was to witness perhaps the start of the British clothing industry being undermined by imported foreign products. Prior to that date, the dress zip fasteners which Barney purchased from trimming merchants were always made by a UK company called Areo Zips. Suddenly cheap, slimline nylon zips manufactured by YKK, a Japanese firm, appeared on the market. Unable to compete, Areo Zips and other similar British zip manufacturers ceased trading. Within a year or two YKK dominated the British zip fastener trade.

During the 1960s another dynamic Japanese firm was equally successful in Britain. The Brothers Sewing Machine Company manufactured superb, well designed sewing machines. Not only were thousands of their machines sold in Britain; millions more were sold throughout the world. Because of the reliability of the Brothers sewing machines I purchased four of their flat machines at £120 each when I opened a blouse and skirt factory in 1973.

It was during 1959 that A. & B. Hyams began looking for new premises in the Shoreditch area. I decided that once they had made the move, I would leave their company. For some time, I had felt increasingly restless and wanted a change of environment. One change that might have been imposed on me had now been lifted. It was announced in the press that National Service was about to be abolished.

I had mixed feelings about National Service. One moment I was glad that I would be exempt from this commitment. The next moment, I rather liked the idea of wearing a uniform and spending two years in places like Cyprus, Hong Kong and Malaya, but it was my old ambition of joining the Merchant Navy that now interested me.

Seaman friends were urging me to visit the Shipping Federation's offices to enquire about enlisting. I wanted desperately to do so. An ideal date would be the following year when A. & B. Hyams would have moved to Shoreditch and my parents, with whom I lived in Stepney, would have been rehoused to Poplar.

On Friday 10 June, I left A. & B. Hyams, much to Barney and Alfie's regret, but it would not be the last time that the brothers would see me. I remained in contact with them for several years. Besides being excellent employers, I had learnt a great deal from Barney, who I always felt was a kind and patient man. I would never forget that it was he who had taught me how to cut garments accurately and the art of marker making and, equally important, how to do simple pattern grading.

It was during 1960 that my friends Brian Miah and Alfie Debono, both of whom were trained garment cutters, left the clothing trade to seek better paid employment elsewhere,

Brian was the first to find alternative work. He acquired an interesting job at a Bethnal Green factory which manufactured pewter mugs and jugs, unfortunately his time at this factory was brief and he was sacked.

Brian declined to give the reason why he was considered unsuitable, but I suspect it may have been his increasing inability to concentrate and absorb what was being explained to him. Alfie and I had noticed that our mutual friend's mental awareness was beginning to deteriorate; we soon learnt the reason why.

Brian's older brother Derek informed us that when Brian was a child he had contracted meningitis and that his recently diagnosed health problem was the long term effects of the disease. Though Brian's condition was slowly progressive, he still led a normal life; he lived at home with his parents and three brothers.

After several months of unemployment Brian managed to find a reasonably paid position as a warehouseman in Whitechapel.

Alfie vowed never to return to garment cutting, which he had come to loath. At the local Labour Exchange he was offered a job as a labourer, though he preferred the title 'maintenance hand' at Wapping River Police Station. The police superintendent at the station explained to Alfie that he must be prepared to witness dead bodies been brought ashore having been recovered from the Thames.

'At least 40 to 50 each year,' said the captain of one of the police launches.

The sight of drowned victims, some of whom were in a terrible decaying condition, proved a harrowing ordeal for the 21-year-old Alfie. A few months later he handed in his notice and accepted a low skilled job at a paint factory on the Isle of Dogs.

Aldgate East

The Aldgate dress factory where I was to spend the next six weeks had a depressing, dark atmosphere. As it was below ground level, the basement cutting room had no windows. Fire extinguishers and alarms were nowhere to be seen. Stone steps to the floor above were at one end of the basement, and at the other end a small trapdoor measuring about 18 inches square was cut out of the ceiling and used for lowering fabric. If a fire started on the ground floor, the basement could be a potential death-trap. An added problem was the colony of rats that had gained access via a sewer that ran parallel with the basement. Small piles of rodentcide, probably Warfarin, were placed in the little crannies at various points along the floor. Many of the rats that had been poisoned crawled under the lower shelf of the long cutting table to expire. The smell was appalling.

According to Elsie, a friendly West Indian machinist who worked in the machining room on the first floor, the basement had been infested with rats for years. Elsie was eventually to pay a price for her willingness to venture down into the basement; when confronted by a large rat on the stone steps she jumped into the air and tumbled down the steps, badly injuring her back. My employer Gerald expressed little concern when told of Elsie's accident.

Gerald resembled Fagin without picee (Little ringlets of hair dangling around the ears). Unknown to him, he was often referred to as 'Fagin' by his staff. He operated a successful mail-order business by advertising his garments in the daily press. Like many wealthy people, he had a reputation for meanness.

There were two other cutters working in the basement when I arrived, Dennis and Andy were cousins and both about my age. Unknown to me Andy, the less experienced, had been employed only temporarily and would leave at short notice once a more experienced cutter could be found. Realising I was that cutter, Dennis, unlike Andy, immediately embarked on a campaign to make life unpleasant for me which continued even after Andy had left the company.

Dennis refused to co-operate. If I asked him where a certain pattern was kept, he would merely shrug his shoulders. When he did respond, his reply was always the same, 'see the boss,' which meant I had to make regular trips to Fagin's office on the first floor. Fagin soon became annoyed with these interruptions; he stormed into the cutting room and reprimanded Dennis, threatening that if he wasn't prepared to work as part of a team he would be dismissed. The ultimatum did not create a better working climate – quite the opposite. Dennis became more resentful and soon resorted to sulking and treating me as if I was a nonentity.

I thought the situation was now ludicrous; how could Dennis not communicate with me, especially when we had to work together laying up wide fabric. Believing that I had no option but to appease I asked him if Andy had found new employment. He looked at me fiercely before saying 'No and he is short of money.'

I answered him sympathetically, 'I am sorry to hear that.' Suddenly, he pointed his finger at me vindictively, but refused to look me in the eye.

Speaking bitterly, he said 'You were out of order. Because of your working here, Andy got the sack.'

'I don't know what you are talking about,' I retorted.

He continued to air his grievances, but his tone was slightly modified.

I protested. 'Dennis, there is no way that I would have accepted this vacancy if it meant another cutter would lose his job. I had no idea that Andy would be sacked, all I did was answer an advert for an experienced stock cutter. If I had known from the beginning about Andy's situation, I can assure you I would not have started working here. Jobs like these are ten-a-penny in this area and you know it too. Besides, I am planning to join the Merchant Navy soon.'

My explanation had no effect. His mind was set: I was the cause of his cousin's dismissal. Now that his grievance was in the open, he felt that he was in a position to continually harass me, hoping that if I handed in my notice and left, Andy would be reinstated. But he miscalculated. I had become angry with his unwarranted and stupid attitude.

That afternoon I challenged Dennis to a fight. He appeared startled, but grudgingly agreed that we could meet in the little courtyard at the rear of the factory after we had finished work at 5.30 p.m.

Immediately after my challenge, a quiet period followed. During the late afternoon, I noticed that he was periodically glancing in my direction, perhaps he was trying to assess what type of opponent I would be when we had our forthcoming scrap. I was not worried. I felt certain that I could beat him. Suddenly, just before tea time and totally out of character, he said that if I needed to oil the cutting machine, the little oil-can could be found in a nearby cupboard. An added surprise occurred a few minutes later. As I searched in vain for a missing dress pattern, he appeared alongside the rail and handed me the appropriate pattern; and there were more niceties to follow. During the tea break, he actually offered me one of his sweets.

This sudden change of character was unexpected. What was his motive? I could detect no sign of his previous acerbity, so noticeable during the morning.

Gone was the sneer, the provocative remarks, the negative answers. His attitude towards me was changing for the better. There seemed to be a willingness to co-operate.

Later in the afternoon, Dennis made several attempts at conversation which I gladly responded to. There was a slight nervousness in his voice which almost disappeared once he spoke of his family and girlfriend. Andy was not mentioned. Perhaps Dennis had finally realised that I was not such a bad fellow after all and that my stay would only be temporary, or could it be that he had become afraid, believing that he might come off worst when we had our scrap. The nervousness which had appeared in his speech now spread to his face. I pretended not to notice; unlike me, he had probably never been involved in a fight before. I quickly reassessed the situation. Obviously, we could no longer keep our appointment in the courtyard, so it would be in our best interests if I withdrew my challenge. He was the weaker man and I was no bully. As we slowly put on our coats, I held out my hand to him; the look of anxiety on his face so prevalent a few seconds before was disappearing fast as I spoke.

'Dennis, don't you think we should be friends? After all, we have to work together.'

He shook my hand and smiled for the first time. From that moment I felt our working relationship could only get better.

Fagin's meanness was resented by his female staff. He seemed to ignore the fact that if he invested money in improving the unhealthy and dangerous working conditions in the factory, his staff would be more productive and contented. Because Fagin was a hoarder, the basement cutting room was filled with unusable, outdated fabric. Huge piles of old remnants were stacked everywhere; rails of ancient patterns were occupying valuable space. Much of my time was spent clearing the cluttered cutting table or searching for elusive patterns that were still in use. I spoke to Fagin about the nauseating, strong smell of the dead rats that rose from under the cutting table.

He instantly dismissed my complaint. After a quick glance at Dennis, who was cutting out a lay he added 'Dennis never complains.'

This, of course, was totally untrue; from the moment that Dennis and Andy had started working in the basement several weeks earlier, they had continually pointed out to Fagin that the cutting room was 'running alive with rats', but he dismissed their complaint. Eventually, both cutters had given up trying to persuade him to eliminate the vermin.

Bending downwards, Fagin stuck his head under the cutting table and began to sniff quite loud. After standing up, he twitched his nostrils, looked at me in amazement and said, 'You must be imagining things, there is no smell.'

I was flabbergasted; the putrid smell saturated the entire basement; how on earth could he deny it, unless he was actually being honest and might well be afflicted, like my mother, who had little sense of smell.

A few days later, I was to learn the truth about his nostrils.

Having never heard of Weil's disease (A severe form of jaundice caused by a spirally coiled bacterium found in rats urine) and ignoring common sense that it was most unhealthy to eat food in a basement with rat carcasses and their droppings lying around, I sat on the cutting table to eat a salt beef sandwich which I had brought back from Blooms the local kosher restaurant. Enjoying my snack, I was disturbed by the sudden appearance of Fagin, who came into the cutting room. Placing his nose in the air like a hound trying to pick up a scent, he called out to me 'Ah, salt beef, my favourite.'

I suppose I could have confronted him and demanded how he could smell the beef and not the decaying rats, but realistically, it would be a pointless and wasted effort. Fagin, as Dennis had earlier reminded me, would show no interest whatsoever in spending money and calling in a professional rat-catcher. As far as he was concerned, small piles of rodentcide were sufficient.

My irresponsible employer may have lacked enthusiasm for spending money to get rid of the rats, but there was no lack of enthusiasm for the fairer sex. Although married with two children, I suspected that he made use of local prostitutes.

Within days of working in the basement, I was approached at the cutting table by Fagin. Calling me aside, he asked if I knew of any teenage girls who might be interested in visiting him at his office during the evening after the staff had gone home, 'For drinks and a bit of fun. Naturally it would be in your interest,' he said with a miserly smirk that implied he was offering me shillings and not pounds.

His suggestion offended me; my instant reaction was a cold negative stare, which I hoped would tell him that I could not be bought. Unbelievably, my negative response had no effect. Rather than move away from the cutting table, he remained there. The tapping of his fingertips on an invoice book was an indication that he was serious and wanted a positive reply. I soon gave him a reply, but not the one he wanted. Relishing the thought of being sacked on the spot, my riposte was deadly and aimed below the belt.

'Look mate, you employed me as a cutter, not as a pimp. If you want a shag, visit Graces Alley.'

Incredibly, no eyelid was blinked; he looked neither aghast nor angry and seemed oblivious to what I had just said. This unexpected episode came to an abrupt end when his name was called from the floor above and he bounded up the stairs.

That evening I met my close friend David Upson for drinks at the Nelson's

Head in the Commercial Road. I told Dave how my unsavoury employer had had the temerity to ask me to procure young teenage girls.

'That is illegal' said Dave, who was familiar with the law. Lowering his whisky glass and with tongue in cheek, he mischievously proposed that we should teach Fagin a lesson by introducing him to Rose, a tiny, but muscular West Indian lesbian who frequented the clubs in Cable Street and Graces Alley.

Rose, when short of cash, would sometimes turn to prostitution. Our diminutive friend made no secret that she despised her clients, describing them as 'old wankers'. Spending a short time with Rose could be dangerous. If the punter dared question her prices, smelt, swore, had been drinking or had a repulsive appearance and if Rose was in a depressed mood, which she often was, then the unfortunate punter might find himself being physically attacked and possibly robbed.

Dave and I visualised the scene with amusement, Rose and Fagin alone in his office. His meanness and awful profile would have incensed her. She would have shown him no mercy. Within minutes, he would have found himself wrestled to the floor, kicked or punched in the groin and deprived of his wallet and watch. Of course, if Dave had been in my position, he would never have seriously contemplated arranging such a rendezvous that would place Fagin's life at risk, but I was different. There was a possibility that I might just be tempted to act as a go-between and introduce Rose to Fagin if he approached me once more about supplying young girls. Fortunately, my rebuttal in the basement must have had an immediate effect because he never raised the subject again.

Just a few weeks after I began working for Fagin, I was surprised to find an ebullient David Upson anxiously waiting for me outside the factory at lunch time. Dave, a former seaman, was interested in rejoining the merchant Navy. He grasped my arm, pulled me along the pavement and said 'Come on, Alf, we have to go to the Shipping Federation; they are recruiting.'

I answered him incredulously, 'Recruiting? Are you sure Dave?'

As we increased our pace along Leman Street, he explained that he had met his seaman friend Len Mackenzie in the pub the previous evening. Len had told him the good news.

I was confused. Dave and I had only recently visited the Shipping Federation offices in nearby Prescot Street to enquire about enlisting in the Merchant Navy and had been advised by an official to return in the spring, when there would be vacancies for utility stewards.

Within five minutes we had arrived at the offices, but our elation was short lived. An unsympathetic bespectacled clerk told us we were too late. The Federation had stopped taking on new staff earlier that morning. Noticing our disappointment, a mixed-race seaman approached us by the exit.

'They will take you on in April, man, but pop in meanwhile; you might be lucky and get accepted.'

After we left the building I felt dejected, but not Dave, who was always an optimist like Mr Micawber, on such occasions. He tried to console me. 'Cheer up, Alf. Don't consider it to be time wasted; we tried and we can try again.' He smiled cheerfully. 'Spring will soon be here, mate,' but spring was eight months away and I was becoming more impatient and restless by the day. Instead of travelling east to Tilbury to join a ship, I was heading north to a filthy basement at Aldgate East.

During the evening I drank with Dave at the Prospect of Whitby pub in Wapping. The disappointment that I had experienced at lunch time was soon forgotten. We met two pretty trainee occupational therapists from Bristol. Enjoying their company we sang the evening away. This was therapy at its best. At closing time, we escorted the girls to Wapping underground station. Walking home, Dave suggested that as we both worked near the Shipping Federation's offices, it would be in our interest if we could take it in turns to visit their offices once a week, but at the office we were always met with the same frustrating reply, 'Not at the moment'. Realising it was probably futile to expect to gain entry into the Merchant Navy before the spring of 1961; we made no further visits to Prescot Street.

After Dennis handed in his notice in the middle of July, Fagin attempted to increase my workload. I refused to co-operate. I was already cutting about ten dockets a week, which I thought was sufficient. I explained to Fagin that if he wanted more production, he must employ a second cutter. He walked away complaining of 'Poor sales' and that he could ill afford extra wages. I did not believe him. He was an extremely wealthy man who hated having to part with any money.

Years later, I was exchanging anecdotes with Jack, a Scottish cutter I had worked with at Rosalyn Fashions in Whitechapel. Jack had had more then his fair share of rapacious employers. One incident that he related instantly reminded me of the parsimonious Fagin.

Jack recalled how a previous employer, a certain Mr Lee, once offered him a lift in his car after work.

As they drove down Brick Lane at Whitechapel, Lee was attempting to pull out a small hair that was irritating his nostril. He stopped the car outside a chemist's shop, went inside and purchased a cheap pair of tweezers. Sitting in the car, he managed to remove the troublesome hair. Instead of driving away as Jack expected, his employer went back inside the chemist's shop and returned the tweezers, insisting that they were the wrong size. He also demanded his money back. The shop assistant duly obliged. Episodes like this are not uncommon in the clothing trade.

Now that Dennis had departed, the atmosphere in the basement was less noisy with only one cutting machine in use. The quietness appealed to the rodents, who were becoming bolder. I was startled one morning by a rat that darted through my legs and disappeared down a hole under the sink. During the afternoon I managed to strike a huge unwanted visitor on the snout with my steel yardstick when it emerged from a large cavity that was cut out of the wall and used for storing markers.

It had now become increasingly intolerable for me to work there. Besides the appalling conditions, I was so restless for change.

It was a Monday morning and I went down into the basement to start work. As usual, I would tread heavily on the steps in a vain hope that my loud footsteps would frighten off the rats. After turning on the lights, I was forced to stop in my tracks; at least six rats scattered in every direction. Fresh droppings were in the sink and on top of the lay that I was due to cut out. I knew, at that moment, it was impossible for me to continue any longer in that disgusting, malodorous basement. I was under no contract or agreement with Fagin and he owed me no wages. Fortunately for him, he had not yet arrived; if he had, I would probably have thumped him. Within minutes, I was in the street, regretting only that I would now lose contact with Elsie, who was still at home recovering from her back injury.

At midday, I phoned Fagin and demanded that he should have my P45 ready that evening at 5.30.

He responded by complaining that I had let him down 'Badly.' He also thought that my grievance about a 'few rats' was no grounds for leaving his employ. I was not prepared to discuss the matter with him. When he continued with his attempts to persuade me to stay, I rudely replaced the telephone receiver.

Outdoor employment now interested me, at least until the spring. Fortunately there was a variety of non clothing work available in the East End. I considered becoming a postman, an assistant groundsman in a park, perhaps even a hod-carrier like my father, though I could never match his strength.

By chance, I met a soldier friend, Mike Cassidy, on leave from the Army and visiting old mates in Stepney.

Mike mentioned a new scheme that the army had just introduced. The scheme was designed to attract teenage volunteers. Recruits could sign up for 3, 6 and 9 year engagements. What I found interesting was a proviso in the scheme that allowed a recruit to return to civilian life at any time during his 12 week training period on condition that he paid a discharge fee of £20.

A week after meeting Mike, I became recruit 23688713 in the Grenadier Guards and was based at Pirbright Camp in Surrey.

During the second week of October, I was back in the East End. My good friend Alfie Debono had sent me the £20 which I needed to buy myself out of the army.

(More details of my 10 week army experience can be found in 'An East End Story'.)

The Wills dressmaking factory situated on the corner of Commercial Road and Albert Gardens, Stepney where I began working after leaving the Army, was almost an exact replica of Fagin's basement. The cutting room had poor lighting and was airless and dusty. It was a dismal cellar which you descended into by way of an ancient loosely-fitted wooden staircase. Fortunately, I could detect no smell of rodents, but the cutting room reeked of tobacco. As expected, there were no fire exits or extinguishers. At least in Fagin's basement there was a secondary exit, albeit a small one; you might, by standing on the cutting table, be able to squeeze yourself out of the 18-inch-square hatch cut out of the ceiling that was used for lowering fabric, but here at the Wills factory there was no alternative means of escape if there was an outbreak of fire.

On the very first day that I started work, I retrieved an old bucket from the factory's yard and filled it with water, ignoring the sarcastic remarks of Stan, the other cutter, I placed the bucket under the cutting table close to where I stood.

The directors of the Wills factory were two Jewish brothers, both elderly, short in stature and in poor health. Their personalities could not have been more different. Bespectacled Sidney, the slightly older of the two, was friendly and loquacious. Maurice, ambivert and taciturn, always seemed to be deep in thought.

The brothers rarely came down into the cutting room, except to give us our work dockets.

Thankfully there were no rats present, but Stan, an overweight, heavy-smoking cutter, was present and I soon quarrelled with him once he knew I disapproved of his smoking in the cutting room. Stan was totally irresponsible. Although we were provided with sacks for the cloth cuttings, he chose not to fill them up as he cut out the lay, which should be normal practice, preferring instead to drop the cuttings onto the floor. At the end of the day, he would half-heartedly attempt to sweep up and fill the sacks, but often small piles of his cuttings, discarded newspapers, cigarette ends and fruit peelings were left on the floor overnight. In the morning, I would arrive early and clean up the detritus. Moreover, throughout the day, Stan continually threw still lit matches onto the floor. This bad habit was highly dangerous; it could create an inferno.

My perennial concern about a fire starting in the cutting room was not groundless. The inevitable soon occurred. Late one morning, I was engrossed in cutting out a large lay when suddenly smoke drifted towards me. I immediately switched off the cutting machine and was amazed to see a small but rapidly spreading fire raging at the foot of the stairs. Within seconds, I had grabbed the bucket of now stagnant water, which I had kept for such emergencies, and leapt across the cutting table, nearly spilling water on the fabric. Dousing the flames was no easy task; it was obvious that the fire had been started by one of Stan's discarded matches. I charged furiously up the stairs looking for him, but he was nowhere to be seen; nor were my employers, they were out to lunch.

Stan was the first to return. I castigated him; totally speechless, he made no comment. When he emerged from this brief silent state, he peered over his shoulder. Fearing the imminent arrival of our employers and instant dismissal, he decided that urgent action was now needed to hide the evidence of the fire.

He ushered me down into the still smoking basement and in his haste the sandwiches which he had just bought were dropped to the floor where they remained. I helped him to scoop up the burnt cuttings and sweep up. After apologising profusely, he implored me not to mention the fire to Sidney and Maurice. I reluctantly agreed, but demanded an assurance that under no circumstances would he ever smoke in the cutting room again.

Sighing with relief, he promised that in future his cigarettes would be left at home.

Our smoke free environment lasted about a month, but predictably his promise was worthless and he started smoking again. Believing that I might not be so lucky a second time and might perish if a fire reoccurred, I handed in my notice and left the company, much to Stan's satisfaction.

The thought that I could have lost my life in that cellar made me even more aware of how dangerous old clothing workshops were. Unlike the larger factories in the area that had fire exits, extinguishers, alarms and practised fire drills, these small workshops had no such facilities, especially if the premises had been converted from former dwellings. Such an example was at nearby Albert Gardens, a delightful square of adjoining houses built in the 1840s.

In the square, no less than ten of the houses had been converted into clothing workshops. The cutting rooms in converted houses, which were dotted all over the East End, were usually in the basement or on the top floor. A fire risk was always present, especially in the machining room, where workers had no choice but to sit at their sewing machines, often surrounded by highly inflammable materials which included hundreds of finished garments in plastic bags. Unserviced old steam boilers still in use were within arm's reach and faulty electrical leads criss-crossed the floor causing everyone to tread carefully. Smoking was never discouraged. Complaints by non-smoking staff, worried about the effects of breathing fellow workers' tobacco smoke, were ignored. Many of the employers were themselves chronic smokers.

The memory of the five young Asian machinists who were burnt to death at D. K. Netawear, a clothing workshop in the Mile End Road, during October 1983, is still fresh today. The fire was one of four East End clothing factory fires that occurred over a six-week period. The flames quickly engulfed the Netawear two-storey building. The terrified and doomed women on the first and second floors could be seen from the road screaming at the iron barred windows.

The tragedy caused a public outcry. A spokesman for The National Union of Tailors and Garment Workers said, 'There are thousands [a nonsensical figure] of these factories in the Mile End area, and the fire could have happened in any one of them. The factory Inspectorate is totally inadequate.' The union invited the Employment Secretary, Tom King, to visit East London 'to see for himself the dangers faced by clothing workers every day'. Ian Mikado, MP for Poplar and Bow, demanded an immediate public enquiry into 'these sweatshops and also the cuts in the fire brigade'. Peter Shaw, MP for Bethnal Green and Stepney, criticised the 'sweatshop tradition'. He further added, 'It is time the whole system was tightened up; we must see to it that this kind of tragedy never happens again.' GLC leader Ken Livingstone, who visited the scene of the fire, said, 'Any fire that spreads so rapidly always leaves a question mark, but we must wait for the report by the Fire Brigade'.

At the inquest the following January, a forensic scientist said that the fire had probably been started by a discarded match or cigarette end which had ignited cardboard boxes containing 3,200 plastic coat-hangers and a box of cloth cuttings that were kept by the stairs.

I do not know if any dangerous East End factories and workshops were forcibly closed down by the local authorities following the Mile End fire. The only company which I was aware of that was put out of business because their premises were a fire risk was Sam-Sam Ltd, a small quilting firm, but they were based in Hoxton Square at Shoreditch.

Fashion House in Fashion Street, where I had worked for the gown manufacturer Myers & Co in 1962, also caught fire. Typically, the fire was caused by a carelessly thrown match or cigarette end which landed amongst a pile of rubbish at the bottom of the stairs. Within minutes, the fire brigade had arrived and managed to get the fire under control. Dozens of workers had already got out of the building, but 21 workers were forced to use the fire exit that led to the roof and firemen had to use ladders to rescue them.

Max

I soon began working at a small skirt workshop located near New Road, Stepney. Max, the proprietor, was a elderly widower. Within five minutes of being interviewed by him I was standing at the cutting table making a simple skirt marker. Although the table was only about 15 feet long, there was sufficient space to make a marker for at least four skirts. Max suggested that, at the end of the day, we could discuss wages. He also stated that the position would be just for a short period, as he was planning to retire and move to Tel Aviv to live with his married daughter. 'She is worried about my health,' he chuckled.

Max employed three female staff. Glynis from Barbados, who did the pressing, was a deeply religious woman. Throughout the day, she would quietly sing and hum Gospel songs. The two other women were Greek Cypriot sisters. Both seemed efficient special machinists. Occasionally one of them would swap her role and become a flat machinist responsible for samples and alterations. Flat machining is different from special machining. A flat machinist sews the parts of a garment together and it is highly skilled work that requires several years of practice to be proficient. A special machinist operates several different machines that can overlock a raw seam, fell the hem of a skirt, make button holes and button-sew. Within a few months, a novice worker with no previous experience of the clothing trade, provided that she or he was keen to learn, could soon become quite capable of operating the special machines. A special machinist tends to be paid by the hour or the week and earns lower wages than a flat machinist, who usually works at a piece rate. Max also employed five or six flat machinists who were home workers and lived locally. He would call at their homes each day, delivering bundles of skirts and collecting the finished skirts.

Unlike coat and jacket cutting, which requires a great deal of skill and also the strength to handle heavy rolls of fabric, skirt cutting is relatively simple. The fabric is usually lighter. The garment itself usually has only five parts, three of which are skirt panels, a waistband and a zip placket.

Knowing that skirt cutting is easy, I expected the wages to be considerably lower than those of dress, jacket and coat cutters, but the wages Max offered me at the end of my first day equalled what was being paid to top coat cutters. This generous offer was probably due to the fact that his retirement was imminent and adding a few extra pounds each week to his cutting costs was irrelevant.

A few days after I began working for Max, he told me that he was very pleased that I was economical with the costins and added that 'trying to gain a little cabbage on every docket is necessary, not so much for any profit, but just to cover my skirt losses that seem to occur every week'.

I was curious to know why he should have losses. With few staff and a small production of approximately 750 garments every week, losses due to his machinists having accidents should be negligible. My surprised expression on being told about the losses seemed to make him feel slightly uncomfortable. Blinking rapidly, he glanced at the Greek machinists before speaking quietly: 'I always have this problem of late. I seem to lose about a dozen skirts on every docket.' Eventually I discovered why Max was losing skirts and it was not due to accidents or damages, although they did occur, as they do in all factories. The reason was theft.

It was during the early afternoon when Max had left the workshop to deliver bundles to his outdoor machinists. I was cutting out a lay when suddenly one of the blade sharpeners broke off from the cutting machine and landed on the floor. Earlier Max had told me that if I needed new blades or sharpeners they could be found in the tool box, but he had forgotten to tell me where the box was kept. I searched everywhere for this elusive toolbox, eventually finding it half hidden by remnants under the cutting table. From my position crouching on the floor, I could see under the table and had a clear view of Glynis and the sisters at the opposite end of the workshop. Glynis had the habit of singing quite loudly whenever Max was absent. Her melodious voice sailed towards me. I recognised the spiritual, 'Sometimes I feel like a motherless child'. I glanced in her direction attracted by the song. Suddenly, a movement to her right caught my eye. With lightening speed the sisters were surreptitiously tucking some finished but unpressed skirts into their bags, which had been placed on the floor by their machines. Glynis seemed oblivious to the theft. It was unlikely that she was involved in pilfering. She was far too religious and God-fearing. I stood up, but not before noticing the sisters discreetly zipping up their bags. With my mind occupied with what I had just witnessed, concentrating on the work proved difficult. I switched off the cutting machine but this action caused the sisters to start whispering. Not wanting to arouse their suspicions, I immediately switched it back on.

I knew that Max would return shortly, but informing him about the theft would be awkward for me. Nevertheless, the sisters deserved to be unmasked. They were thieves and had no right to steal from him. Max seemed to me to be a generous employer, undemanding and thoughtful. I imagined that the wages that he paid to Glynis and the sisters was comparable to, if not better than, what was being offered elsewhere. He trusted his staff implicitly, yet two of them chose to abuse his trust, perhaps over a long period.

Glynis, did the pressing by an open window. Suddenly she shouted to me that Max was calling my name from the street. I was pleased; this would be an opportunity for me to explain to him in private about the sisters' activities. I went down the stairs and found a heavy-breathing and sweating Max sitting on a sack of machined skirts by the doorway. He looked exhausted. 'Help me to carry these skirts upstairs, Alf.'

Obviously, this was not the right time to mention a delicate matter. I swung the sack onto my back; it was extremely heavy.

At 5.30 p.m. the sisters hurriedly left the premises, followed by a weary but still singing Glynis. With Max and me alone in the workshop, this would be an ideal moment to expose the sisters, but being tactful was essential. I had no idea how he would respond to what I was going to reveal. There were two choices available to me: I could tell him directly that I had witnessed the sisters stealing. Alternatively, I could merely imply that he might be employing dishonest people, but refrain from disclosing names. The second choice seemed appropriate.

I spoke slowly. 'Max, I have been thinking about your skirt losses; have you ever considered the possibility that they are being stolen?'

I had barely finished the sentence when he replied quite loudly, 'Stolen, did you say stolen?'

His tone implied disbelief. He continued, but looked and sounded agitated.

'Never, never, nobody would steal from me, nobody. I know my ladies, they are all good people.'

My god, I thought, the man is so trusting; surely he cannot be that naïve. He shook his head and again emphasised that the losses were due to his staff, both indoor and outdoor, having accidents that resulted in skirts being damaged.

Speaking defensively, he added, 'I am not the only one; all factories have this problem.'

His rejection of my accusation of theft occurring surprised me. When he again shook his head I thought that it was appropriate to change the subject, but I still believed it was important to bring to his attention a very serious matter of which he seemed unaware, or was he? Maybe he did realise that the sisters were stealing from him, but because they were fast and efficient workers he chose not to sack them. It was also possible that in order to keep his little business on course until retirement he was prepared to look the other way and write off the losses, especially as he was now, through my efforts, obtaining some cabbage on every docket.

After our conversation was over I put on my duffle coat and was about to leave the premises when Max stopped me by the door and said. 'Don't

52

concern yourself my boy; be happy. I know what I am doing; am I really an old Meshuggenah?' (Yiddish for madman)

'Of course not, Max,' I replied.

Although I would not raise the subject of theft again, I remained concerned because of the presence of the despicable sisters.

I liked Max. He had a good heart and his little acts of kindness were most welcome. There was always a hot drink waiting for me when I arrived at work in the morning. He would shake his head in amazement, knowing that I had just walked from Poplar.

'If only I had the stamina,' he lamented.

Never once did he fail to offer me a selection from the variety of fruits that he consumed daily with a passion.

'Jaffa oranges,' he proudly boasted.

'Are they fresh from the Kibbutz?' I joked.

When I mentioned that I was fond of Jewish food, he smiled broadly. The next morning he told me not to go to the café at lunch time. I suspected that he had a little treat in store, and what a treat it was.

At 1 p.m. I switched off the cutting machine. There, placed on the table for Max and me to enjoy, was an enormous plate of delicious latkas, chopped liver and salt-beef sandwiches. He also offered me hot Russian tea, which I had never tasted before. Perhaps this feast was Max's way of showing his gratitude. I knew that he was pleased with my ability to achieve tight costins and gain between 5 and 10 per cent cabbage on every order. This surplus enabled him to complete all dockets.

The sisters continued to steal as if it was their perquisite, but they were now taking some precautions. It may have been the case that this loathsome pair suspected that I was not totally unobservant, because they now seemed to be restricting their furtive activities to late afternoons, usually just before they went home and preferably when the noisy cutting machine was switched on. My head may have been lowered, but not my eyes. I was quite capable of cutting safely and still being aware of what was happening elsewhere in the workshop.

The weeks passed quickly. Soon it would be time for Max to roll up his tape measure and remove his apron for the last time. I was glad that he had a loving daughter in Israel who was willing to look after him. With advancing years and declining health, living alone in London might be detrimental for Max.

It was at a lunch time during Max's final week. We were sitting on the cutting table, enjoying what was to be the last of our weekly Jewish luncheons, this time boiled gefilta fish, pea soup and bagels, when he explained to me his current plans. He had agreed a price and would sell his business to Chris, who was the husband of one of the Greek sisters. Glynis would stay on and I could also remain, if I so chose.

'On one condition;' he hesitated before he spoke again. 'I have been asked by Chris if you would teach his brother-in-law, Nicos, to cut. He will shortly be arriving from Cyprus.'

'Of course,' I replied, 'But only for the foreseeable future.'

Glynis seemed a little upset during Max's last hours as the outgoing proprietor of the skirt factory. Not once did she sing or hum all day. I had become quite accustomed to her pleasant voice. A few weeks earlier, she had invited me to watch her choir practise at a Hackney church. Politely, I refused, but became interested when she offered a sweetener: the choirmaster had two very attractive daughters.

David Upson and I wore smart clean clothes when we were introduced to the daughters at the church. Glynis must have been myopic, far from being attractive, the sisters, overweight sopranos, were hideous.

Our excuses for leaving were probably not believed. Dave felt faint and I had a sudden stomach upset.

Once outside in the churchyard, we bolted. Within 15 minutes we were sitting drinking in Dirty Dick's, recovering from our 'ailments'.

Max's imminent departure was of little interest to the heartless sisters. They seemed unconcerned and hardly spoke to him all day. I hoped that whatever the price Max had agreed with Chris it would be adequate, but his machinery was old and the workshop was in need of repair. Chris may have acquired the business for a pittance.

When it was time to stop work at 5.30 p.m. Max placed his arm around Glynis's shoulder and gave her a wage packet and a small envelope; it was probably a financial gift. Turning to me, he handed me my wage packet, whispering in the process, 'There is a little extra inside.' I thanked him and we shook hands. He looked relaxed and contented and he also promised to send Glynis and me postcards from Israel.

I left the workshop with Glynis, who was in an angry mood. Outside in the street, she gripped my arm and spoke alarmingly.

'I can't stay here, Alfie, and work for those bloody bitches; they are thieving cows. I can tell you, Jesus won't forgive them.'

Although I thoroughly agreed with her choice of words, I was quite surprised by her unchristian outburst.

As we walked towards the pedestrian crossing, I explained to her that I thought I was the only one who was aware that they were stealing. Again she gripped my arm and we stood still for a moment.

'Alfie, I have always known. I may be short-sighted, but I still saw them. I pretended not to notice.'

I asked her if she had informed Max.

'Yes, I did, twice, but he did not believe me, he trusted them. He is a good man, Alfie, very rare.'

I waited until she had crossed the road before turning round and heading in the direction of Poplar. I could not but wonder what the atmosphere would be like in the workshop on Monday morning, knowing that Max would no longer be there.

Throughout the 1960s the East End clothing trade was undergoing change. Like Max, many of the older factory proprietors were retiring, selling their businesses or closing them down. The more ambitious, who still had the energy, were opening up fashion showrooms in the West End and leasing out their factories. During this period, I noticed that there was a general lack of interest amongst the children of these factory-owners in taking over and continuing the family businesses that their hard-working parents had created. Alfie and Barney Hyams' sons were typical examples; they showed no enthusiasm for the 'shmatta game'.

This widespread attitude was in most cases welcomed by the parents, who preferred and encouraged their children to enter the professions rather than spending their lives managing a clothing factory in Whitechapel. Medicine, accountancy and the law were favoured options.

I once spoke to a retired Shoreditch coat maker, who gave me a graphic account of the ongoing problems which he had faced when he was in business.

'Okay, it's part and parcel of the game having to deal with unreasonable staff, but I had to be a confidant, advisor, judge and peacemaker too, and that was time-consuming. If you only knew how many times over the years I had to step in between feuding women trying to cut each other up with their scissors, always over a bloody window. One woman wants the window closed because she feels a draught, the woman sitting opposite her wants the window open because she feels hot. So what happens? They start arguing; the next minute they are rolling on the floor trying to cut each other. As I just said, it was always over a window, but the biggest worry for me was trying to find enough dockets when the game got slack. It was terrible having to put off staff just after Christmas. Okay, it was only temporary, but it gave me sleepless nights. Then there were the times when I would receive a bad cheque. Can you imagine what it felt like going to the bank to draw cash to pay the wages only to be told that the cheque was worthless? The aggravation made me ill. Once I caught pneumonia and was laid up on my back. The phone rings; it's someone from my factory telling me that the delivery of coats that we sent to the West End that morning had all been returned from the showroom; they would not accept them. Their excuse was that the coats were not up to my usual standard. The governor in the showroom went bonkers and threatened non-payment over late delivery. So what did I do? Crawl out of my sickbed and go to work. Sure, I made a few bob out of the game, but it also gave me blood pressure, diabetes and a dodgy ticker. If that wasn't enough, over the years I have been spat on, kicked, punched and even stabbed in that factory. Believe me, the game can be a killer.'

When he had finished his painful reminiscence, he proudly showed me photos of his two solicitor sons, both in cap and gown. 'Thanks to the Almighty, my boys had the good sense to see what the game did to their old man. Believe me, it was a relief for me and my wife that they never wanted to be part of it.'

The stabbing of employers by members of their staff in East End factories is unusual. The only case I can recall was alleged to have involved Jack Pasha, a veteran Stepney clothing manufacturer. I have no idea whether the incident did occur or was spurious, but the same story was related to me in at least two different factories. I was told that Pasha had become totally dissatisfied with one of his new employee's less than perfect pressing. The employee, a West African, was so upset that garments were continually being returned to him for repressing and also having to suffer the humiliation of Pasha's severe criticism, he went berserk. Grabbing a pair of tailor's scissors from a nearby bench, he plunged them deep into Pasha's shoulder. Pasha, tough as old boots, stood his ground and instantly withdrew the blood-soaked scissors from his shoulder. Confronting the African, he bellowed, 'If you want to stab me, do it properly'.

I worked for Pasha in the 1970s, but only for a short trial period. I did not like the atmosphere at his factory; it was too gloomy, the staff unfriendly and Pasha too abrasive. His departing words to me were uncalled for. He predicted that I would 'walk the streets and find no work'.

Pasha may have been a successful and established businessman, but he was no prophet. Within minutes of leaving his factory I had found work in nearby Cavell Street.

The vacuum created by the departing Jewish factory owners was soon to be filled by other hard working minorities, the Greek and Turkish Cypriots who, for some time, had been seen in ever-increasing numbers in the East End clothing factories. These immigrant machinists, men and women, worked extremely long hours. Not content with finishing at 5.30pm like their English counterparts, they would always take bundles of garments home, machining late into the night and throughout the weekend.

Within a few years first the Greeks and later the Turks became factory proprietors themselves. The success of the Turkish Cypriots was noticed by their kinsmen in Istanbul. Eventually, Turks from the mainland were arriving in London, often clandestinely, and were soon opening up coat and jacket factories not only in the East End but in North London too.

When I walked up the stairs to what was now Chris's workshop on the Monday morning, I felt a little apprehensive. Once inside, I could see that change had occurred over the weekend; the walls had been white-washed and the windows and floor had never looked cleaner. The entire workshop, neglected by Max, now seemed brighter and fresher. Extra ceiling lights had been fitted. A bench of six new sewing machines had been installed. An additional pressing unit was clamped to the floor, indicating that my new employers were planning to double their production. Four new Greek workers, one man and three women, had their heads lowered and were furiously machining the skirts. Glynis had not yet arrived. I could not see how, as a large lady, she was expected to squeeze into the tiny area that was now allocated to her. Being late was unusual for Glynis; maybe she had had a premonition and saw what was happening here and wanted no part of it.

The man sitting at the overlocking machine got up, came over to me and said 'Me Chris, you Alfos, yes?' His breath reeked of tobacco. We shook hands; his grip was strong. Pointing to one of the sisters, he said, 'My wife, Eleanor; everybody say you top cutter. I pay good money, you see.'

As I approached the cutting table, I looked back at the entrance, half expecting to see Glynis enter, but there was no sign of her.

When we stopped for tea at 10am, the phone rang. Chris answered it, but his English was failing him. He called out to me. 'Alfos, come speak here.'

I knew immediately that it would be Glynis. She spoke calmly and precisely.

'Hello Alfie, how are you, my dear? Listen Alfie, I have found a new job at Dalston Junction, so I won't be coming back; please ask Eleanor to have my cards ready for Friday evening so I can collect them.'

I handed the receiver back to Chris and gave him the message. Unsure whether he fully understood, I repeated the message. Shrugging his shoulders, he boasted, 'Not problem, I am good presser you see.'

Removing his cardigan, he instantly went over to the pressing unit where Glynis would have stood. A huge quantity of unpressed skirts were piled high. Grabbing one of the skirts, he immediately started to press. I noticed how confidently he used the steam iron.

During that first week Chris demonstrated his adroitness. Throughout the days and presumably late into the evenings, he would be pressing, felling and overlocking, jumping from one machine to another. It was quite possible that he was even familiar with the cutting process. His ability to be flexible was essential, since it guaranteed that the daily production would not be held up. No doubt, once the business expanded, he would be forced to employ extra pressers and special machinists to relieve his enormous workload. With four new staff taken on and the factory open seven days a week, more dockets were needed to be cut. I was approached to do overtime, but declined. Chris refused to pay the minimum time and a quarter for extra hours worked; so much for his earlier promise to pay me 'good money'.

To obtain the additional cutting, my employers engaged an evening cutter who would continue with my work after I had finished at 5.30 p.m.

The standard of this man's cutting was extremely poor; he was incapable of cutting a straight line. Much worse, corners were rounded off, important nips that should have been no more than a quarter of an inch deep were now half an inch, which would result in the machinist having to take wider seams, consequently the garment's measurements might become small. It was evident that the lays were being cut out at tremendous speed with little or no care involved. To these Greeks quantity, was required not quality.

I would eventually meet this evening cutter. It was none other than Nicos, the sister's younger brother, whom I was supposed to teach cutting. I suspected that he had been on a crash course in stock-cutting and that Chris was the teacher.

Besides skirt production the factory was now manufacturing dresses and blouses which they accepted from other suppliers. This was a wise decision. If the Greeks were not able to obtain sufficient skirt dockets, they could then increase their dress and blouse production to make up for the loss.

This flexibility was not always available to coat and jacket manufacturers, they were very vulnerable during periods of slackness; they had neither the necessary machinery nor the trained staff to produce other types of garments, such as dresses or separates. Sometimes desperate jacket makers would attempt to manufacture gents' trousers, but they were not always successful. In most cases, these employers would be forced to lay off staff and close their factory doors for a few weeks until the trade recovered.

Nicos was now based in the workshop full time and like Chris and his sisters he would work a 14-hour day. Having already learnt how to operate the special machines, Nicos was determined to master all aspects of cutting, including marker making and pattern grading. Despite disliking these Greeks and counting the weeks that I had left to work in the factory before enlisting in the Merchant Navy, I considered it to be part of my job to co-operate with Nicos. I thought that with his limited cutting experience he would appreciate my advice, but never once did he seek it. Perhaps it was Greek pride or tradition that prevented him. After all, I was a 20-year-old, 10 years his junior.

Because there was only one cutting machine available, Nicos, who spoke excellent English, insisted that he should do all the cutting himself. Furthermore, he would also be the marker maker. My role would be that of his assistant, helping with the laying of fabric and bundling.

It seemed obvious to me that once Nicos felt he was capable of managing the cutting section, I would be dismissed, but it was of no consequence to me; stay or leave, I did not care. Soon David Upson and I would fulfil our dream, which was of a life on the high seas.

Now that I was relieved of the cutting and marker making, I was in a position to observe how confidently Nicos handled the cutting machine. As expected, he would attempt to cut out the lays at a fast pace – a dangerous habit, as every experienced cutter knows. Before the week was out he had cut his finger. Refusing to visit the nearby casualty department of the London Hospital, he asked Eleanor to substitute a piece of white canvas for a bandage; ignoring the blood that began to trickle down his finger and my offer to finish cutting the lay, he carried on working, but at a reduced speed.

I would have thought that the accident would have taught Nicos a fundamental lesson that if he continued to cut fast and erratically, he would injure his fingers again, but not so. The moment the canvas bandage was removed, he began cutting at an ever faster rate.

Nicos had no idea what he was doing. Instead of standing up close and slightly to the left of the cutting machine as he operated it with his right hand, he would stand back and over to his right. This awkward position restricted the full use of the left elbow, forearm and outstretched fingers that was needed to keep the fabric flat as he cut around the patterns.

I estimated that it would be just days before he had another accident – perhaps, this time, a more serious one, but I was wrong. A mishap occurred within hours. Whilst cutting along the selvedge of the lay, he somehow caused the cutting machine to topple off the table. It crashed to the floor, shattering the ten inch blade. Thankfully, nobody was in the path of the flying bits of razor-sharp blade. Chris jumped up from his bench and screamed at Nicos in Greek. Nicos, rather than accept his punishment, started to argue with his brother-in-law. The sisters decided to join the fray. They both rushed over to the cutting table shrieking at the two men, Eleanor began waving her scissors menacingly in the air. While the four of them were remonstrating, I lifted the cutting machine back onto the table. The engine had seized up and the drop-guard was badly bent. Chris angrily threw his cigarette to the floor, put on his jacket, grabbed the cutting machine and carried it down the stairs. Nicos immediately looked out of the window and made a rude gesture. Eleanor gasped, and tried to clip his ear. The situation here was ludicrous. Accidents like this should never have happened. Chris knew that I was a 'top cutter', yet he insisted that Nicos, who had little cutting experience, cut out the dockets. His decision was sheer folly.

Within the hour, Chris had returned with an Eastman cutting machine that he had hired. Incredibly, rather than asking me to finish cutting the lay, as I expected, he allowed Nicos to continue with the new machine. With one eye on Nicos, I continued with the bundling, but remained fearful that another calamity was imminent.

Some time later, Nicos switched the cutting machine off for several minutes. He seemed hesitant. I suspected that he had made a mistake, perhaps a major one. He glanced at me for a moment. His expression was that he might need my advice, which of course, I would gladly give, but no assistance was called for.

Again, I asked myself, was the reason pride? Maybe he disliked giving the impression that he was incapable of rectifying his mistakes. Whatever the reason, it was foolish. If he was prepared to disregard an opportunity to make use of my experience when he needed it most, he could find himself in serious trouble.

Anxious to find out what damage he might have done, I said to him, 'Nicos is there anything wrong?'

Instead of answering me, he responded quickly by switching the machine back on. No attempt was made to rectify what I now believed was an error. He then moved the Eastman machine to another part of the lay and carried on cutting. That decision was most unwise; he should have stopped cutting immediately. It might well be the case where the entire remainder of the lay's marker would have to be altered to create sufficient space to re-cut whatever part he had damaged. To allow Nicos to continue with the cutting would greatly reduce the possibility of rectification. I knew at this point I had to intervene.

When I called his name a second time Nicos rudely answered 'What now?'

His reaction did not surprise me; the rudeness was probably caused by frustration, brought on by his incompetence, rather than by being interrupted by me.

I retained my composure and said 'Nicos, can I have a word with you?'

This time his tone was less irritable. 'What is it you want, Alf?'

I came straight to the point but adopted the polite and tactful David Upson approach.

'Nicos, first I would like to say that I know for certain that a mistake has occurred and secondly, you must realise that I have had five years cutting experience and have cut out hundreds of dockets.'

Before I spoke again, he walked over to his tray, lit up a cigarette and nervously glanced at Chris, who looked very annoyed. No doubt his brother-in-law was still upset over the cost of having to hire a cutting machine while the one that had been damaged was being repaired.

I quickly examined Nicos' work. There was, as I suspected, a serious cutting error; somehow, he had managed to lob off the round end of a Peter Pan collar.

It was not my intention to embarrass or provoke him, but I was curious to know how he was going to overcome the problem of the damaged collar. Again, a careful choice of words was called for.

'Nicos, can I ask you about this collar?' He paused for a moment. His reply was almost inaudible.

'Maybe it could be re-shaped and made smaller.'

When I realised what he was suggesting, I gasped at his naivety.

'That solution would never work Nicos; you can't have half of this docket with a much smaller collar, even if the blouses were completed in that state. The showroom would never accept them; all the garments would be returned to Chris, and he would be charged for the entire docket; furthermore, he might never be allowed to sub-contract for them again.'

A subdued Nicos muttered, 'What do we do next?'

I knew exactly what we had to do next. With no fabric left, the only solution was somehow to find sufficient space in the partially cut marker to fit in the new collar. With the aid of scissors and cellotape, I began to re-arrange the marker.

A silent Nicos, whose pride seemed to have disappeared, stood by, scrutinising me as I worked. It took me some time before I finally managed to create adequate space to mark in a new collar.

Nicos agreed that I should finish cutting the lay. We just had to get through this day without further problems.

Chris must have noticed that Nicos had made a mistake. Fortunately for Nicos he made no attempt to find out what the problem was. Not once did he look up from the overlocking machine; he seemed to be working at an incredible speed.

After I cut out the collar, Nicos carefully inspected it by running his fingers around the edge.

Turning to me, he said 'It's perfect.'

The following day, we had prepared another lay of blouses for cutting. This time, Nicos would cut it out. He made no objection when I offered to give him a little instruction. I was determined that any instruction would be more than just a few tips. I wanted it to be an important lesson, hopefully one that he could learn from and put to practical use. It was the right moment. Chris had left the factory to deliver bundles to his outdoor machinists. I began by demonstrating the correct way to stand slightly to the left of the cutting machine, particularly emphasising the all-important use of the left hand. I also showed him my method of cutting out the always difficult collars, pointing out that a blouse which had a badly cut collar would instantly be spotted and rejected by a quality controller.

Nicos seemed to grasp the importance of what I was attempting to explain and looked confident when he proceeded to cut the lay. His cutting was now less erratic than before, but it was still too fast. A few minutes later, he switched the machine off and allowed me to examine the sleeves which he had cut out. I could not fault them. Before switching the machine back on he complained that I had made him feel a little uncomfortable by standing too close and watching him as he worked; he also insisted that I should inspect the entire lay after he had finished cutting rather than every five minutes.

At the opposite end of the table I began to prepare the labels for bundling; from this position I could study how he handled the cutting machine. Having me standing some ten feet away, he did seem to be able to concentrate much better.

When I eventually inspected his work after he had finished, I could see that there was some deviation where he had cut along a straight line and several of the nips were too deep. These types of errors would be eliminated if he slowed down his pace. I mentioned these points to him, but he made no comment.

Over the next few weeks, the standard of his cutting improved considerably. There was no doubt in my mind that if Nicos cared to follow my instructions, albeit begrudgingly, he would, in due course, become an accomplished cutter. However, developing marker making and pattern cutting skills would take much longer because the companies that Chris sub-contracted for supplied their own markers and retained their patterns, but in the future there would be opportunities to master these allied skills. He could, as I suggested, learn a great deal by studying and remembering the layout of the markers; alternatively, he should make sketches of them for future reference.

During April I made one of my fortnightly trips to the Shipping Federation at Prescot Street.

Unfortunately, due to other commitments David Upson decided to postpone rejoining the Merchant Navy.

An official at the federation whom I had known from my previous visits remarked 'Persistency pays off; you're in the Navy now.'

He wrote down my name on a card and told me to return at the end of the month to accept a vacancy as a utility steward on a P & O ship.

Having no idea what a utility steward was, I asked an elderly seaman, who was about to join a queue, what exactly were the duties of a utility steward. He rattled off several tasks that included kitchen portering, serving at a hotplate and potato-peeling. 'All galley work mate, not a bad job and plenty of grub.'

Whatever the work entailed, no matter how menial the position, I would not complain. At long last, my dream of joining the Merchant Navy would be a reality.

The next day was Friday. The excitement of knowing that I would soon be in the Merchant Navy made it difficult for me to concentrate at work. Fortunately most of my morning was spent bundling, so there was little chance of my making mistakes.

At midday, I assisted an impatient Nicos to lay up a huge docket of ladies' shirt-blouses. The fabric and marker has been supplied by a company for which Chris had just started sub-contracting.

Just before the lunch break, it suddenly occurred to me that the marker, which was for three shirt-blouses, had not been checked. I had overlooked Barney Hyams' important rule. 'Always check other people's markers before cutting, preferably the moment you have access to the markers.'

I immediately suggested to Nicos that we should spend a few minutes examining the marker. My suggestion caused him to snap 'The marker is fine, let's get a move on.'

He was, as usual, in a hurry, determined that we should finish laying the 200 runs of fabric before I stopped work at 5.30 p.m.

When I entered the factory after lunch Chris, who was sitting at an overlocking machine, indicated with his fingers that I should go over to him. I stood in front of his machine, but the sight of his decaying teeth and the odious smell emitting from his mouth forced me to lean backwards.

He spoke just four words. 'Alfos, you finish tonight.' Before I could answer him, he looked down and increased the speed of his overlocking; an obvious signal for me to return to the cutting table.

Because I was due to hand in my notice in two to three weeks time, being given the sack was meaningless to me and finding work in another factory for a short period would be easy. I knew that by 10 a.m. the following Monday I would be working elsewhere.

Nicos showed no interest or concern when I told him that Chris had sacked me.

'He is the boss and he makes the decisions,' he replied coldly.

We finished laying the fabric shortly before 5.30 p.m. I would spend my last few minutes working in this factory fastening the marker with steel T-pins. Suddenly Nicos switched the Eastman on and started to cut the lay. His impatience annoyed me. He should have waited a few minutes until I had fully secured the marker.

When I attempted to place the T-pins in the section of the marker where the front bodices were located, I discovered to my horror that none of the bodices were paired. My God, I thought; we have a serious problem here; 200 runs of fabric which had a distinct right and wrong side had been layed right side up, but the marker did not pair. I had assumed earlier, when Nicos had told me that the marker was 'fine' he had thoroughly checked it for any mistakes. Apparently he had not.

While Nicos was cutting the lay, I snatched the cutting docket from his tray and there, in bold print and underlined, were instructions that as the marker did not pair, the fabric must be layed to pair. Nicos, in his haste, had not bothered to read the note.

Although it was 5.30, and time for me to cease working for these people, my conscience would not allow me to leave the factory until the marker was rectified. I raised my voice.

'Nicos, would you switch off the cutting machine for a moment.'

He did not seem to hear me or he chose not to. I asked him a second time to switch off the machine, but still there was no answer. Suddenly, my wage packet came flying through the air and landed on the edge of the cutting table in front of me. Chris had thrown it; I reached out to grab the packet, but it was too late; vibrations from the Eastman machine had caused it to sway for a second before it fell to the floor.

Chris's action infuriated me. In the past, employers had always handed me my wages, sometimes saying 'thank you'. I picked up the wage packet and as I did so, Chris shouted 'Alfos, Alfos.' Rather than practise his English, he made a gesture with his nicotine stained forefinger, which was pointing at me and then at the exit. I interpreted this ill-mannered gesture as an order to leave the premises, but I was not quite ready to leave. Opening the wage packet, I took out the P45 and began to count the money inside, but there was something wrong. I found that there was a discrepancy of about 25 shillings. Questioning Chris why this was so, he replied rudely, 'You not question me, cash wages complete.'

I reacted angrily to his blatant lack of consideration and demanded that he pay me the 25 shillings at once. Eleanor and her sister appeared alarmed by my loud voice. They shouted at Chris in Greek and he responded by shouting back. Nicos continued with the cutting, even though their squabbling must have disturbed him. Being rude seemed natural to Chris; he stood up, snapped his fingers and demanded my wage packet. He quickly counted the money inside, wrote down the amount in his notebook and gave me back the packet. Struggling with his English, he said 'Okay, you come next week, me speak accountant.'

Although still incensed, my restraint held, but only just; I took a deep breath, unclenched my fist, grabbed my duffle coat and, without another word being said, went over to the cutting table to advise Nicos to stop cutting immediately and alter the marker. Nicos was well aware that I was trying to attract his attention, but he refused to switch off the cutting machine.

Chris and his sisters were looking up at me, wondering why I had not left the premises.

As Nicos had no intention of stopping work to speak to me, I left the cutting table and walked towards the exit. Glancing back just before leaving the workshop, I noticed Nicos reaching for his cigarettes. He looked in my direction, but chose not to return my wave, which was not unexpected as he had made no secret of the fact he resented my working there, even so, ignoring me now I was leaving was beyond the pale. If this naïve man had only uttered a simple word of goodbye, or managed to wave back; I would have returned to the cutting table, paired up the front bodices and then tried to persuade him to allow me to cut the delicate collar stands. If he had attempted to cut them, the result would be disastrous, as the stands would be so badly shaped that the machinists would not be able to use them, but it was too late now. These unpleasant people had deliberately provoked me into wanting to leave the factory as quickly as possible. By my remaining silent, and not informing Nicos that the marker did not pair, a catastrophe would now occur, but I did not care and felt no guilt whatsoever.

Once outside in the street, the loud Greek music and the faint sounds of the sewing machines caused me to look up at the factory window. It was now 5.45 pm; in a few hours time, when Nicos's devastating mistake would become apparent, different sounds, much louder than the bouzoukis, would have filled the ears of passers-by. Thankfully, I would not be around to witness the drama unfolding, but I could imagine the scene vividly. When the curtain rises, we see Nicos, who has just finished cutting the lay and is about to make preparations for bundling. It is quite possible that he does not realise how badly he has cut the collar stands. During 40 years of cutting different types of garments, without question shirt collar stands proved the most difficult to cut accurately, as they did for most experienced cutters. Nicos then moves along the cutting table and makes the shocking discovery that none of the front bodices are paired. He realises that the entire docket of 600 shirt blouses has been ruined, cannot be salvaged and are destined for the dustbin. Chris, of course, must be informed. No doubt he will immediately go berserk, causing the sisters to become hysterical. The ensuing uproar will be like an earthquake, much worse than when Nicos had previously allowed the Eastman machine to topple off the cutting table.

Perhaps Nicos might be able to avoid becoming ensnared in the turmoil by fleeing from the factory, or seek refuge under the cutting table.

I decided not to return to the factory the following week to beg for the 25 shillings that was owed to me, I was not impecunious and there was a strong possibility that the Greeks might try to involve and blame me for the ruining of the shirt blouse docket, although they had no proof. Chris could put my 25 shillings aside. He would now need every penny. This small amount could go towards the huge cost, possibly totalling several hundred pounds, that he would surely have to find as compensation for the loss of 600 shirt blouses.

I still felt very angry when walking home to Poplar, but the cold April air soon started to calm me down, allowing pleasant thoughts to enter my head. That evening David Upson would meet me at the Green Parrot in Grace's Alley. Later, we would visit the Prospect of Whitby for a glorious sing-song.

Marco Gowns

The next morning I phoned Marco Gowns of Bow. This firm was advertising for a stock cutter in the East London Advertiser. An elderly man's voice answered. The conversation was brief.

'How long have you been a cutter?' 'For five years.' 'When can you start?' 'This Monday morning.'

'Good. Be here at 8.30. We are situated at Paton Close, directly behind Poplar Civic Theatre.'

Having secured a job for the remaining two to three weeks before I joined a ship at Tilbury I could relax.

The evening looked promising. David Upson's lover, Madeline, had invited me to a party at her flatlet at Aldgate East, where I was to be introduced to her friend Lucy.

The following Monday I started work at the Marco Gowns' factory at Bow. The £10.00 a week wages that I was offered was sufficient for my needs.

The business was owned by three Jewish brothers, each of them six foot tall, overweight and in their mid-60s. A fourth brother seemed not to have reached their heights; his sobriquet was 'Tiny' because of his short stature. Tiny had no connection with the business, preferring a career as a boxing referee.

Two of the brothers managed the busy machining room on the first floor. The third brother was permanently seated in a small office in the cutting room on the ground level. There were two other cutters, both Jewish and in their late 40s. Alfie Hart, the more senior of the two, acted as an unofficial foreman. Besides being a very experienced cutter, he was a skilled marker maker with a draughtsman's eye for detail.

Alfie soon proved to be the friendliest of men and was instrumental in making my short stay so pleasant. At every opportunity this amiable man wanted to chat to me. He too had the misfortune to have once worked for Fagin, whom he described as a 'tight git'.

Ultimately, it was the ubiquitous rats in Fagin's basement cutting room that forced Alfie to hand in his notice. Lionel, the other cutter, was the complete opposite of Alfie. He was an unfriendly man. Even though I was no threat to his position he still refused to speak to me. I was surprised to learn that he once studied to be a doctor, but had failed the preliminary examinations. 'His mind wanders,' whispered Alfie.

Because Lionel was prone to making mistakes due to his lack of concentration, he was discouraged from cutting the dresses, but he was allowed to cut canvas and staflex (Fusible interlining.) The few markers that he did make were messy, due to endless pencil erasing. The machinists would frequently complain that he was always putting wrong size labels in the dress bundles, which caused utter mayhem.

According to Alfie, our employers had attempted to sack Lionel over his incompetence, but each time he had cried like a child, successfully pleading with them to give him one more chance.

I was soon to witness Lionel being confronted by an angry machinist who had returned a bundle of dresses that contained wrong size labels. In desperation, he denied that he had made the bundle, suggesting to her that 'It was the boy's work.' (Me) I listened in amazement. Alfie, who was standing close by and had heard every word, shook his head in disbelief.

Pathetic as Lionel was, I could not be annoyed with him, but I did feel uncomfortable at being referred to as a boy. Fortunately, I always had the prescience to initial the back of my labels when I did bundling. So demolishing his accusation was easy. Respecting his age, I gently informed him that as the labels were not initialled by me, I was not responsible. He looked at me stupefied; refusing to apologise, he mumbled some excuse before shuffling away. Despite this incident, I enjoyed working for the brothers. Cutting their garments was simple. The dockets were not large or complicated and I was under no pressure to work fast.

During a lunch break at the end of my first week, Alfie and I were sitting on the cutting table. There was a lack of chairs and stools in most cutting rooms. We were discussing a recent serious fire that had occurred at Jaydays Mantles of Raven Row, Whitechapel. The fire had started under the cutting table and quickly spread throughout the factory. The sixteen employees had to flee the premises, followed by the manager, who had received burns to his fingers when he attempted to put out the fire.

Lionel suddenly interrupted our conversation, 'The fascists will, of course say it was a Jewish lightning; they usually do.' Alfie instantly rebuked him; 'What are you talking about Lionel? Most arsonists work at night when buildings are unoccupied.'

Listening to the two men, I learnt something new. I vaguely remembered 'Jewish lightning' and 'King David's lightning' being mentioned elsewhere but I had no idea that 'Lightning' was clothing-trade slang for an arsonist. I asked Alfie if he knew the origin of the term 'Jewish lightning.' He mulled over my

question for a moment and said, 'If my memory serves me right, Jewish lightning was originally associated with a notorious Jewish opportunist named Leopold Harris who, during the 1930s, for a fee, would start a fire in a business premises, which enabled the governors to cheat their insurance companies. That bugger Harris brought shame to the Jews. Of course, the publicity was ammunition for Mosley's blackshirts.'

Wanting to find out more about Leopold Harris, I obtained a book entitled *The Fire Raisers* by Harold Dearden. The book was originally published in 1934. It seems that Harris was a corrupt fire assessor and the main driving force behind a gang of some twenty crooks who conspired to set fire to shops and warehouses with the aim of defrauding insurance companies. Harris's activities were eventually exposed to the police by a former member of the gang. At the subsequent trial in 1933, which lasted for seven weeks, Harris and fifteen other defendants were found guilty and jailed. Harris, the ring leader and mastermind, received the longest sentence, fourteen years penal servitude for crimes which included conspiracy to commit arson, conspiracy to defraud, arson in respect of ten fires, ten cases of obtaining cheques or money by false pretences and three cases of attempting to obtain money by false pretences.

Early in May I returned to the Shipping Federation to collect my seaman's record book and union membership card and have a brief medical examination. An official at the federation advised me to join my ship, the P & O Liner S.S. Orontes, at Tilbury as soon as possible.

I hurried back to the factory. The three brothers, who were pleased with my work, were sorry to see me leave, but they assured me that a vacancy would always be available if I decided to return. Alfie was sad, too, though he understood that I 'needed to see a bit of the world'. He gave me his East Ham address, insisting that we should keep in touch. Years later, I tried to contact him, but it was too late; an acquaintance of his told me that my old friend had passed away.

After being discharged from the 'Orontes' early in August, I spent a few days relaxing at home. During this short break I became bored and was keen to start work again. I had already decided that I would miss the next voyage of the 'Orontes' beginning in the middle of August, but rejoin the ship in November for what would probably be her last sailing. After 36 years at sea she would be broken up. (I have written about my three month voyage on the Orontes in *An East End Story*.)

The main reason I chose to remain ashore for the next few months was women. Having had no contact with the fairer sex during the previous three months, they were now constantly on my mind.

Although I had no experience of cutting coats and jackets, I was well aware how physically demanding the work can be, but according to Ted, a cutter friend of mine who worked at a Whitechapel jacket factory, cutting garments there was simple and no different from cutting dresses and separates. He had already spoken to his employers, who were prepared to offer me a job as a stock cutter at twelve pounds a week.

I accepted their offer, knowing that my stay there would only be temporary. Inevitably, I found the enormous rolls of fabric too heavy to lift and carry. Laying up the fabric perfectly straight on the fold proved far from simple. The technique required much more skill than laying up fabric on the open, which was the way that I had always worked in the past. Also, I found it cumbersome to use chalk and wax to mark the patterns directly onto the fabric. It seemed to me that this method was not very accurate. I preferred making paper markers but at this factory I had no option but to follow the standard working procedure. Another problem was working so close to the busy Hoffman pressing machines. From the time that I arrived in the morning, until I finished work at 5.30 p.m., it was impossible to avoid the ghastly smell that rose from these machines.

I soon learnt from fellow cutters that there was a thief operating inside the factory: jackets were being stolen. The driver was the most likely suspect. Besides delivering the finished jackets to the West End showrooms; he was responsible for taking bundles of cut garments to the outdoor machinists and collecting their finished work.

It happened during an afternoon, the driver was just about to swing a sack of bundles on to his shoulders and begin his outdoor rounds, when my employers suddenly appeared alongside him and demanded that he open his sack. Reluctantly he agreed and hidden inside the sack were two expensive jackets. The driver was instantly dismissed and given a severe warning that if ever he stepped inside the factory premises again, the police would be notified.

After severely bruising my fingers yet again trying to lift the heavy rolls of fabric on to the cloth-unwinding rail, I came to the conclusion that coat and jacket cutting was not for me. I handed in my notice, collected my wages, insurance cards and P45 and left the factory feeling relieved. My tenure at the factory had lasted six miserable weeks.

Being out of work did not bother me at all. I felt relaxed and contented; I had some money in my pocket and a little savings in a Post Office account and, most importantly, November, which was the month when I could rejoin the Orontes at Tilbury, would soon arrive.

Whilst working in Whitechapel, I had always enjoyed walking home to Poplar via Stepney Way or Aylward Street. This leisurely stroll was particularly enjoyable and relaxing; intermittingly I would gaze into the distance at the tower of St.Dunstan's church, clearly visible above the trees in the churchyard.

Aylward Street was one of Stepney's oldest thoroughfares; many elderly East

Enders, including my parents, still preferred to call this street by its former more attractive name, Charles Street.

The George Tavern, situated on the corner of Aylward Street and Commercial Road, is still in business after 300 years of continuous trading. At the eastern end of Aylward Street, embedded like a jewel in ancient soil, stands the early medieval St.Dunstan's Church, complete with its famous red ensign hoisted high above the bell tower.

Because for hundreds of years, seamen had been worshiping at St Dunstan's, the church has historically been referred to as the 'church of the high seas'. Even now I have a lingering childhood memory of Aylward Street.

In the early summer of 1947 Stepney borough housing department decided to rehouse my family from our 1930s-built one-bedroom flat at Carr Street 'Buildings' to a pre-First World War three-bedroom terraced house in Jane Street. The task of removing our furniture and belongings was given to my father who somehow managed to obtain an old barrow and would single-handedly transport our furniture from east to west Stepney, a distance of two miles.

My dad, a gentle and timid builder's labourer, was 37 years old. He was only 5ft 5 inches tall, but he had the strength of an ox. Two to three times that day, without any assistance whatsoever, he made the long, arduous journey. He would have to carry the furniture down from our first-floor flat, load it onto the barrow and then, with me, a slightly excitable six-year-old, sitting on top of the barrow, push it to Jane Street. Once there, unaided, he would unload the barrow. Throughout that day he worked like a beaver. I can recall only one instance when my dad stopped pushing the barrow for a few moments; he sat down on the kerb and wiped his brow. An elderly lady came out of her house and gave him a glass of water.

For me, this journey to Jane Street seemed like a great adventure, especially when we passed through the unfamiliar bomb-scarred Aylward Street where I could see children playing on the bombsites and in derelict houses. How I wanted to climb down from my perch and join them, but my dad's instruction was to sit perfectly still and hold on tight to the sideboard.

When I arrived home late Friday afternoon after my final nostalgic walk from Whitechapel, I felt that because my mother was in poor health I would not worry her by mentioning that I was now unemployed. Mum's whole life had been one of poverty and hardship and now, when things should have been easy for her; with her children in early adulthood, working and bringing much needed money into the home, her health was deteriorating fast.

Fortunately, my resourceful elder sister Sylvia, who was still living at home, was in a position to do the cooking, housework and to lovingly care for mum during her final years.

Sclare & Lee

In the autumn of 1961 I returned to work in Rampart Street, Stepney after an absence of six years. The local labour exchange had found me a position as a stock cutter at Sclare & Lee, a successful Jewish family business that manufactured medium price dresses. Standard Tailors, for whom I had worked during the evenings after school in 1955, had vacated their premises situated at the bottom of the street and had moved to another factory at Greatorex Street, Whitechapel. Rampart Street was full of businesses associated with the clothing trade. There were several factories manufacturing coats, dresses and separates. Quill & Stein, skirt-pleaters, were on the corner and next door to Mo's tiny snack bar was Steinberg buttonholes, which operated from a small workroom on the ground floor of a three storey house. Steinberg's made buttonholes for local tailoring workshops whose owners could not afford to purchase expensive buttonhole machines.

Morris Lerner, the proprietor of Mo's snack bar, was blind. It was inspiring to witness this cheerful and confident man serve customers. His hearing and touch were so acute; he could skilfully handle cash and make tea, coffee and toast. A young female assistant would prepare the sandwiches.

Whenever it was busy at Mo's during the lunch break, several of us clothing workers would move on to the larger and less crowded Platt's Café in nearby Commercial Road. In the café I often sat next to Keith, a local dress cutter and Johnny, the buttonhole hand. Johnny worked for his brother-in-law, Bernie Steinberg.

After finishing our meal, we invariably embarked on a brief discussion before returning to work; on this occasion, Johnny and I were comparing the latest war films on general release. Johnny, the most unassuming and modest of men, suddenly surprised me by casually mentioning that in 1942 he had served in the Eighth Army during the North African campaign.

Johnny preferred not to reveal too much about his personal role in the Second World War, but with a little coaxing from Keith he did say that he and his comrades admired the courage and tenacity of the German soldiers. His attitude towards the Italian army, Germany's hapless ally, was derisory. To him the Italian troops in Libya were undisciplined, cowardly and more of a liability to the Germans than a useful ally.

'Often during combat, the Ities would either run away or surrender.'

He spoke bitterly when he recalled seeing the injuries of released British prisoners of war. I expected him to name the Germans as the perpetrators, but no, he was adamant that the brutality had been inflicted by Italian prison guards.

Apparently, several people working in Rampart Street thought that Bernie Steinberg may have been suffering from a mental illness, but I did know that an extremely excited Bernie was seen running up and down Rampart Street shouting, 'I have won the football pools, won the pools. I am rich.'

Sadly there were no winnings for Bernie, he later realised that he had misread his coupon.

If Bernie was a sick man, his illness could have been a major factor that contributed to his eventual suicide.

When Johnny arrived for work on a Monday morning there was no sign of Bernie. He began to search the premises and when he entered the backyard, he made a terrible discovery. His brother-in-law was lying lifeless on the ground; he had thrown himself out of one of the upper windows.

Occasionally I would buy fruit and soft drinks at Mick and Alf Cohen's tiny 'hole in the wall' kiosk, at nearby Cannon Street Road. The kiosk really was a hole in the wall, filled to the ceiling with boxes of fruit, cigarettes, soft drinks and no doubt the proverbial mice too. There was no standing room inside the kiosk, so the brothers had to stand at the door to serve customers. The business was established in the mid 1930s and was open until 4 a.m., seven days a week, 365 days a year. Mick worked the dayshift and Alf the nightshift. Taxi drivers, night workers, and patrolling policemen were frequent customers.

The Cohen's also had a lucrative trade selling condoms to the local prostitutes.

During the summer months, Mick could be seen sitting outside the kiosk with folded arms, guarding the fruit which was displayed on a long table. There was occasional theft, mainly from vagrants and gangs of children. I once witnessed an outraged Mick throw a mouldy orange at a scruffy character who was attempting to steal bananas.

It was a Saturday evening during the late spring of 1974; I had just collected a packet of three from Alf; he seemed slightly agitated. As I was about to leave, he suddenly gripped my arm and pleaded with me to 'hang around for a few minutes'; a drunken, fractious Somalian was refusing to pay for cigarettes.

When he eventually paid for his purchase and staggered away, I asked Alf, who was a small man in his mid sixties, why he did not employ an assistant to work with him on the nightshift; he shrugged and replied, 'Usually I can look after myself'. Alf did not seem to me to be capable of looking after himself. If he had been capable, he would not have asked me to wait until the Somalian had gone away.

I thought Alf was foolish; he should have realised how dangerous the area had become. A few years earlier, his brother Mick had been badly beaten up and robbed outside the kiosk in broad daylight. He never recovered from the beating; twelve months later he was dead.

At 4 a.m. on Friday the September 27, 1974, David MacLean , 25, and Andrew Barbour, 22, brutally attacked Alf as he was about to finish his shift; he died on the pavement. The killers grabbed packets of cigarettes and a few pounds from the till and fled. Within days, the two men were arrested. They were later put on trial for Alf's murder

When the police searched the cramped kiosk, they discovered a huge amount of cash hidden amongst the cardboard boxes. Many of the wads of bank notes, including old white five-pound notes, were in a poor condition, having been affected by mildew. It took a team of police officers seven hours to count the money; the final total was £110,000. Later, the police did a routine inspection of 67 year-old bachelor Alf's sparse, council flat at nearby Christian Street, but the only food they found in the larder was a small tin of baked beans.

A few days after the murder, David Upson and I sat drinking in the Mackworth Arms, the Irish pub just a few yards from the kiosk; we were saddened by the news of Alf's death. We both regarded Alf as a kind and inoffensive man who would not hesitate to give his regular customers credit, occasionally, Dave in the past had made use of this concession.

Sitting at our table at the Mackworth was an Irish acquaintance. The three of us were at a loss to understand the reasons why Alf hoarded a fortune inside the kiosk.

'Perhaps he didn't trust banks,' suggested the Irishman. Another Irishman, at the next table overheard his remark; he leant towards us and said 'No way, Michael; the old boy was a miser.'

Laughing cruelly, he added, 'He will be the richest man in the cemetery.'

'Maybe it was tax avoidance,' said Dave soberly.

I had no opinion why Alf felt the need to hide money, but it did seem tragic to me that a harmless, elderly little man had spent seven nights a week for the previous forty years, standing at his kiosk doorway in all weathers and then had to suffer a barbaric death. The kiosk remains closed to this day.

Working for Sclare and Lee at Turner House in Rampart Street would prove an unforgetable experience. The factory was divided into two parts of equal size. One section was a cutting and designing room, the other was for the machining and finishing of garments. The managing directors of the company were Mr &

Mrs Sclare and Alan, their 'enfant terrible', ambitious son.

Mr Sclare senior, usually referred to as 'Old man Sclare', was a slight, gaunt figure with hunched shoulders and a pergameneous brown face. Never once did I see him without a tape measure around his neck or a cigarette in his mouth. The loud persistent cough that ravaged his chest was probably a symptom of his lung cancer; years of excessive smoking had caused irreparable damage to his lungs.

'I don't see why he has to go to America for private treatment. Is not our Health Service good enough for him?' I found this remark by a cynical machinist distasteful.

Undeterred by his cancer, old man Sclare was a great fighter with strong will power. He worked tirelessly to try and make his business a success. His wife, who came to the factory most days, seemed to play a lesser role. She was mainly involved with samples and new designs. Her increasing deafness caused a few thoughtless people to be impatient with her. Although, in her early fifties, she still looked very attractive. Speaking little she used her large eyes with great effect to show her train of thought. Sometimes, you would find her staring at you, but not in an unpleasant way.

Aubrey, old man Sclare's elder brother, was once a successful businessman, but went bankrupt due to his compulsive gambling. Now reduced to the status of the factory sweeper-upper; short in stature and with a slightly lop-sided lugubrious face, he always looked a dispirited man. The same old shabby jacket and cap that he wore every day may have belonged to his grandfather. He could have been mistaken for a tramp. I suspected that his in-laws saw him as an embarrassing presence. Sometimes, a few of the staff, including Bill, the foreman cutter, were unnecessarily rude to him. Their attitude annoyed me; I liked Aubrey and considered him to be a friend.

I soon had the first of several confrontations with the imperious Bill, who insisted that as I cut out the lays, I must throw the cuttings to the floor, rather than place them into sacks (A practice which I always disliked) 'So Aubrey can sweep them into sacks and take them outside.'

I refused to comply; having to tread over piles of cuttings on the floor, while operating a 10 inch blade cutting machine, was potentially dangerous. You could trip up and bring the cutting machine crashing down on top of you. Bill's irresponsible instruction would have alarmed Barney Hyams, who had ingrained in me from an early age that safety was paramount in a cutting room. I had always adhered to his advice, as it was based on experience and common sense. Moreover, I felt that I was creating unnecessary work for Aubrey, who was not a young or strong man.

My defiance infuriated Bill, who instantly accused me of being 'stubborn and childish', but I was impervious to his accusation because I knew I was right.

A little later Bill became further enraged when he noticed me still putting the cuttings into the sacks and then tying them up. He marched into the adjacent machining room, probably to complain to the boss about my 'stubbornness', but rather than old man Sclare emerging and reprimanding me as I expected, only Bill appeared. He looked saturnine; an indication that our boss was far too busy to be interrupted or concerned with trivial matters. I felt elated, but not for long. Aubrey leaned on the cutting table. He emphasised his words. 'To keep the peace, Alf, you had better do what Bill wants.'

I thought for a moment before replying, 'No way, Aubrey, Bill is clearly wrong and if a factory inspector or a fire prevention officer made a surprise visited to this factory and saw me throwing cuttings to the floor, Mr Sclare could find himself in deep trouble. And another thing, you should not allow Bill to humiliate you.' Aubrey waited until Bill had gone into the office; he spoke quietly. 'Do me a favour, Alf; to keep the peace, just do what Bill wants. I know he is an arsehole crawler; he thinks that just because he has worked here for twenty years, he is indispensable. He keeps hinting to my brother that he wants a gold watch for long service. If I had my way, I would give him a long service present, his cards.' Aubrey's tirade had an immediate effect on me; I burst out laughing. Bill heard my laughter; he stepped out of the office and glared at me disapprovingly for a moment before going back inside.

Fearing that I might ignite more ill feeling if I remained 'stubborn', I decided that I should keep the peace, swallow my pride and agree to Bill's demand, but as a precaution, to lessen the possibility of an accident, I would throw the cuttings to the floor periodically rather than continually as I cut out the lay.

My relationship with Bill was now permanently sour, although during my very first morning at the factory he had been most helpful in getting me organised. He gave me a dress sample with its docket and patterns, made space for me at a cutting table, offered me a choice of scissors and directed me to where my rolls of fabric were.

The first marker that I made was for two dresses. Bill carefully examined the marker and, finding no errors, he gave me the go ahead to start laying up the fabric. He walked away, but returned a few minutes later. Before speaking he looked across to the entrance, as if he were expecting somebody to arrive.

'If you hear a loud banging on the door, don't be alarmed, it will only be Alan, Mr Scare's son.' 'Why should I be alarmed?' I enquired. Bill glanced at the entrance a second time before whispering.

'Alan is crazy. He wants his father out of the business; he thinks he can manage it better himself; gives the old man stick all day long and sometimes they fight.'

I did not have to wait too long to witness the bitter, strained relationship and in-fighting between father and son that was to continue with various degrees of intensity for the four months that I worked at the factory.

At 10 a.m. we stopped for tea and I sat on the cutting table opposite the entrance. Within minutes, somebody outside on the landing began to kick the door violently, causing it to vibrate. Suddenly, the kicking stopped. All was quiet for a moment; then the door started to vibrate again, but this time the sound was like that of a shoulder being used. I wondered if I was about to come face to face with the 'enfant terrible'. I looked around at the other staff but no-one was looking at the entrance. Bill, noticing my anxious look, came over to me and said, 'The door is unlocked, but because it is not wide open when Alan arrives, he goes berserk; rather than turn the handle to let himself in he prefers to break down the door.'

Bill spoke wearily, 'I suppose I'd better let the pest in.'

He walked over to the door, pushed it open and in stepped a dark haired man in his late twenties. He appeared anguished. In the next instance Mr Sclare, who had been alerted by the noise, rushed into the cutting room brandishing a pair of scissors like a dagger and shouting 'I will kill you, kill you.' Alan immediately took off at the sight of his father charging towards him and started to run around the long cutting table with his father in pursuit. During the chase, the scissors were thrown at Alan along with any other object that Mr Sclare could grab from the cutting table. Aware of these flying objects overhead, I wondered if I should put on my coat and leave the premises. Alan eventually darted into the office, followed by his mother, who had stood by helpless to intervene. Mr Sclare leant against the cutting table. He appeared breathless and began to gently rub his chest; the upheaval must have caused him pain. I picked up his tape measure that had fallen to the floor. He shook his head at me, perhaps because I looked concerned, unlike the other cutting staff, who all seemed nonchalant. Or were they? Possibly they had been advised to look away whenever father and son clashed. Too many watching eyes might somehow encourage the drama to get worse.

What kind of factory was Sclare & Lee? I had never experienced this kind of environment before.

Each day was much the same in the cutting room; a slight disagreement or difference of opinion between father and son would quickly develop into an acrimonious argument. On one occasion their shouting was so loud that concentrating on the cutting was impossible; the only remedy was to plug my ears with screwed up little bits of paper.

I grew to dislike Alan intensely; he seemed to be constantly and deliberately provoking his father into an explosive rage. As the weeks went by, like the rest of the cutting room staff I became accustomed to the daily feuds and would look away whenever they occurred.

During a lunch break at the beginning of November I left Rampart Street in a hurry and made my way to the P & O Shipping Company's office in Leadenhall Street. I was keen to rejoin the 'Orontes' for her last voyage. Unfortunately the only vacancy on offer was that of a potato peeler – a position I promptly rejected.

I left the P&O Shipping Company's offices a little disappointed, but not unduly worried .Being a registered merchant seaman, I could return again at any time in the future. Meanwhile, I had to get back to the Sclare & Lee factory before the lunch break was over. No doubt if I was late Bill would give me grief. To him, being five minutes late would be inexcusable. Predictably, he was poised just inside the entrance when I returned a few moments after 2 p.m. He scowled at me, tapped his finger on his watch and snapped 'You're late'.

'So what?' I replied impudently. His obnoxiousness knew no bounds.

Within seconds, my duffle coat was off, my apron was on and I was laying up the fabric.

My looking and feeling on edge was noticed by Aubrey, who was sweeping up close by. He deliberately swept the cuttings towards me and when just a few feet away he told me to 'relax and calm down'.

Although the foreman was a constant irritant and the ongoing rows between Mr Sclare and Alan could sometimes be a major distraction, I was able to cope working there. Cutting the garments was not difficult. As with Marco Gowns, their dockets were not large or complicated and I was more than compensated for having to tolerate the odious Bill by the presence of the amiable Aubrey. However, liking Aubrey and admiring the indomitable Mr Sclare was not enough to prevent me from handing in my notice.

I had become bored with the same daily routine and would look for a more fulfilling job. Moreover, my desire to work on a ship was beginning to wane. This loss of interest was partly due to my wanting to attend evening classes to study maths and English grammar, but also, the swinging sixties had arrived: 'la dolce vita'. For David Upson and me, the sixties would become a decade of wine, women and song. Besides frequenting the marvellous dockside pubs, namely the Prospect of Whitby, the Eastern Hotel and Charlie Brown's, we were meeting so many fun-loving females. Our social and sex life was never better than in the 1960s.

Of course, Bill was glad that I would now be leaving, but he could still not resist the temptation to be rude to me. I needed to find a dress pattern to make a new marker, but the patterns were not kept in chronological order. Dozens of them were hanging on rails near to where Diana the frantic pattern maker worked.

Diana was always extremely busy; she seemed to be perpetually harassed by the Sclares to produce an endless stream of patterns for samples and new designs. Because her time was so precious, I would try and avoid disturbing her and search for the patterns myself. Perhaps I was taking a little longer than usual to find the pattern. This delay was noticed by Bill and gave him an opportunity to make his move.

'Don't be stubborn Gardner, ask Diana for the pattern.' His tone was provocative.

Diana appeared surprised by his rudeness.

Ignoring Bill whenever he antagonised me was now my standard practice. I continued to search for the pattern until I found it. When I returned to the cutting table, an exasperated Bill was striding towards the machining room, no doubt to complain yet again to Mr Sclare about my 'stubbornness'.

Bill was unable to reach the machining room; he had to step aside for an angry looking Mr Sclare, who walked quickly past him carrying an unfinished dress. Alan was standing by the sample table when his father came up to him and threw the dress on to the table. Alan, now joined by his mother, began to check the garment's measurements; almost immediately the three of them started bickering. A still fuming Bill gave me an insidious stare, but I took up the challenge and stared back. It was very tempting for me to punch his mouth; he deserved it. Once again the ever-observant Aubrey must have read my truculent thoughts. He moved towards me dragging a sack of cuttings along the floor.

My diminutive friend quipped 'Alf, just ignore the crawler.'

His voice was barely audible, drowned out by a ferocious quarrel Alan was now having with his parents over the ill-fitting dress sample. Their shouting was deafening.

In due course I was to witness an incredible scene inside the cutting room. Alan had arrived late and he seemed upset that his mother was not in the office. Suddenly but not totally unexpectedly, like a town crier, he started to raise his voice.

'Where is my mother, where is my mother?'

After this initial outburst was over, rather than disappear back into the office he remained by Diana's table and started to shout again, but much louder than before. Diana covered her ears. As always when disturbed by Alan's regular tantrums, old man Sclare dashed into the cutting room and tried to silence him. This time, the 'enfant terrible' was slow to react when he caught sight of his father racing towards him. Alan attempted to run away, but he was too late; Mr Sclare managed to grip him by the back of his collar. Grabbing a pair of scissors from the table, he frogmarched him towards the office.

Alan struggled to break free, but was unable to do so. With a mighty heave, his father pushed him into the office, where he fell to the floor. After the door was slammed, a noisy fracas ensued. The crashing and banging inside caused the wooden partitioned office to shake violently. I feared for Alan's life.

'This is serious' shouted Bill. Now aided by Aubrey, he attempted to force open the locked door but was unable to do so; I was called to assist. We managed to break down the door and were confronted by a shocking sight; Alan was spread-eagled on the floor, pinned down by his father, whose hands were around his throat. Mr Sclare kept lifting Alan's head up and forcing it back down, shouting 'I will kill you, kill you.' Bill and Aubrey managed to pull Mr Sclare off of his son. Although a sick man, Mr Sclare was still physically strong. Meanwhile, I crouched down and removed the scissors that were embedded deep in the wooden floor by Alan's neck. Mr Sclare was placed in a chair. Alan quickly stood up and he seemed unaffected. No doubt he had experienced episodes like this before and would do so again. Brushing himself down, he calmly went into the cutting room and spoke to his mother, who had just arrived.

It took some time for Mr Sclare to get his breath back, he was so distressed from this latest shock to his system. Whenever he lost his temper, he would clutch at his chest, as if the aggravation had disturbed something inside.

I was baffled as to why Mr Sclare chose to continue working in this 'loony-bin'. Surely his health was of the utmost importance? Was there nobody influential enough to persuade him to retire and hand over the business to his ambitious son? It was harrowing to see the old man's tortured face during his clashes with Alan. I began to wish that Jewish lightning would strike the factory and burn it to a cinder. Perhaps then Mr Sclare would be forced to retire. Who knows, he might then go off with his wife and embark on a world cruise and enjoy what time he had left. My thoughts travelled back to six months earlier, when I had worked in the scullery of the S.S. Orontes. During fire drill, when we crew left our posts and made our way through the passenger decks to man the lifeboats, I noticed how healthy and contented the elderly passengers seemed as they relaxed in their chairs on deck. Why could Mr and Mrs Sclare not be like those passengers enjoying the autumn of their lives? But somehow I didn't think they ever would. I imagined that Mr Sclare would carry on working with his failing health and daily confrontations with Alan until he became too ill to continue. I hoped he would survive for several years; perhaps he did.

In late September 1962, several months after I left Sclare & Lee, I saw Mr Sclare one Saturday lunch time as I returned to the East End on the top of a number 15 bus. I had just been to the Royal Opera House at Covent Garden and bought a ticket to see Verdi's 'La Forza del Destino'.

As the bus stopped at the traffic lights near Mansion House, there dressed in a brown casual jacket and all alone emerging from the underground station, was Mr Sclare. He appeared relaxed and at peace. I quickly wound down the window, thrust out my arm, called his name and waved. He looked up, smiled and waved back.

I was still not ready to re-enlist in the Merchant Navy. My evening classes were going well and my social life was excellent, mainly due to David Upson, who would never miss an opportunity to 'chat up' unescorted girls at our dockland haunts. 'He who hesitates is lost' was his motto. Perhaps my motto was 'you lead and I follow'.

Spitalfields & Whitechapel

'In dealing with a foolish or stubborn adversary, remember your own mood constitutes half the force opposing you.'
Austin O'M0alley. (Keystones of Thought)

Shortly after leaving Sclare & Lee I spotted a vacancy for a garment cutter being advertised in the local press. The company, Greycloth Limited, manufactured rayon dresses.

I spoke to somebody on the telephone about the vacancy; his impatient and business like tone suggested that he did not suffer fools gladly. With lightning speed, he rattled off a few details about the job; it was well-paid; there was plenty of overtime available and, if I was an experienced stock cutter, I should come along to the factory at 8.30 the next morning for an interview with the managing directors. He gave me the name and the address of the company – 54 Artillery Lane, Spitalfields – and before I could state my name the receiver was replaced. I expected that if the directors considered me suitable they would ask me to start work immediately.

I arrived at the Greycloth factory at Artillery Lane the following morning at 8.30 for my appointment with the managing directors. Apparently, they had not been informed that I would be coming for an interview.

The two directors, both Jewish, seemed unperturbed by my visit. Wanting to create a good impression, I offered to return at a more convenient time, but they insisted that I should sit down in their office. I suspected that they were desperately looking for an experienced cutter.

There seemed to be at least twenty-five years difference in the men's ages: they may have been father and son. The older man was tall and barrel-chested. The younger man, who was short and slim, suddenly stood up, opened the office door and called out, 'Shar, Shar, bring three coffees please'. A few minutes later, an Asian man brought in a tray of coffee and biscuits.

In between sips of coffee I answered several questions, which included how long had I been a stock-cutter, who was my last employer and did I have a driving licence? Surprisingly, they did not ask me what my reasons for leaving Sclare & Lee were, but it did occur to me that the moment I left their office, they might phone old man Sclare for a verbal reference. They also wanted to know if I could make markers and grade patterns.

I explained that I had made hundreds of markers and could do simple grading.

'What exactly do you mean by simple grading?' enquired the younger man. Feeling self-assured, I said 'It's not a problem for me to increase or decrease a pattern's size but I can not make an initial pattern from a new dress sample.'

To emphasise my capabilities, I repeated that I could only do simple basic grading.

The directors seemed satisfied with my explanation.

'By the way' said the younger man 'You don't need to make markers here. They will be made for you by our manager Mr Carter, who we will introduce you to shortly.'

The older man went on to talk about their business, which had been established in Spitalfields for many years. They were manufacturers of medium-to-better-priced dresses and skirts. Approximately 70 per cent of their production was exported overseas; the remainder was for the home market. The company was growing rapidly and soon they would be forced to look for larger premises. We discussed wages and conditions. On offer was £14 per week for 40 hours worked and I would be expected to cut approximately 1500 dresses a week. If the job interested me, I could start work immediately. I replied that I was interested and would like to come in for a trial that very morning.

'Good' said the older man; he quickly got up from his chair, opened the office door and shouted down the passage 'Shar, Shar, would you please bring Mr Carter here.'

A few moments later, a stern-looking man aged about fifty entered the office. His voice was easily recognisable: he was the same person who had answered the telephone the day before when I enquired about the vacancy. Instinctively, I felt I did not like this man. First impressions are usually wrong, but occasionally one gets it right. Perhaps my judgement was biased because Carter's voice and profile were very similar to that of Bill, the odious foreman at Sclare and Lee.

After a brief introduction and a handshake with Carter, whose grip was cold, I closed the office door and followed the briskly walking manager along the passage to the cutting room. In another room nearby I could hear women's voices and the sound of sewing machines.

Shar, the Asian man, was using a handbrush to sweep the dust from the long cutting table. He reacted nervously to the sudden presence of Carter, who instantly growled at him 'Come on cha waller, move it; you should have finished that job ages ago.'

Now visibly annoyed, the manager snatched a wooden yardstick from the table and, using his outstretched arm and with wide sweeps, swept the remaining dust from the cutting table. The cloud of dust he created nearly engulfed Shar, who coughed, clasped a remnant over his mouth and quickly moved away.

Carter removed a marker from under the cutting table and gave it to me.

'It's a marker for three dresses.'

With the same yardstick, he tapped at rolls of wide fabric lying on the floor.

'I want this cloth cut and bundled by tomorrow morning; my overlockers are running out of work.'

He pointed to Shar, and said 'Cha waller can help you with the laying up.'

I turned to face Carter and said 'Do you mind if I have a quick look at your marker first?'

'I do mind' 'he replied impatiently 'All my markers are sound, okay?'

Of course it was not okay. No experienced cutter would ever cut out a lay without first examining the marker. I also wanted to have a look at the docket to see what quantities were needed for the lay.

'Do you have a work docket?' My question caused him to glance at me suspiciously.

'You don't need dockets here' he replied impatiently. 'You just lay up what I tell you to lay up, do you understand?' I understood perfectly what he wanted, but failed to understand the necessity for him to be rude. Perhaps his nasty attitude was the result of having to deal previously with incompetent cutters. He then pointed to some cut stayflex piled high on a bench.

'That stayflex is for your bundles, okay?'

While he spoke, Shar was busy unwinding the underlay paper on the cutting table.

With cold piercing eyes, Carter watched me as I unwound the marker. Seemingly satisfied that Shar and I were about to start laying the fabric, he began to walk away. But he stood by the door to observe us for a moment before leaving the cutting room.

I was determined to examine the marker, even though Carter thought it unnecessary. It would take me no more than a few minutes to make sure all the patterns paired and none were missing. I quickly scanned the marker. Some of the back bodices were slightly off grain and there were also a few alterations. Carter had used a ballpoint pen rather than a pencil and consequently he could not erase his alterations. He had tried scribbling tiny crosses on the wrong lines which resulted in parts of the marker being messy and confusing.

Great care would be required when cutting out the lay. I measured the width of the marker – it was nearly 54 inches wide, the same width as the fabric. The marker should have been made one inch less to make allowances for any fabric that became narrow.

Just as I finished checking the marker, Carter came back into the cutting room; there was a look of anguish on his face. 'Haven't you started laying up yet?' he snapped.

I replied loudly 'I beg your pardon?' but there was no answer; he was too busy tut-tuting.

As I rolled up the marker, Carter stood close by with the yardstick firmly in his hand. He looked intimidating. After tut-tuting again, he headed towards the door, but not before reminding me that the lay must be cut, bundled and made ready for the following morning.

'If necessary, we must work late tonight.'

I was not prepared to work late into the night, I would stay until 7 p.m. and no more. It seemed odd to me that the directors had failed to mention that their cutters might be expected to work exceptionally long hours. Providing there were no problems with fabric becoming narrow, and Shar was an able assistant, it was possible that by the time we stopped working at 7 p.m., the first bundles of cut dresses would be ready.

Shar soon proved to be an excellent assistant: never once did he tug at his selvedge edge, which made my work much easier. Often time can be wasted if you are given an inexperienced or heavy-handed assistant who has a tendency to tug at their selvedge edge, which, in turn, disrupts your more important straight edge. You then have to spend valuable time re-straightening your own edge and this problem can be aggravated if the fabric becomes narrower than the marker.

As we were laying up the fabric Shar seemed reluctant to talk. Eventually, I did manage to coax him to speak, but he constantly looked towards the door, no doubt fearing that Carter might suddenly come in and reprimand him for talking to me. He had worked at the factory for approximately a year, ever since he had arrived from West Pakistan. I asked him if he knew why the previous cutter had left. After glancing yet again at the door, he whispered 'because of Mr Carter; he sick man, not nice man'.

I was confused by his answer. Did he mean that Carter was physically or mentally sick? There was no obvious sign of an illness. A little later Shar explained that he had seen at least six cutters come and go since he had joined the company. It was not necessary for Shar to struggle with his limited English to try and explain why the cutters had left. The reason was obvious; none were able to tolerate Carter.

We finished the lay by mid-afternoon. None of the rolls of fabric were narrow. If they had been, I would have had to spend time altering the marker, which would have entailed losing precious time.

With great speed I cut out the lay. The pace that I worked at would have caused Barney Hyams to raise his eyebrows. Meanwhile, Shar had prepared the zips, tickets and labels that were needed for the bundles. By 7 p.m., we were tying up the first of the bundles. It was now time to stop work and go home, but Shar insisted, probably through fear of Carter, that we stay a little longer and carry the bundles to the deserted machining room next door and place them in the overlockers' racks.

The next morning, I arrived early for work. A grim looking Carter overtook me in the passage and went into the office; he failed to acknowledge me when I said 'good morning'. Perhaps he was about to give the directors an appraisal of my work; if snubbing me in the passage was an indication that he was not satisfied with my work, it was unlikely to be a highly favourable report.

When I entered the cutting room, Shar was crouching on the floor dragging rolls of fabric out from under the cutting table. Presumably, he was preparing this fabric for my next lay. Suddenly, Carter appeared. Noticing my duffle coat on the pattern rail, he instantly ordered me to remove it. His order was petty, but I complied and hung my coat on a nail hammered in to the wall. Turning to Shar, who was still crouching on the floor, he shouted 'Why the bloody hell didn't you get all of this cloth out last night, you bloody twit?'

He snatched the yardstick from the cutting table and struck it hard across Shar's backside. The Pakistani yelped in pain. Still gripping the yardstick like an outraged teacher threatening to use his cane on an unruly pupil, and only a few feet away, he raised his voice at me.

'Finish the bundling quickly, and then call me; we are behind schedule.'

I reminded Carter that I was not due to start work for another fifteen minutes; he looked at his watch, glared at me fiercely, and stormed out of the cutting room muttering what sounded like an imprecation.

If Carter thought I was being pertinacious so be it, but my being assertive was an absolute necessity.

Carter had to be made well aware that, unlike Shar, passivity was not one of my weaknesses. Under no circumstances would I ever tolerate his bullying and abusive language.

Shar had finished removing the fabric from under the cutting table and had hurried next door to the machining room to sweep up before the female workers arrived.

With ten minutes to spare before starting work, I sat on the cutting table and started to read my newspaper, but I was disturbed by the appearance of the older director, who came towards me smoking a cigar.

After saying good morning, he smiled and handed me an envelope. 'It's an invitation to our staff Christmas dinner.'

I thought this invitation premature; I had only worked at the factory for just a single day and Christmas was several weeks away. A question entered my mind; could it be that Carter had actually given the directors a favourable report of my work? After I thanked him for the invitation. He leaned on the cutting table, puffed away at his cigar for a moment, and then asked me what did I think of the job so far.

Not much, would have been my truthful answer, but instead I remarked, 'The work is straightforward, but I have to be honest and say I find Carter difficult.'

A sullen expression appeared on his face; a sure sign that he knew that I had no plans to stay.

Describing Carter as being difficult was an understatement; in reality, he was a nasty bully who deserved a good thrashing.

'You have to realise, Alfred' he spoke quietly, 'Mr Carter is unwell. He has to go into hospital soon for an operation.' I could have pointed out to him that Carter did not seem unwell when he used the yardstick on Shar's backside.

Before he left the cutting room, the director insisted that I should visit his office during the lunch break, 'For a quick chat.'

It took me some time to finish the bundling. Shar refused my offer to help him carry the bundles next door to the machining room.

'When Mr Carter here, not your duty my friend to carry. When Mr Carter go home, our duty please.'

Shar was adamant that he required no help, so I took a two minute break to visit the gents. When I returned to the cutting room, Carter was holding a marker in one hand. With his other hand, he was using his trusted yardstick to sweep the residue of dust from the cutting table.

'Are you ready to start work now?' he hissed. 'Start work now?' I growled 'What do you think I have been doing for the last hour, picking plums?'

His reaction was startling; his mouth opened wide and his eyebrows shot upwards, as if pulled from above.

I felt pulled too, towards the exit. Carter remained speechless for a moment. It was unlikely that he was used to being answered back by a young upstart.

When he spoke again, his tone was still provocative. 'That's your cloth, okay.'

He pointed to the rolls of fabric lying on the floor, thrust the marker into my hand and barked, 'You and Char Waller start immediately on this docket, it's urgent.'

Refraining from barking back and keeping calm was probably the right reaction, though the I was tempted to retaliate.

I did a quick analysis. I had walked all the way from Poplar to this factory and had done an hour's work. It made sense if I could keep my temper suppressed and try and tolerate Carter for the remainder of the day, then at 5.30 p.m. collect my pay for two days' work.

Carter left the cutting room in a huff, leaving Shar and me to start laying up the fabric, but first, despite Carter's obvious objection and Shar's increasing nervousness, I had to follow the standard correct procedure of spending a few minutes scrutinising a new marker for possible mistakes. I was certain that if I cut out the lay and then discovered some pattern was missing, it would be an excuse for Carter to have me dismissed without wages. Many cutters I had known over the years had lost their jobs because they failed to pay sufficient attention to their markers.

Steve Cohen, a cutter friend, was a prime example. Steve once made an enormous mistake when he cut a docket of 200 pairs of ladies corduroy slacks.

Corduroy, the most difficult of fabrics to handle, can be a cutter's nightmare. The right side of the fabric's ply is very smooth one way; the opposite way is rougher and darker; the reverse side is slightly coarse. When you have layed the fabric right side up, it requires much skill to prevent the section you are cutting from moving and sliding away. Laying corduroy to pair rather than right side up is always the best option. That way the fabric tends to grip better, resulting in less movement and sliding. As a rule, corduroy garments are made with the smooth ply pointing downwards; for example, from the garment's waistband to its hem. If a marker maker had mistakenly reversed some or even one pattern when making a corduroy marker and a cutter did not spot the error before laying up the fabric and cutting out the lay, the end result could be calamitous.

Although Steve Cohen was an experienced cutter, somehow he broke the cutter's code, the number one golden rule that was designed to prevent the cutter and possibly the marker-maker from being sacked. He went ahead, layed and cut a huge docket of 200 ladies corduroy slacks without first checking the prepared marker. If Steve had spent just a couple of minutes checking the marker before proceeding to lay up the fabric, he would have instantly noticed that the marker maker had mistakenly interlocked the patterns.

When Steve came to make the bundles after he had cut the lay, he realised the enormity of the error; the ply of the slack's fronts was smoother and lighter in colour, while the ply of the backs was rougher and darker. His Turkish employer went 'absolutely ballistic'.

As before, Carter's second marker was for three dresses. It was a total mess; there were so many alterations, as well as one sleeve not pairing and a small back neck facing missing, a common error when a marker is made with undue care. Carter had also failed to leave sufficient allowance on the outer edge. Fortunately, there was a small area of surplus in the marker that the missing neck facing could be squeezed into, and pairing up the sleeve would be simple, but there might be problems if the fabric became narrow.

I found Carter's attitude baffling. He was urging me to cut the dockets quickly, while giving me poorly made markers which would inhibit the cutting process. Moreover, he resented me checking his work, which in most factories is a standard and necessary practice.

As I began to roll up the marker, Shar became fidgety and seemed eager for us to start laying the fabric.

It suddenly occurred to me that he was probably worried that if Carter suddenly appeared and saw him not working, he could be on the receiving end of Carter's vile tongue, or even his yardstick. Although Carter was a despicable manager, I still felt duty bound to make sure that the marker was rectified before cutting. Carter, who had left the cutting room five minuets earlier, must have sensed that Shar and I had not yet started laying the fabric. I glanced to my right and there he was moving quickly towards us and looking menacing. He halted in front of me and shrieked, 'What are you bloody doing, playing games?' Shar panicked and took a step back. I faced Carter and spoke forcibly.

'The reason there is a hold-up is because your marker is not quite right.'

Unwilling to answer me, he began to roll up the marker. Once again, I was at a loss to understand his lack of concern. When he placed the marker aside, I immediately asked him if he would alter the marker or should I. Carter's piercing stare that Shar was so well acquainted with had no affect on me.

He raised his voice. 'You just carry on working until I tell you otherwise.'

With my sense of rectitude intact, I replied 'I cannot carry on working. You must tell me who is responsible for rectifying this marker; you or me.'

Carter reacted angrily, his voice louder than before. 'If you don't start work right now, you can clear off.'

At this stage, my patience finally ran out and I raised my voice, 'Who do you think you are fucking shouting at, mate?'

Unaffected by my stance, he stood within a foot of me.

Modifying his tone, but pointing his finger just inches from my face, he replied vehemently, 'I am not your mate, sonny, put on your coat and clear off.'

I responded to his provocation by giving him a hard shove. He went backwards and tripped up on the rolls of fabric still lying on the floor. The fabric broke his fall.

Carter did not stand up and confront me as I expected, instead, he clambered under the cutting table and emerged at the other side beside a startled, wide-eyed Shar.

Obviously, my time at this factory was now up. I grabbed my duffle coat and left the cutting room.

The office door at the end of the passage was slightly open and I went inside without knocking on the door; the two directors were sitting at their desks. I directed my fury at both of the men.

'I have had enough of Carter; would you please pay me for a day's work.'

The directors looked aghast; although it was probably not the first time that an enraged cutter had burst into their office and complained about Carter's behaviour. The older man was the first to speak. 'What on earth has happened, Alfred?'

I was still seething with anger. 'How can you expect me to work with a maniac like Carter?'

The director remained silent for a moment. There was no doubt in my mind that he was accustomed to his manager being described disparagingly. The younger man stood up and sat on the edge of his desk.

With folded arms and a quizzical expression he remarked, 'Is Mr Carter really that insufferable Alf?'

I shook my head in disbelief; 'Insufferable? He is a nutcase.'

The older man sighed, perhaps he had sighed many times behind that desk in recent months.

He spoke wearily; 'We have to be honest Alfred and admit that you are not the first cutter who has found our manager, to quote your own earlier words, difficult,' and probably not the last, I thought.

Leaning back in his chair, he frowned before speaking.

'In hindsight, I suppose we should have mentioned to you yesterday that Mr Carter will be leaving us shortly on medical grounds. We are aware that because of the nature of his illness he has recently become somewhat temperamental.'

Somewhat temperamental would not be how I or Shar, if his English had been more fluent, would have described Carter. Somewhat malicious was more accurate.

The older director signalled to his younger colleague to close the door. Speaking a little louder than before, he continued, 'Usually, Mr Carter co-operates with the cutters, as he should do, but as I just said a moment ago, he is a sick man. We do realise that when the pain is severe he can become impatient and irritable. All of us here must make allowances for his occasional bouts of irrational behaviour.'

Sounding optimistic, he said 'Looking to the near future, we have a new man coming soon to take over Mr Carter's duties. He is a very experienced manager and certainly approachable. Now if you are willing to remain with the company until Mr Carter leaves us, I am sure that you will find the atmosphere here much better.'

The director was right; the working climate could only improve with a new manager in charge, but my mind was made up. I was not prepared to stay for one moment longer. Apart from what I thought was an unsatisfactory explanation of Carter's illness, the directors had been a little irresponsible. They should have pointed out to me during the interview the day before that Carter was a sick man. If they had, I would have curtailed my fury and not have pushed him to the floor. Moreover, I wondered, if they had known of my serious altercation with Carter just minutes earlier, would they have still wanted me to stay on? Probably not. Common sense told me that to continue working with Carter was ludicrous. It would only lead to more confrontations.

After a further attempt to persuade me to change my mind proved futile, the older director took out a small cash box from a drawer in his desk; he opened it, removed some money and gave me five pounds.

This amount was much more than I had expected. Three pounds would have been adequate. I offered to give him back two pounds, but he refused to accept it.

'By the way, Alf' said the younger director, 'Would you mind leaving us your address, so that we can contact you in the future?' I agreed and wrote it down in his notebook.

Once outside in the passage, Carter's loud voice could be heard scolding Shar in the cutting room.

The directors would never contact me, but I did hear from Shar; he sent me a 1962 New Year card.

Within minutes of leaving Artillery Lane, I was outside Fashion House in nearby Fashion Street. There, on the staff wanted sign of Myers & Co, Gown manufacturers, were vacancies for stock-cutters.

I went up the stone stairs to the first floor of this reasonably modern building. After I had rung the factory bell, a short, fat, balding man with an oval face opened the wide door.

He yawned before speaking, his voice was sonorous. 'Yes, can I help you?'

I spoke politely, 'I am enquiring about the vacancy for a stock cutter.'

He yawned a second time and beckoned me to follow him into his office. He sat his portly, ageing frame on a well-worn chair, while I sat on a rickety stool. He kept perfectly still, his face inscrutable.

After the perfunctory questions were over, he seemed satisfied that I had sufficient cutting experience. Yawning continually, he managed to say 'I will pay you 13 pounds a week; if you work well, there will be an increment in a month's time. When would you like to start?'

I replied at once 'Right now, if possible.'

After yawning yet again, he forced himself up from his chair and we left the office.

On the factory floor by the windows that overlooked Christ Church gardens, two cutters were at work; I wondered if they too were recent arrivals. I looked around as the boss led me to a small cutting table.

Half of the factory floor was occupied by machinists, special machinists, pressers and cotton cleaners. There were perhaps twenty-five female staff of all ages; some of the younger workers were quite pretty.

'At the moment' said the boss sheepishly, 'You can be our stayflex cutter.'

He gave me a small marker and pointed to rolls of white stayflex in an adjacent rack.

'Cut about a hundred runs.' He yawned once more before ambling back to his office.

The 36 inch wide marker for neck and armhole facings was very well made. Whoever had made the marker had done an excellent job; all the facings paired and fitted in well, but not too compact; an ideal little marker, deliberately made easy for the cutter.

Laying the stayflex was relaxing and beneficial. By late morning, the lingering anguish that I had felt since leaving Artillery Lane was now replaced by a feeling of guilt. The more I reflected on that awful altercation with Carter, the more ashamed I had become.

At 1 p.m. a bell rang and the machines were switched off. Bob, an elderly cutter, recommended the Maltese café in Fashion Street. I bought a sandwich and coffee there, consumed it quickly on the premises and decided to wander down Fashion Street.

Just like Artillery Lane and many of the neighbouring streets in the area, Fashion Street was associated with the clothing trade. Besides dressmaking factories, there were ladies' and gents' tailors, two beachwear manufacturers, an embroiderer, a shop selling tailors' trimmings and another shop where they repaired sewing machines. Other trades included a signwriter and a fancy box maker. There were also two ladies' hairdressers and a rag merchant.

I turned left into Brick Lane and left again into Fournier Street. The street looked dirty; several of the old Huguenot houses seemed neglected and were in need of repair. Continuing the circle, I turned left into Commercial Street and saw a group of men on the pavement outside Christ Church. The men were watching two drunken vagrants having a fight just inside the church gardens. The spectators were laughing and egging the men on. Every time a blow was struck, it delighted the onlookers.

With a few minutes to spare, I went back inside the factory. From the windows which overlooked the church gardens, I could see other vagrants joining the fray.

Throughout the afternoon there was no sign of Myers the boss. Being a newcomer, I thought that he, or an assistant, would have liked to have checked my work, but nobody came over to my table. Either the boss had left the factory or he was having a nap in his office.

After cutting the stayflex, I knocked on the office door to enquire about my next assignment, but there was no answer. I placed my ear to the door and could hear the unmistakeable sound of snoring. Bob signalled to me to knock much harder. Eventually, my loud banging did the trick. Myers thunderous voice boomed out 'Come on in.' After explaining that I had finished cutting the stayflex, he looked at his watch and said

'For the remainder of the afternoon, you can help Malcolm.' He seemed to be dozing off as he spoke.

Malcolm, a freckled-faced man in his early thirties, was cutting out a lay of dresses. He suggested correctly, that I should start cutting from one end of the lay and he from the other end and then meet somewhere in the middle. Just before 5.30 pm, we had managed to cut the lay.

I left the factory with Bob. Outside in the street, he told me that he always travelled by the underground to his home at Bow.

'And you are actually going to walk all that way to Poplar?' he said incredulously.

'Of course' I replied, 'Walking keeps me fit; besides, I save on the bus fare.'

As I walked home I felt satisfied that my first day at Myers & Co had gone well. The conditions at the factory were acceptable, the work had been relatively easy and the wages offered were reasonable. Adding to my satisfaction was the thought that Christmas was not far away, which meant parties, girls and wonderful sing along evenings at the Prospect of Whitby, accompanied by David Upson.

Arriving home that evening after an hour-long, two and a half mile walk had left me famished.

Being almost twenty-one and still growing, I seemed to be constantly hungry. It took me just minutes to devour the food that mum had prepared. My hearty appetite might have worried other parents; it certainly concerned my friends, in particular David Upson, who ate so little himself. His appetite, by his own admission, had been permanently suppressed by excessive drinking and smoking.

Within five minutes of finishing my dinner, I had given mum three pounds from the five pounds which I had earned at the Greycloth factory, had been to the Sussex Arms on the corner and bought her a bottle of stout and was crossing nearby stink-house bridge on my way to the evening institute at Mile End, where I was studying Maths and English. (Stink-house bridge is the old iron bridge that crosses the Limehouse Cut at Upper North Street. Adjacent to the bridge and on the bank of the cut was the Frederick Allen Chemical Works. The awful smell which was discharged from this factory saturated the area.)

The days went very quickly at the dress factory. Although Myers seemed to spend most of his time in the office, the production ran smoothly. I was never quite sure who was in charge of the machining section. Whoever he or she was, they certainly were good managers; rolls of fabric would regularly arrive at the factory and rails of finished dresses would be continually dispatched to West End showrooms.

When not cutting canvas and stayflex, I would usually assist Malcolm with laying the fabric, cutting and bundling. During my first week at the factory I made a number of attempts to start a conversation with Malcolm when we worked together, but to no avail. If I mentioned current affairs, politics or the cinema he seemed to show little or no interest. I wondered if he was just reserved and humourless by nature or had a great deal on his mind, although he did smile when I tried to capture a tiny mouse that emerged from under the cutting table.

During afternoon tea the following Friday, Myers came over to the cutting tables and, without saying a word, he gave Malcolm, Bob and me our wage packets. After his customary yawn he went back to his office.

The three of us checked our wages and suddenly Malcolm became jubilant and said 'I have had a pay rise'.

Bob looked glum and muttered 'I haven't'.

After the tea break was over, Malcolm and I continued to lay up a docket of wide fabric. I had hoped that he might have retained the jubilation that he had shown during the tea break but he remained reticent. However, all was to change.

With just half an hour left, before we finished work for the day, Malcolm suddenly became talkative. First he asked me if I had a regular girlfriend, to which I replied, 'Not a serious girlfriend, but I am seeing a number of girls.' He then wanted to know how old I was and did I still live at home.

Malcolm's unexpected but welcome change of mood seemed odd; he did not seem to me to be somebody who was capable of showing any interest in his workmates, least of all of asking them personal questions.

A little later, he decided to reveal some facts about his own life. He had recently married Rachel, his long-time girlfriend, and they were living in a tiny basement flat in a large Victorian house in Stoke Newington. The accommodation, which he described as cold and draughty, may have been former servant's quarters. He believed that the flat had remained empty for over twenty years.

'How do you know that?' I asked.

'Because when we cleaned and decorated the flat prior to moving in, we found dozens of old newspapers dated 1939 and also pre-war gramophone records in the cupboards.'

My question 'How do you like married life?' seemed to induce an instant change of mood; he frowned and said 'I can take it or leave it.'

Perhaps I had inadvertently touched a sensitive point. By the time we finished work at 5.30pm, he had withdrawn into a pensive state.

Malcolm was uncommunicative the following Monday morning. We spent several hours working together, but he hardly uttered a word. At lunch time, Bob and I and some of the machinists went to the café. Malcolm would stick to his daily routine and sit alone on the cutting table eating sandwiches.

Inside the café, one of the women asked me how I could work with a 'Miserable git like Malcolm.'

Bob's aspersion followed, he described Malcolm as being an 'odd bugger'. Sitting there listening to them, David Upson's advice came to mind 'Where ignorance is bliss, it's folly to be wise' so I refrained from adding to what I thought was negative criticism of Malcolm. Bob may have given up trying to befriend and humour our colleague, but I had more patience and could easily tolerate Malcolm's long periods of silence. Probably other people in the factory shared Bob's belief that Malcolm was unfriendly. I believed differently. After just one week working with Malcolm as a team-mate, I had come to the conclusion that because his mind was totally occupied with what I assumed to be personal problems he unwittingly gave the impression that he was aloof and distant.

The next day, I was to witness a complete change in Malcolm's persona; he would finally abandon his taciturnity and become loquacious. What brought about this change was a simple image.

I had come back early from the café at lunch time. Malcolm was standing by the windows gazing out across Christ Church gardens. Having failed so many times in the past to engage him in conversation, I thought it was time to try a new tactic. I was curious to see how he would respond when I showed him a photo of one of my occasional girlfriends in a bikini. He took the photo from me and, after looking at it for a moment, he placed it on the cutting table, then instantly picked it up for a closer look. The effects of scrutinising the photo were startling. His normally mournful expression had now changed to a lecherous stare.

I tried to retrieve the photo but he held it tight for a few seconds before releasing it.

'Cor, your girlfriend is a beauty,' he said enviably.

'Just one of my girlfriends 'I bragged.

'You have more?' he gasped.

Feeling cock-a-hoop, I said, 'Of course.'

His appetite was wetted, 'How many more?'

'Three or four and a couple in reserve,' I deliberately exaggerated the figure.

'As many as that?' he said in disbelief.

Continuing with the charade, I replied chauvinistically 'Maybe, one day, you can see some more photos of my conquests.'

What he said next seemed like a demand: 'You must show them to me tomorrow.'

During the tea break the next morning, I handed a delighted Malcolm an envelope that contained several photos. Some of the images were of girlfriends past and present and a few were of David Upson and me posing with various females.

After meticulously and gleefully examining the photos, he shook his head and spoke gloomily: 'How I am missing out on life.'

A thought entered my mind: what would his wife have said if she had overheard him?

At lunch time, Malcolm decided to accompany me to the café in Fashion Street, where I was obliged to answer several of his questions.

'Where did you and your friend meet all those girls?'

'Tell me more about the Prospect of Whitby.'

'Is it safe to drink in Charlie Browns?'

When Bob and one of the female pressers joined us, I hoped that Malcolm would end his interrogation, but he continued unabated. He may have been oblivious to our colleagues' sudden presence, but I was not. Our conversation was private. Gulping down my tea, I stood up and made an excuse that I had to make a phone call, but Malcolm followed me outside and posed a final question on the pavement.

'If you and your friend David are drinking at Limehouse this weekend, would you mind if I come along too?'

It was inevitable that Malcolm would ask me this question so I had an answer already prepared.

'Unfortunately Malcolm, I can't say yes without first speaking to Dave.'

He seemed disappointed with my explanation, but his mournful expression soon disappeared when I promised to speak to Dave that very evening and see if we could arrange something.

Throughout the afternoon Malcolm and I worked separately, so I was spared the ordeal of having to answer his probing questions, but during the tea break he would again insist that I answer questions and give opinions on subjects that ranged from dockland pubs to the female form and the odds of catching syphilis with women you hardly know. At the end of the break, I realised that I had probably made a mistake in allowing him to see the photos.

During my long walk home to Poplar after work, I began to have reservations about whether to mention to Dave later that evening at the Prospect of Whitby, that Malcolm had expressed an interest in meeting us on Saturday night. Apart from the fact that Malcolm was a married man, I was beginning to wonder if he really was, to quote Bob's description, an 'odd bugger'. Only a few days earlier he had seemed to be a melancholic, silent type and now he had become intense, talkative and very interested in the opposite sex. Inevitably, I had reservations about how he would conduct himself if Dave and I invited him to come along with us when we toured the docklands pubs, especially at the marvellous Prospect where the atmosphere was full of laughter and song. It was risky not knowing how he would behave up close to women with whom we were trying to make contact. If he received a cold shoulder from one of them would he just accept it, or might he turn nasty, be rude, sulk, and perhaps even create an unpleasant scene? Who knows?

Over the years, Dave and I had performed well as a team; my friend had refined a successful method of putting his 'threepenny bit in'. Politeness was always the most important rule. If girls were not interested when we approached them in the pubs, we would simply excuse ourselves and move away, but if they did respond favourably, we would immediately offer them drinks. The conversation would be light-hearted at first and then Dave, with his incredible wit and perfect timing, would soon have the girls in fits of laughter. Never one for telling cheap, ribald jokes, he told original funny stories, usually about himself. At the end of the evening the girls would have had enjoyed themselves so much, in most cases, that they were quite willing to meet us again.

Dave agreed with me that it would probably be a mistake to allow Malcolm to accompany us when we visited the Limehouse pubs the following Saturday evening. There was a possibility that he might jeopardize our well-tried and tested routine.

Strolling up Fashion Street the following morning, I spotted Malcolm chatting to a stranger outside the factory. When I approached the entrance, the stranger shook hands with Malcolm and walked away.

As Malcolm and I went up the stairs to the first floor, I told him a little lie, that I had been unable to meet David Upson the night before. He made no comment, which I thought was strange. Hopefully, he had now lost interest in socialising with Dave and me. Hesitating for a moment before opening the factory door and speaking enthusiastically, he said 'I have just found out about a fantastic pub in Islington'.

'You have?' I replied, with the minimum of interest.

'It's the Pied Bull. Have you been there?'

I shook my head, 'Never heard of it.'

Malcolm and I spent the first part of the morning cutting out a large docket. With intense concentration required, it was impossible to chat. Stopping for tea at 10 a.m., I sat on the cutting table and quietly read my book.

Half way through the break, Malcolm appeared alongside me. It would now be question time, or so I thought, but there were no questions forthcoming. He was in a generous mood and offered me biscuits. Noticing my book was of popular Italian operas caused him to distort his face as if he were in pain.

'Love-a-duck, Alf, you don't like opera do you?'

My face became a little distorted, too. 'Well I certainly don't like rock-an-roll rubbish that's for sure.' Still feeling generous, he suggested that I should travel with him up to his home that evening after work and pick out any pre-war 78 records that I wanted before he 'dumped the lot'.

Responding to my lack of interest, he added 'There are some opera ones by a guy called Caruso.'

His offer now seemed promising.

For the previous five years, I had been collecting operatic arias sung by famous tenors. Believing that I might be able to obtain some rarities for my growing collection, I accepted his offer.

Sitting on the bus that took us to Stoke Newington, Malcolm again mentioned the Pied Bull pub. Apparently, an acquaintance of his who worked in Fashion Street had told him that he had recently visited the pub, where he had met a woman who was unaccompanied and drinking alone. Later he went back with her to her lodgings and stayed the night. The same acquaintance also said there were several unescorted women at the bar who were quite willing to accept drinks and dance with strangers. Encouraged by his acquaintance's success, Malcolm thought it would be a great opportunity if the pair of us visited the Pied Bull the following evening 'to try our luck'. Although a little tempted, I turned down his suggestion and explained that I had already made arrangements to meet David Upson at Charlie Brown's.

A brief moment of silence followed. 'Then I will go alone,' he said dryly.

When we arrived at his flat, he introduced me to Rachel before going into another room, presumably to collect the records. Rachel gave me a welcoming smile and apologised for her husband's rudeness.

I liked her instantly; she was tiny and slim with dark wavy hair, but her pretty face was partially obscured by thick rimmed glasses. She soon proved to be a punctilious hostess who insisted that I sit down at the table and sample her home-made cheesecake. While I chatted to her contentedly, I could not but wonder why, after being married for just a few months, her husband was unashamedly ready to betray her.

When Malcolm came back into the lounge he was carrying a large wooden box full of 78 records and old books. I helped him to gently place the heavy box onto the floor. In between taking deep breaths, he said,

'Take your pick, Alf.'

I rummaged through the box and found a few recordings that I liked. Each record I chose had faint scratch marks, but for a collector these operatic items were treasures. The books were in poor condition. Mildew and mice had taken their toll and only one small book was worth retrieving, a Penguin ABC of the world's trouble spots of 1938. After another cup of tea and accepting Rachel's invitation to call again, I left the flat with the records and book in a carrier bag. A brisk walk took me to Dalston Junction, where I boarded the 277 bus for Poplar. Getting off near the Eastern Hotel, I went inside and met David Upson in the saloon bar.

Dave was familiar with the Pied Bull, which he described as a 'pick-up joint, used by old pros'.

He also advised me to warn Malcolm to avoid the pub 'like the plague'.

I did convey Dave's message to Malcolm the next day, but he instantly dismissed the warning as hearsay, arguing that the woman his acquaintance had met at the Pied Bull was just a lonely divorcee and 'definitely not a tart'.

He also confirmed that he would be visiting the pub after work.

At 5.30 p.m. I left the factory with Bob. In nearby Commercial Street, Malcolm could be seen running along the pavement to catch a bus. I hoped, for Rachel's sake, that it would only be buses that her husband would be catching that evening and not gonorrhoea.

The next morning, arriving too early for work, I stopped by at the Maltese café in Fashion Street. Sitting there, alone and staring out of the window, was Malcolm. He looked dejected, perhaps a sign that his visit to the Pied Bull the previous night had been a disappointment, or even a disaster. I hoped he had remembered the French letters. After scowling at me when I sat down opposite him, he spoke sharply.

'I suppose you want to know how I got on last night.'

'Not really' I replied equally sharply.

Modifying his tone, he added 'Well, it was a waste of time.'

I expected him to say no more, but he wanted to continue talking.

With time to spare before we started work, Malcolm began to relate the events of the night before. It seems that when he arrived at the Pied Bull, the bar was near empty. To compensate for what he thought was going to be a wasted evening, he attempted to 'get off' with the barmaid. When his efforts proved unsuccessful, he decided to finish his drink and leave. Suddenly, three women in their early thirties, came into the bar; two were dark-haired, the third a blonde. They bought drinks and sat by the juke box. Attracted by their laughter, he gave the women a prolonged glance. To his surprise, he received inviting smiles from all three and realising there was an opportunity for a possible dalliance, he ordered another drink and went over to the juke box to play some records. As he passed their table, the blonde with 'big gold circular earrings' gave him a wink.

A little later, after he had sat down at an adjacent table, the same woman who had given him the wink leant across to him, her accent Scottish. 'Want some company, friend?'

Accepting the invitation Malcolm brought his chair to their table.

After several rounds of drinks, paid for by Malcolm, the two dark- haired women left the bar to visit another pub nearby. Shortly afterwards, Malcolm found himself being induced back to the blonde's flat 'for a night cap'.

It seemed obvious to me that the woman was a prostitute and not a lonely divorcee. If Malcolm was unable to tell the difference, he was a fool. With minutes left before 8.30am, we left the café. As we approached the factory entrance, he explained that the blonde rented a small terrace house not too far from the pub.

'When we went into the bedroom she offered me whisky, which I refused. We undressed and got into the bed. After about five minutes, I heard a faint noise coming from inside a wardrobe that had a gaping crack in its door; when I heard the noise a second time, I jumped off the bed.'

At this stage of Malcolm's account, we were interrupted by Bob, who had been walking up close behind; with typical cheeriness but totally off-key, he sang 'O what a beautiful morning, O what a beautiful day'. Spotting a group of machinists just ahead, he overtook us; one of the women quickly moved sideways when he tried to tickle her ribs. Bob's own ribs received more than a tickle from a well-aimed, and not too gentle, prod from an umbrella tip. The assailant, a firebrand presser, shouted at him to 'bugger off, you silly old sod'.

As Malcolm and I walked up the factory stairs, he continued with his story, but I began to find his predicament amusing.

'The blonde said that the noise in the wardrobe was mice but I did not believe her; that was when I saw the eye.' I interrupted him, 'an eye?'

'Yes, I could see an eye peering through the crack in the wardrobe.'

I was tempted to tease him and enquire if it might have been Rachel hiding inside poised to catch him in the act.

When we reached the factory's entrance, Malcolm suggested that we talk later. At tea time, I went over to his table, intrigued to know who was inside the wardrobe. 'I just don't know' he replied, scratching his head 'I was so scared I just grabbed my clothes and ran; maybe someone was about to attack and rob me.'

Restraining myself from laughing at the unfolding farce, I pretended to be serious by suggesting that the eye could have belonged to a voyeur, or worse, a blackmailer armed with a camera. Malcolm, realising that I was probably teasing him, sneered at me. 'It was no laughing matter; I had to get dressed on her doorstep, and to cap it all, the bitch opened the window above and threw out a milk bottle, which nearly hit me.' I had no sympathy for him. It was unlikely that the episode had taught him a lesson; he was determined to indulge in extra-marital relations at the earliest opportunity.

Malcolm did not return to work after the Christmas break. I feared the worse. Bob wondered if the 'odd bugger' might have found a better paid job elsewhere. I thought that was unlikely. Malcolm never indicated to me that he was unhappy with his salary or the conditions at the factory; moreover, he had only just received an increment. Somehow, my thoughts kept returning to that eye peering out at him from the crack in the wardrobe.

Malcolm was irresponsible and naïve. It was quite possible that he had paid a second visit to the Pied Bull and he may have been waylaid later or involved in some incident. There could be other reasons for his absence; perhaps the most plausible was that he was ill. No doubt, in due course, Bob and I would be informed why Malcolm had not returned to work.

The next morning, Myers came over to the cutting table where Bob and I were laying fabric and explained that he had just received news from Rachel that Malcolm had been involved in an accident. He was in hospital, but had regained consciousness. All he could remember was walking alone down a side street, when a small boy riding his bicycle on the pavement crashed into him. He had no recollection of striking his head on the ground. Malcolm's account of what had happened to him was probably true. Of course, there was a remote possibility that his head injury was not the result of being struck by a boy on a bicycle but by a milk bottle thrown from a window.

With Malcolm still recuperating at home, the boss was spending more time on the factory floor. He made an effort to make a few markers and, on a couple of occasions, he helped Bob to lay the fabric.

For somebody who was short, obese and enjoyed dozing in his office, it must have been particularly irksome to suddenly find yourself spending hours pacing up and down at a cutting table. Bob found it an ordeal working with him. Bob also warned me that once the boss started to tire he became irritable and very rude.

Bob's warning had little effect on me. I considered myself to be hardworking and conscientious; not for one moment would I tolerate rudeness, no matter what the consequences were.

It was inevitable that I would have my share of working with the boss. Our collaboration came sooner than I expected. He would assist me to lay up some wide fabric. Not only was my new partner slow on his feet but he tugged at his selvedge, which made it difficult for me to keep my carefully laid selvedge straight.

Politely, I advised him not to tug the fabric too hard and he responded by giving me a look of disapproval. Perhaps he had misunderstood or misheard me, because he continued to tug at his selvedge. Then I made a fatal error; I gently suggested that he was just a little heavy-handed and that he should hold the fabric as if it was as light as a feather. This time I received more than a look of disapproval. He responded angrily, raising his powerful voice: 'Don't you be impertinent and tell me what to do. I am the governor here, not you.'

Keeping calm, I explained that it had become awkward for me to maintain a good selvedge edge.

Speaking less rudely he replied, 'If you are incapable, then I will keep the edge straight.' A moment later we swapped places and I became the assistant.

Moving crablike along the cutting table with his humpty-dumpty figure, sour expression and puffing and panting in the process, brought smiles to the faces of Bob and some of the women workers.

When a cutter and an assistant lay up wide fabric together, as a rule they work directly opposite each other, enabling them to spread out the fabric more easily and spot any damages and flaws. Because of the difficulty Myers was having trying to keep his selvedge straight, and his heavy-handedness and lack of experience, I was continually waiting for him to move along the table.

When I suddenly yawned he glared at me, which I thought strange coming from somebody who might be inflicted with a mild form of encephalitis lethargic (Often referred to as sleeping sickness). However, in later years, a friend suggested that, in all probability, Myers had been suffering from narcolepsy, which is a condition often found in pre-diabetic people.

Having forgotten what I had been taught on the parade ground at Pirbright camp-to yawn with my mouth closed, I made the mistake of yawning yet again. It went not unnoticed by Myers who snapped nastily at me.

'I don't pay you good money to sleep on the job; if you want to sleep, you can go home.'

I was flabbergasted by his remark.

'Then I'd better go home' I retorted.

'You can stay until 5.30,' he growled.

I growled back 'Not on your Nellie. I will leave right now.'

'Suit yourself,' he replied dismissively.

Myers turned around to a startled Bob and called him over to take my place. As he did so I walked away, but not before reminding Myers that I would return on Friday to collect my pay, insurance cards and P45. He scowled but made no comment.

Leaving Fashion Street and turning right into Brick Lane, I spotted the words 'Cutter Wanted' on a piece of cardboard stuck on the shopfront window of B.& S. Katz & Co.Dressmakers. I crossed the road and rang the bell.

A girl with an angelic face opened the door and let me in. She pointed to a door that led to a basement and said, 'the manager is downstairs'. As she spoke, the familiar sound of sewing machines could be heard coming from an adjacent room. I went down the wooden steps and found myself once again in a tiny cutting room with no fire escape. A mousy smell was present and a cigarette end was on the floor: a potential fire trap.

Katz, the managing director, seemed a pleasant man of about 40 years of age. He explained that he had recently started interviewing applicants for the position, but none had sufficient experience in cutting expensive dresses. Leaning on the table, he asked me several questions, including how many years I had been a cutter, whether I could make markers and grade patterns, what wages I was expecting and where and for whom had I worked previously and, finally, what were my reasons for leaving.

The last question was difficult to answer. I was unsure if I had just been sacked, or had left voluntary. In theory, I suppose, I had reacted to the threat of being dismissed by dismissing myself.

I replied somewhat reluctantly 'I have just left a job in Fashion Street, following a dispute with the boss.'

He paused for a moment, before saying, 'Can I ask you what the dispute was about?'

I hesitated before saying 'I was accused of being lazy.'

He removed his spectacles and began cleaning the lenses with his handkerchief; as he did so he smiled and said, 'Everyone who works in Fashion Street is reputed to be lazy.'

At least Katz had a sense of humour, a refreshing change from my recent employers, who seemed incapable of even smiling.

'Have you ever cut quality garments?' he said, emphasising the word quality.

Before I had a chance to reply, he handed me a dress sample which was part of his current production; I placed it half on the table, but it slid to the floor.

'Whoops, there goes my profit' he joked.

I picked the dress up and apologised for being careless.

Because the garment was intricate and well-made, unlike any garment I had ever cut in the past, I thought it essential to give a truthful answer.

'Unfortunately, my experience is limited to cutting cheap-to-medium dresses, but it's not a problem for me to cut expensive dresses. I take great care with my cutting.'

After Katz placed the garment back on a rail, we went upstairs to the ground floor and stood by the exit.

I expected him to say that I was unqualified for the post, citing my lack of experience. Also, he could have been influenced by the accusation of laziness. Instead, he surprised me by saying 'I don't believe that you are a lazy fellow at all, so I am prepared to give you a chance to prove that you're not. All I ask is that you cut accurately and not make your nips too deep.'

'That's fair enough' I replied.

He looked at his watch. 'Come in on Friday morning at 8.30 for a trial and let's see how capable you are.'

I knew exactly how capable I was and most importantly I had the capability to recognise unsafe working conditions. If he thought that I might be interested in working there permanently, he was making a mistake.

I had no intention of ever working again in a subterranean cutting room that had no fire escape, but I was prepared to work at his factory just for one day. I could earn a few pounds and at the end of the day pop into Myers factory and collect my outstanding wages and, if there was still time left, quickly make my way to nearby Alie Street and enquire at Marshall Walker, a gown manufacturer which for some time had been advertising for stock cutters.

'An ominous sign,' said David Upson, who believed that unfilled vacancies were usually 'not worth a light'. I assumed he meant that the pay and conditions which these companies offered was so inadequate that they were unable to attract workers.

Katz was just finishing making a dress marker when I arrived for work on the Friday morning.

He was well organised. The fabric that I needed for the lay was stacked up against the wall. The work docket, scissors and yardstick were all neatly laid out on the cutting table and he seemed quite impressed when I insisted on having a quick look at his marker.

After I had checked his work, he remarked wistfully, 'If only more cutters would check their markers.'

It was impossible to find fault with the marker, all patterns paired and were perfectly on grain. The width of the marker was 44 inches; thankfully, he had made the marker 1 inch narrower than the fabrics' 45 inch width. Being 5 foot 10 inches tall, I could manage on my own to lay the fabric. 'I am pleased you have long arms,' quipped Katz.

He waited a few moments until I started to lay the fabric. Seemingly satisfied that I was capable of working unsupervised, he said, 'Right, you are on your own.' At 10 a.m. he returned and was accompanied by Jean, the girl with the angelic face, who handed me a cup of tea. Katz suggested that if I needed anything, I should speak to Jean.

There were several questions that I would have liked to have asked her, none of which were work-related.

After Katz had examined how straight I had laid the selvedge edge, he gave me a nod of approval. Moments later he left the cutting room, followed by Jean, who gave me a departing smile.

Her smile captivated me; suddenly, working here below-ground with no natural light or fire escape seemed tolerable, at least for the next seven hours.

During the late morning, just after I had started cutting out the lay, Jean came back down into the cutting room. She went over to a rack in the corner and removed a cardboard box which contained labels and size tabs. My heart started to flutter at the sight of this lovely apparition. Unable to concentrate, I switched off the cutting machine; the sudden silence caused her to stop counting the labels. Turning around, she smiled and said, 'How do you like working here?' Her voice was warm and sensual. Mesmerised by her beauty, it took me a couple of seconds to answer her. I decided not to mention the dangerous working conditions, but I did say 'Working here is not bad at all, but I am only on a day's trial.'

Jean explained that she was a special machinist and sometimes helped with the bundling. This was exciting news, as it meant that we might be working quite close to each other during bundling, possibly even before the day was out. She smiled again before placing the cardboard box back in the rack and going up the stairs.

I was mystified, I had not expected to meet a beautiful girl like Jean working in a small factory in Brick Lane. She seemed out of place. Her accent was refined and her poise and walk elegant. She reminded me of the gorgeous middle-class nurses I had seen in the wards at the nearby London Hospital.

Lunch time soon arrived. With three quarters of an hour free time, I left the factory and hurried down Fashion Street, hoping to meet Bob in the Maltese café. Perhaps he had news of Malcolm or had any information about Marshall Walker, the gown manufacturers in Alie Street. Bob had told me that for the past thirty years he had worked in many factories in the Aldgate East area. During the Second World War he had been based in Petticoat Lane cutting thousands of uniforms and greatcoats for the armed forces. So there was a slight possibility that at some stage he might have cut garments at the Marshall Walker factory.

Bob had started work at Myers & Co quite recently. With his affable nature, he soon proved to be popular with the machinists. A contented man, not the least ambitious, he had never learned to make markers or grade patterns, he was happy just remaining a humble stock cutter. Married but childless, like his wife he enjoyed 'beer, and bingo'. Usually he spent Saturdays in and out of his local betting shop, gambling only on favourites. Sometimes his horses and greyhounds 'came home', but, like most punters, he usually lost money.

There was no sign of Bob in the café but, to my amazement, sitting comfortably and drinking tea was Malcolm. He looked as if he had just recovered from being involved in a scrap. There was a plaster on his forehead and a bruise above one of his eyes. I took my coffee and sandwich over to his table and sat down. He was in a relaxed mood and spoke first.

'Hello, Alf, I have just been to collect some wages and they told me that you had had a row with the boss and left. Bob looks as if he has worked his toches (buttocks) off. Anyway, how have you been?'

'Never mind me, Malcolm, how are you?'

'I am feeling fine, just the odd headache, that's all.'

'Surely, you're not considering returning to work so soon?'

'I can't talk about work at the moment; maybe I will finish with this trade. When I was in hospital, I thought about setting up a clothes stall in Petticoat Lane.'

I realised it might be a little delicate to questioning him about how he came to have a bruised forehead, but I was interested to know more about the accident.

'You can't remember anything at all, about what happened to you?'

'I knew you were going to ask me.' He seemed slightly agitated.

'But I really was knocked to the ground by some tyke on a pushbike; don't you believe me?'

'Of course I believe you,' but my tone may have suggested otherwise.

Because he seemed crestfallen, I held back from asking him if, before the accident, he had made a second visit to the Pied Bull; a change of subject was called for.

'Tell me Malcolm, how attractive were those nurses?'

As expected, his dejected look quickly disappeared and he replied cheerfully, 'They were crackers, just like some of the girls in your photos.' Now totally at ease, my friend spoke willingly. 'It was a strange experience, waking up in that ward. At first, I could not remember my name, where I was living and how I came to be in the hospital, but I did know I had a bloody painful head.'

'It must have been quite a shock for Rachel to find you in that state.' I remarked. He seemed somewhat amused when he replied 'When I came round for the first time, there was this strange, little tearful woman sitting by the bed and holding my hand.' 'You didn't recognise her?' I said. 'No, not at all, I pulled my hand away and asked her who she was; then she told me her name was Rachel and that I was her husband.'

'How embarrassing for you both' I said, with a half smile. 'It was more than embarrassing, it was shocking; the thought that I was married to a woman who I had no memory of caused me to have a kind of seizure and I nearly passed out.'

It was difficult to restrain myself from laughing.

After a few days in hospital he regained his memory and Rachel had been allowed to take him home.

Malcolm and I left the café together and shook hands on the corner. He crossed the busy Commercial Street to catch a bus to Stoke Newington and I headed for Brick Lane. Walking slowly back down Fashion Street, I tried to visualise what the future had in store for Malcolm. He had just spoken of giving up cutting and becoming a market trader, probably on the assumption that selling ladies clothes from a stall might be an opportunity to meet women. Inevitably, any future infidelities could lead to a break-up of his marriage. If Rachel were to divorce him, he might well regret it for the rest of his life.

Much to my disappointment, there was no sign of Jean when I returned to the factory.

Katz followed me down to the basement and began to examine the parts of the garment which I had cut out. I felt sure that he would find no fault with my cutting.

When he had seen enough of my work, he took off his thick-rimmed spectacles before speaking.

'Your cutting is excellent Alfred, first class, but your nips are far too deep.'

I thought his criticism odd; my nips were never more than a quarter of an inch deep, anything less and the machinist might not have noticed them. After Katz had left the basement, I spent a few moments checking every one of the nips; none were deeper than a quarter of an inch. I began to wonder if there was a possibility that the spectacles he was wearing may have actually magnified the size of the nips.

The moment Katz's mentioned the nips; I knew he had decided that I was unsuitable for the job.

At 3.30 p.m. the sewing machines on the first floor were switched off; it was tea time. The sound of footsteps could be heard coming down the stairs; hopefully it would be Jean bringing me a cup of tea, but I was to be disappointed a second time. No Jean or tea; it was Katz who came into the cutting room, followed by Ted my cutter friend with whom I had worked at the Whitechapel jacket factory.

Ted immediately and discreetly signalled not to acknowledge each other. Katz began to ask Ted the same type of questions that he had put to me a few days earlier. Calling me aside, Katz quietly explained that this new cutter would now continue with my work and that I could go home. After thanking me for coming in for a trial, he took out his wallet and gave me three pounds.

I was aware that Ted was an experienced cutter, besides having immense strength which had proved to be an asset when lifting heavy roles of fabric; he was a talented marker maker.

It seemed strange that Ted, who could have commanded a much higher salary by being in charge of a modern cutting room, should find himself being interviewed for a lowly paid job in a tiny basement in Brick Lane. The only conclusion that I could come to was that he must have noticed the vacancy sign in the window as he passed by and, on an impulse, rang the bell. Of course, an added incentive must have been the lovely smile of Jean, who probably opened the door.

Collecting my wages at Myers & Co was an unpleasant experience. Myers refused to let me step inside the factory when I rang the bell.

'Just wait there' he growled.

After what seemed like a twenty-minute wait, Myers opened the door and thrust my wage packet, insurance cards and P45 into my hands. Ignoring his rudeness, I turned around to go down the stairs; suddenly, he bellowed, 'Don't ever work in Fashion Street again.'

Responding angrily to what I perceived to be a threat, I rushed back at the still open door and raised my voice, 'Just you get back into the sty where you belong, you fat pig.'

Fearing what might come next, he quickly stepped backwards and accidentally bumped into Bob, who was about to leave the premises. Bob, alarmed that I might physically attack Myers, shuttled me down the stairs and into the street. As we walked down Commercial Street towards Aldgate East Bob explained that he, too, had handed in his notice following a dispute with Myers.

'He was implying I wasn't pulling my weight, so I told him to shove the job.'

Bob was not interested in accompanying me to the Marshall Walker factory to enquire about the cutting vacancies 'Don't waste your time going there Alf; they pay lousy wages.'

Ignoring his and David Upson's warning, I was prepared to waste my time and see what Marshall Walker had to offer. If their 'lousy wages' were twelve pounds or less, the job would not be worth considering. Just before Bob and I arrived at the entrance of the Aldgate East subway, he told me that he had an appointment that very evening with the owners of an expanding dress factory at Mile End. This firm desperately needed additional cutting staff and, depending on their experience, stock cutters were earning on average fourteen pounds a week.

'Listen to me Alf 'he spoke urgently, 'I am already late for my appointment. Don't bother with Marshall Walker, just come with me to Mile End instead. We could be on to a winner.' I declined to accompany him.

Bob soon realised he was using up valuable time trying to get me to change my mind. He quickly wrote down his phone number on the back of my wage packet, suggesting that I should call him in a few days and let him know how I 'got on'. Before dashing down the subway's stairs, we shook hands and wished each other good luck. Bob's advice was probably correct, but I was determined to check out the Marshall Walker factory.

There were other reasons why I was interested in working at the Aldgate East area. The Shipping Federation was close by, convenient for when I wanted to rejoin the Merchant Navy, and I could meet David Upson during the lunch breaks. A ten minute walk would have taken me to Cannon Street Road, where he worked. Lastly, I wanted to try and make contact with the lovely Jean; how and when was yet to be decided.

I crossed Aldgate High Street and took a short-cut through Half Moon Passage and emerged in Alie Street just a few yards from the Marshall Walker factory. The building's structure was unusual; it did not seem like a factory, more like a disused cinema.

I rang the bell and was invited in by a friendly and smiling tea lady. As she escorted me to the managing director's office, I asked her if the factory was a former cinema. 'Nearly right' she replied, 'It used to be a dancehall.'

The director had left his office and was on the factory floor. I followed the tea lady into a vast noisy machining room. 'There he is' she said, pointing to a dapper, smartly dressed man who was distributing wages to the staff. The tea lady went over to him to explain who I was. She soon came back with a message, the boss was extremely busy and unable to interview me but I should just 'turn up for work at 8.30 a.m. on Monday'.

After an hour long walk from Poplar the following Monday morning, I reached the factory at about 8.15.

I followed the managing director to the cutting section which comprised three long tables in front of a raised area that was probably once a stage. Before being called away by his forelady, he explained that Maria the designer would arrive shortly and that I should assist her to cut samples. I immediately explained to the director that cutting samples was not the position I was applying for, it was stock-cutting.

Ignoring my explanation, he spoke reassuringly, 'Don't worry Alfred, it should only be for today.'

Within minutes, a short, slim man with dark wavy hair and in his mid thirties came over to one of the cutting tables. He took off his coat, put on an apron and poured himself a hot drink from a flask. Facing me, he said 'Wotcher mate, I am Phil the cutter.'

If Phil was the cutter, what would be my role? I began to wonder if the director was being shrewd, perhaps he thought that he could persuade me to be the regular sample cutter, but persuasion would not work. If he needed a sample cutter he should advertise for one. Possibly he had, without success. Sample cutting is unattractive work; most stock cutters seem to have an aversion to cutting samples and I was no exception. It could be very frustrating working alongside a designer/ pattern-maker, especially if she was uncooperative, inefficient or working to a tight schedule. Often problems emerge when cutting samples. There could be a fault with a new pattern, it might be badly made, parts could be missing; sometimes wrong information is given to the cutter regarding the appropriate fabric, interlinings and labels. It is stop-and-start work, having to continually interrupt the pattern maker for guidance. Another reason why stock cutters try to distance themselves from sample cutting is that they just don't seem to have the patience that is required for the job. Stock cutters rarely encounter the problems associated with sample cutting; their work is not stop-and-start but reasonably straightforward. Usually, the cutters are given prepared markers, occasionally they make the markers themselves and sometimes an assistant is required to help them to lay up wide fabric. After the lay has been cut out, the cutters would be expected to separate the parts into bundles. Depending on the size of the docket and how skilful the cutter, the whole process should be completed within a day.

'You flow with the tide,' said Bob.

Perhaps stock cutting is repetitious and mundane but it is still preferable to sample cutting.

It was almost 8.30 a.m. and Maria had yet to make an appearance. I gazed around the huge factory. Most of the space was taken up by sewing machines, special machines and pressing units. Gradually at first, a stream of women workers arrived and sat down at their machines. Their average age was about forty. The absence of younger workers on the factory floor seemed to me to cast doubt on a 1961 Department Of Employment report which suggested that, in the Shoreditch and surrounding areas, 45 per cent of the girls who left school that year were working in local clothing factories. If the report was accurate, at least a few of those school leavers would have made their way to the Marshall Walker factory; but there was no sign of young people working here. Suddenly, loud music from the radio could be heard, it was time to start work. Phil was helpful; he showed me where to hang my duffle coat and gave me a remnant to make an apron. 'You will get on fine with Maria, she rarely makes mistakes.' What Phil said disappointed me and instantly confirmed my suspicion that the director was indeed being shrewd.

Maria, the Greek Cypriot pattern maker, had short black hair, dark eyes and an immobile expression. She rarely smiled and spoke little. Whenever she stood still for a moment to collect her thoughts, her whole being resembled that of a statue. Throughout the day, Maria worked silently and assiduously. Never once did she give me insufficient information to cut her samples and I soon learned to respect her professionalism. Because she was so busy, I did not want to be a hindrance, or even worse a nuisance by interrupting her, unless it was absolutely necessary. Using my initiative was best suited here and fortunately I encountered few problems. When I did seek Maria's assistance, she instantly stopped working to advise me. Despite her reticence, I liked Maria; she was co-operative, polite and always precise. Phil was right that Maria was a perfectionist who made few mistakes.

Cutting samples on my first day proved less of an ordeal than I anticipated, thanks to Maria's efficiency.

By the end of the day, I had cut out no less than ten different garments, none of which had proved difficult or complicated. Earlier the director had spoken briefly to Maria and the eyes of both had been focused on me as they nodded. I pretended not to notice, but assumed they were nods of approval.

At 5.30 p.m. I quickly left the factory; there was no time to speak to the director about wages; that matter could be dealt with the following day. I made my way to Brick Lane, determined to try and make contact with Jean. Within five minutes, I had positioned myself outside the Odeon cinema, just a few yards from Katz's factory. If Jean came out, I would boldly approach her and ask for a date. It did occur to me earlier that I could have phoned Katz and asked to speak to Jean direct, but I was unsure of the consequences. Would Katz allow me to speak to her, would she even answer the telephone if she knew it was me, and what if I was rejected? It would be so easy for her just to say 'no' and replace the telephone. At least in Brick Lane, face-to-face, I might be able to persuade her to agree to a date.

'Persevere until you get refused, then walk away,' David Upson had said when I had sought his advice about women in the past. 'Always try and humour them and make them laugh, but for God's sake don't be serious, or they will probably tell you to get lost.'

By 6 p.m. neither Jean nor Ted my cutter friend or any of the other staff had emerged and, shortly afterwards, Katz came out and locked up the premises. I had arrived in Brick Lane too late; Jean had already gone home.

During my second morning at the Marshall Walker factory, the director called me into his office and explained that because both he and Maria were satisfied with my work as an 'able sample-cutter'. He was prepared to offer me an 'excellent wage', but he failed to mention a figure. Smiling broadly, he added, 'Cutting samples isn't that bad, is it Alfred?' 'But you engaged me as a stock cutter,' I replied.

His smile quickly vanished; lost for words, he began to tap his fingers on the desk.

'Yes, of course, em,well, em, perhaps you and Phil can take it in turns to cut the samples, em, how does that sound?'

His smile returned when I reluctantly agreed, though Phil may not have liked the new arrangement.

Clasping his hands together as if he had just concluded a successful deal, he said 'Good, let's get back to work, shall we?' I refused to leave the office until I knew what the 'excellent wage' was.

'Eleven pounds ten shillings.'

'How much?' 'Eleven pounds ten shillings.' 'No, I can't work here for that amount.' His jaw dropped, 'You can't?' 'No I can't.' I replied irritably.

Bob was right; Marshall Walker's reputation for paying 'lousy wages' was intact.

Scratching his forehead, he said 'Well, maybe I can increase it to twelve pounds a week.'

I quickly assessed the situation. Perhaps I could have argued for more money, citing cutter friends of my age who were earning between twelve and fourteen pounds a week, but my tenure at his factory would only be temporary. The moment I made contact with Jean, I would hand in my notice. So I decided not to bargain but just accept his offer.

Over the next few weeks, I would intermittently stroll up and down Brick Lane hoping to meet Jean. Sometimes I would arrive early in the lane before starting work; at other times for longer periods, especially at lunch times, but she was never to be seen.

Usually on a Friday Phil and I would spend our lunch break at nearby Petticoat Lane market. After a tasty snack at the Jewish delicatessen, we would make our way slowly back to Alie Street. One day, while in the market, Phil recognised a woman who he had not seen for some time. She was extremely pretty and in her early thirties. They greeted each other warmly; names of mutual friends and incidents from the past were recalled. As they spoke, I noticed that there was sadness in her eyes and voice. After the woman spent a few minutes in our company, she looked at her watch, gasped and said, 'I really must get back to the office.' As she walked quickly away Phil, seemingly keen to meet her again, called out, 'We are usually here on a Friday.' He watched her disappear into the crowds.

There was a tinge of sadness, too, in Phil's voice, as he explained what had happened to his lady friend. Twenty years previously, as a young teenager, she had come home from school and discovered her widowed mother had been brutally murdered by an ex-lover.

The loss of her mother had had a profound effect on her young mind. In her eyes, all men were cruel and inhuman; they were to be feared, avoided and never trusted. It was only when she reached early adulthood and with tremendous support from girlfriends, that her mistrust of men became less, but when boyfriends dared to mention marriage, she would shy away and immediately end the relationship.

I began to wonder if Phil might have been one of those former boyfriends she had rejected.

That same lunch time I recognised an attractive girl in the market. It was Jean; she was strolling past the stalls linked arm-in-arm with a strikingly handsome youth. When they stopped to buy fruit, she looked in my direction. Though just a few feet away, I was not recognised. It felt a little hurtful not to be recognised and acknowledged by somebody who was constantly in my thoughts. Adding to this pain was the sudden realisation that I had been a fool to believe that Jean might be interested in me; after all, who was I to her? Why should she remember me? We had only met briefly several weeks earlier in a small, airless basement. I was just one of several nameless stock cutters who had come and gone in quick succession. How I wished it was me who was with Jean that day in the market, but wishful thinking would not produce results. She was already 'spoken for,' as David Upson would remind me that evening.

When Phil and I arrived back at the factory after lunch, I handed in my notice. The director was dismayed; he offered to increase my wages by ten shillings a week, which I immediately rejected. Not discouraged, he raised the figure to a pound, but still I said no. He complained that it was unfair of me to give just a few hours notice when the factory was very busy with lots of samples and dockets to cut. His shaming me was successful; I agreed to stay on for another week.

My last few days at the factory went extremely slow; each day seemed like a week. The director made full use of my time. I cut dozens of samples, but no small dockets. When Friday finally arrived, I could not leave the factory fast enough, almost failing to say goodbye to Maria and Phil.

The following Monday morning, I walked in a leisurely fashion along the Commercial Road towards Aldgate East. I felt optimistic that I would soon find a cutting position that suited me. Approaching Cannon Street Road, I saw David Upson getting off the bus. It was good to see that my friend had made a full recovery. Over the weekend, he had been struck on the head with a beer bottle whilst having a fight with a Jamaican seaman at the Golden Lion pub.

As I continued walking west, the familiar voice of the singing window cleaner could be heard behind me. Seated on his bicycle, with a bucket hanging on the handlebars and his ladder strapped dangerously sideways across his back, he would sing his regular song 'O what a beautiful morning, O what a beautiful day.'

This song, from the musical 'Oklahoma' was a particular favourite of Bob's, who regularly sang it in Fashion Street during the mornings on his way to the factory.

If pedestrians or people standing at a bus stop failed to smile and acknowledge the singing window cleaner or worse, gave him a negative look, he would retaliate and resort to insults, usually beginning with, 'you miserable sods'. Some recipients of his sarcasm did force a smile; others shouted back scurrilous remarks or gave a rude gesture. I was there in Commercial Road when he had had an accident. As he cycled past the bus stop near the Troxy cinema in full voice, he struck the kerb and was thrown head first over the pavement railings. The fall may have temporarily affected his vocal cords because on subsequent occasions when I had spotted him, his mouth had been firmly shut, but now he was back on form, his voice as strong as ever.

Once I had reached Aldgate East, I started to walk back in an easterly direction along the Whitechapel Road. Dozens of clothing factories were located in the road and surrounding streets; coat and jacket factories would be bypassed. I soon found what I was looking for, a gown manufacturer on the second floor of large business premises was advertising for a stock cutter. Finding no bell or knocker at the entrance, I used a penny coin to tap hard on the steel door, and when there was no reply, I listened carefully, but not a sound could be detected. This was peculiar; I would have expected to have heard voices, the radio, the vibrating sounds of sewing machines. The silence was soon broken by the door being pushed open. A familiar face appeared and stepped outside; it was the van driver of William Gee Limited, a Hackney-based tailors' trimmings merchant.

The driver recognised me, too; 'You're wasting your time, mate, old Big-ears don't pay the wages.'

He left the door ajar before disappearing down the stairs. Cautiously, I went inside, expecting to find myself in a typical clothing factory with sewing machines and pressing units. Instead, there was no machinery or staff; just stacks and stacks of fabric piled high.

I was confused. The premises did not seem like a factory, more like a cloth warehouse; and where was 'Big-ears', who I assumed was the governor.

Raising my voice, I called out 'Hello, hello,' but there was no answer. I waited a moment before repeating 'Hello, hello,' and this time there was a response. A distant voice called back, 'I am coming.'

The footsteps came closer. Suddenly a tiny grotesque man with enormous ears, dark slanting eyes and a pointed chin appeared from behind one of the stacks of fabric. His looks suggested that he might be an Armenian. but his accent was local.

'Can I help you?' he said with a disarming smile.

'I am enquiring about the stock cutting vacancy.'

Still smiling he replied, 'Yes, yes, can you grade patterns?'

'Simple grading, yes, and I can make markers, too.'

'Good, good; let me show you what I am cutting; by the way, the wages are thirteen pounds a week.'

He also asked me if I was Jewish born. To which I replied 'No, but I know quite a few Yiddisher words.'

I followed him down the centre of the factory. Hundreds of rolls of fabric were in racks and lying on the floor. The absence of workers and sewing machines indicated that he might be operating some kind of cutting service or fabric storage. We stopped at a massive cutting table, perhaps 30 feet long. A dress lay had partially been cut out. Still retaining his smile, which seemed to be a permanent feature of his face, he said, 'Can you cut this lay for me?'

'Of course.'

I took off my duffle coat and switched on the ancient cutting machine, but because the machine had no self-sharpeners I switched it off.

'Any problems?' said bewildered Big-ears.

'How do you sharpen the blade?' I replied.

'With this.' He handed me a well-used sharpening stone before walking away.

After a clumsy and frustrating attempt to sharpen the six inch blade, I proceeded to cut out the lay.

Within minutes, the blade became blunt again; it required constant sharpening.

After an hour or so, I managed to finish cutting the lay, but I had forgotten my golden rule, the absolute requirement: before cutting a marker not made by myself to always check the marker for possible errors; hopefully there would be none.

Big-ears did not answer me when I shouted 'I have finished.' Either he was sitting in some sound proof office behind the stacks of fabric or he had left the premises. The latter was probably unlikely, considering that I was a stranger.

Again I shouted 'I have finished' and still there was no reply. After a few minutes waiting by the cutting table, I decided to look for the elusive governor, but he was nowhere to be found; the only sign of an office was a telephone on a small desk by the entrance.

Like a magnet, I was drawn to the steel door; instinctively, I knew it would be locked.

After trying unsuccessfully to force open the door, I sat down on a stool by the desk.

The situation here was dangerous; what if there had been a fire on the premises?

Big-ears had no right to lock me inside the factory and he should have told me when he was leaving.

The little man was totally irresponsible. I felt enraged and would confront him the moment he returned.

After a few frustrating moments sitting at the desk, I stood up and began to explore the huge factory floor. Near the cutting table I discovered two doors partially concealed by a pile of fabric that reached the ceiling. One door was a fire exit; above it a plastic sign read: THIS DOOR MUST BE KEPT OPEN DURING WORKING HOURS. The sign had been ignored; the door was locked and its crash bar secured by chains and a padlock. The second door led to a disgustingly filthy latrine, where I saw rodent droppings on the floor and spiders scattering in every direction. The smell was awful. The toilet pan and the small sink were encrusted with dirt; the taps had seized up; a string had been substituted for the cistern's pull chain and no toilet paper was available. I left the cubicle, sat on the cutting table and wondered what on earth I was doing in this factory.

Eventually a smiling and apologetic Big-ears rushed into the factory and explained that in his haste to collect some fabric from a West End showroom, he had totally forgotten to inform me that he was leaving the premises. I accepted his explanation but insisted that under no circumstances must he ever lock me in again. He apologised once more for his 'increasing forgetfulness.' His memory loss may have been genuine; he suddenly remembered that he had left his van full of rolls of fabric parked outside the factory. Reluctant and grim-faced, I followed him down the stairs to the street. Unloading lorries and vans and then having to carry the often heavy rolls of fabric up flights of stairs was a task I always disliked. It could be precarious work; several times over the years, while carrying fabric on my shoulder, I have tripped up, lost my balance and fallen down the stairs. On one occasion, a huge roll of bonded moss crepe had fallen off a cutter's shoulder. It bounced down the stairs and, like a battering ram, struck me hard in the chest. Bruises to my neck and collar bone were a regular occurrence. Years later, after decades of carrying fabric, my abdominal wall had become weakened, resulting in two hernia operations. Never once did I receive sick pay or compensation.

After working at the factory for a few days, it occurred to me that I was being taken advantage of as very little cutting was required and most of my time seemed to be spent loading and unloading the van.

For a qualified cutter, it felt demeaning to have to take on the role of an unskilled labourer.

Big-ears attempted to pacify me when I listed my complaints, starting with the filthy latrine. He listened attentively, promising that I would soon be able to concentrate just on marker making and cutting. He would hire a part time cleaner and a young 'Shlepper' (Yiddish for somebody who carries or drags) to do the manual work. He also promised, that once he had organised his business on a better footing, I was to be offered a 'fantastic deal'. He refused to give a date when he would hire additional staff, saying only that the changes would take place sometime in the near future. I was not satisfied with his promises. Impudently, I demanded to know the exact date, but again he said that he was unable to say for sure. It was obvious to me that his evasiveness was a sign that he had no intention of keeping his word.

At the end of my fourth day, a day entirely spent carrying rolls of fabric from vans up two flights of stairs and then placing them in racks, I came to the conclusion that there was no future for me at this factory. I would leave Big-ears employ the next day, which was Friday.

My last day was as demanding as the previous four days. The soreness in my shoulder was so painful that it felt as though it had been dislocated. If only I had had the strength of my father, a lifelong hod carrier.

Rubbing my shoulder at the end of the day, I collected my wages and told Big-ears that I was resigning. For once, his perennial smile disappeared and he wanted to know my reasons for 'this sudden decision'.

'As if you don't know why,' I remarked indignantly.

Too tired to air my grievances, I made my way towards the exit with Big-ears following me. When we reached the steel door, he asked for my telephone number 'For future reference.'

I explained that we did not have a telephone at home.

'Then your address, please.' He asked appealingly.

Wearily, I flopped down on the stool by the desk and wrote my address in his notebook. I waited for a moment while he read it before standing up and slowly staggering down the stairs and out of the building.

Never did the Whitechapel air taste so good. That Friday evening, I took the bus home to Poplar.

The next morning, after an uncomfortable night's sleep, due to a throbbing shoulder, I was woken by my anxious mother, who handed me a telegram, but her anxiety was short-lived; the telegram was from Big-ears requesting me to call at his factory as soon as possible.

Later that day, I met David Upson at the Golden Lion pub and showed him the telegram. I explained that even though I had spent the previous five days shlepping cloth for a peculiar little man, curiosity was tempting me to return to Whitechapel. 'Maybe I might be offered this fantastic deal.'

Dave found it amusing when I described myself as a shlepper; he too often made use of Yiddish words.

After listening to my description of the poor conditions at big ears' cutting room, he gave his verdict.

'There won't be a fantastic deal Alf. Just tear up the telegram.'

I should have listened to my friend.

As I approached big-ears factory on the Monday morning, the little man was in the street unloading rolls of fabric from his van. He was breathing heavily when he asked me to assist him.

Tapping my shoulder I growled, 'It's still sore after schlepping your cloth all last week.'

'Excuses, just excuses' he sneered. 'Just one load each and it's finished.'

Several loads later, and after stacking the fabric in piles on the floor, Big-ears offered me coffee from a dirty flask, which I promptly refused. Hygiene was not one of his priorities.

We sat on the cutting table and I listened in disbelief as he outlined his proposal.

A leading West End fashion house was desperately short of sample cutters. I would apply for a vacancy.

Once based there and having access to new sample designs, I was to discreetly make sketches of these designs and make notes of the relevant fabric and costins. On my way home from the West End each evening, I would stop by at his factory and hand him the sketches.

My first reaction to this fantastic deal was to kick him in the kishcus. (Guts)

Perhaps he was a meshuggeneh because he seemed oblivious to the fact that he was asking me to commit a crime, to be a gunif (thief).

Adopting the role of a willing accomplice, I asked him, 'How much gelt for each sample?'

'Two pounds.' 'Make it three pounds and we have a deal.'

He answered me abruptly. 'Who do you think I am a shiemiel? (Simpleton) Two pounds or nothing.'

It was becoming difficult to maintain the charade without laughing. I got down from the table and said firmly 'Okay, you have a deal.' After rubbing his hands gleefully, he walked with me towards the exit.

He sat down at the desk and quickly wrote the name of the West End fashion house in his notebook, tore out the page, gave it to me and suggested that I should visit the company immediately.

'And if possible, start work today and report back to me this evening.'

Believing that we had made an agreement, he grinned and opened the steel door for me to leave. But the grin soon disappeared; I demanded some fare money, 'because the West End is too far for me to walk'.

Not expecting these sudden costs, he growled 'Yes, yes, all right.' He turned his back on me before taking out his wallet. After a crisp pound note was thrust into my hands, I hurried out of the factory.

At least I had earned a pound for unloading the van. Big-ears would never contact me again.

Pridewear

In the late spring of 1962, shortly after leaving big-ears factory, I visited a girlfriend at her tiny bed-sitter near Dalston in Hackney. Noticing that there were several clothing factories in the locality, I decided to explore the area for possible employment. Although Hackney was too far to walk to from Poplar, the two boroughs were linked by the 277 bus route.

Above Jands Modes Ltd, a gown shop at 83 Kingsland High Street, was Pridewear Ltd, a small dress factory. Several vacancies were advertised on their sign, including one for a stock cutter. The factory entrance was at the side of the shop front.

As I approached the door, a formidable looking Jewish lady, with wide hips and smoking a cigarette, came out of the shop. She eyed me up-and-down and said 'Are you a cutter?' Her tone was not discourteous.

I smiled and replied 'How did you guess?'

She smiled back and said 'Just go up the stairs and speak to my son, Brian. He is the governor'.

I walked up a well-trodden wooden staircase to the first floor. The two rooms had been converted into a pressing department. Pressers, finishers and cotton-cleaners were busy at their work; suddenly, a tall, pear-shaped, dark haired man in his late twenties appeared from behind a dress rail and came towards me.

I immediately recognised him; he was Brian Shack, a friend of Alan Sclare, the 'enfant terrible'.

Like his mother, Brian instantly knew I was a cutter; speaking with a perfectly modulated voice, he said, 'Are you interested in the cutting vacancy?'

'Yes I am.'

He signalled me to follow him. We sat on stools by the window that overlooked the High Street; I politely refused his offer of tea. After lighting up a cigarette, he asked me the inevitable three questions; could I make markers, grade patterns and where had I worked previously. Answering the first two questions was easy; the third was difficult; my recent work record was abysmal. If I listed the numerous companies that I had worked for since leaving the Merchant Navy, he might consider me to be a time-waster. Nevertheless, I did mention Sclare and Lee, adding that I had seen him (Brian) a couple of times at the factory speaking to Alan Sclare. My mentioning Alan seemed to distract him from wanting more details about my other employers. After telling me a puerile joke about some incident in Alan's distant past, he went on to say that his own company, Pridewear Ltd, 'every garment made with pride', was a 'cmt' factory.

I was not quite sure what he meant by cmt. Noticing my puzzled expression, he explained that the term was a standard abbreviation for 'cut, make and trim'. I still did not fully understand the term, but I wanted to give him the impression that I did; replying confidently, I said 'Oh yes, of course.'

When the telephone rang he stubbed out his cigarette before answering it. This breathing space was an opportunity to try and evaluate what my chances were of being offered work. It was difficult to assess; possibly yes, possibly no. After he replaced the telephone and spent a few moments with his staff he lit up another cigarette and returned to the stool, which squeaked under his weight.

While he spent a moment inhaling the cigarette and collecting his thoughts, I began to sense that he might just offer me the job. When he spoke again, I knew immediately I was accepted.

'We subcontract for fashion companies in the West End. They supply the material and samples and we cut, make and trim the garments; our production is about a thousand dresses a week, which we need to increase substantially. I should mention that we are planning to move soon to new, and larger, premises nearby.'

Before continuing, he paused for a moment to inhale the cigarette.

'The working hours are 8.30am to 5.30pm. Overtime is available most days, including Saturday morning and the wages are £15 per week.' He concluded by suggesting that if I was interested I could start work the next day. I was very interested. £15 was more than I had been offered in other factories, and there was overtime too. My only concern was whether I was capable of doing the job properly.

As I had agreed to start work the next day, Brian asked me to follow him upstairs to the cutting room to meet Ron Atkinson, his foreman cutter and assistant manager, 'so that you can have a word with Ron and he will explain about the cutting'.

The second floor was the machining room; perhaps a dozen female workers sat at various types of sewing machines. Like the staff in the pressing room on the first floor, the women seemed contented as they worked.

The cutting room, which was situated on the top floor, was identical in area to the floors below. Each floor originally had two rooms that had been converted to one.

There were two cutting tables, one of which was no more than five yards long and it was pushed against the wall. The second table, double its size, took up the full length of the oblong shaped room, stretching from the windows that overlooked the High Street to the window at the rear that faced the back yard.

Brian introduced me to Ron before returning to the pressing room.

Ron Atkinson looked about thirty. He was not tall but his handsome face more than compensated for his lack of height. Patiently, he showed me a well made dress marker that he had just completed. He explained that he would work at the small table and be responsible for grading patterns, marker making and cutting small dockets and I would cut the bulk of the weekly production, including interlinings and, when necessary, make my own markers. There were other duties, too. I would have to help him to load the finished garments onto the van for Brian, who would deliver them to the West End. We would also unload any fabric that he returned with. These additional duties would occur most days.

The thought of earning £15 a week seemed to overrule my previous abhorrence of shlepping fabric.

I was very impressed with Ron; he was so friendly and easy to talk to. It was as if I had known him for years. I knew from the moment that I walked into the cutting room that we would have a good working relationship. Not only was he blessed with good looks and a kind nature, he was incredibly talented. I soon began to appreciate his expertise. After National Service in the Royal Air Force, he had enrolled at a fashion college, where he studied design and pattern making. He had worked at Pridewear for about five years. I could only marvel at his skills. Just a quick glance at a particular garment displayed in a shop window, as he drove home to Colindale in North West London, would be sufficient for him to make a mental note of the design. He could, from memory, create a well-crafted pattern. If required, he would cut out the sample using identical or similar fabric and finally, although his experience with sewing machines was limited, he had the ability to put together a perfectly fitted garment, an exact replica of the one displayed in the shop window.

Satisfied with all that had been explained to me and having no questions in mind, I said goodbye to Ron, assuring him that I would start work the next day. I left the factory feeling jubilant.

Mrs Shack, still smoking a cigarette, was fitting a dress on a mannequin in the shop window; she returned my smile as I passed her shop front.

Walking past Ridley Road market towards Dalston Junction, I felt extremely pleased with myself, knowing that I would be happy working at Pridewear. Both Brian and Ron seemed to be exceptionally nice people, the complete opposite of some of the ghastly characters that I had met in factories recently. Having a good memory can have its disadvantages; how could I ever forget the parsimonious Fagin, the odious Bill, the revolting Carter, the awful Myers, the despicable

Chris and the snide Big-ears; but in those same factories I had had the good fortune to have met genuinely likable people, such as Alfie Hart, Aubrey, Max, Shar, Glynis, Bob, Maria and Phil. I felt so buoyant about my future prospects I could not wait to tell David Upson the news that at long last I had found a suitable job.

In my eagerness to work at Pridewear, I had ignored the fact that the working conditions at the factory were not altogether satisfactory. The cutting room and the machining and pressing rooms had no fire escape. Brian, Ron and several of the women workers were smokers. Shlepping fabric from the street to the top floor would be tiring and it seems that a single toilet was shared by the staff at both Pridewear and Jan's Gown shop, but Brian was planning to move soon to larger premises nearby. Hopefully, the new factory would be on the ground floor with modern facilities.

The next morning, at 7.30, I boarded the 277 bus at the southern end of Poplar's Burdett Road. Travelling by bus to work was an unusual experience for me; since leaving school six years earlier I had always walked to work. The journey to Dalston took about twenty minutes. With plenty of time to spare, I wandered through Ridley Road market before stopping for tea and toast at Tanzi's Italian café directly opposite the Pridewear factory.

My first morning at work went surprisingly quickly. Ron had prepared a double dress-marker for me; the style was a 'Swiss Miss'. This pretty little cotton dress had short puffed sleeves, a full, gathered skirt and eyelets down the centre of the bodice.

I set about laying the 45 inch wide fabric with a zeal I had not felt since my days at A. & B. Hyams.

I was determined to prove that I would be an asset at Pridewear; under no circumstances would I make any mistakes – but it was not to be. A couple of months later, I completely ruined a docket of 200 dresses.

Sitting by the window at lunch time enjoying my sandwiches, I noticed a sleek, bright red sports car stopping outside Jands's shop; its door opened and out jumped Brian Shack. A few curious pedestrians had gathered on the pavement to have a closer look at this unusual but impressive car. Ron also looked out of the window. He told me that Brian was one of the very first customers to purchase the world famous E-Type Jaguar in 1961; the cost was £2,000. Brian's wife Eleanor eventually became the owner of a sports car, too, but she had to be content with the inferior and less expensive MGBGT.

Sensing that I was keen to do overtime, Ron allowed me to start work at 8am and stay until 6.30 p.m. I needed money desperately; my savings amounted to just a few pounds in my pocket. Rather than borrow from David Upson, I had recently pawned two suits which had been bought during better times.

A woman behind me in the queue at the Crisp Street market pawnshop in Poplar was pledging some sheets; she tapped me on the shoulder and whispered 'Watch him, the old git is a Scrooge.'

Her description of the gaunt pawnbroker was justified; as he carefully examined the suits, he was continually tut-tuting. Shaking his head he said, 'The guts have been knocked out of them.'

I could have knocked the guts out of him; the suits were new and had never been worn, but he still advanced me two pounds. Ron expressed incredulity that I had visited the pawnshop.

My first pay packet, which included overtime, was about £18 after deductions. I was thrilled, having never earned so much for one week's work. My first priority would be to increase the amount of money I could give to my mother each week, starting that very Friday I would also collect my suits from the pawn shop and, over the weekend, invite David Upson for a tasty curry at the Gulistan, a little Asian restaurant at 218, Commercial Road, Stepney. Dave and I had dined there many times since we became friends in 1959.

Perhaps the Gulistan, a two-man business that consisted of a cook and a server, was not the most hygienic of establishments. The server, an elderly Lascar, wore the same green jumper with holes in the elbows seven days a week, but the lamb curry was excellent and cheap. Never once did Dave or I suffer any ill-effects after eating there.

Still feeling generous when we left the Gulistan, I refused to allow Dave to buy any drinks when, at his insistence, we toured the Cable Street clubs. My preference would have been an evening spent at the Prospect of Whitby, singing alongside the off-duty nurses but, for that evening, it would be Dave's choice.

Though my friend and I no longer drank regularly in Cable Street, he still felt the occasional need to visit the area to 'check out the latest gin joints', but entering these gin joints, which were patronised by unsavoury characters, could be risky, especially when violent arguments and fights occurred. It was no joy for me having to stand so close to pickpockets, dope peddlers, pimps and prostitutes.

A few months earlier, Noel Morgan, a drunken seaman, received fatal stab wounds when he was involved in a fight with staff at Abdulla's Somalian Café in Ensign Street. As a precaution, I would always follow Dave's advice to avoid eye-contact with strangers in Cable Street.

We spent the evening drinking at the Green Parrot, The Rio Club and probably the 'Black Roses Café Bar'.

Rosetta Jackson, an African woman, was the proprietress of the café bar; fearless and pugnacious, she looked very strong, with a wide V-shaped back and muscular arms. She had to be tough, especially when dealing with aggressive, unemployed seamen, who would intermittently ease their way unnoticed into her bar and pester customers for drinks and money.

The atmosphere could be tense, with sinister-looking Maltese men coming and going. Drugs were being openly sold and prostitutes bartered with Rosetta's clientele.

Dave and I would eventually boycott the café bar. My friend suspected that a regularly smooching couple were probably undercover police on a surveillance operation.

'The last thing we want, Alf, is to be here if the police raid the joint.'

His observation may have been accurate; the police did raid the premises and Rosetta was arrested for possessing 42 packets of hemp and a loaded revolver.

As I was totally happy working at Pridewear, time seemed to pass very quickly. With regular overtime available, my net wages was an average £22 a week.

'Invest in unit trusts,' advised David Upson, when he saw my fat wage packet.

Like many clothing subcontractors Brian relied on 'cabbage'. Usually Ron managed to achieve tight economical costins and as a result cabbage made up at least 10 per cent of Pridwear's production. Without the profit obtained from the sale of cabbage, Brian may not have been able to keep his business viable; the making price he received for his dockets was often inadequate. Time and time again, he would be on the telephone pleading with his suppliers for extra money; five shillings, three shillings, even a shilling. He was not always successful.

There were other frustrating and disappointing periods for Brian, especially when he had to accept dress dockets that required their front bodices to be embroidered or pint-tucked.

Finding specialist firms that could do this processed work and had spare capacity proved difficult. The problem was always the same: we would cut out a docket of several hundred dresses, send the bodices to the embroiderer and then wait for a delivery. Invariably the deliveries did not come when we needed them most.

Time and time again embroiderers and pin-tuckers failed to keep their promise to make regular deliveries. Meanwhile, Brian's suppliers would be constantly harassing him to complete the docket; they, in turn, had customers waiting for their orders. One of the small specialist firms that we dealt with was Commercial Embroideries, whose workshop was above Bloom's, the famous kosher restaurant in the Whitechapel Road.

Kublin, the owner of Commercial Embroideries, never kept his word. He would collect the bodices from us, but not before Brian had persuaded him to give us a date when we could expect the first delivery. Kublin foolishly committed himself to a date, knowing full well that it was a commitment he was unable to keep. When he did make a delivery, it was not, for example, 50 sets of bodices on a Monday, but just 20 sets the following Friday. Similar small quantities of the order were delivered over a period of several weeks. Brian soon became extremely annoyed at the embroiderer's incessant failure to keep his word. Kublin would furtively sneak into the cutting room, leave the embroidered bodices on the cutting table and then attempt to leave unnoticed.

I was given strict orders by Brian to notify him the moment the embroiderer arrived and, if necessary, try to physically prevent him from leaving. The second part of this order was ludicrous and would be ignored. Besides, Kublin was a big strong man. If an enraged Brian was prepared to confront him over inadequate deliveries, let him do so at his peril.

Kublin often arrived at the factory in a harassed state; he admitted that the main reason why he could not give us more support was because he was unable to find skilled staff. All I could do was advise him to accept a part, rather than a whole docket from us, and not to promise exact delivery dates. During these minor crises, Brian somehow managed to keep his suppliers at bay, but only just.

Because Ron was a master craftsman who hardly ever made mistakes, I had become complacent and would not always check his markers thoroughly. Ignoring my golden rule and believing that Ron was infallible was to have dire consequences for me. I made a gigantic and costly mistake.

Ron had made a treble dress marker, but the patterns did not pair. Either I had failed to examine the marker correctly or did not follow his instruction to lay the fabric to pair. I went ahead and layed the fabric right side up and cut out the lay which totalled approximately 200 dresses. As so often, cutting errors are discovered during the bundling process. A cold shiver swept through my body; none of the front bodices paired. I just could not believe that I had made the same mistake that Nicos had made.

I frantically searched under the cutting table to see if there was more of the same fabric to cut 200 front bodices, but there was none. A terrible sense of failure gripped me. I was an incompetent idiot who was about to be sacked. Ron quickly realised that I had done something wrong.

With my head lowered in shame, I explained my mistake. He came quickly to my table, to see if he could help, but there was nothing he could do. Reluctantly, Ron summoned Brian from the pressing room.

Trepidation now engulfed me; severe punishment was inevitable and imminent. Either I had to purchase the 50 to 75 yards of fabric that was needed to recut new fronts, or I was to be kicked out of the factory. The latter seemed more likely. No doubt tomorrow morning I would walk to Aldgate East and start looking for work. Alternatively, perhaps I should visit the Shipping Federation and enquire about finding work on a ship.

My costly mistake could not have come at a worst time for Brian. He had recently lost money by allowing a travelling salesman friend to sell his cabbage to gown shops all over London. This friend had accumulated a great deal of money on these cabbage sales but rather than pay Brian he absconded.

A grim-faced Brian came into the cutting room and stood motionless at the cutting table. For a few moments, he just stared at my cut out lay. Whatever punishment he had in mind, I would accept it. Perhaps a punch in the eye was forthcoming. The seconds ticked by, but still he did not speak; when he finally spoke to me, his tone was surprisingly mild.

'Alf don't ever make a mistake like that again.' Turning to Ron, he said 'We can sort this problem out later; give Alf another docket.'

I was totally amazed at Brian's reaction to what I considered to be a catastrophe. It seemed strange; he had every right to sack me or demand compensation for my incompetence, but he chose not to. Could it be that the look of utter despair on my face caused him to show leniency? I would never know; even Ron was unsure. Whatever the reason, I was deeply grateful.

Brian may have been incredibly lenient to me, but the same kind of benevolence was not always available to future employees, especially the drivers. In July 1962, three months after starting work at Pridewear, I was working late one evening when shouting in the street attracted me to the window. Huge crowds had gathered on the pavement at the entrance of Ridley Road market. Large numbers of police were present, some on horseback. When the crowds surged forward, the police tried to keep control, but scuffles broke out. I wondered why the CND, which I had thought was a peaceful organisation, were trying to hold a demonstration at Ridley Street market of all places, but it was not the CND who were in the market, but Sir Oswald Mosley and his Union Movement supporters. Mosley was given no chance to make a speech. Within minutes of arriving his opponents had surrounded him and he was kicked and punched viciously to the ground. The police immediately called off the meeting.

It was always a pleasant experience for me to sit by the window at lunch time and gaze at the hustle and bustle below. One day, I spotted an older and slower 'Right Ho' pushing his heavily-laden barrow. Irish Mary, the elderly vagrant from Bethnal Green, was also to be seen. Her thin stature seemed more stooped than before. I wondered why these two characters were so far north.

Mary was loitering outside the London Co-operative store opposite. When a rag-man on a horse and cart stopped outside Tanzi's café for a few moments, Mary seized the opportunity to do some trading.

The rag-man made no objection when she ripped off her dirty camel-coloured jacket and swapped it for a long, dark green coat that she had pulled out from amongst the rags. With great speed she put on the coat, fastened up the buttons, stuck her nose in the air and paraded herself like a model in front of the laughing Co-operative window-dressers.

Early in August 1962 a generous Brian Shack allowed me a few days holiday with pay.

Much of my free time was spent at Shadwell Park, reading and enjoying the passing river traffic. On one of these halcyon days I brought Danny, my 16-month-old nephew, with me. My sister Sylvia reminded me that at some point her son would probably need to sleep.

With Danny seated on my lap, we took the bus to Watney Street market, where I bought lemonade, biscuits and a magazine from Fielding's stationery shop. Fifteen minutes later, we arrived at the park. Danny, now in an excitable mood, ran happily across the grass. After endless rides on the swings and the roundabout and a frolic with other toddlers in the sandpit, he spotted the paddling pool. I soon learned that young children had to be held tight; Danny had to be restrained from dashing into the pool. When he eventually started to tire, we sat on a riverside bench near the circular ventilation shaft of the Rotherhithe Tunnel and drank the lemonade. The biscuits, too dry and unsweetened for him to enjoy, were thrown to the ubiquitous pigeons. It was pointless trying to attract his attention to the endless stream of ships, tugs and barges, for it was the swans and ducks that fascinated him most. As he was struggling to keep his eyes open, I picked him up and rocked him in my arms. The lapping of the waves on the foreshore and the gentle drone emitted by the ventilation shaft had an immediate effect; he fell asleep.

The following lunch time, I returned alone to the park but no benches were vacant, so I left for the nearby Prospect of Whitby, where the vista from the riverside terrace was superb. Having an incredible thirst, I drank two to three pints of beer in quick succession. Sitting on the river wall with my legs dangling over the side, I was joined by three medical students, probably from the London Hospital in Whitechapel. One of the students spotted an animal's skull on the foreshore below; he insisted that it was a sheep's skull.

'Don't be a clot, can't you see it's a pig?' said a second student.

Sitting next to me was the third student; he was adamant that it was a goat's skull. Noticing that I was amused by their discussion, and speaking with a soft Welsh accent, he asked me if I had an opinion on the scull. 'Perhaps it was a dog, a Great Dane' I replied naïvely.

Maintaining their interest, the three students climbed down the steel ladder that was fixed to the wall and began to examine the skull's bone structure by the waters edge.

While they argued amongst themselves, I swung my legs around to face the terrace and found myself admiring the bone structure of an attractive fair-haired teenage girl with Nordic features. She sat directly opposite me on one of the barrel seats. Her companion, a man in his fifties, wearing an enormous gold chain around his neck, was trying unsuccessfully to hold her hand. When their glasses became empty, he managed to persuade her to have another drink. The moment he went into the saloon bar, the girl got up, came over to the river wall and stood just a few feet from me. After lifting herself up onto the wall, she turned her head and gazed out across the river. Stimulated by the effects of the beer and David Upson's advice 'A faint heart never won a fair lady' I asked her if she was Swedish; she smiled and replied in perfect English,

'Nearly right, I am Norwegian.'

'Are you studying in London?'

'No, I am an au pair.'

Fearing that her companion might reappear at any moment, I had to put my threepenny-bit in quick.

'If you come here during the evenings, there is a wonderful atmosphere; everybody sings along to a Hawaiian band.'

Her eyes opened wide. 'Does that include Saturdays?'

'Saturday evenings are extremely popular.'

'Okay, I will come with a girlfriend this Saturday.'

I quickly added 'And is she like you, Norwegian, very pretty and speaks fluent English?'

She smiled, 'Of course, all three.'

This unexpected but welcome interlude came to an abrupt end; her stern looking companion came towards us carrying a small tray of drinks and glaring at me.

Rather than give him the impression that I was an opportunist, which of course was true, I politely tried to engage him in a trivial conversation, but he totally ignored me. I was a persona non grata.

He sat on the wall between the girl and me and slyly turned his back sideways in an attempt to obscure my view of her, but I was unperturbed. There was a good chance that I would have a close view of her the following Saturday evening.

Before leaving the Prospect, I waited until the medical students had climbed back onto the terrace. One of them had retrieved the skull. To my question, might it have been a dog's scull? The Welsh student replied,

'Definitely not, nor was it a sheep, a goat or a pig.'

I declined his offer to examine the skull. With my interest diminishing fast, I asked him if he had any idea what it might be. The students answered as one, 'an ox'.

With her companion's back still a barrier, it was too difficult for me to indicate to the Norwegian girl that I was about to leave. After a few moments I finished my drink said goodbye to the students and left the terrace, using the narrow exit to the street.

Having consumed too much beer, I felt slightly drunk walking along the busy and dangerous highway. Usually, beer makes me hungry. The thought of a tasty pie and mash at Watney Street market caused me too increase my slightly wobbly pace. Within the hour, I had left the pie-and-mash shop feeling contented and a little sleepy. The afternoon had gone well; besides spending a pleasant couple of hours at the Prospect of Whitby and meeting an attractive girl, I had just consumed a delicious meal. But this feeling of well-being was about to be shattered.

Turning into Chapman Street and passing Fielding's shop. I saw a crowd of people, mostly women, standing on the pavement directly opposite a stationary lorry. Something dreadful must have happened.

As I approached the crowd, the wailing of distressed women could be heard. At the rear of the lorry, I was horrified to see the lifeless body of a small boy lying in the road; a blanket had been placed over him, but the top part of his face could be seen. Suddenly, I found myself panicking; the boy looked like Danny; was it Danny? My heart started to pound rapidly and my knees started to knock together uncontrollably. Painful questions flashed through my mind. What was Danny doing here, where was Sylvia, his mother, why did she not hold his hand? An elderly woman, noticing my anxiety, gripped my arm. As the ambulance screeched to a halt, the lorry driver, whose heartbroken face I can recall to this day, had been kneeling by the little boy. He gently lifted him up, and as he did so, more of the boy's face was revealed. It was then that I realised it was not Danny. Once the ambulance had left the scene, my knees stopped knocking. Mingling with the crowd, I listened to what was being said by witnesses. A picture soon emerged.

Because Chapman Street is an exceptionally narrow street, the lorry was very close to the kerb and travelling at no more than five miles an hour, due to the close proximity of the market. Apparently, as it passed the two little boys, who were playing 'piggy back' on the edge of the pavement, the younger of the two toppled off of his brother's back and landed in the road, where he became fatally trapped under the rear wheels of the lorry.

When I returned to work the following Monday morning, a tearful Marie Decosta, who was one of Pridewear's pressers, came into the cutting room and explained to Ron that her nephew, David Cohen, just four years old, had been knocked down and killed at Watney Street market. Aware of her grief, I thought it would be too insensitive to mention that I had seen the little boy lying in the road.

Always fearful of making another mistake, I took great care with my cutting and marker making; it was unlikely that Brian would give me another chance if I did something wrong. I worked carefully and conscientiously. My efforts were soon appreciated. With Ron's approval, Brian, who had a trusting nature, gave me a set of keys to open and close the factory. An extra pound a week was offered for this commitment.

Now that the production was increasing by the week, Brian found it extremely difficult to manage the factory, particularly when so much of his daily routine was spent on the road supplying work to his outdoor machinists and delivering the finished dresses to the West End showrooms. In order to dispense with these time-consuming duties and spend more time inside the factory, he decided to employ a driver.

Ron, too, often assisted with the driving. It may have been the swinging of the heavy sack of bundles onto his back that caused his sciatica. The excruciating pain would radiate downwards and affected both his legs. Desperate for a cure, he went to see Sir Reginald Watson Jones, a Harley Street consultant.

After twelve expensive sessions of deep X-ray treatment and no improvement, he sought the services of a Chinese acupuncturist, who had converted his garage into a clinic. After several visits to the acupuncturist, Ron found that the pain was less severe. Eventually, he would become pain free.

Brian Shack's relationship with his drivers was always acrimonious. The drivers were much to blame for the acrimony. In between their various collections and deliveries, they would often 'take liberties'.

Typical were the unofficial breaks, when they would disappear for long periods, occasionally using Pridewear's van for their personal use.

Our first driver, James, liked to call himself 'Jessie James'; He came from Antigua and was big, clumsy and highly superstitious, believing in voodoo and witchcraft. He tried to convince Ron and me that in Antigua there was a baby born with a gold tooth. Though married and with a young child, he had a mistress named Betty, who lived with her husband Wally at Stoke Newington.

James drove the van at great speed, sometimes finishing his rounds quickly, so that he could spend an hour or so with Betty at her home. His visits were carefully planned; he always made sure that Wally, who did shift work, was out of the house when he called.

When James was not driving, he would assist me to lay up fabric and help with the bundling. He was unable to concentrate sufficiently, but usually his mistakes were minor and easily rectified. If the phone rang, his ears would prick up in anticipation. Sometimes the call would be for him and usually it was Betty, advising him when it was safe to call at her home. Ron, who would receive all incoming calls to the cutting room, had become familiar with Betty's voice. Believing that he could imitate her, he decided to play a practical joke on James, with me in collusion. We devised a plan. After the staff had gone home, Ron would go downstairs to the machining room directly below the cutting room and use the phone there to ring me; I would hand the receiver to James, who would be told by a distressed Betty that her outraged husband had just discovered that she was having an affair. Our joke went well; James placed the receiver to his ear and looked alarmed as he listened to Ron's now feminine voice.

'James, James, we are in trouble. Wally has found out about us. He's got a gun; he's coming round to get you; I am going to do myself in.'

James, now visibly panicking, shouted down the receiver 'Don't do that, honey, don't do that.'

Dropping the receiver, he rushed over to the window and looked out. He returned quickly to the receiver and once more pleaded with 'Betty' not to harm herself. Again he went over to the window to see if there was any sign of Wally. By the window, there was a small opening in the floor which was used for dropping bundles of cut dresses to the machining room on the second floor. Standing so close to this opening, I could hear Ron's voice below, but incredibly, James did not hear him. Ron, determined to continue the charade, was now attempting to give his histrionic performance even more realism by quickly changing his uncontrollable giggling into loud sobs. As James hurried over to the window a third time, he almost skidded to a halt; he suddenly heard the sobbing rising up from the opening in the floor. Realising he had been fooled, he slammed the receiver down before cursing Ron and me. Flopping down on a stool and in between taking deep breaths and wiping his sweaty brow, he made an appeal.

'Please man, never, never do that to me again.'

'Jessie James' would receive another shock, but this time it was not the result of a practical joke. Thieves stole Pridewear's loaded van of dresses just prior to James setting off for the West End.

A few hours later, the van was recovered minus the garments. Now concerned that the thieves were still in the area, Brian ordered me to stand guard outside the factory whenever the van was being loaded. His concern was not unfounded. A few weeks later, while James was making a delivery to a showroom near Oxford Street, the same thieves must have followed him to the West End. Unable to steal the van a second time they left a note on the windscreen threatening to kill James and 'that geezer (me) outside the factory'.

James was not a brave man; after reading the note he became absolutely petrified. Somehow, he managed to drive back to the factory where he parked outside the entrance. Too scared to get out of the cab, he just sat there, continually sounding the horn until Brian and Ron were alerted. They managed to assist an extremely distressed James into the factory and it took several hours before he finally calmed down.

During the evenings I felt slightly nervous standing at the bus stop at Dalston Junction waiting for the 277 bus that would take me home to Poplar. Often, late at night, I was the only person at the stop and that was when I felt most vulnerable. If the thieves were going to carry out their threat to kill me, this would have been the right moment. All pedestrians who passed by had to be considered potential killers who might try and stab me in the back and my only defence was alertness and a cut-throat razor borrowed from David Upson. Fortunately for James and me, no attempt was ever made to harm us.

As the months went by, James's occasional forgetfulness and not always carrying out his duties properly aggravated Brian and their relationship eventually deteriorated. In between sacking and immediately reinstating him, Brian decided to try a new tactic; instant fines would be imposed every time James made a mistake. Though this tactic was more of a threat than an intention, it had the opposite to the desired effect. James felt bitter and humiliated and he told me that once he had found a new job, he would leave.

In between subcontracting for West End fashion houses, Brian, who had a brilliant eye for current fashion trends, began to purchase limited amounts of fabric. His plan was to manufacture small amounts of his own garments and he quickly became quite successful at this new enterprise.

As the months went by, we were manufacturing more and more of Brian's garments, which included dresses, blouses, skirts and slacks. Two new companies: 'Miss Impact' and 'Wots Its Name' were created to cope with the increased volume of work.

Now that Brian was making the move away from CMT to manufacturing under his own label, finding larger premises became his top priority. In late 1963, he finally found a factory nearby that was suitable.

Just around the corner from Pridewear was Crossway. At the bottom of this little street stood a disused Victorian chapel that had recently been occupied by the North London Handbag Factory. The proprietor, a Mr Langford, originally a refugee from Poland, had decided to cease trading.

David Upson, who worked as a framer for D. & W. Handbags at Stepney and was aware of the high quality of Langford's products, could not understand why the factory had closed down when the industry was flourishing. Whatever the reason, it was unlikely to have been the unsparing beating that Langford had recently received at the hands of Bill Bishop. Bill was the husband of Kay, Pridewear's diminutive Irish tea lady and cleaner.

The Bishops lived just a few yards from the handbag factory. One day,

Langford, for reasons that I have forgotten, threw a bucket of water over Kay's young son, Paul. When Bill, a former amateur boxer, saw his drenched son, he charged into the factory. It was all over in seconds; he attacked Langford and left him black and blue and lying stunned on the floor.

I felt sad when Brian relocated his business to Crossway. I had become attached to the old cutting room, despite its unsuitability, which included a roof that leaked alarmingly. Each evening Ron and I would place buckets on the floor and hope that any dripping rainwater would not change its course and land on the fabric. The wiring had been neglected; I would regularly receive electric shocks from a faulty light switch and there was the cold. With no heating installed, the cutting room was like a refrigerator during the winter months. Ron managed to obtain a small electric heater at the onset of the long severe winter of 1962/63. We would ration its use; for the first hour, the heater was placed by his table, then it was unplugged and repositioned near my table. We would repeat this hourly ritual throughout the day.

There was no room for an office at the factory. Pridewear's accountant, Eric Finklestine, who changed his surname to Farley, would arrive at the factory every Friday morning to prepare the wages, but he had to be content with the use of a small table in the cutting room.

The new factory at Crossway had all the facilities that Brian needed for his expansion plans. The first floor would be used for machining and pressing. By the entrance was a large office. There was also a small canteen, toilets and a stockroom. The enormous semi-basement would be the cutting room; with enough space for three long tables. At the rear there were two rooms that could be used for storage and adjacent to these was a washroom and a WC. The only outdated facility was the solid-fuel heating system, the boiler of which was situated in a large coal bunker in the yard. Every morning throughout the winter, Ron or I would be responsible for cleaning out, stoking up and lighting this enormous boiler.

Once established inside the new factory, Brian's cut, make and trim production would come to an end. Although Brian retained Pridewear as a manufacturing unit, all our dockets would now be supplied by his burgeoning fashion companies: 'Miss Impact' and 'Wots Its Name'. A third company 'Magnificent Dresses' was also created. Brian's business expanded rapidly and additional staff were engaged.

Silvia Bronson, a designer and pattern cutter, was the first to arrive, followed by a team of travelling salesmen, who would sell Brian's garments to retail outlets all over the country.

One of the large rooms at the rear of the cutting room was converted into a packing and dispatch unit. The room was next to an exit that led to an alley but situating this unit so close to the alley was a mistake since the alley would be an ideal route for a dishonest employee to smuggle out garments from the dispatch room.

Again Brian's trusting nature was abused. Noel, a head packer, was discovered stealing. His face was devoid of shame as he was escorted off the premises. Instead, he held his head high and smirked as he passed through the cutting room.

James had now left Pridewear, much to my regret. His successor, Ken, a 'Cape coloured', came to London from South Africa via the Merchant Navy. He looked like an Argentine gaucho with his dark curly hair, elongated face and pencil-thin moustache. By coincidence, Ken and I had met before, through our mutual friend David Upson. Ken was a reformed alcoholic. I thought it likely that because his hands sometimes trembled, it was possible that, at some stage, he had experienced the DTs (delirium tremens).

Dave had also experienced the DTs in the past, which included some weird hallucinations. He described to me how, during a drunken state, he had foolishly taken a hot bath.

'When the steam disappeared, I saw an exact replica of myself sitting opposite in the bath; no matter how much I blinked, the image was still there. If I smiled, it smiled back; if I rubbed my nose, it did the same. It was as if I were looking in a mirror. Then I dozed for a few minutes; when I woke up, the image had gone.'

I had become quite friendly with Ken. He invited me to have dinner with him and his fiancée Irene at their Dalston flat. At the flat, I was introduced to Irene's close friend Helen, a divorcee, who was at least ten years my senior.

The next evening, I hoisted a laughing Helen on to the cutting table. An hour later, and just before I locked up the factory for the night, I made sure that there was no indentation left on top of the lay.

Ken, like his predecessor James, followed the same pattern of taking far too long with his driving duties – perhaps he was visiting Irene during his working hours. As expected, Brian became extremely annoyed with Ken over his absenteeism. He ordered him, in no uncertain terms, to speed up his collections and deliveries. Ken did make the effort to improve his time schedule but it was not enough to satisfy Brian, who threatened to sack him if he did not give his total commitment to the job. But Brian's demand for total commitment went too far.

Irene and Ken finally decided to get married. The wedding was arranged to take place at a local church on a Saturday at 10 a.m., however, Brian had other ideas. He insisted that Ken must first work on the Saturday morning and complete his outdoor machinist run before he had any thoughts about getting married.

Ken, fearing that he might lose his job if he refused, decided to comply. Irene was absolutely furious. She warned Ken that if he did not get to the church on time, she would never want to see him again.

At 9.55 a.m., a near-exhausted, perspiring Ken, carrying a huge sack on his back, staggered into the cutting room. The sack, along with the carnation in his lapel, slid to the floor. As he quickly made his way towards the exit, he shouted 'I am married to this cursed job'.

I calculated it would take him just three minutes to reach St Mark's Church. Driving the van at great speed, Ken just managed to get to the church on time. A few weeks later, and after being offered a better paid van driving job elsewhere, he handed in his notice.

Brian's character was difficult to define; I could not understand why he could be so heartless at times, yet at the same time have an admirable, though sometimes irresponsible, nature. He trusted his employees implicitly. Even newly engaged staff were often given positions of trust, without their references being checked.

Pridewear's third driver was an opportunist who took advantage of this loophole. He came into the factory one morning, ostensibly looking for work; Brian immediately offered him the driver's vacancy.

During the afternoon, this unknown man was asked to make a delivery of dresses to the West End. As he climbed into the driver's seat of the van, he must have wondered what fools we were at Pridewear. He never made the delivery. Later that day, the van was found abandoned, minus the garments.

With orders flooding in for 'Miss Impact' and 'Wots its Name' original designs, Pridewear could not cope with the increased volume of work. Brian would have to make use of the local Greek and Turkish clothing sub-contractors. In order to assess the standard of their work, we followed a well tried procedure used by most garment manufacturers. First, we would give the sub-contractors a bundle of cut dresses – never more than twelve garments. Usually this initial small amount was made reasonably well, but when we gave the contractors a follow-up docket of the same style, often totalling several hundred garments, the quality of their work was far from satisfactory. Notable problems were incorrect measurements and poor pressing. Time and time again we would return finished garments to these factories for rectification. Gradually, during these early days, from the dozens of factories that we experimented with, we selected only those whose production was on-par with Pridewear's high standard. Brian was determined to sustain the growing reputation of 'Miss Impact' and 'Wots Its Name' for producing well made garments.

In October 1965 my mother, who had been ill for several years, died suddenly.

Accepting her death was very painful; most of her children had been born during her late thirties and mid forties, so my brother and sisters and I never knew her as a young and healthy mother but only as a middle-aged mum who was often ill. Her children loved her dearly and not a day goes by when she is not in our thoughts.

After my mother's death I became restless. It was the same kind of restlessness that I had felt during my last months at A. & B. Hyams. The Merchant Navy was once more in my thoughts; I made enquiries at the Shipping Federation about re-enlisting, but there were no vacancies. I also thought about going into business with David Upson and we discussed the possibility of forming a partnership. Our plan was to obtain a coach and take tourists around the famous dockland pubs, but unfortunately this idea never materialised.

In the spring of 1966 a small complicated telephone switchboard had been installed in the cutting room. If Ron was unavailable, I would have to answer all incoming calls, but I found the switchboard difficult to use. I kept pressing the wrong buttons. Brian, who spent most of his time upstairs in the machining room, suddenly appeared in the cutting room looking extremely annoyed and accusing me of continually cutting him off during conversations. I suggested to him that perhaps he should relocate the switchboard to his office, where it rightly belonged.

He responded nastily 'You should use your brain and learn how to operate the machine.'

Annoyed at being insulted, I put on my jacket, threw the factory keys on the cutting table and walked out of the building. When I returned to the factory a few days later to collect my wages, P45 and insurance cards, Ron tried to persuade me to stay on, but I refused to listen. I had already found a new job at A. Simmons Limited, a small firm of dressmakers at Vartry Road, Stamford Hill.

Stamford Hill

Stamford Hill was the furthest north that I had ever worked. The 106 bus from Poplar would take me to just a stone's throw from Vartry road. The factory, small and purpose-built, lay back from the road. Its cutting section consisted of a single long table. The proprietor, Simmons, who was short, fat and bald, seemed much older than his forty-five years. He looked, spoke and expressed himself just like Sam the Hoffman presser, who worked at Standard Tailors.

I was so sure that they were brothers I asked him if he was related to Sam but he said no.

Simmons employed only freelance cutters on a weekly, part-time basis. The arrangement suited me.

A temporary part-time position would give me an income, plus a couple of free days a week to look for other, more rewarding work.

'I will make all the markers for you' said Simmons, as he unravelled a 45 inch wide marker.

'And you can lay, cut and bundle, and for that, I will pay you fivepence a dress. How does that sound?' Having never been a freelance cutter before, or done piece work, I had no idea if fivepence was the going rate. I just nodded and said 'Okay'.

I glanced at the marker; it was a total mess and resembled the many carelessly made markers that I had seen in other factories. If Simmons had used a pencil instead of a ballpoint pen, he could have erased his mistakes, but using a pen meant he had to resort to marking little crosses on unwanted lines.

Over the years, I came to regard these little crosses as the signature of an incompetent marker maker. As in the past, I would have to be extra careful when cutting out poorly made markers. Alternatively, I could make the markers, but Simmons would have to pay me a fee. While we stood by the table, I asked him if he would pay me more money if I were to make the markers.

He looked at me mystified. 'Is there something wrong with the marker?'

I picked up a yardstick and pointed to the little crosses.

'There is a possibility that your alterations might confuse me when I cut out the lay.'

Simmons did not seem to be offended by my directness and criticism of his work.

After admitting that he had made 'a bit of a cock up with the marker' he agreed that we could negotiate a price for future markers.

At the end of my first day, I had finished cutting and bundling a docket of just over three hundred dresses. A smiling Simmons came over to me; he had a notebook in his hand.

'I have just done a calculation. Alf, do you know you have earned six pounds today?'

I too had done the calculation and according to my figures the total was just under six pounds ten shillings. When I queried the discrepancy with him, he thought that I had made a mistake. Opening his notebook, he showed me what he had written down; it read 312 dresses x 5d = £6.

'I am afraid your figures are incorrect' I said firmly but politely. 'At least by ten shillings.'

When he checked the figures in his notebook a second time, he realised that his figures were indeed wrong.

I accepted his apology, but it seemed ridiculous that on my very first day I would have to question him about my earnings; perhaps an ominous sign but I hoped not.

The next day, I earned no more than three pounds. The disappointment showed on my face.

'You have to take the good with the bad,' said Simmons gruffly.

For the next month, I did take the good with the bad, because it was convenient for me to do so. Although I worked on average three days a week and my daily pay was never more than seven pounds or less than three, I was reasonably satisfied. Working as a freelance cutter enabled me to claim my pay at the end of each working day, a concession which I managed to persuade a reluctant Simmons to agree to and was absolutely necessary. Jack, my Scottish friend who, as a piece work cutter, had been 'ripped off' in the past by crooked factory owners, strongly advised me to always demand my wages on a daily basis.

'Never let them hold your money Alf, especially the bubble and squeaks.' (Factory slang for Greeks).

Simmons employed a small team of pressers and special machinists. There were no flat machinists at the factory. All of the flat machining was done by local women working at home.

Whenever Simmons left the factory to call on his outdoor machinists, he would leave his elderly father 'in charge'.

But Simmons senior was incapable of being in charge. He was a little hard of hearing, had poor eyesight and was really only capable of performing simple tasks. The machining staff never once sought guidance from him during Simmons' absence; they were used to working unsupervised. Sometimes the old man would help me to lay up the fabric. Short, stocky and with a well-lined face, he may have been eighty years old. He never changed his old grey flannel trousers that seemed to reach his chest line rather than his waistline. I had to be patient when he assisted me as his movements were slow and mechanical, but I always enjoyed working with him. He was a happy character who continually chuckled. He thought I was Jewish because of my constant use of Yiddish words and my daily ritual of dashing off at lunch time to the local Jewish delicatessen to buy salt beef or chopped liver sandwiches.

Noticing me eating my sandwich, he said 'You must be Jewish, Alf, only Jews eat salt beef.'

I tried to explain that I was a Shaygets (a non-Jewish young man) and that many of the customers waiting to be served inside the delicatessen were Gentiles who, like me, appreciated delicious Jewish food, but he did not believe me. If he was convinced I was Jewish, I was quite happy to accept it.

Like many men of his generation, Simmons senior had served in the First World War. Occasionally he spoke of his experiences in the trenches during the battle of the Somme. He mentioned that several of the non-commissioned officers were 'momzers' (bastards). Chuckling away, he recalled that one particular sergeant was so hated by his own men that 'they bumped the momzer off'.

'They did what?' I said, looking surprised, 'I don't believe you.'

Still chuckling, he continued 'We were supposed to be firing on the Germans, but instead somebody fired at the momser'. It was difficult for me to believe that this friendly old man had witnessed, and approved of, the shooting of a sergeant, though he might well have wanted to. He was probably just trying to humour me. A little later, I told him about my own brief experiences in the army and that some of the brutal NCOs that I had known deserved to be bumped off. I was in no doubt that with five million men in the British army during the Great War, some non-commissioned officers must have been shot in the back by men under their command. For a Tommy Atkins who might have been ill treated by an NCO, what greater opportunity to settle old scores than in a battle situation?

My two free days each week were spent wandering around the East End knocking on the doors of clothing factories looking for work. Passing through Fashion Street, I saw Myers walking along the opposite pavement. I did not expect him to recognize me after four years. He stood still for a moment and snarled at me, which I thought strange; I had always believed that Jewish people were incapable of harbouring petty grudges. Rather than ignoring him, I stupidly stuck two fingers up in the air.

During my wanderings I noticed that there were less cutting vacancies being advertised on factory signs than there had been when I last trudged the same streets in 1962. In the local press a few of the major clothing companies were no longer regularly advertising for staff and there seemed to be a marked decline in Jewish-owned clothing factories in the area, especially in Hackney.

One weary factory owner explained to me that it was now impossible for him to compete with the local Greek and Turkish companies. 'I am in shtook (Deep trouble) because of these shysters.' He complained that his Cypriot rivals not only had modern machinery and a hardworking and uncomplaining workforce, they could undercut his making price by a minimum of 30 per cent.

'Let them earn their shekels (Money /coins) while they can, so that they can build their big villas and orchards in Cyprus, but you wait and see, my boy, before the century is out, the shmatta (Old clothes) trade in London will be no more; eventually all the shmatta will be made abroad.'

He was to be proven right; by the mid 1990s clothing manufacturing in the East End had all but disappeared. I had no luck finding a job that interested me and I attended several disappointing interviews with factory employers. In most cases, the working conditions were below standard or the wages inadequate, particularly at the skirt factories. As in the past, I avoided coat and jacket companies. I had no desire to bruise my fingers ever again trying to lift heavy rolls of coat fabric onto the cloth-unwinding rail.

It would have been possible for me to find employment in a Greek or Turkish factory, but because many of these factory owners had a reputation for being devious and untrustworthy I felt reluctant to work for them. It was a common and ever increasing practice for crooked Cypriot garment manufacturers to remain in business for six months only. During this period these unscrupulous manufactures would avoid paying rent, gas, electricity and phone bills and keep for themselves much of their employees deducted income tax and national insurance contributions.

In due course the redundant employee would receive an unexpected demand from the Department of Health and Social Security for their missing contributions. Almost overnight the bankrupted employer would offer a financial incentive to one of his former employees or a relative to open a clothing factory under a new name. These hirelings were mere puppets for their former boss who would be based in the factory organising the production with impunity and as planned, milk the profits to the last penny. Six months later the phoney employer would be ordered by his master to declare himself insolvent. Within a short space of time the whole process would invariably start again. The Inland Revenue and the Department of Health and Social Security were well aware of this widespread practice, but were unable to curtail it. One can only speculate how many luxury villas with fine orchards in Cyprus were purchased with illegal profits obtained from this scam.

As the weeks went by, Simmons began to offer me less work, sometimes only a day or two.

He probably had cut a few of the dockets himself, which was understandable. Having less work did not concern me that much. I had plenty of savings from my high earning days at Pridewear, so I had no immediate financial worries, although I did feel that it really was time for me to make a greater effort to find regular employment, but where? I had walked the streets from Mile End to Aldgate East without much success. Perhaps it was time for me to leave the clothing trade while I was still young.

I had also thought about going into business.

There was a tiny coffee and sandwich bar to let at Beak Street, W1 which interested me. David Upson promptly advised me against the idea. 'For somebody who can't make a pot of tea or spread margarine on a slice of bread, you suddenly want to be a caterer. Listen to me, Alf, forget the coffee bar and stick to cutting.'

My friend need not have been concerned. I was well aware of the pitfalls of starting a business that one knows so little about; nevertheless, I was still curious to find out more about the coffee bar.

Dave, thoughtful as ever, said 'Okay, if you're determined to have a look at the coffee bar, this is what I suggest. We will travel up to the West End this Friday evening, you can go on to Beak Street, then meet me later in the French pub, but for God's sake don't commit yourself without speaking to me first.'

The next day, I returned to Simmons's factory. As usual, Simmons senior was very pleased to see me and he wanted to know what I had 'been up to'. I waited until we were laying up the fabric before explaining that I might be renting a coffee bar in the West End.

Pointing at me, he chuckled. 'You see, I knew you were Jewish. You're going into business already.'

Simmons must have been eavesdropping on our conversation because immediately after I had finished eating my sandwich at lunch time, he came over to the cutting table and said 'Is it true Alf, that you might be renting a coffee bar in the West End?'

I replied cautiously 'Yes, it's true I have been toying with the idea. In fact, I have an appointment with the owner this Friday evening.'

He came a little closer, and whispered 'If you need a partner, how about me?'

I was given no chance to reply as he was continually whispering.

'I can see, Alf, you're like me. You have become disillusioned with this trade, the long hours, the stress and aggravation, always false promises and for little financial reward.'

His prattle confused me. In the past he had never expressed any disillusionment with his business, quite the contrary. I could recall that on my very first day of working for him, he had mentioned how the clothing trade continued to fascinate him. It was unlikely that owning a small dress manufacturing business would make him rich, but I am sure his income was sufficient to give him a high standard of living. Even though I had yet to give him an answer, he seemed to have taken it for granted that we could be partners. Simmons gazed upwards for a moment and smiled, as if he was visualising himself being elsewhere. After rubbing his hands together, and still whispering, he said 'I can just see us behind the counter, happily serving customers. Can I help you sir; please take a seat madam, two sugars or one?'

His wishful thinking suddenly came to an end; he was distracted by his father who gave him tea and bagels. After the old man had shuffled away, I thought it wise to question Simmons to see if he was sincere.

He listened carefully as I spoke.

'If you are interested in operating a coffee bar, it would result in your having to close this factory. Are you really willing to take a chance and embark on a business venture that you know so little about?'

Before answering me, he focused his eyes on his staff who were about to finish their lunch break. When the women switched on their machines, he explained that he had to be realistic and look to the future. His father, owing to his great age, would not be able to continue working for much longer and the few staff that he employed would soon be of retiring age.

His explanation was not believable and only confirmed my suspicion that he was just a daydreamer. Of course, his father was old, but he contributed so little to the running of the business it was unlikely that the production would be affected at all if he were to retire and although the female staff may have been middle aged they were not due for retirement for several years.

Rather than continue our conversation, Simmons suggested that we should talk later.

During the afternoon tea break, a smiling Simmons came over to the cutting table. He spoke brazenly. 'As prospective partners, don't you think that I should accompany you to the meeting with the coffee bar owner?' It was news to me that I had a prospective partner.

I answered him dryly 'I don't recall our discussing the possibility of forming a partnership.'

'I thought we had' he replied slyly.

'No I can assure you we did not.'

He adopted a persuasive tone. 'Look Alf, lets go along to meet the vendor of the coffee bar and see what it's all about; we have nothing to lose.' He was right, we had nothing to lose. I wrote down the address of the coffee bar and gave it to him; he agreed to meet me in Beak Street at precisely 7pm the following Friday. Satisfied with the arrangement, he hastily left the factory to call on his outdoor machinists.

It meant little to me whether he kept our appointment. Already, my interest in starting a business venture was beginning to wane and I started to question my motives in detail. Did I really want to rent a coffee and sandwich bar? probably not. Did I want a business partner other than David Upson? probably not. With so many doubts in my mind, I should have phoned the coffee bar owner immediately and cancelled our appointment, but it was too late now as I had already made arrangements with Dave and to meet Simmons in the West End. Also, it would be an opportunity to visit the Soho pubs with my friend.

Our West End excursion would be an interesting change from our regular Friday evening tour of the dockland pubs.

I spent the remainder of the afternoon separating the cut lay into bundles. Once you had devised a system that minimised mishaps, it was possible to let your mind wander a little and concentrate on other matters, but what occupied my mind more by the hour was the realisation that I might have made a mistake in initially mentioning to Simmons senior that I was planning to rent the coffee bar. Had I inadvertently encouraged his son to contemplate closing down his factory to look for an alternative business? I glanced at Simmons's father, who was slowly sweeping up at the opposite side of the cutting table. He stopped for a moment to wipe his forehead; leaning on his broom he nodded at me and gave his customary chuckle. He was such a contented old man. With the speed of a snail, he would set about his various duties, sometimes answering the telephone or cutting loose cottons from the finished dresses; he would also make the tea for the staff. 'Call me Char Waller' he joked; no doubt a reference from his army days. I disliked the expression 'Char Waller'; it reminded me of the revolting Carter.

As I watched the old man sweeping up, I could not but wonder what would happen to him if his son did close the factory and he suddenly found himself not working. Would a sedentary life style have an adverse affect on his health? I had read that many healthy elderly men who were forced to retire soon developed all kinds of physical ailments. And what of Simmons staff? They could find themselves unemployed, though finding suitable employment in neighbouring clothing factories would not be that difficult. Possibly I was being too concerned with probabilities.

When I finished work at 5.30 on the Thursday evening, a jubilant Simmons gave me my earnings and confirmed our appointment to meet outside the coffee bar at Beak Street the following day at 7 p.m.. After saying cheerio to Simmons senior, I left the factory with a visceral feeling that I would never return to work at Stamford Hill.

On the Friday evening, David Upson and I travelled on the 25 bus to Oxford Street, where we went our separate ways. Dave was familiar with the pubs around Soho's Dean Street. Periodically, he would leave the East End and seek out old acquaintances who drank in the Golden Lion or the adjacent York Minster, otherwise known as the 'French pub'. I reached Beak Street just before 7 p.m. and stood outside the coffee bar. There was no sign of Simmons. I looked through the window and was startled to see Simmons talking to a man behind the counter whom I presumed to be the proprietor. This was odd. Our arrangement was to meet outside the coffee bar and then go inside together for my appointment with the proprietor.

When Simmons spotted me at the window he quickly ended the conversation and came outside. He looked totally disappointed. Waving his hand dismissively at the coffee bar, he whispered, 'It's not a good proposition. I am going home.' He tried to side-step me on the pavement, but I blocked his path. Furiously, I laid into him.

'Listen Simmons, we were to meet outside at 7 p.m. What the devil are you playing at? Do you think I am a shmuck? You had no right to meet the proprietor without my being there.'

What he said next was a calculated lie that enraged me even more.

'I thought our arrangement was to meet at 6 p.m. As you did not turn up, I went inside and spoke to the manager.' It was now blatantly obvious that Simmons had deliberately arrived early to find out if it was a worthwhile proposition to rent the coffee bar for himself. He had no interest in becoming a partner with me; he had used me in a devious manner. I could, and should, have struck his face for lying. Instead, I elbowed him aside and headed in the direction of Dean Street to meet Dave in the French pub.

A few days later, Simmons phoned me at home and said 'I have plenty of work for the next few days'.

Refraining from being rude, I merely stated that my new rate for cutting garments was now tenpence rather than the previous five pence. He immediately replaced the receiver.

Stepney & Poplar

Between Philpot Street and Cavell Street along Stepney's Commercial Road there were at least ten clothing factories. Whilst I was in the area looking for work, I enquired at these factories to see if there were any stock cutting vacancies, but there were none.

At the end of this parade of factory premises Fordie Sadie, a Jamaican rag and waste paper merchant, had his warehouse.

Middle-aged Fordie was bald and rotund. He lived in a small house by the railway bridge at the southern end of Anthony Street just yards from my old school, St. George-in-the-East, Cable Street. Fordie Sadie, an extremely kind and jolly man, was very popular with local children. As a child and usually on a Sunday afternoon my friends and I would abandon our bombsite playgrounds and gather outside Fordie's house, where we would call his name 'Fordie, Fordie, Fordie'. Within a minute the curtains of a first floor window would be drawn and a smiling Fordie and his wife would look out. What followed was the usual routine. Seated at the open window, Fordie would toss out fruit. Dozens of apples, pears, oranges and bananas would be caught by our little hands. When no more goodies rained down, a still smiling Fordie and his wife waved goodbye to us and closed the window.

David Upson was instrumental in finding my next job. His company, D. & W. Handbags, had moved from Cannon Street Road to a modern factory at nearby 54 Cavell Street. Dave had noticed that C. & H. Fashions, just a few doors away at number 50, were advertising for a part-time cutter and he urged me to enquire about the vacancy, adding that he had seen some 'pretty girls going into the factory'. I needed no further encouragement.

Cavell Street connected Commercial Road in the south to the Whitechapel Road in the north.

The street was named after the famous British nurse Edith Cavell who, in 1895, became a probationer at the nearby London Hospital. In 1907 she accepted an appointment as matron of a nurses' training school in Brussels. At the outbreak of the First World War the school became a Red Cross hospital. By 1915, Brussels was occupied by the German army. The Germans allowed the hospital to continue to treat wounded Allied and German troops. During this period, besides nursing the sick at the hospital, Edith Cavell unwisely became involved in helping British and French soldiers who were stranded behind German lines to escape to neutral Holland. The Germans soon learnt of her involvement and she was arrested along with fellow organiser Philippe Baucq. After a court martial, they were both sentenced to death and shot.

Though part residential with a small park, Cavell Street had several clothing factories, including dress, skirt and shirt manufacturers. Other trades were ladies' and gents' tailors, cloth merchants, a tailors' trimmings shop, a furrier, an embroiderer and two handbag factories.

Edith Cavell would probably have disapproved of number 20. It was the Missud café, a grubby Maltese establishment that attracted many prostitutes and pimps.

C. & H. Fashions operated from a large, ground-floor factory in the back yard of a three-storey house. The front room on the ground floor of the house was used as a second cutting room, the upper floors were a private residence.

Harry, the boss, was massive. Vastly overweight, with an enormous girth, his wife, whose name I cannot recall, was of equal proportions. Neither of them seemed to do any physical work in the factory. Throughout the day, they just stood or sat around. The business seemed to be managed by their two capable and efficient foreladies, one Jewish and one gentile. The production was mostly pleated dresses and skirts.

Producing pleated garments could be a time-consuming practice. Before the cut skirts were sent to a pleating company, the hems had to be stitched. When the skirts were returned from the pleaters they were encased in tissue paper, which was then removed. Without careful labelling there was a risk that confusion could arise, with skirts and bodices being wrongly paired.

Harry employed about twenty women machinists and pressers; the only man was Frank, a middle-aged cutter. This cutter could have earned a living as a Will Hay look-alike. He was an exact replica of the eccentric and lovable comedian, but Frank was neither eccentric nor lovable. He was a nasty, embittered man who had a reputation for being difficult and uncooperative. Fortunately, he was based in the factory and I worked in the small cutting room that overlooked Cavell Street, so any contact between us would be minimal.

I soon learnt that Harry was very popular with his workforce. With satisfactory working conditions and reasonable wages paid, none of his staff seemed to have any grievances.

Just a few days after I started working there, one of the young machinists, a tall, blonde, good-looking girl, came into the factory one morning in a distressed condition. While walking down Cavell Street, she had been 'touched up by a Pakistani'. Harry and some of the machinists tried to console her. Through her tears the girl explained that the offender, whom she had seen on previous occasions in the street, either lived or worked locally.

For the next few days, the girl's two older brothers escorted her to and from work. Before the week was out, she spotted the culprit in the street. When she pointing him out to her brothers, they ran across the street and began to kick and punch him. One of Harry's machinists, who witnessed the incident, explained to the staff that the brothers gave the Asian man 'a good hiding'. The girl's attacker was never to be seen in Cavell Street again.

Whilst working for Harry, I became an outpatient at the ear, nose and throat clinic at the nearby London Hospital, where I received treatment for a nasal condition; Part of the treatment was sub-mucous resection, which involved boring holes through the mucous membrane inside my nostrils to make a wider breathing channel. This treatment seemed to me to be somewhat primitive. I sat up close to a doctor whose legs were apart. He began to spray a liquid anaesthetic inside my nose; after a few minutes, my nostrils were suppose to become numb. Well mine were not numb when the doctor stuck a red hot, thin implement the size of a knitting needle up my right and then my left nostril. Besides the pain, the smoke and the sizzling noise, the whole experience was not helped by a small group of fidgety and seemingly uninterested medical students seated around the doctor. One of the female students winced when she saw the blood trickling down from my nose; another student appeared to grin when my head reeled back in pain. After my nostrils had been plugged with gauze to stop the bleeding, I was sent away.

Within the hour, I was back in the factory and the concerned Jewish forelady used a wet handkerchief to clean up any remaining blood that was left around my nose. While she did so, I made a disparaging remark about the medical students, whom I thought lacked sensitivity. Suddenly she became a little downcast and, standing slightly away, she said 'My son was never like those students when he studied medicine at King's College Hospital. He was a kind and caring boy, who would have made a wonderful doctor, had he lived.'

Quietly, I repeated her words 'Had he lived.' Holding back her tears, she explained that although her son had been in previous good health and only in his early twenties, he suddenly became ill and 'Just wasted away.' I could have kicked myself for mentioning the medical students. If only I had known about her son.

Working alone in the cutting room was an enjoyable experience. I could listen to the radio as I worked and if ever I needed assistance to lay wide fabric, one of the young women workers was assigned to help me. 'You lucky devil' said David Upson to me as he sipped his whisky at the nearby Mackworth Arms.

Originally, Harry had offered me two to three days work a week, which was now increased to four. The only problem that I encountered when cutting the skirts was the nipping of the waistline. They were complicated nips which had to be very accurate, as necessary guidelines for the pleater. If the skirts were nipped too deep or just one nip was left out, chaos could ensue.

Harry had no knowledge whatsoever of patterns, marker making or cutting and consequently he sometimes failed to give me sufficient information about the all-important nips. He seemed to believe that, as an experienced cutter, I should 'just get on with the job'. Usually I did, to the best of my ability, but there was one occasion when I had no option but to seek advice from Frank, the inimical cutter. As expected this advice was not forthcoming. I spoke politely.

'Frank, I am sorry to disturb you but I need a little information about some nips.'

There was a slight delay before he answered me. Peering over the top of his spectacles, he growled.

'I want to make something clear to you right now; I am not here to nurse you, do you understand?'

I did not expect his answer to be so severe and disturbing memories of my confrontations with Carter returned.

'And I am not asking you to nurse me' I retorted, emphasizing the 'You.'

He looked away, uninterested, but I refused to leave his table until he co-operated with me. Again I asked him for advice.

'All I need from you is a little information about nipping the skirts of the crystal docket.'

Harry, who was looming in the background, had become alerted by my slightly raised voice; he lumbered slowly towards the cutting table. Frank spotted him, too. Perhaps fearing being reprimanded, he quickly removed a skirt pattern from a nearby rail and spoke quite loudly so that his boss could hear:

'All the information about the crystal pleats are written on this pattern. If it's too intricate for you to work out, let me know.' Harry, now believing all was well, by-passed us at the cutting table.

I was in no mood to mollify Frank after this sudden phoney attempt to assist me. I snatched the pattern from his hands and strode past Harry, who now appeared a little concerned at my grave expression, but he made no comment. Now having the relevant information, I could finish the marker and start laying the fabric, which would take me several hours to complete.

My encounter with Frank had been inevitable and possibly a similar confront-ation would occur again, but for the moment there were much more important things on my mind, such as listening to the second test match between England and their old adversary the West Indies that was being broadcast live on the radio.

Two to three years earlier, at Pridewear, Ron Atkinson had introduced me to the joys of listening to ball-to-ball cricket commentary on the Third programme. Working alone and undisturbed that Friday, I could enjoy the cricket.

Like hundreds of thousands of cricket lovers, I listened spellbound as Tom Graveney, recalled by England after an absence of three years, gave a brilliant and memorable display of batting genius. Caught by Allan at the wicket, just four short of a century, Graveney silenced his critics, who thought that at 39 he was incapable of resisting the fiery bowling of Sobers, Hall and Griffith.

My best friend, David Upson, was fond of cricket too, but he would miss this memorable test; he was recovering in Poplar Hospital. A few days earlier he had crashed his motorbike into a pedestrian crossing.

As I sat by his bedside, Dave promised me that he would never drink the 'crazy wine again'.

Sandwiched between D. & W. Handbags and C. & H. Fashions at 52 Cavell Street was Bernard's Drapery and Bargain Store. This tiny shop was no bigger than a large pantry. Bernard, who had noticed me looking in his window during a lunch break, appeared at the doorway and tried unsuccessfully to entice me inside to buy some 'cut price shirts'.

A few days later, after collecting my wages from Harry, I returned to the shop and a delighted Bernard sold me some cheap shirts and vests. Over the next two months, I would visit the shop several times

Bernard was a classic 'spieler'. Once he started to yap and was at full throttle it was difficult to interrupt him or leave the shop. I liked him despite his arrogance and uncompromising views on politics, the National Health Service, exports, imports, unfair Japanese competition and even the price of bread.

Like Simmons senior he, too, thought I was Jewish. I suppose because I had worked for Jewish people for the previous ten years, I had inadvertently adopted certain Jewish modes of expression and idiosyncrasies.

Instead of my purchasing two pairs of socks Bernard, with his effusive sales talk, managed to persuade me to increase it to half a dozen. As I was a 'special customer' I received a discount.

Rather than allow me to leave his shop, he began to praise Frank Sinatra, who had just married the actress Mia Farrow, 29 years his junior.

'That's what it's all about, plenty of sex, keeps an old man young and puts lead in the pencil.'

Lamenting a lost opportunity to have his 'own way' with a young penniless 'Shiksa' (Yiddish for a gentile female, often used in a derogatory way).

'She came into the shop looking for a couple of items; but she had no gelt (Money) and wanted credit. I told her that I could not afford to give credit. The next minute she is leaning on the counter moving her little toches from side to side, offering me a short time in exchange for the merchandise.'

My short time in the shop was up, lunch time was over and I had just a few minutes to return to work. 'Before you go' said Bernard with a sigh, 'I was a fool, I should have accepted her offer, I could have done anything to her, anything I wanted, anything.'

Suddenly the sound of a faint cough caused me to look to my right and there, tucked away in the corner at the end of the counter and camouflaged by surrounding and hanging garments, was a teenage girl whom I recognised, it was Bernard's daughter. She stood silent with her eyes fixed downwards.

As I left the shop, I gave her a second glance; our eyes met briefly. She seemed embarrassed and quickly looked away, which was understandable. It must have been an ordeal for her to have just listened to her father relating the unsavoury incident.

When I first met Harry's factory cleaner Violet, I was cutting out a lay. It was incredible; for a moment I thought that I was seeing an apparition of my mother who had died nine months earlier. Though a little younger than mum, Violet was of the same short stature. The resemblance was striking – dark hair, dark eyes and a high forehead. I wondered if they were distantly related. Violet looked ill as she swept the cutting room floor. Suddenly she stood still for a moment, leaned on the broom and clutched at her stomach. I could see that she was in pain, but she denied it when I asked her if she was unwell. Sad memories of my own mother also clutching at her stomach returned. It was cancer of the womb that caused her death. I hoped Violet did not have the same disease.

I stayed at C. & H. Fashions for about six weeks. The moment the factory experienced a slack period, Harry laid me off. He was genuinely sorry to have to do so and he asked for my recently acquired telephone number promising that as soon as the trade 'Picked up' he would give me a call. No call was ever made.

My finding work the next day was due to the Oschman family. The Oschmans were cloth cuttings collectors but unlike 'Right Ho', who pushed a barrow, they used an open-top lorry. Mr Oschman was diminutive, nimble, very strong and, at times, irascible. His twin sons, Martin and Roger, were of the same height and build as their father. The fourth member of the quartet was Bill Hodnett, Mr Oschman's son-in-law. Bill, tall and dark-haired, was of London Irish stock. This unassuming, deeply religious, gentle man was one of the nicest people I had ever met.

My first contact with the family began five years earlier, when I was working at Sclare & Lee. Throughout the 1960s and 70s they would collect the cuttings from Pridewear and virtually every other factory that I worked at in the East End.

Bill thought I was an excellent 'sack tie-er-upper'. For somebody like me, who found it difficult to tie his shoelaces properly, the complement was quite an honour.

The day after I left C. & H. Fashions, I began roaming the Whitechapel area looking for work. In one of the side streets I came across the Oschmans heaving sacks onto their lorry. I asked Bill if during his travels he had noticed any factory signs that were advertising for stock-cutters.

Bill was aware of one factory, T. & J. Blake, a dress-manufacturing company situated in Poplar High Street, just two hundred yards from the Oschman's own warehouse. With his customary thoughtfulness, Bill suggested that, as they were about to leave for Poplar, I should climb on to the back of the lorry for a free lift. It was surprisingly comfortable sitting among the sacks and I was content to sit there all day, but within ten minutes we arrived at Poplar High Street.

My quick interview with the managing directors of T. & J. Blake went well. The Blakes, like Harry and his wife at C. & H. Fashions, were pleasant people. They instantly offered me the job. Though the wages were not good, it was a modern, clean factory with excellent working conditions and just a ten minutes walk from my home at Cordelia Street. I agreed to start work the next day.

Because of the vast difference in their ages, I thought that the Blakes were father and daughter. In fact, they were husband and wife. The only time I can recall seeing them speak together was when Mrs Blake scolded her husband over what I considered to be a trivial matter. Their marriage might have been one of convenience.

Mr Blake, with his immobile, lizard-like face, was in his late sixties; he always seemed distant and spoke little. His large bosomed wife had a dual role. Part of her day involved designing dresses, the remainder of her time was spent managing the machining section. During the tea breaks, she would relax and sit amongst the machinists and join in their gossip. She adored the female impersonator Danny La Rue, whose cabaret show she had seen many times. I began to visualise Mrs Blake coming away from the theatre with sketches and notes of Danny's 'fabulous frocks' with the intention of incorporating them into her own designs.

The dockets which I was given at the factory were usually small quantities and never more than 50 garments.

I calculated that the total amount of garments that I cut out each week could be no more than four to five hundred. The other cutter, who preferred to be called Lofty, produced a similar amount. With such a small production, I could not see how the Blakes' business was viable. The cost of renting such a large factory floor and with a workforce of approximately twenty five, the wages and overheads bill must have been considerable. I could easily have cut much more if the cutting section had been better organised but a great deal of time was wasted between finishing and starting new dockets. Patterns, fabric and cutting instructions for my next docket should have been made available so that I could continue working without stopping. It became frustrating trying to find out from the Blakes what my next docket was. Trying to locate Mr Blake was often difficult; he seemed to be in and out of the factory for much of the day and it felt uncomfortable having to interrupt Mrs Blake when she was busy working on her samples or trying to keep the production on course.

My now standard 'What would you like me to do next Mrs Blake?' usually brought on a momentary blank stare. Collecting her thoughts, she would return with me to the cutting table and spend several minutes looking through a folder of uncut dockets, before deciding what would be my next job.

I suggested to Lofty that an ideal situation would have been for us to work on our own initiative and decide what to cut next. His response was 'Why bother, I am not bothered,' but I was bothered. I felt that we should liaise with the Blakes and possibly work out a weekly cutting plan. Alternatively, either Lofty or I should be responsible for preparing the markers and sorting out the fabric for several dockets in advance. Inevitably, his reaction was lukewarm.

Lofty, who was tall and in his mid thirties, had an objectionable nature. He made it quite clear to me on the very first morning when I started work that if and when the Blakes had insufficient dockets to cut, it would be me and not him who would be laid off. I assured him that such a prospect did not concern me at all. Almost in the next breath, he bragged about the affair he was having with a married woman, to which I listened without interest. Possessing an awful nasal-sounding voice did not stop him constantly singing as he worked. I was spared the ordeal of having to have any contact with him during the breaks; he would crawl under the cutting table, stretch out his long frame and have a nap.

Lofty's quiet snoring never distracted me whenever I sat on the cutting table enjoying my sandwiches, but one lunch time sobs rather than the familiar faint snores came from under the table. When a watery eyed Lofty emerged a little later, he told me that his mistress had recently given him 'the bullet'.

A thought entered my mind: if only his own wife would give him the bullet, too.

Eventually, I did manage to speak to Mr Blake about the possibility of trying to streamline the cutting process; he reacted favourably to my initiative. 'I think that is a very good idea, Alfred. I would certainly like to have a meeting soon with Lofty, you and my wife too, so that we can discuss the matter.' The meeting never took place. Within a few weeks, Lofty's prediction came true; it was me and not him who was laid off when the Blakes found that they had fewer dockets to cut. My own prediction was not quite as accurate as Lofty's. I estimated that because the factory was not well-managed, the business could not survive for longer than a year. I was wrong; it lasted two years. In 1968, I noticed the Blakes' sign had been removed. A new ladies' clothing manufacturers, P. & H. Haring, occupied the premises. Now out of work, I began to knock on factory doors.

My friend Bill Hodnett was sympathetic when I stopped by at his warehouse in Poplar High Street. Although he was unable to recommend any vacancies, he thought that I should consider contacting Ron Atkinson at Pridewear.

'Because the factory is very busy Alf.'

My reply was emphatic. 'I won't go cap in hand Bill.'

As the Oschman's weekly visit to Pridewear was now due, he offered to mention to Ron Atkinson that I was unemployed. I declined his offer and explained that Ron was no fool; he would know instantly that I was using him as an intermediary. I gave Bill my telephone number. He assured me, that during their rounds, he and the twins would keep their 'ears and eyes open for cutting vacancies'. After my friend made a promise to phone me if they 'Spotted anything of interest' I thanked him for his concern and left the warehouse.

That same afternoon I went for an interview with the proprietor of a small dress factory near Commercial Street at Aldgate East. A young Sikh with a stammer led me down a wooden staircase to a cellar cutting room. As I descended the stairs, the familiar musty smell that I first encountered at Fagin's factory rose upwards. The smell was a clear indication that rats or mice were in residence. The Sikh lad told me to wait by the cutting table while he notified the boss of my arrival.

I surveyed the surroundings. The cellar was approximately 20 feet square and a heavily stained and torn carpet partially covered the floorboards. The cutting table was not well constructed, its rough, uneven surface, which was cracked in places, would have made it difficult, and even dangerous, for me to manoeuvre the cutting machine. In one dark, damp corner, a fungus growth had spread up the wall and only a fool would have dared to look inside the WC, which had the word 'bog' scribbled on its door. An ominous and perilous sign were the big sacks of fabric cuttings which had been left lying close to the exit. Inevitably, the cutting room had no fire escape or extinguishers.

I needed to get out of this depressing oubliette immediately. Suddenly, the sound of heavy footsteps could be heard coming slowly down the stairs. The young Sikh appeared first, followed by a diminutive, thick set man smoking a cigar. He could have been either Greek or Turkish; his English was poor and not easy to decipher, but by getting him slowly to repeat himself I managed to understand what he was trying to say.

'You cut me 2,000 one week, Singh boy help.'

My wages which he called 'Good money' was a paltry £20 per week. He used his fingers to describe my working hours.

'In morning, start you eight, finish you six; Saturday, start you eight, finish you one.'

Pointing his finger at me, his tone became authoritative, 'If not cut 2,000, you no good, I no pay good money.' Rather than bend his finger backwards or tell him to fuck off, I wished him good afternoon and bounded up the stairs.

Before leaving the area, I decided to visit David Graham, who owned a tailor's trimming shop in adjacent Commercial Street. I had known David for about ten years; A.& B. Hyams was a customer of his, as was Pridewear. There was a slight possibility that David might just know if any of his customers were advertising for stock cutters. David thought it unusual that with my experience, I should be walking the streets looking for work, like Bill Hodnett, he too suggested that I should contact Pridewear.

'I am sure that Brian Shack would not hesitate to re-employ you Alfred.'

David also gave me a list of factories which he thought might require a stock cutter. Included in the list were Marshall Walker, B.& S. Katz and Myers & Co, and the remaining factories were situated close by. I took the list, thanked David for his kind assistance and left the shop.

None of the factories on David Graham's list were of any interest and not all were advertising for stock cutters. It was the same old story; either the wages were very low or the working conditions appalling. One ghastly, smelly workshop that I visited had been a former stable.

Years later, when David Graham amalgamated his business with William Gee Limited, one of London's oldest and largest trimmings companies, he offered me a job as a travelling salesman.

'On condition, Alf, if you don't mind me saying so, please smarten yourself up and wear some decent clothes.' Being an 'inveterate and contented scruff,' as David Upson would accurately but affectionately describe me, I had to refuse the offer.

During the 15 years that Aycut spent as a dress manufacturer he operated from four different East End factories. This photo of me was taken at his factory in New Road, Stepney

The late Bertie Latchman

Etam. For two years, Etam and I worked alongside each other at the same table. Not only was he a highly skilled cutter, he was always cooperative, polite and friendly.

Christmas at Good Gear Ltd.
On my right are Salith, Satnum and Nejla. Little Connie the chain-smoking Maltese overlocker is on the extreme right

Ada busy at her four-threader

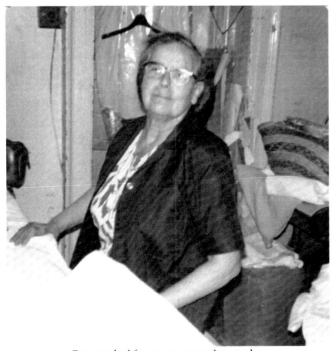

Emy worked for me as a part-time packer

Betty and my sister Sylvia were highly skilled machinists

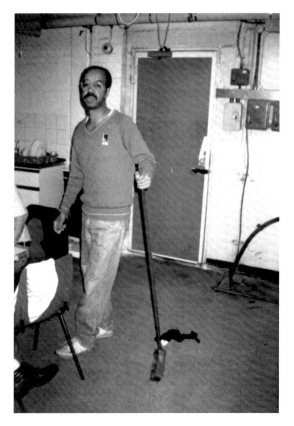

The late Rashid

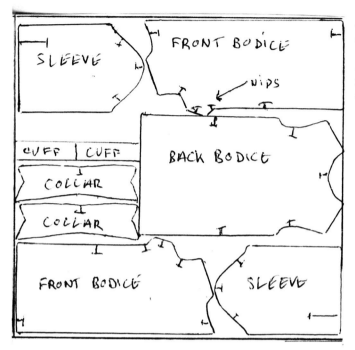

As the fronts and sleeves do not pair in this single shirt Blouse-marker, the fabric must be layed in pairs.

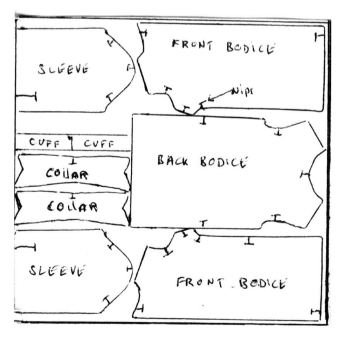

This marker for a single shirt-blouse is ideal for a plain fabric. The fabric can be layed right side up, wrong side up or layed in pairs. Under no circumstances could this marker be used for a printed one-way fabric.

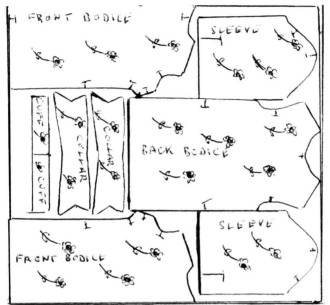

As can be seen by the way I have made the marker, it is designed for a printed one-way fabric. The fabric can also be layed in pairs.

Tools of the trade. Eastman cutting machines

Many years ago, I applied for a cutting vacancy at this now closed clothing factory in Commercial Street, Spitalfields, but the working conditions were so ghastly that I did not accept the position.

From the windows of the Myers factory (centre), I would gaze out at Christ Church Gardens. It was by the trees in this photo that the popular American writer Jack London stood in 1902. He took several photos of the poverty-stricken homeless men, women and children who were 'sleeping or trying to sleep' on the benches.

60 Cannon Street Road, Stepney. In 1983 I began working for Aycut Eral, whose company Good Gear Ltd was based in this building.

In 1961, Greycloth Limited, rayon-dress manufacturers, occupied 56 Artillery Lane, Spitalfields.
The cutting room was situated at the rear of the black-painted shop front on the right. I survived working there just one day.

One can see by these vacancy signs that there was a shortage of skilled clothing
workers in the East End during the 1950s.
Philip Gold's factory (top) was in Fieldgate Street, Stepney and Messrs I. Stadler's
factory was situated in nearby Commercial Road. Philip Gold's facilities included
congenial working conditions, a canteen and even sunbathing on the roof.

54 Cavell Street, Stepney. Throughout the mid 1960s David Upson worked as a framer for D & W Handbags, which occupied this entire building. To the right of the building was C & H Fashions where I was employed as a stock cutter during the summer of 1966.

61-75 Alie Street, Stepney.
This huge former clothing
factory has remained empty for
many years. It is unlikely that the
premises will again be used for
light manufacturing.

Falcon Works, Copperfield Road,
Bow.
I have unpleasant memories of
working at the New Image factory,
which was on the first floor.

Ever since Alf Cohen's murder in 1974, his hole-in-the-wall kiosk at Cannon Street Road, Stepney has remained bricked up.

In January 1855, Mr George Spill, the owner of the 'Old Farm-House' waterproof factory at Stepney Green, received an urgent government contract to manufacture 45,000 waterproof suits and boots for British troops fighting in the Crimean war. The suits consisted of leggings and capes with sleeves attached and a hood that could be drawn tight around the neck. There was an additional order for several thousand pairs of waterproof ground sheets.

The working environment seems to have been far superior to that in many East End clothing factories during the 1960s.

Back at Pridewear

*When one is happy, there is no time to be fatigued; being happy engrosses the
whole attention.*
E. F, Benson, (The Author's Kalender, 1915.)

The days passed quickly and although I was unable to find a decent job, I
remained optimistic.

Sometimes Bill and the Oschmans would sound their horn and wave from
their lorry as they drove past. I met them when they came out of a factory in the
Commercial Road. Bill, with his typical thoughtfulness, offered me money to
buy 'a cup of tea and a sandwich'.

My optimism paid off. I received an unexpected and most welcome phone
call from Ron Atkinson. It was unlikely that David Graham or Bill had spoken
to Ron about my situation, because I had specifically asked them not to do so.
Therefore I presumed it must have been a coincidence.

Ron explained that Brian Shack had recently opened a showroom in Mortimer
Street near Oxford Circus and would be spending much of the week there. He
(Ron) was now the production manager. The present cutting room manager,
Charles, had been given one week's notice. Ron refused to disclose over the
telephone why the manager was unsuitable. Ron went on to say that he and
Brian thought that if I were interested, I could return and take charge of the
cutting room. I was extremely interested. He suggested that I should come
to the factory the next morning and have a meeting with Brian to discuss the
position.

Prior to my meeting with Brian and Ron the following morning, I had
breakfast at Hedges' café which was situated at the western end of Sandringham
Road, just a hundred yards from Pridewear's factory at Crossway. Mr and Mrs
Hedges, who were in their early sixties, had created an efficient and cosy eatery.
The ambience was made more relaxing by four aquariums filled with colourful,
tropical fish. The kitchen, open and at the rear of the dining area, was spotlessly
clean and an old lady, said to be in her mid nineties, did the washing up.
Throughout the previous four years, I had been a regular customer at the café,
especially at lunch times. With at least six freshly cooked wholesome dishes on

the menu and a variety of 'afters', all at an exceptionally low price, the café had become a favourite with the local office and factory workers.

The Hedges were so pleased to see me return after an absence of several months, my hearty breakfast was 'on the house'.

Brian and Ron were also pleased to see me, as I was them.

The three of us sat in the office to discuss my role as the new cutting room manager. Thankfully, there was no mention of my earlier confrontation with Brian and my walking out of the factory. It was the present and not the past that Brian was concerned with.

I listened carefully as they outlined a list of my duties. The list seemed large, but not daunting.

I would be in charge of Danny and Joe, both of whom were full time experienced cutters.

Ron would require a minimum of 2,000 garments cut every week. Any excess production would be collected and made by Pridewear's regular local make and trim factories. I would be responsible for dealing with these factories. Besides making the markers, I would have to produce economical costins for Miss Impact's continuous stream of new samples. In order to achieve this, it was essential that I closely liaise with Sylvia, the designer, who would be based in the cutting room. I would also oversee all fabric that was delivered to the factory and keep an up-to-date stock check. The ordering of trimmings, which included zips, buttons, stayflex, marking paper, etc, would be undertaken by me. My contact with the packing and dispatch staff would be minimal. As a key-holder, I would unlock and lock the cutting room. Brian offered me a generous salary; he also pointed out that overtime would be unlimited and available seven days a week.

At the conclusion of our meeting, Ron asked me if I had any questions. I did have one which may have been imprudent, but I needed to know why Charles had been given the sack.

Brian allowed Ron to give me the answer in just five words 'He lacked experience and commitment.'

After I agreed to start work the next day, Brian stood up and left quickly for his showroom at the West End and Ron took me downstairs to the cutting room. My heart sank. The same switchboard that I had not learned how to operate properly, and which I blamed for my hasty departure from Pridewear several months earlier, was still on the desk. It looked intimidating as ever, but this time, I was determined to master its use.

The two stock cutters were busy cutting out lays and neither of them noticed Ron and me come in. Charles, the tall manager, was quietly making a marker. Ron introduced me to him. As we shook hands I could not but wonder if beneath his smile and friendly manner there was a little animosity towards me. Some people who found themselves in a similar situation might feel humiliated, having just been given the sack and then been asked to stay on with the company for a final week to work alongside their successor.

While I spoke briefly to Sylvia the designer, a fair-headed, dapper man in his mid thirties came into the cutting room. He went over to Ron and gave him some dockets. Sylvia gave the man a negative glance and whispered to me 'That little man is Carl, an American, our latest driver.'

It was time for Ron to return to the machining room. I stayed behind and chatted to Charles while he carried on making his marker. He assured me that he did not feel bitter about being dismissed; on the contrary, he had no regrets that he was leaving.

'They expected a lot from me but weren't prepared to pay a top rate, that's why I never showed any interest or enthusiasm for the job. If Shack had made it worth my while, my attitude would have been different.'

Pondering for a moment, I began to feel that Charles's complaint did not ring true. Brian always paid fair wages to his staff and certainly the salary that he had just offered me was quite good. Maybe the truth was that Charles felt embarrassed or even ashamed to admit that he was unsuitable for the job.

I left the factory with a little smile on my face. It felt great that I was coming back to work at Pridewear and be part of Ron Atkinson's team. I was tempted to skip and dance along Kingsland High Street. Jand's Gown shop came into view. Mrs Shack, never to be seen without a cigarette was, as usual, dressing a mannequin in the window.

My first morning back at Pridewear involved looking through the numerous dockets that required markers and placing them in priority. It took me some time to locate the required patterns; they were hung on several rails. In the old days I had kept the patterns in a strict chronological order so that it would take me just a few seconds to find any pattern I required.

Charles was co-operative and only too pleased to let me take charge now that his responsibility for managing the cutting room had been removed.

During the morning a delivery of fabric arrived. Instinctively I followed the two cutters, Joe and Danny, towards the exit to help with the unloading of the van. Charles called me back.

'Alf, you have been a cutter for too long. As the manager, you're exempt from shlepping cloth.'

After ten years of shlepping cloth, that concession was most welcome.

I returned early from Hedges' at lunch time and was startled to find Charles and Carl wrestling on the floor. Joe and Danny were sitting on the edge of the cutting table enjoying the spectacle. More of a test of strength and skill than a real fight, Charles, the much taller man, was not as strong or quick as Carl, who fought like a terrier. As it was still lunch time, I chose not to intervene. While they continued to roll on the floor, I gathered from Danny that the two men often antagonised each other by name-calling.

Charles had a large nose, and for some time he had been on the receiving end of Carl's acerbic jokes about its size. Charles would retaliate by referring to Carl as a 'Shortarse.' The wrestling ended once it was time to start work.

Late in the afternoon, while I was speaking on the telephone, Bill and the Oschman brothers arrived; smiles appeared on their faces when they saw me. Almost in unison, they called out 'He's back.'

It would take the trio just a few minutes to collect the sacks of cuttings and be on their way. I replaced the telephone just in time to speak to Bill before he left. 'Isn't it strange Bill? Just after I spoke to you in Poplar, Ron phoned me to ask if I wanted to come back.'

With a twinkle in his eye, he replied, 'It wasn't me.'

'Maybe, you sent Ron a telepathic message,' I joked.

As I spoke, he was lifting a heavy sack onto the edge of the cutting table before lifting it again onto his shoulder. Carrying it towards the door, he turned partially round and remarked 'Alf, I think we are definitely going to see you stay here for the next few years.'

My friend was right. I would remain at Pridewear until 1970.

Within a short period of being put in charge of the cutting room I managed to increase the number of garments being cut each week. This increase was achieved by maximising the full use of Danny and Joe. They would no longer have to spend time sorting out the fabric for their dockets, or do bundling; this work would now be done by me. Because of my ability to make markers quickly and willingness to stay late, I had time to spare to take on these additional tasks and in many cases I would cut their stayflex as well.

The number of garments cut over a six day week rose from 2,000 to 3,000. Ron did not have sufficient staff to cope with the increase, so, the surplus was subcontracted out to local Greek and Turkish factories.

During my first week at Pridewear Carl, the driver, decided to join me for lunch at Hedges. I was glad he did. It was an opportunity for us to have a friendly chat. He was forever in transit. Throughout the day he was in and out of the factory. If he was not on his outdoor 'machinist run' he would be making deliveries to the Miss Impact showroom; he was also Brian's chauffeur.

When we left the café, he insisted on inviting me to the nearby Castle pub for a 'quick drink'.

I immediately asked him if it was wise to drink and drive the van, but he laughed at my concern and boasted 'I can knock back a bottle of Scotch before the conk (Charles) can drink a cup of coffee.'

Carl refused to allow me to spend any money in the pub. David Upson, a habitual whisky drinker, would have been aghast at the amount of spirit that Carl consumed. In a ten minute spate, while I drank just a half pint of beer, I counted no less than twelve whiskies that he gulped down in rapid succession.

Incredibly, I could detect no sign of drunkenness as we walked back to the factory. He may have been sober, but I thought it totally irresponsible of him to drive with so much alcohol in his system.

Over the next couple of weeks, at his insistence, I met him two or three more times at the pub, usually after leaving Hedges' at lunch time. On these subsequent visits his drinking was reduced to no more than three or four whiskies. He always refused my offer to buy the drinks and I soon began to wonder if his generosity masked an ulterior motive. He also invited me to have dinner at his nearby council flat and meet his family.

'They have heard so much about you. Sherrie, my wife, and my daughters can't wait to meet you.'

Half heartedly, I accepted his invitation, which was for a Friday evening after we finished work.

At his suggestion, a quick visit to The Castle 'was essential, before we had dinner'.

At the pub I had a pint of beer, while Carl drank whisky with abandonment.

With her sunken dark eyes and hollow cheeks, Sherrie looked frail. When she spoke, her voice was soft and weak. Carl's two young daughters were polite and well behaved. Candie, the eldest and no more than twelve years old, served the dinner.

I was curious to know how Sherrie had met her husband. It seemed odd to me that Carl, an ex-fighter pilot in the American air force, who had flown on combat missions over Korea (or so he claimed), should now be employed as a van driver and living in a council flat in Stoke Newington.

Instead of Sherrie, Carl chose to explain. He spoke in a matter of fact way and the details were brief.

After his term of duty in Korea was over, he was stationed at an air base in England. Whilst on leave in London, he met Sherrie. It was a simple enough explanation, though I would have liked to have known more. Carl was an intelligent and articulate man. If he could fly aeroplanes, why did he choose to drive a van? What were his future plans? Would he eventually settle with his family in America? Earlier in the pub I did ask these questions, but he became evasive, merely pointing out that he had 'plans on board'. Because of his reticence, I quickly changed the subject.

After we had finished the superb dinner, the table was cleared and a pack of cards was produced. Candie and her young sister soon proved that they were capable rummy players. While we played cards, Carl continued to drink endless whisky. Throughout the evening, I had a recurring feeling that he had something on his mind, which he wanted to discuss with me. Each time I thought he was about to utter the words, he would change his mind. I wondered what he wanted from me. Was it a loan? If so, I would have refused; did he see me as a prospective business partner? He did say earlier in the pub that he had 'plans on board,' but business deals would not have interested me. Most likely, it was something to do with work, but what?

By 9 p.m. the huge amount of whisky that Carl had drunk had begun to take affect and he started to doze. His daughters had already retired to bed; both girls made me promise that I would return one evening soon.

I stood up from the table; it was time for me to leave. Not to disturb her husband, Sherrie led me quietly to the door. I thanked her for a most enjoyable evening and gladly accepted the invitation to have dinner with her family the following week.

It did not take me too long to ascertain what Carl had wanted to say to me at his flat. He had hoped that by being my friend and buying me drinks in the pub and inviting me back to his flat for dinner and to meet his family, I could be bribed into turning a blind eye to a little dishonesty he was engaged in, but he misjudged me.

Every Saturday morning he would arrive at the cutting room at 7.30 and clock in. A few minutes later, he would discreetly leave the building by way of the rear exit. Just before 5.30 p.m. he would return and clock out. I allowed this moonlighting to continue for a week or two, hoping that he would stop it of his own accord, but he made no attempt to do so.

Sitting in Hedge's café, I told him bluntly that this activity was wrong and that it was inevitable that he would be found out and probably sacked; he was also placing my position in jeopardy. If Ron or Brian believed that I was aware of his moonlighting and had not reported him, there was a possibility that I, too, might be dismissed.

Carl selfishly ignored my warning and continued to get paid for hours not worked on a Saturday. He gambled that as a 'friend' I would not expose him. I felt impotent; he had laid a trap and I had fallen into it. Nevertheless I was determined to see an end to his moonlighting, but felt reluctant to report him to Ron. Eventually it was the two cutters who forced me to act.

Both Danny and Joe were conscientiously employees. Working every Saturday, they too had become aware of Carl's dishonesty and strongly disapproved of it. Danny threatened to leave if Carl was not 'slung out' and Joe, the tall, usually mild-mannered West Indian, was equally annoyed; he wanted to 'tan Carl's hide'.

It was to be an unpleasant experience for me to have to expose Carl, but there was no alternative.

Ron had no idea that Carl was dishonest. Thankfully, there was a remedy. Rather than notify Brian, who would have instantly dismissed the driver, Ron restricted Carl's working hours from Monday to Friday.

When war broke out between Israel and the Arabs in June 1967, Carl immediately bought some Israeli war bonds. I suspect that the purchase was more to curry favour with Brian than from any sympathy for Israel.

Carl eventually followed the same pattern as his predecessors, none of whom ever stayed longer than a year; he began looking for another job. Suddenly Carl handed in his notice and left Pridewear. He also left his wife and children and moved away from the area.

That same year, Danny and Joe left Pridewear simultaneously. Both had lost interest in cutting garments and decided to leave the trade. Luckily, we had an abundance of dockets already cut, but not for long. New cutters had to be found quickly.

Tall, gangly and newly married, Ronnie Radlett was the first replacement cutter. Because Ronnie rarely smiled and seemed distant, he gave the impression that he was an unfriendly character, which I soon learnt was not the case. He simply preferred to be left alone to get on with the job. Dependable and assiduous, he constantly produced high quality work and never made mistakes, unlike Danny and Joe, who were sometimes a little careless with their cutting.

The second cutter we engaged was bespectacled, 5 feet 5 inches tall, Shanthilal Patel. He looked more like an academic than a factory worker and preferred us to call him Sid. He originally came from Kenya, where his parents were once wealthy Nairobi shopkeepers. Following the Kenyanization of trade and the professions that began in the mid-1960s Sid's parents, along with thousands of other Asians, were forced out of the country.

Sid had limited cutting experience. He tried to impress me by attempting to cut the dockets quickly and inevitably he made some serious errors. I warned him to slow down and concentrate on cutting accurately. Now that the cutting room was producing less cut work, I could not afford to spend time continually checking and rectifying his work. Ron soon threatened to sack Sid if the standard of his work did not improve. Thankfully, Sid heeded the warning. Realising that it was unlikely that he would be dismissed if he cut less dockets each week, he slowed down his pace and gradually his mistakes became less frequent. However, from time to time, as I bundled his work, I would still discover poorly shaped sleeves or armholes. Eventually, after my two or three pep talks and tips on cutting techniques, he became more skilful. Although the standard of his cutting would never be on a par with the quality of Ronnie Radlett's work, it was acceptable.

Sid was extremely ambitious – the work ethic was in his blood. He made no secret of his belief that one day he would have his own factory. He considered himself lucky to be working at Pridewear. It was an opportunity for him to learn about the trade and also to earn reasonable wages. Like me he worked seventy hours a week, and even then he wasn't satisfied. Often he would leave the factory late in the evenings, dash off to a local Greek or Turkish factory and work until the early hours of the morning, cutting their dockets.

Reminiscing to Ronnie and me about his life in Kenya, Sid explained that because of his appearance many Africans mistakenly thought he was a doctor. They would stop him in the street and ask for medical advice. Ronnie now called him Doctor Sid, but Sid surprisingly preferred the title I gave him, Doctor Crippen. Of course, he had no idea who the infamous doctor was.

Brian's business was flourishing; so much fabric was arriving at the factory that I was beginning to find it difficult to cope with the ever-increasing amount of work that was expected from me. We now had at least a dozen sub-contractors who had to be kept regularly supplied with work. Because several of the contractors had no cutting facilities at their workshops, they could only accept bundles of cut garments to make and trim.

The remaining larger factories which had cutting tables were in a position to cut, make and trim our dockets. As it was Brian's strict policy never to allow dress patterns to leave the premises, these contractors were unable to make their own markers. Thus denied the opportunity to obtain valuable cabbage, their markers were always made by me and given to them when they collected their fabric.

I asked Ron if he would consider engaging recently unemployed David Upson as a trainee cutter/stockman to oversee the incoming fabric deliveries and allocate fabric for the sub-contractors. Ron thought it was a good idea and quickly obtained permission from Brian to offer Dave the job.

I went to see my friend that same evening. Dave liked the thought of our working together. I explained that it would be an opportunity to learn stock cutting. Approximately a third of his working day would involve shlepping fabric; the remainder of his time would be spent assisting Ronnie Radlett and Doctor Crippen to lay fabric. He would also be taught how to cut stayflex and, later on, progress to cutting simple dockets. Though Dave was thin and regularly suffered from recurring bronchitis, he was quite strong, so the shlepping would not be that arduous and whenever there was ever a large delivery of fabric, the two cutters would help him to unload the van.

The next morning at seven, Dave and I drove up to Crossway in his turquoise

Berkely Special T-60. He had recently bought the car second-hand from somebody in Wapping for £60.00. This quaint little three-wheeler had two seats and just enough space to fit a very thin person in the bucket seat. I was sorry when he sold his powerful Tiger Triumph 600 motorbike, complete with a sidecar. Several times over the years I had enjoyed being snuggled up inside the sidecar with a young female, while Dave had to be content with her friend on the pillion.

Within weeks of starting work at Pridewear, Dave, with his warm personality, became friends with Ronnie and Doctor Crippen. Both cutters were only too pleased to have him as their assistant layer-upper and bundler. They also had my permission to try and teach Dave to cut stayflex.

My friend was quick to lean the basic skills of cutting, but he was extremely cautious when handling the cutting machine; this cautiousness resulted in his working at an exceptionally slow rate, which did not please Ron. Fortunately, as the months went by Dave gradually managed to build up his confidence and increase his speed. He soon became a valuable asset to me in the cutting room. I was able to delegate much of my dealings with the sub-contractors to him. Sylvia was also relieved of her busy schedule of designing and pattern making. She was given an outstanding assistant. Martin Shoban was the right man for the job; not only was he an incredibly fast and accurate pattern maker, he quickly formed an excellent working relationship with Sylvia. He must have been contented at Pridewear because he stayed for eighteen months. I may not have agreed with his left-wing views or appreciated his love of folk music but, as a person he was kind and likeable.

Martin took his music seriously. His folk group 'Sam's Friends' was semi-professional. The friends were Martin the guitarist and Billie his vocalist girlfriend. Sam was Billie's pet spaniel.

Dave and I went to a few of their 'gigs'. For somebody like me who was obsessed with opera and had an ignorant tendency to dismiss music other than classical music as total rubbish, these gigs, contrary to my expectations, were quite pleasant experiences.

Sometimes Martin would temporarily depart from 'Sam's Friends' and perform solo, strumming his guitar and singing at a couple of pubs in Fleet Street.

I preferred the small upstairs bar at the Tipperary, opposite the offices of the Daily Express, where Martin appeared on Friday evenings. It was convenient for David Upson and me to visit him there, for we both had girlfriends who lived and worked in nearby Holborn. We also went to see him at the King Lud at the bottom of Ludgate hill. The pub's regular singer, Mick Emery, would not have been out of place in any dockers' pub. He sang Irish ballads with gusto; refusing to use a microphone, his loud husky voice reverberated around the huge crowded bar. Mick seemed very popular with the clientele, who enthusiastically applauded him whenever he stopped for a 'beer break'. Martin, who sang next, received no appreciation or applause. Singing, in a weak voice, a tuneless song dedicated to Billie caused a group of overall-clad compositors standing next to me at the bar to let loose a volley of sarcastic remarks.

Martin soon became part of the cutting room 'clan'. After eating his sandwich at lunch time, he would join the two cutters, Dave and me for a game of football; the pitch was the space between the cutting tables, our football, screwed up newspaper. He also enjoyed visiting the dockland pubs. Although born in Stepney, he had no idea such lively riverside pubs existed. Dave and I often took him, Ronnie and Doctor Crippen on a tour of 'our patch'.

At the Prospect of Whitby they enthusiastically joined in the all-encompassing singing. Our workmates may have been with us at the Prospect in January 1969, when Dave and I joined a large crowd of students on the pub's riverside terrace. We were outside to heckle the crew of an East German cargo ship moored opposite. The ship was waiting for the high tide, which would have enabled it to enter the nearby Shadwell basin. The crowd was outraged over the death of Jan Palach.

The young Czech student had committed suicide in Prague's Wenceslas Square by pouring petrol over his clothes and then setting himself alight as a protest at the Russian invasion of Czechoslovakia and the crushing of President Dubcek's liberal government.

'Dubcek, Svoboda, Dubcek, Svoboda.' Dozens of chanting voices were carried by the icy wind across the Thames. The solemn looking crew standing on the deck could only stare back at us.

I invited Martin to come along with me to one of the weekly dances that were held at the London Hospital's medical students' hostel in Philpot Street. It was there that I introduced him to an attractive New Zealand nurse. In return, he allowed me the use of his small flat in Highgate for a night of passion with a gorgeous raven-haired physiotherapist.

'Quid pro quo,' joked David Upson.

All of us at Pridewear, with the exception of Brian Shack, were sorry when Martin handed in his notice.

It was inevitable that he would leave; there were no prospects at Pridewear to further his career. Besides the lack of opportunities Martin had little respect for Brian, whom he considered to be a ruthless businessman.

This lack of respect would, in time, develop into a loathing, especially after he had witnessed Brian's heartlessness towards his staff.

One of the packers, an Asian man from South Africa, had received news that his father had died suddenly in Cape Town. Rather than have to work on a Friday until 10pm, he had asked Brian if he and his brother-in-law who also worked in the dispatch department, could leave early to attend a memorial service that his two brothers had arranged and which was to be held at their flat that same evening. Brian flatly refused and insisted that they must stay late and finish dispatching the orders. On another occasion, in the presence of Martin, Brian had dealt harshly with an ailing David Upson.

In 1968 Dave, who was experiencing a severe attack of bronchitis, became a victim of the influenza epidemic that swept the country. Ron and I advised him to go home and rest, but he would not listen. Gradually his condition worsened until he hardly had any stamina left to continue with his work. Finally he decided it would be sensible if he went to see his doctor for 'A tonic.' Unfortunately, Brian thought otherwise. Either he did not care or he did not realise how ill Dave was. Whatever the reason, it did not prevent him from savagely remarking to my best friend, 'The only time you will ever leave this factory is when you are so ill you have to be carried out on a stretcher.'

Dave, with his obliging and passive nature, agreed to work on. Aided by his little whisky flask and by my relieving him of cutting and shlepping fabric, he somehow managed to muster just enough strength to help Ronnie and Doctor Crippen lay fabric and to assist with their bundling. After four or five days of these light duties and regular swigs of whisky, he started to recover.

I was aware that Martin had planned to teach the art of pattern cutting in the future. Within a few years he had achieved his goal. Shortly after leaving Pridewear, he enrolled at a teachers' training college, where he met and married Jenny, a pretty fellow student. After qualifying, he accepted a post as a lecturer at the London College of Fashion. He would remain on the staff for many years. During this tenure, he wrote a dozen technical books on pattern cutting and allied subjects and even found the time to be a consultant for the United Nations. His expertise in setting up training programmes, teaching pattern cutting, grading, production and sitting on examination boards would take him on assignments to many developing countries, including Syria, India, Bangladesh, Sri Lanka, China, Thailand and Vietnam.

Martin gave up lecturing at the London College of Fashion several years ago, but not to retire. Still energetic and passionate about his profession, he decided to open an independent pattern-making school in Islington. The void that Martin left at Pridewear would never be satisfactorily filled.

Our next pattern cutter was Ann Howard, the granddaughter of the famous British film star Leslie Howard. Ann was a very attractive young lady who was not unnoticed by us red-blooded males in the cutting room.

Unfortunately Ann, a recent graduate from a Fashion College, did not have sufficient experience to do the job properly. Some of Sylvia's creations were very complex and would have required somebody of Martin's calibre to master. In her haste to cope with difficult designs and the sheer volume of work that she was expected to undertake, Ann became a little careless and forgetful, which resulted in her sometimes producing an ill-fitting pattern. Appearing dismayed when she realised her errors would cause her to gaze around the cutting room as if she were appealing for assistance. Though I worked at the opposite end of her table, I had no useful knowledge of pattern making, so I was unable to offer any advice. However, Ron, who was a talented pattern maker, could have assisted her, but he was always extremely busy in the production room and could not be disturbed.

Ann was reluctant to discuss any of her problems with Sylvia. I had been aware for some time that there was little contact between the two women; their conversation was usually brief. This lack of communication was in the main due to Sylvia, who seemed to me to be deliberately distancing herself from Ann. As the weeks went by, Sylvia's aloofness and coldness became even more apparent. David Upson, a keen and accurate observer of human nature, confirmed what I had already begun to suspect; Sylvia was envious of what Ann had and she lacked – attractiveness and a sensual femininity.

Ultimately, Ann's short stay with us was not a happy one. In the right environment, working alongside people with whom she could communicate, her nascent pattern-making ability would have developed and not be inhibited as it was at Pridewear.

With Brian's business booming he needed continually to produce new designs. One of the rooms at the rear of the cutting floor was converted into an additional design workshop and three new designer/pattern-makers, two women and a man, were installed there. Victor, the jovial but sardonic van driver who worked for the pleaters, Quill & Stein, and regularly delivered our pleated skirts to the cutting-room, promptly nicknamed the two women designers Olive Oil and Tugboat Annie.

Within weeks of these new employees starting work, we began to have a problem with fabric shortage.

The shortage was soon traced back to the design workshop. The three designers had no idea how important it was to make a note of the exact amount of fabric they were using for their samples and they would invariably cut off lengths of fabric from rolls and fail to mark back on the tickets how much they had used. In some cases, they would mislay the ticket. I appealed to them to take greater care and to inform David Upson what and how much fabric they had used, but they made no effort to comply. This irresponsible and lax attitude created a great deal of extra work for Dave. Though the amounts of fabric involved were small, he often had to measure whole rolls that had a ticket missing before it could be collected by the sub-contractors.

Sometimes exasperated contractors would phone me and complain that because there was less fabric on some of the rolls than indicated on the tickets, they were unable to complete their dockets, and that I must alter their dockets accordingly. Again I returned to the design workshop and asked the designers, politely but firmly, to mark back on the ticket how much yardage they had used.

Tugboat Annie, the worst culprit, objected vehemently to what she termed my 'constant interrogation'. I realised we were fighting a losing battle with this troublesome trio. Eventually I was forced to raise the matter with Brian; He seemed very concerned when I spoke to him on the telephone, assuring me that he would 'deal with the problem', but I continued to receive complaints from the sub-contractors. Fortunately for me, the design workshop did not last long. The three designers were not very talented; they created few original samples. Either Brian dispensed with their services or they resigned of their own accord. It was a welcome relief for Dave and me when they left. Following their departure we received no more complaints from the sub-contractors.

Keeping an exact record of fabric in the cutting-room was always one of my top priorities. Dave ably assisted me in keeping the record up to date. Having this information at hand, I knew exactly, at all times, which fabric was currently being used by the cutters, what fabric was stacked under the cutting tables and what fabric had been collected by our sub-contractors. Brian had an exact copy of the list which he kept in his office at the showroom. So when Jeffrey, one of Brian's young travelling salesmen, implied that I was stealing and selling fabric, I was able to demolish his accusation easily.

It was about 8 p.m. when Jeffrey suddenly appeared in the cutting room. I was making a marker.

He stood by my side, eating ice cream from a tub.

In between scooping out the ice cream, he said, 'I have been told that if I need any cloth, I should come and see you.'

'I beg your pardon?' I replied; he edged a little closer and lowered his voice.

'Somebody told me that I should see Alfie, if I need a bit of cloth.'

At this point, I began to feel very uncomfortable and a little annoyed. I raised my voice slightly and said, 'I am afraid you have been given the wrong information and have come to the wrong factory'.

I expected my rebuttal to send him away, but he just stood there. A moment later, he leant against me and repeated what he had just said. I glanced across the cutting room at David Upson, who was quietly making bundles; he looked up. It was unlikely that he could hear our conversation, but he knew by the expression on my face that I had become angry. Unnoticed by Jeffrey, my friend signalled to me to keep calm.

I should have grabbed this unwanted visitor by the scruff of the neck and thrown him out of the factory; instead, I turned around, looked him squarely in the eye and spoke in a tone which he would understand.

'Listen Jeffrey. I want to make something absolutely crystal clear to you right now. I have never borrowed, stolen or sold one single inch of cloth from this factory or any other factory and I would suggest to you that you get out of this cutting room while you can.'

Following my riposte, he moved a little distance away from me, placed the now empty tub on my table and smirked as he spoke.

'All right, all right, Alfie, keep your shirt on. Can't you see I am only joking?'

This salesman was not joking, he was deadly serious. I turned my back on him and continued making the marker. Jeffrey said no more. He stood silently at the table for a moment, then, like a snake, he quietly slithered away towards the exit.

It was difficult for me to concentrate on making the marker. How dare Jeffrey suggest that I was dishonest and who was this person or persons who he had claimed to have spoken to? But I knew no such people existed. Surely Brian would not have sent him to test my honesty? It was not possible. Both Brian and Ron had known me for five years and trusted me implicitly. They knew that I would never steal a reel of cotton, let alone a roll of fabric. As soon as Jeffrey had left the cutting room, I phoned Ron at his home and explained what Jeffrey had just said. Ron advised me to immediately contact Brian, who was still at the showroom, and report the incident. Brian was outraged. As soon as Jeffrey stepped inside the Miss Impact showroom the following morning he was dismissed.

On reflection, I should have demanded an immediate enquiry. Jeffrey should have been forced to come clean and explained his motives, but at the time I was satisfied that he would no longer be with the company. His unfounded accusation had cost him his job.

During this period we were exceptionally busy at the factory. Dave, Doctor Crippen and I and sometimes Ronnie Radlett, too, were often cutting seven days a week.

Because of our extended working hours we were just managing to cut enough dockets for the machining staff and also for our sub-contractors, who depended on us to keep them regularly supplied with work. If ever we were overwhelmed by the sheer volume of dockets to cut, we could make use of the Bowline Cutting Service, a Dalston Lane based company. Bowline employed skilled cutters and they offered a twenty-four hour delivery service. Unfortunately, owing to my stupidity, this company ceased trading with Pridewear.

I had felt sorry for Bowline's hard-working little driver. He had a habit of constantly complaining about his job. 'The effing wages are not worth a bean, the effing hours are long and my effing back is killing me.' After the driver had finished loading the rolls of fabric onto his van, he came over to my table to collect the marker. Without thinking of the repercussions, I casually mentioned to him that Pridewear was in need of a driver and that if he was planning to leave Bowline, he might consider applying to work for us. He replied almost before I had finished speaking, 'Wot's the wages, guv?'

'I am afraid I don't know, if you're interested, you will have to speak to Mr Shack or Ron, upstairs.'

He hesitated for a moment before answering me 'I will fink about it guv; I gotta go. See yer.'

He took the marker from me and dashed out of the cutting room. A little later, he returned with his boss and two other men, whom I assumed to be cutters. They were carrying our rolls of fabric that the driver had just collected. After they had placed the fabric on the floor, the boss gave me the marker. He appeared to be upset and I asked him why he had returned the fabric. His answer was sharp and precise.

'I can't do business with a firm that is trying to poach my staff.'

Momentarily lost for words, I replied, 'I am afraid I don't understand. What exactly do you mean, trying to poach your staff?'

I glanced at the driver as I spoke; he immediately looked away, turned around and hastily left the cutting room, followed by the two cutters. The boss remained by my table. After scowling at me, and pointing his finger vindictively at my face, he repeated his complaint.

'You have no right to offer my driver a job.'

Because his accusation was in part true, I felt compelled to give an explanation.

'I am sorry if you believe that I offered your driver a job, but that was not quite true. I did not offer him a job. I have no authority to offer him a job. Your driver gave me the impression that he was about to leave your employ. I simply informed him that as Pridewear was in need of a driver, he might be interested in applying to work here, once he had left your company.'

My unexpected visitor was in no mood to be reasonable. Whatever I might have said it would have had no effect; he had me over the ropes and he knew it.

Thankfully, the ever watchful David Upson was at hand. Making an excuse that he needed my assistance, he called me over to his cutting table.

The Bowline boss must have realised that our conversation was over, because he hurried out of the cutting room.

I reported the matter to Ron; he was unconcerned. Bowline was not the only cutting service available to us. Like Dave and me, Ron thought that the driver was a 'chancer', who gambled that by informing his employer that he had just been offered a job at Pridewear, the employer might value him a little bit more and hopefully increase his wages.

We would never know if the driver's gamble was successful, but I had learnt a lesson. In future I would try and leave matters concerning recruitment to Brian and Ron.

Bowline's ceasing trading with us was an inconvenience which didn't last long. By increasing our working hours in the cutting room yet again, we were soon producing enough cut dockets to keep Ron and our sub-contractors satisfied.

Ever since leaving A. & B. Hyams in 1960, I had remained in contact with Barney and Alfie. I had much affection for my old employers. They had always been kind and fair to me during the four years that I had worked for them. Without Barney's expert knowledge, which he had instilled in me at an early age, it was unlikely that I would now have the experience to manage a busy cutting room. So when I received an urgent phone call from Barney for assistance, I had no option but to comply. His business had began to experience a slack period. Without immediate dockets, he would be forced to lay off staff.

On my recommendation, Brian agreed to give A. & B. Hyams a sample docket.

At the appointed time Barney came to see me. I knew that he had recently suffered a mild heart attack, but he looked well and still had much enthusiasm for the trade.

Curiosity attracted him to have a look at the marker I had just made. His roving eye would have instantly spotted any mistakes. It was as if the clock had been turned back a dozen years. Every marker that I had made at A. & B. Hyams had been personally checked by Barney.

'No cabbage here, no bunce whatsoever,' he joked.

'Well, I was fortunate in once having a good teacher,' I replied with tongue in cheek.

I gave him a bundle of cut dresses and explained Pridewear's standard practice that applied to all new sub-contractors. He would first make just a small quantity of dresses to see if the quality of his work was acceptable; I had every confidence that it would be. A. & B. Hyams had been successfully manufacturing dresses for nearly twenty years and were experts in their field. I would have liked to have chatted longer, but this was not the right moment to reminisce about the past; we could leave that for another time. Barney had to rush back to his factory at Bethnal Green, make the samples and then take them to the Miss Impact showroom.

As predicted, Brian liked the standard of his work. The next day, Barney returned to the cutting room and we gave him a cut docket of the same style.

For the following few months, A. & B. Hyams made, on average, 300 dresses a week for Pridewear.

When Barney's regular suppliers became busy and started to send him new dockets, he would only work for us intermittently and finally he ceased working for us altogether.

It felt good that I was in a position to assist Barney and Alfie during their difficult period. They gave me a present that was much appreciated – a little plastic container that was filled with boiled gefilta fish, my favourite Jewish food.

It was brought to my attention, probably by Bill Hodnett, that T. & J. Blake was also experiencing a difficult period. With Brian's permission, I contacted Mr and Mrs Blake and offered them work. They managed to complete a small trial docket of dresses for us, but their work was not up to a satisfactory standard.

Kay, Pridewear's diminutive Irish cleaner was a happy soul. Ronnie Radlett and I would constantly tease her and Kay probably realised that because we worked such long hours a little laughter and distraction was inevitable. As Kay swept around the cutting tables, she had to run the gauntlet of having her ribs tickled and elastic bands being flicked at her. We took advantage of her fear of mice. I would tie cotton to a small piece of dark fabric and place it in her path and as she approached the fabric the cotton would be pulled. Believing that it was one of the resident mice darting along the floor would cause her to shriek. Ronnie once picked her up and placed her inside a large oblong cardboard box and tied it up. Being released shortly afterwards, she leant on her broom and burst into uncontrollable laughter. She loved our antics and would never complain.

Kay had been afflicted at birth with undeveloped legs and as a child she had to endure several operations. After her shin bones were cut through, her legs were forcibly stretched to allow the shin bones to grow longer and then reconnect.

This painful treatment left her with a severe limp. Her husband Bill worked as a maintenance man at Queen Mary College, Mile End. Occasionally, he would do repair jobs at the factory, but there was one repair job that Bill was unable to cope with. The ongoing vibrations from the sewing machines on the floor above had weakened part of the cutting room ceiling. An area of heavy plaster, approximately ten foot by five foot, came away from the ceiling and crashed 15 feet down on to the exact spot where Doctor Crippen had been standing just seconds before. Had I not called him away to collect a new cutting docket from my table, he might have been killed or suffered a serious head injury.

Brian arranged for two workmen to quickly hammer wood sheeting across the damaged ceiling..

'A cheap botched job,' remarked David Upson.

Meanwhile, more cracks had appeared and began to spread outwards from the sheeting. Brian was informed, but he made no attempt to have the remainder of the ceiling surveyed to see if there were any possibility that more plaster could fall down. Luckily for my staff no plaster broke away.

Like my parents, Bill was born in the shadow of Stepney's Saint Dunstan's Church. As a young lad in the late 1930s, he knew the mentally disabled ginger haired boy who had fallen into the Limehouse Cut and drowned. Bill was also familiar with the cruel rhyme us local children used to sing.

'Ginger nut fell in the cut. A fish came up, and swallowed him up. And that was the end of Ginger nut.'

Kay brought a large holdall of dark orange crew neck jumpers into the cutting-room; she had bought them cheap 'From a man in the street.' The jumpers may have been stolen. Ronnie, Doctor Crippen, Dave and I each bought two jumpers. These sales allowed Kay to make a small profit. 'Ouch,' yelped Dave, when Kay prodded his ribs with her broom. He had teasingly called her a 'fence'. A few days later, Kay's new career as a part time fence ended as quickly as it had begun; she was at the receiving end of a policeman's wagging finger.

It was a Monday morning; I unlocked the cutting room at the usual time 7.30. Going inside, I was shocked to discover that every roll of fabric, totalling several hundred, had been removed from under the cutting tables. Never did this huge factory floor look so bare. My first reaction was to assume that Brian Shack, for whatever reason, had arranged for the fabric to be collected the previous evening. It seemed peculiar that I had not been informed. At least the cutters could continue with their partially cut out lays.

Cautiously, I went into the rear room that backed onto the factory's narrow alley that led to the street. The door was firmly locked but the adjacent window had been smashed. Three or four of the thin, hollow metal tubes that were fixed across the window and contained the burglar alarm wiring had been forced off, but not before the wiring had been rerouted, thus allowing the circuit to remain unbroken. The large gap in the window was big enough for the thieves to get through and pass out the fabric. I had to make a decision what to do next. Should I try to contact Brian, wait until Ron Atkinson arrived at 8am, or notify the police?

On hearing footsteps behind me, I was surprised to see Brian Shack walking towards me. This was strange, since being based in the showroom at the West End; he rarely came to the factory. If he did pay us a visit, it was usually late morning.

In a slightly excited state, I explained to Brian that we had had a break in.

He failed to answer me. After gazing nonchalantly for a few seconds at the vast empty cutting room he said, 'I suppose we had better phone the police'.

His seemingly unconcerned response was puzzling.

Within minutes the police arrived and began an investigation.

During the 10am. tea break, Kay and those of us who worked in the cutting room and all wearing our new dark orange jumpers were standing close to the friendly and garrulous detective who was attempting to obtain fingerprints from around the broken window. Perhaps ignoring protocol as he worked, the detective was quite willing to explain to us about the various criminal activities that were occurring in Dalston and Stoke Newington. Stopping work for a moment to sip his tea, the detective eyed us each up and down.

He must have noticed that we were all wearing the same dark orange jumpers. With his eyes firmly focused on Kay and wagging his finger to emphasise a point, he said, 'Do you know that, in every factory in this area, there are always people who are selling knocked off gear. We might not always nab them the first time, but you can bet your bottom dollar we catch them in the end.'

Poor Kay; the broom that she was leaning on seemed as if it were about to snap and her rosy cheeks had turned grey.

Later that day, after the police had left, a nervous Kay asked me if I would 'advise the boys not to wear their jumpers for the time being'.

Because our work load in the cutting room was ever increasing and Dave had proved himself to be a useful cutter, I thought that the time had come to find a replacement to relieve him of his shlepping duties.

Brian and Ron Atkinson were not against the idea. I was to inform them if I found a suitable applicant.

During the early summer of 1969, the cutting room door bell rang; I answered it and was confronted by a forlorn man who looked like a younger version of the actor Ronald Coleman. He spoke appealingly:

'Do you have any vacancies?'

Before I had a chance to answer him, Dave, who was standing directly behind me, whispered in my ear, 'Take him on, Alf, we need extra help,' but I hesitated in offering him a job; his slight build seemed too fragile to carry heavy rolls of fabric.

Again Dave whispered, though this time louder than before, 'Take him on, Alf, we need a storeman.'

Not to disappoint my friend, I asked the stranger if he had ever done any manual work.

He replied confidently 'Yes I have, I did road repairs and I also worked in a chocolate factory.'

It was evident that he desperately needed a job.

I opened the door wide and said 'Okay, come in and I will give you a trial.'

A grateful and jubilant Dave rubbed his hands together.

I wondered why Roger Bullock, a middle-class university graduate with a classical degree and more recently a school teacher, would want to work in a grubby basement factory, but Roger enjoyed his new role as Pridewear's stockman. With enthusiasm he would receive the rolls of fabric that arrived daily at the factory and he soon became very organised and efficient when allocating the fabric to Pridewear's cut, make and trim factories. He looked an amusing sight when he carried out his duties. There was no dark orange jumper for him to wear. His code of dress was a maroon, crushed velvet *Lungi* (Long piece of fabric which is wrapped around the waist and extends to the ankles.) Enjoying the camaraderie in the cutting room, it was inevitable that he would join Dave and me at 'Dirty Dick's' and the Prospect of Whitby after work. Roger's tastes and politics were conservative and his ever abiding love of Wagner, cricket, real ale and the occasional woman would never diminish.

On 5th November 1969, Dave, Roger and I stood around a bonfire with some off duty staff nurses from the Royal Free Hospital; later we went back to their flat at Finsbury Park.

Sitting on cushions on the floor with drinks in our hands was most enjoyable, particularly for Dave, who was also playing 'hiding the thimble' with one of our hosts. Unfortunately for Roger, no spare women were available to keep him company that evening, and he had to be content with reading to us extracts from Samuel Beckett's 'Waiting for Godot'.

In the early summer of 1970, Ronnie and Doctor Crippen left Pridewear. They had been offered well paid stock cutting jobs at Shubette Ltd, a dress company based at Old Street in north London. Dave would join them soon afterwards. The moment Dave had left Pridwear, a saddened Roger removed his crushed velvet apron. He had lost all interest in remaining a stockman and would leave at the earliest opportunity. He expressed no desire whatsoever to return to teaching.

Although, I would still socialise with my former workmates in the evening, the cutting room now seemed an alien place. I had spent so much of my time in the factory over the previous four years; Roger would remark that I had made the cutting room my 'Home,' but I was determined to leave too. My plan was to have a two week break and then apply for a part time job as a stock cutter at Burns & Lux, a Hackney blouse factory. This company offered very flexible working hours, which appealed to me.

Ron Atkinson was baffled as to why his entire cutting staff had left or were about to leave. He described the ongoing departure of the cutters as a 'disease', but the reasons were simple. The wages that Brian was now paying his cutting staff were inadequate. The three cutters had become disillusioned having to work very long hours to earn 'decent wages'.

Ron would have preferred me to stay; he agreed, as did Brian, that over the past four years, I had worked 'very hard'.

Within days a successor was found to take my place. I agreed to Ron's request to stay on for a further fortnight to show the new man the ropes.

Roger also handed in his notice. He had found a job with a well known computer firm and living in London enabled him to stay in regular contact with Dave and me.

Ron Atkinson's career at Pridewear would eventually come to an end. After fifteen years of loyal service, he lost his job when Brian Shack went bankrupt. In 1973, Brian discovered that two of his employees who were in charge of Miss Impact's dispatch department were cheating him on a large scale. Unknown to Brian, these employees owned a gown shop and for the previous two to three years had secretly sent thousands of Miss Impact's newly-made garments to their shop. So vast was their scam, it ultimately led to Miss Impact/ Pridewear's liquidation. I could not understand why Brian's accountants had not spotted the embezzlement earlier. I learnt later that the thieving employees were none other than the cousins whom Brian had so cruelly denied the right to attend the memorial service held for their father four or five years before. It was possible, that the thieves' motives, besides the obvious greed, may have been revenge.

The cousins were arrested, put on trial, found guilty and promptly jailed, but the damage that they had inflicted was devastating. Brian was unable to pay his creditors. The Miss Impact showroom and the Pridewear factory was closed down and the workers, including Ron Atkinson, were laid off without being paid any outstanding wages. Eventually Ron, like thousands of other highly skilled workers was made permanently redundant by the decline of the British clothing industry.

Shortly after Miss Impact/ Pridewear went into receivership, Brian Shack became a manager at Quorum, the Chelsea based fashion house founded by the famous designer Ossie Clarke.

Burns & Lux

The Burns & Lux factory was situated in the Long Street Industrial Estate at Hackney. The estate, built in 1958, was one of several in the Hackney area owned by the Greater London Council.

At Long Street there were 60 work units, ranging in size from 1,000 to 5,000 square feet. The work units were well serviced, with modern lifts, washrooms and toilets on every floor. There was also a resident caretaker and a team of porters who kept the estate immaculately clean.

Of the 60 work units, twelve were occupied by clothing manufacturers. Other light industrial trades on site included handbag and hat makers, furriers, wood-machinists, turners, furniture manufacturers and engineering and electronic companies. At unit 8, I spotted an old school friend, John Bullman.

John was a carpet layer. Since leaving school, he and his younger brother had worked for their father, who was the managing director of Bullman & Sons, Carpet Contractors. Often with lightning speed, the Bullman brothers would unwind a huge roll of carpet on the ground in the courtyard and cut it into shape.

Because for some time Burns & Lux had been advertising for a part-time stock cutter I expected the wages, to quote my friend David Upson, to be 'not worth a light', but earning high wages during the summer of 1970 was not my immediate priority – working fewer hours was.

Ever since I had spent an enjoyable short holiday in Guernsey earlier in the year, I began to tire of having to work 70 hours every week. I was not a married man with a family to support; I had no mortgage, debts or commitments. I longed to work part time for the foreseeable future and learn to relax more. Perhaps revive old aspirations like learning to play the piano, study the Italian language, read books and write poetry. Instead of taking up these interests now that the opportunity had arisen, I foolishly placed them aside in favour of spending much of my spare time in the pubs and pursuing numerous women.

David Upson warned me, 'If you're not careful, Alf, this over indulgence might push you into a pit of permanent dissipation.' Dave's advice was ignored. I was just not prepared to give up the succession of pretty girls I was having affairs with.

My relationship with Sue a wealthy 22-year-old divorcee was now over. She had learned 'from a mutual friend' that I was 'bedding', Rita, a lithe, sensuous, guitar playing Anglo-Portuguese girl. Perched on the pillion of Rita's motor bike, much to Dave's amusement, may not have been as comfortable as sitting in Sue's white open top sports car, and Rita's modest pied-a-terre at Richmond in Surrey was cramped compared to Sue's large house in north-west London, but Rita had an appealing, gentle nature, unlike Sue, who was strong-willed and assertive.

After Rita's eventual departure, I had meaningless brief relationships with girls from Germany, Spain and Yugoslavia. Later in the year, my rampant promiscuity was brought to a halt – I contracted non-specific urethritis, a venereal disease.

'I told you to be careful,' said David Upson, shaking his head.

After successful treatment at the London Hospital, I made the decision that my insalubrious lifestyle must immediately end. Abstaining from womanising was now essential, at least for the foreseeable future.

Victor Sims, the director of Burns & Lux, offered me a part time stock cutting job, totalling 30 hours a week, which was spread over three days. I would have to clock in and out each day.

As the sagacious David Upson predicted, the wages were meagre, just twelve shillings an hour.

Victor, a mild mannered, polite man, was in his early 40s. Each week his company manufactured two to three thousand ladies' shirts and blouses. Approximately a third of the total was exported to Scandinavia; the remainder was sold to wholesale London warehouses.

The production methods at Burns & Lux were quite advanced compared to those of other blouse factories. After a lay of shirts was cut and bundled, the bundles were given to a special machinist who operated a four-thread overlocking machine. A four-threader was a time saver that had a dual purpose, as it could overlock and flat stitch at the same time. The blouse sleeves and the bodice, known as the shell, were put together by this machine. Other factories that did not have four-threaders had to pre-overlock the shell, which then had to have the same seams stitched by a flat machine. The shirt collars were also made inside the factory; it was an absolute requirement that collars were made accurately. A shirt or a blouse with a badly made and ill-fitting collar would never sell. Years of experience had proved to Victor that few of his outdoor machinists were sufficiently skilled to make perfect collars. For fitting the collar and the cuffs onto the shell and machining the hem these home workers were paid a low rate. The workers were in no position to complain; probably they were grateful that they could earn a little money while their children were at school.

Each day Victor would arrive at the factory at noon. Along the route from his home at Bromley in Kent he would visit his outdoor machinist to deliver and collect work. The machined shirts that he brought back were then buttonholed, buttoned, pressed, packed into boxes and delivered to customers.

During Victor's absence from the factory, the managing of the business was left to three men, one of whom was Maurice, his 82 year old father.

Maurice was too old to do physical work and normally remained in the office for much of the day.

The second man, Albert Joseph, was a 51-year-old bachelor. Albert would open up the factory at 7.30 each morning. He was in charge of the cutting section and liaising with the machining staff. Finally, there was tall, bear-like Clive Purchase, a well spoken factotum in his late thirties. His duties varied, he would receive visitors to the factory, including buyers, travelling salesmen and drivers making deliveries. He sometimes supervised the packers and occasionally made markers for the cutters.

It soon became apparent to me that these three men had a profound dislike for each other and this resentment would frequently inhibit their working relationship.

I never found out what had caused the rift between Maurice and Albert. Its origin was a mystery and seemed to have occurred several years previously. The two men avoided speaking to each other and when they did speak, the conversation was always brief.

Maurice, who had established the business in the 1940s, despised Clive, whom he regarded as an interfering busybody who had far too much say in Burns & Lux's affairs. This view was shared by Albert, who resented Clive's presence in the factory. At every opportunity, Albert would attempt to demean Clive, usually before he had arrived for work. Albert would make much capital out of Clive's habitual forgetfulness and propensity for making mistakes. Sarcastically, he would accuse Clive, who was a sergeant in the Middlesex Regiment's territorial unit, of deliberately avoiding being a 'real soldier' by missing out on national service. Perhaps Albert, too, could have been accused of avoiding national service. Although twenty years of age at the outbreak of the Second World War, he had served in the Home Guard for five years, mainly at an Ack-Ack gun battery at Dagenham in Essex.

Clive, an articulate and well-read man, regarded misogynist Albert as a devious agitator and Maurice a spiteful old man. There was some justification in Albert's criticism of Clive's forgetfulness and marker making ability. Clive sometimes paid scant attention to ascertaining the exact width of the fabric, and consequently his markers were too wide. This carelessness created unnecessary work for the cutters, who had to alter the markers before proceeding to lay up the fabric. Moreover, these markers were not always paired or on grain and small facings were often missing. I wondered if Clive had a crooked eye. Albert was also prone to make mistakes with his markers, but I always allowed myself sufficient time to carefully check their work, thus preventing serious mishaps.

The long-suffering Victor was well aware of the ever increasing, mutual animosity displayed by the three men, but he seemed unable to change its course. There was also another ongoing problem that he had to contend with, a problem of his own creation. Because he could ill afford to pay his women workers high wages, several of them made no effort to work hard. Supplementing their low wage was a daily, three shilling luncheon voucher. The women were each paid by the hour and there did not seem to be a regular timetable for when they started and finished work.

All of the flat and special machinists and the pressers too – about a dozen women – were grouped together in one corner of the factory and they constantly chatted throughout their work period. Woe betide anyone who plucked up enough courage to tell them to be quiet; even Victor seemed powerless to control them.

Marion, whose job it was to make bundles and sometimes assist me to lay up the fabric, sympathised with the women. 'What you expect from the women, Alf? If Victor pays them pocket money instead of a decent salary he can't complain if they don't work conscientiously.'

Like the rest of the staff, my time was calculated to the nearest minute. If I worked 29 hours and 56 minutes, I was paid for that amount and not for thirty hours; four minutes pay would be deducted. The daily, three shilling luncheon voucher, just sufficient to buy a cheese sandwich and a cup of tea, was also denied to me, but I was under no obligation to remain at Burns & Lux; I stayed because it was convenient for me to do so.

Apart from Marion, my only contact with other female workers was with Julia, a diminutive Danish born overlocker who spoke English with a charming French accent, a legacy of living in France for many years.

'Little Julia,' with her round, slightly lined face and an abundance of dyed blonde hair, held down by a ribbon, looked like a gypsy fortune teller. She had an immensely kind nature and in due course I became very fond of her.

Because Julia was not Hackney born, looked different and spoke with a foreign accent, she was considered by some of the machinists to be an oddity and often left out of their conversation. Not that Julia cared; she had no interest in boring gossip, the comings and goings of the machinists' children or discussing the previous evening's episode of 'Coronation Street'.

Though childless, Julia was happily married to John and living at Stamford

Hill in North London.

The couple were devoted to their dog. Like Ronnie Radlett, they kept an Old English sheepdog.

Eventually, I became a matchmaker; I arranged for Ronnie's dog 'Blue' to mate with Julia's 'Lady.'

The liaison was a success and 'Lady' eventually produced ten pups. As part of the agreement, Ronnie received one pup, which he promptly sold. Julia seemed to have forgotten that, as the matchmaker, she had promised me a pup too. I refrained from reminding her of her promise.

With her vast knowledge of greyhounds, Julia gambled frequently. Besides visiting the greyhound tracks at Clapton and Hackney, she was a regular lunchtime punter at the bookmakers near Long Street. She seemed to have a continuous winning streak. Albert, another inveterate gambler, was the opposite; he always lost money betting on the horses.

Julia related to me how Albert, who used the same bookmaker, would stand close by and gaze with envy whenever she collected her winnings. Being jealous of Julia and seemingly disliking women in general was probably the reason why Albert resented her so much. He could be incredibly rude to her. There was one occasion when Albert was particularly nasty to Julia. She had made the unforgivable mistake of trying to speak to him as he listened to the racing results on his transistor radio.

Listening to these results at 4.30 p.m. was a daily ritual that was sacrosanct to Albert. In a threatening tone, he told her never to interrupt him again. As she walked away, both Marion and I heard him clearly mutter 'bloody bitch.' Julia heard him, too, but her nature was so passive, she ignored his remark.

Albert was increasingly rude to me, too, possibly because I irritated him by continually calling him over to the cutting table to rectify errors on his markers. Like Julia, I too made the grave mistake of distracting him at the wrong time.

It was almost 4.30pm, and Albert had just inserted new batteries into his transistor radio and was about to switch it on when I appeared at the opposite side of his table and politely asked him if he could just 'Spare me a moment to inspect the marker'.

He responded by giving me the negative expression which he usually reserved for the female staff.

After tut-tuting and hissing 'later, later', he placed the radio to his ear and with his other hand indicating that I should return to my table. His response annoyed me and I had to restrain myself from snatching the radio from his hand and treading on it, an act which would have been welcomed by every other employee in the factory.

After turning off the radio and tearing up his betting slips, a sure sign that yet again his horses had failed,

he left the cutting room to visit the washroom on the landing outside. I followed him to the washroom with the intention of giving him a strong warning to stop being rude to me and Julia.

When he came out of the cubicle and saw me standing there by the washbasins with my clenched fist, and looking menacing, he turned around and went back inside the cubical and locked the door. I immediately banged on the door and shouted 'Come out, you little weasel.' There was no answer, so I banged on the door again; this time he did emerge. Ignoring me, he began to wash his hands in the basin; while he did so, I tried to get his attention by prodding his bony shoulder. Turning around to face me, he discharged a volley of abusive language. At that point I grabbed him by the throat and pushed him against the wall; eye to eye, his spectacles slid to the bottom of his nose. After I had warned him that if ever he was rude to me or Julia again he would receive a thick ear. I left the washroom and went back inside the factory.

When Albert appeared a few minutes later, I was surprised that he did not report my assaulting him to Victor. Instead, he calmly came over to my cutting table and asked me what was wrong with the marker. I stood aside as he rectified an error. Following my altercation with Albert, I found that he was now distancing himself from me; no doubt, along with Maurice and Clive, I was somebody new he could dislike.

Being disliked by the 'despicable Albert' did not concern me at all; at least he was no longer rude to me. However, it was not the case with Julia. He was nasty to her at every given opportunity.

Patricia, another female employee, was also the victim of the foul-mouthed Albert. The distressed woman fled the factory in tears. These incidents always seemed to have occurred when Victor was out of the factory.

At lunch time Patricia's outraged husband Mike charged into the bookmakers where Albert was placing bets. Quick thinking customers in the shop managed to restrain Mike from physically attacking Albert. There was a further episode when Albert's seemingly uncontrollable nastiness caused him serious problems. He had upset Gloria, a plump special machinist. Gloria overheard him make a remark about her figure. When she relayed the remark to her husband, he came into the cutting-room the next day, grabbed Albert around the neck, forced his head down on the cutting table and threatened to decapitate him with the cutting machine.

Pressure was put on Albert's neck yet again, but this time it was mistaken identity. Julia, who was present at the time, witnessed the incident. It was 5.30 p.m. and Albert was just about to go home when suddenly a burly Greek looking man dashed into the factory, gripped Albert's neck with both hands, pushed him up against the wall and demanded wages which he claimed was owed to his wife. A terrified Albert, who had a slight heart condition, gasped 'not this factory, not this factory'. The intruder refused to listen; he screamed, 'Just give me her wages.' Albert pleaded, 'Leave me alone, can't you see I have weak heart?'

When the grip on his neck was tightened, Albert had the prescience to feign a heart attack. As he began to slide to the floor, the man ran out of the factory. Although shaken, Albert was not hurt. Victor, who had been away on business for much of the day, arrived shortly afterwards.

I had never regarded Victor's octogenarian father, Maurice, as a 'spiteful old man'. On the contrary, he was always pleasant and courteous to me. Two or three years earlier he had undergone surgery for colon cancer. Now a widower, he lived alone in a City of London apartment. Maurice's neighbour was the redoubtable Evening Standard music critic, Sydney Edwards.

Much to Albert's annoyance and Clive's amazement, Maurice would regularly amble out of the office and lean on my cutting table, be it while I worked or when I sat on the same table during the tea breaks. He enjoyed talking to me, as I did to him. Perhaps he sensed that I found elderly people interesting. We would chat about various subjects. Maurice thought that I was some kind of expert on the river Thames and the docks, which, of course, was not the case.

'You kept your word,' he said with an appreciative smile, when I showed him my copies of Whistler's famous 1859 etchings of the Thames waterfront.

He kept his word, too, by passing on my note to Sydney Edwards. The critic had written that Maria Callas once gave seven encores after a concert at the Royal Festival Hall and that no other artist had ever equalled that figure. My note to Sydney Edwards was brief.

'Not quite true Mr E. The great Swedish tenor Jussi Bjoerling was obliged to give no less than ten encores following his recital at the same hall in the early 1950s.'

During one of his rare, friendly moments, Albert gave me a warning. 'Never accept a lift in Maurice's car.'

Although I usually brought my own car to work, I was still curious to know why Albert had warned me.

'Because,' he replied with a smirk, 'The old sod is a menace on the road. He is too old to drive and he can't see properly, and he sways side to side as he drives along.'

I did not take Albert's warning too seriously. I thought it was just an opportunity for him to mock and criticize Maurice.

Eventually, I did take up Maurice's offer of a lift when my car was in a garage being serviced.

Within a few minutes of sitting in the sage green, Ford Consul car, I realised that Albert's warning should not have been ignored. Not only was Maurice exceeding the speed limit by driving at fifty miles an hour, he was driving on the wrong side of the road.

I may have been Maurice's favourite employee and highly regarded by Victor, who thought that I was an efficient cutter, but in the eyes of Albert and Clive, I was a 'clever dick' and too 'cocky by half'. Their biased opinion of me was irrelevant.

Maltese born Tony was a Burns and Lux packer and he was also responsible for the daily emptying of our bins of cloth cuttings into the skips in the courtyard. Occasionally, he would assist cutters to lay fabric.

Tony was about 25 years old and extremely muscular; he looked Greek rather than Maltese.

While we were laying up fabric for the first time, Tony told me that his father had recently been killed in a road accident. After I had offered my condolences, he went on to say that just prior to the accident, his wife and young son had also lost their lives when the car they were travelling in went over a cliff top in Malta and crashed onto the rocks below. I was surprised how he could speak in such a matter-of-fact way without a trace of emotion in his voice. I would have expected that a man who had just lost his wife, son and father would have expressed some sadness as he related the tragedies, yet there was none. I began to suspect that Tony might not be telling me the truth, but for what reason, I had no idea. Clive, who was working nearby may have been eavesdropping because he discreetly grinned at me.

After Tony had returned to the packing table, Clive confirmed my suspicion that Tony had indeed told me a fictitious tale.

'Never believe what Tony tells you, he is a compulsive liar; far from being deceased, his wife and baby are very much alive and living in Southampton; and his father is alive too, he lives with Tony in a flat off the Hackney Road.'

Totally perplexed, I asked him why Tony would want to lie to me, a complete stranger.

Before replying, Clive glanced at Tony, who was quietly packing the blouses into cardboard boxes.

'The reason is, as far as I can surmise, he just likes to get sympathy from new employees, but they soon get to know he is just a harmless simpleton.'

Having accepted Clive's explanation, I thought no more of the matter until a few weeks later, when I realised that not only was Tony a liar, he was also a thief. I had witnessed him on several consecutive days slyly dropping blouses into the bins of cloth cuttings. He would quickly conceal the blouses by sprinkling the cuttings over them before dragging the bins outside and down to the

184

courtyard, where he would empty the bin's contents into the skip. Either he had an accomplice who would retrieve the blouses or he himself would collect them during the evenings after work.

If I had spotted Tony pilfering within just a short time of working at the factory, then other workers must have noticed him too.

As a new employee, rightly or wrongly, I did not feel it was my responsibility to inform Victor about Tony's activities. Besides, it was not necessary for me to be an informer. I knew that because each day he was stealing about half-a-dozen blouses, it would only be a matter of time before he would be caught.

Most factory pilferers who take the odd item remain undetected but once they become greedy and attempt to steal more, greater risks are taken and carelessness sets in. Once that happens, they are soon found out, and instant dismissal usually follows.

Tony and I had lunch in Capitalli's Italian café opposite Shoreditch Church. I explained to him that I had seen him several times stealing blouses and that it was highly probable that other staff were aware of his thieving. He responded by chuckling and shrugging his shoulders. I tried to emphasise the seriousness of the matter by giving him a friendly warning. 'Be careful, mate. If Victor, Clive or Albert suspect that you are on the fiddle, they might lay a trap to catch you in the act.'

Tony showed no interest when I advised him a second time to stop stealing. Again he shrugged his shoulders before replying, 'Who cares? Let them sack me.'

I emphasised that it might not be that simple an added, 'If you are caught and the police are notified, you might be arrested, put on trial and, if you're found guilty, you could find yourself in prison.'

'They will never catch me,' he bragged. 'But maybe you're right; I should ease off for a while.'

I hoped my warning would have forced him to ease off permanently, but it was not to be. His easing off for a while lasted less than twenty four hours.

The very next day I saw Tony snatch with great speed about four or five blouses from the packing table and drop them into one of the waste cuttings bins which he was due to take down to the skip.

Apparently, Clive had witnessed the theft, too. Tony's fate was now sealed. While he was in the courtyard, he was being observed by Clive at the window. At 5.30pm, Tony said good night to me and left the factory; just a few paces behind him followed Clive. Five minutes later, Clive returned with the stolen blouses.

It seems that once inside the lift with the waste bins, Tony would remove the blouses and use string to tie the blouses into a bundle. Another piece of string would be attached to the bundle like a lead and the blouses would then be put back into the bins. After he had emptied the bin that contained the blouses into the skip, he would make sure that the end of the lead was within arm's reach. After Tony finished work in the evening, he would return to the skip and use the lead to haul out the loot.

Tony must have received a severe shock when he turned around at the skip with the blouses tucked under his arm, and was confronted by Clive, who instantly demanded the blouses.

To Tony's question, 'What is going to happen now?'

Clive replied authoritatively, 'You can leave right now, and don't ever come back.'

Victor's mild reaction to Tony's thieving and dismissal was typical and expressed in just six words.

'What a silly boy Tony is.'

My intention of remaining at Burns and Lux as a part time stock cutter was proving difficult; the company was very busy with lots of orders. Victor asked me to increase my working hours, which I did for a short period, but I was not happy. Eventually, another part time cutter was engaged and I was able to return to my usual 30 hours per week.

Pereiodically I would spend my two free days working at different garment factories in Hackney and the surrounding areas. My previous aversion to work at Greek Cypriot factories changed and I registered at the (GCCMA) Greek Cypriot Clothing Manufacturers Association.

This association had several full or part time stock cutting vacancies on its books.

Occasionally, at the various assignments that I was sent to and much to my delight, David Upson would be working at the same factory.

Since leaving Pridewear, Dave had worked at numerous clothing factories in the Dalston area. Because he lacked sufficient stock cutting experience and had very limited ability to make markers, he was unable to find suitable long term employment. He just drifted from one low paid job to another.

I suggested to my friend that he should visit the Star Employment Agency adjacent to Aldgate East station. This agency only recruited clothing workers and the vast majority of their vacancies were situated in Stepney and Bethnal Green.

The thought of being interviewed by what I described as 'young and attractive' receptionists appealed to Dave and he eventually visited the agency.

That evening I tracked him down at the Eastern Hotel, where he was in a relaxed mood. Before I had arrived, he had attempted, unsuccessfully, to strike up a conversation with the latest 'mysteries'.

These mysteries were three unescorted Scandinavian young women. They were crew members from timber ships moored at Montague Myers wharf, at the nearby Millwall docks.

Not disheartened because he had received the 'cold shoulder' from the women, his eyes were directed at two slim, mixed race girls who had just come into the lounge bar and sat near to our table.

After several minutes of trying in vain to make contact with the girls, using his old 'language of the eyes' routine, his attention was directed at me.

'You tricked me Alf, enticing me to the Star Agency. Those receptionists weren't young and attractive, far from it, they were old and matronly.'

His accurate description of the receptionists caused me to giggle. After buying my friend a large whisky, I was forgiven, but I was keen to know the outcome of his visit to the Star Agency.

'On a serious note, Dave, did they offer you anything at all at the agency? '

'Well, they sent me to a large dress factory at Stepney Green for an interview which lasted about 10 seconds. The boss opened the door and asked me if I could grade patterns. When I said no, he just slammed the door in my face.'

Dave dismissed my suggestion to return to the Star Agency to make a formal complaint.

Having doors slammed in your face by rude or arrogant factory bosses was an experience I particularly detested. Dave and I were always extremely polite when enquiring about vacancies, but we could not always expect the same cordiality from employers.

Just prior to my friend's visit to the Star Agency, I had accompanied him to Shoreditch High Street. He had seen a dress cutting vacancy being advertised. Unknown to Dave and me, this factory was on the fourth floor of a fancy goods warehouse that had no lift.

The factory's loosely fitting vacancy board was fixed to the wall just outside the street entrance.

Vacancies being advertised included flat and special machinists, pressers and experienced stock cutters. When we reached the fourth floor, Dave, who was recovering from bronchitis, felt a little breathless. Before ringing the factory doorbell we waited a few moments until he recovered.

Almost immediately, a dark haired, bespectacled man in his late thirties opened the door. I assumed he was the governor. After giving us a negative stare, he said 'Yes?'

Dave was rudely interrupted in mid flow as he enquired about the cutting vacancies.

'The position is filled,' snapped the man and the door was closed and bolted.

The blatant, unnecessary rudeness of this man incensed me. Dave and I did not deserve to be treated in this way. Against my friend's advice, I rang the bell; the same man opened the door. This time I spoke.

'If the vacancies are filled, why are you still advertising and wasting people's time? '

He did not answer me; instead, he looked down at my foot which I had pushed forward to prevent him from closing the door,

'I am waiting for an answer' I demanded.

'Would you please remove your foot,' he replied nervously.

'I will remove my bloody foot when I'm ready,' I retorted.

At this stage, he must have realised that I would not budge. Rather than threaten to call the police or shout for reinforcements from inside the factory to evict me, he gave me an answer, which was probably the first thought that came into his head. His excuse that he was too busy to remove the stock cutting advert on the board did not ring true. Having said my piece, I slowly withdrew my foot and descended the stairs. Vandalism was on my mind: I would remove the vacancy board and destroy it.

Dave tried unsuccessfully to persuade me from using my jack-knife to prise the board from the wall.

The board, old and with its paint peeling off, was easily removed.

Standing on the stairs, I stamped on the board until it broke into several parts. After picking up the pieces, I took them back up the stairs and placed them on the ground outside the factory door. It was tempting to ring the bell.

Twenty minutes later, Dave and I were enjoying a quick half at Dirty Dick's.

Reflecting on climbing the four flights of stairs to reach the factory, my friend remarked 'I am glad I wasn't offered a job at that factory, Alf, can you imagine having to schlep rolls of cloth up those stairs, it would have killed me.'

Dave was now desperate to find regular work at any cost. He would travel around the East End in his little secondhand Reliant van enquiring at various clothing factories for possible employment, but every time he explained to prospective employers that he had little marker making experience, he was turned away. Eventually, he managed to persuade the managers at Good Grooming Ltd, a blouse manufacturing company based at Stratford in East London, to engage him as a stock cutter. The wage that this company offered was, according to my friend, 'chicken feed', but Dave was in no position to complain, especially when he was told that all the markers were made by Good Grooming's foreman.

I urged my friend to grasp at every opportunity to learn marker making. If necessary, he should take short lunch breaks and spend the remainder of his break experimenting and making simple blouse markers. Dave thought it was an excellent idea. He sought and gained permission from his employers to do this.

Providing he practised in his time and not the company's time, they would not object. But Dave's initial enthusiasm soon waned. Sacrificing his lunch breaks did not last long, because he was much more interested in spending lunch time at the Green Man pub just a few doors from the Good Grooming factory.

He had become very popular with the pub's staff, especially with the young blonde landlady, who found his humour highly entertaining. I once joined him at the bar, where he and the landlady sat on stools. Delirious with laughter at Dave's funny jokes, she leant backwards and lost her balance. Dave, who had a glass of beer in one hand and a cigarette in the other, attempted to prevent her falling by using his head like a buttress behind her shoulders, but his movements were too slow. She slid to the floor, bringing my friend crashing down with her. If the carpet had not been thick, they could have injured themselves. The landlady, whose bosom had been soaked by a gin and tonic, got up and laughingly scampered to the kitchen. Dave looked as though he had just surfaced from a barrel of beer.

After working at Good Grooming for several months Dave learnt, 'by trial and error' how to make his own markers.

'I did make a few mistakes at first Alf, but I think I got it right in the end.' Dave was offered no increment from his employers.

A few days before his factory closed for the Christmas holiday, I met Dave for a lunch time drink at the Green Man pub. At a nearby table sat some local warehousemen, who were comparing their end of season bonuses. Receiving bonuses was a rarity for me, as it was for Dave.

'But not this Christmas' said my friend, who had adopted that half grinning expression which normally meant that he was amused at his own misfortune.

'My generous boss has just given me a tenner.'

He explained that while cutting out a lay, he had heard his name being called. Switching off the machine, he looked up and saw his passing employer throw a small white packet at him, which landed by the cutting machine. It was his 'Christmas box', a packet of ten cigarettes, 'and a cheap brand at that'.

'Now you know why your boss drives a Rolls Royce,' I remarked caustically.

Dave replied by shrugging his shoulders; despising miserly and heartless employers was not in his nature.

With the arrival of the New Year, Dave made a series of resolutions that he was determined to adhere to. Because he was continually receiving low wages, he could ill afford to squander any spare cash that was left over after he had paid his mother her 'Weekly dues.' His plan was to refrain from dipping into 'The kitty' and to find an evening and Saturday job. Drinking at lunch time would come to an end; visits to the pub would be restricted to a quick half at the weekends, but sadly he refused to smoke less and save money on his hefty cigarette bill.

My friend's attempts to find part-time work were not successful. I knew it would be just a matter of time before he became despondent and apathetic. As the weeks went by, his financial situation worsened and he even considered selling 'Daisy' his beloved little Reliant.

I was very fond of the battered old van. Besides being a useful means of conveyance, Dave and I had spent many happy hours squeezed inside with various women. Daisy also served as an occasional drinking den. We once parked just a stone's throw from Arbour Square Police Station. If a policeman had peered through the window and had seen Dave, me and two Australian girls drinking the 'crazy wine', we would have been arrested.

Dave did not have to sell his van; I managed to find him a part-time job. Over a six-month period, I had been spending two or three evenings a week, and occasionally during the day, cutting dress dockets for L. & M. Fashions at the Angel in Islington.

The owner of the factory, Greek Cypriot born Jimmy Onoufriou, was a former sub-contractor for Pridewear.

Jimmy made no objection when I asked him if Dave could replace me as his regular part- time cutter.

I had enjoyed working for Jimmy; he was a happy character who never complained, became annoyed or demanded that I worked at a greater speed, and he was always appreciative of my efforts to produce cabbage from every docket. At the end of the day, without a second thought, he would stuff ample pound notes into my hands.

Managing Jimmy's factory was left to Lulu, his hard working wife. Not only was Lulu a skilled flat machinist, she could operate the special sewing machines as well. Jimmy's role was limited. Like so many of these Cypriot husband and wife teams, the wife would be in charge of the production while her husband would act as the driver and help out in the factory.

In between driving the van and nipping out to the betting shop during the day, Jimmy would assist with the pressing and cotton cleaning.

Dave, with his customary cautiousness, took great care when cutting L. & M's dockets. It soon occurred to me that Jimmy, although he never mentioned it, probably would have preferred a much more experienced cutter than Dave.

Rather than see my friend having to work late into the night, I suggested to Jimmy that I should assist Dave so that he could finish early. Jimmy agreed, as did Dave, who was most grateful that I would be his assistant. He offered me a share of the wages which he received from Jimmy, but I refused. My only fee would be a quick half in Dirty Dick's after we left the L. & M. factory.

Several months after working part time for Jimmy during the evenings and at weekends, Dave and I were travelling up Great Eastern Street, Shoreditch, on our way to L. & M's, when he suddenly parked his van outside the Dori Skirt factory, which was advertising for a stock cutter.

Dave went inside the factory and ten minutes later he came out smiling and giving me the thumbs up sign. Sitting inside the van, he explained that he had been offered a job.

'Just stock cutting, no marker making, five pounds more than I am earning at Good Grooming and plenty of overtime, too.'

That same evening after we had finished work at the L. & M. factory, we drove quite fast to Dirty Dick's where we celebrated Dave's change of fortune, not with a quick half, but with several sherries and a couple of pork pies.

Dave promptly handed in his notice at Good Grooming. His bosses made no attempt to persuade him to stay.

I was pleased that Dave had, at long last, found suitable employment. Now that my friend was in a position to cease working for Jimmy, I felt that I had no alternative but to revert to being L. & M's evening cutter, but after a few weeks I was bored with having to travel up to the L. & M. factory, especially now that summer had arrived.

Jimmy understood when I explained that I could not continue working for him for much longer.

'I only wish I was in your position Alf,' he remarked glumly. My successor was none other than Ron Atkinson.

Jimmy Onoufriou eventually became duped by investigative journalists from a leading London newspaper. The journalists were preparing an article on the ever increasing cabbage trade which was causing a mini crisis in the clothing industry.

A number of directors of well known fashion houses, which included Mary Quant, Feminella, Quorum, Fiona Fashions and Samuel Sherman, had become very concerned that their sub-contracting factories were obtaining too much cabbage from the dockets which they had been given. The amounts varied between 10 and 20 per cent.

There were two major problems for these fashion houses. First, much of the cabbage was newly designed garments which had been produced by fashion houses at great cost. This cabbage was being sold cheap to shops, boutiques and market stallholders who, in turn, were selling the garments at about half of the wholesale price that the fashion houses were charging their retailers.

The second problem was that much of the cabbage was reaching outlets before the fashion houses could dispatch the same style to their regular customers.

Masquerading as newly established boutique owners who were interested in purchasing cabbage, undercover journalists visited several Turkish and

Greek clothing factories in North London. One of these factories was L. & M. Fashions.

Because of the consistently high quality of L. & M's production, Brian Shack, now the managing director of Quorum, had retained the services of Jimmy after Miss Impact/Pridewear had gone into liquidation.

Jimmy was a little suspicious at first when the bogus cabbage buyers arrived, but he soon agreed to sell them some cabbage. He offered them a classic Marie France blouse which was part of Quorum's latest collection. The reporters bought three blouses at £6 each. Jimmy took the precaution of first removing the Quorum label. Following the sale, 'The cabbage buyers' received some advice from Jimmy.

'These Quorum blouses usually retail for about £25 each. You can, if you so choose, sell them for whatever you want to, but I would advise you not to be too greedy; work on 100% profit, not 200%.'

Before the reporters left, the unsuspecting Jimmy suggested that they should call again next week, when he would have some new and different cabbage.

The reporters immediately took the three blouses to the Quorum showroom at Chelsea, where Brian Shack confirmed that the blouses were indeed part of Quorum's new range.

Brian, who as a former clothing sub-contractor, had for years relied on and benefited from a regular supply of cabbage, explained to the journalists that the cabbage trade was an 'abomination' and he went on to say that selling cabbage cheap had caused an upheaval in the industry. He further added that, in an attempt to get his sub-contractors to co-operate with Quorum, he had offered to buy back the cabbage at double the making price, but few had taken up the offer.

The expose in the press about the cabbage trade, in which both Brian Shack and Jimmy Onoufriou were featured, had no lasting affect on the working relationship between the two men. Quorum continued to supply L. & M. with regular dockets, despite knowing that cabbage was still being obtained.

I became a little restless during a two week break from Burns & Lux. The riverside benches at Shadwell Park, where I had sat for many lazy hours quietly reading or gazing at the passing river traffic, had become uncomfortable and there was no regular woman to keep me company.

Bobbie, my recently departed Yugoslavian girlfriend, could have been contacted if I had been prepared to be 'serious about our relationship,' but being serious with any girl at that stage of my life was out of the question. I was too busy enjoying my bachelorhood. Also, Bobbie was now living at Reading, which was too far from the Aldgate pump.

This pump, formerly David Upson's landmark, was now my boundary mark.

At the beginning of my second week's break from work, I had walked to Stratford in East London with the intention of obtaining a ticket for the Theatre Royal's current production. As I passed the Good Grooming factory in Stratford High Street, I paused for a moment and glanced at their vacancy board. The company was advertising for stock cutters. A thought flashed through my mind: to end my restlessness, would it be possible for me to work there for a few days before I returned to Burns & Lux?

I rang the factory bell, stepped inside and stood by the entrance, where I was interviewed by the two directors. During the short interview I gave my standard answer to the usual question.

'Yes, I could grade patterns and make markers.'

The directors must have been desperately short of experienced cutters, because they failed to ask me where I had worked before and what were my reasons for leaving. Probably my confident answers impressed them for they also suggested that I should start work immediately. No wages were mentioned. When the factory closed at 5.30 p.m. the directors would have made an assessment of my capabilities and would then offer me a salary accordingly. Whatever wage they offered it would be acceptable.

The directors were very different in appearance. One of them was tall, slim and dark haired, he moved about very quickly. The second man was older, slower and overweight; his facial features were those of a retired pugilist; it was probably he who had thrown the packet of cigarettes at David Upson.

Keith, the self assured production manager was the same Keith I had known several years before, when I had worked at Sclare & Lee and he had worked at a neighbouring factory. He was one of a group of local clothing workers who would meet at Platt's café in Stepney's Commercial Road.

Keith could remember Johnny, the buttonhole hand, but had no recollection of me, despite our having chatted at the same dining table on numerous occasions.

I followed Keith across the large factory floor to where the cutting tables were situated. The factory was a modern, one storey building. Approximately two thirds of the floor was occupied by the machining, pressing and despatch staff. At least 30 workers, mainly women, were employed there. The remaining space was the cutting section. The fluorescent lighting above the long cutting tables was insufficient and the whole area had a gloomy appearance.

Keith gave me a docket and a blouse marker which he had just completed. We checked the marker together and it was, as I expected, perfectly made. The fabric was too wide for me to lay single handed, so Joe, the nimble, middle-aged driver, was assigned to be my assistant. Another cutter worked at a nearby table;

he made no attempt to acknowledge me, but we did exchange a few brief words at lunch time.

As Joe and I were laying the fabric, a sour faced woman brushed past and went into a tiny room next to the cutting tables, sat down at a desk by the open door and sipped a cup of tea. Joe quietly explained to me that the woman was the wife of one of the directors and she was also 'supposedly, the company's designer'. During the morning, whenever I glanced in her direction, the woman glanced back. She did not seem to me to be doing any designing; her desk was bare. I could see no sketch or notebook, no pencils, coloured crayons or piles of fashion magazines that she could browse through to induce creativity. She just sat there, back hunched, her elbows resting on the desk and her cheeks cupped in her hands, or sat bolt upright like a silent owl perched on a bough. Her eyes seemed to be constantly directed at me. I soon began to find her presence increasingly disconcerting and wondered if her real role was not that of a designer, but an overseer. It could be that in the past the company had encountered problems with indolent cutters or even pilferers, but I was neither indolent nor a thief. It may also have been the reason why the other cutter was reluctant to talk to me during working hours.

Two days of being observed by a sentry, as I worked, had become unbearable. I collected my pay and left the company.

Minuet Fashions

'The work will show how to do it.' (Estonian proverb)

When I began working in the East End clothing trade in 1956, 99 per cent of the business was Jewish owned, but with the passing years new immigrants – Greeks, Turks and Asians – began to dominate the industry. Few English employees in the trade aspired to become factory owners and even less reached management level, but there were exceptions. My friend Victor Clarke worked for his father, who had a small gent's trouser workshop in Whitechapel, and the Fullerton brothers, whom I had known from schooldays, opened a dress manufacturing factory in Bethnal Green.

In 1973 I would join their ranks and become a clothing manufacturer too.

At the beginning of that year I began developing an interest in opening a small clothing workshop and employing staff. My first priority was to find cheap premises to rent.

David Upson thought that my starting a business was an excellent idea. 'Providing that your sums are right, but always remember, Alf, it's not how much money you might make, its how much money you might lose.' I agreed with Dave. I could not afford to lose any of my limited funds. I had always worked hard and tried to save a little money, so whatever business venture I undertook it would have to be financially viable.

When not working as a part time stock cutter at the Burns & Lux blouse factory in Hackney and other clothing factories nearby, I would trudge the streets around the Shoreditch area looking at empty factories and workshops; none were suitable, they were either to large or very expensive and very few of the older workshops had modern facilities which included clean toilets, running hot water and fire exits. Several of the older workshops which I inspected were infested with cockroaches, rats and mice.

Somebody must have informed 'Turkish John' of John-Kay Fashions based in Islington that I was looking for a business premises to rent. It was a Saturday evening when he phoned me.

'Alf, come to my house tomorrow afternoon, I have a factory for you.'

I had known John for many years. During the 1960s he was one of Pridewear's stalwart sub-contractors.

John had converted empty rooms in his large house into a small factory. His staff, numbering about six, were all young Chinese women.

Not only did these women, who were probably illegal immigrants, work from early morning until late in the evening six days a week, they were also being accommodated at John's house, for which they paid him rent – food may have been provided too. It was unlikely that John offered them a fair wage. After he deducted rent for their lodgings, the residue left in their pay packets must have been no more than a meagre allowance.

John and his wife's avariciousness paid off. They had accumulated so much money from their business that they were able, like scores of their enterprising and often unscrupulous countrymen living in London, to purchase a villa complete with orchard in Cyprus.

Because John did not have a cutting room at his house, he could only accept cut work dockets.

He always arrived at the Pridewear factory much earlier than the agreed time to collect his docket. Invariably, the docket was not quite ready, which resulted in him becoming extremely impatient and agitated.

The same desperate pleas were repeated time and time again.

'Alf, my girls are waiting to work.'

'Alf, my girls are sitting at empty machines.'

'They need to work, otherwise I will lose them.'

'I have to find their wages every week.'

Eventually, I gave up my attempts to persuade John to leave the cutting room and to return a little later when his docket would be ready for collection. He seemed to believe, that once he left the premises, I would offer his docket to another sub-contractor. He also refused to move away from the cutting tables, preferring instead to watch the cutters as they bundled his work and the longer he waited in the cutting room the more anxious he became.

The moment the bundling was completed, and with assistance from the cutters, the bundles were placed in sacks and quickly carried to his car. It was normal practise for John to phone me a couple of days later, imploring me to have another docket of cut work available the same day. I had become accustomed to dealing with demanding and awkward sub-contractors. Initially, when I became Pridewear's cutting room manager, I would often react irritably to contractors like Turkish John, who were constantly harassing me, but with the passing years. I had learnt how to contain my irritation.

On the Sunday afternoon, following John's phone call the previous evening, David Upson and I travelled up to his home at Islington.

Earlier, Dave had warned me not to trust John.

'Be careful Alf, he might have an ulterior motive.'

He also expressed doubts about Islington being a suitable area to open a clothing factory.

'Keep searching around Shoreditch Alf. You know the area, your contacts are there and it's easy for staff to reach, and don't forget Dirty Dick's is just around the corner.'

I should have listened to my friend. It was not a factory that Turkish John was offering me, but a grim, damp cellar below his house. The ceiling was extremely low; there were no power points and the only lighting was a single fluorescent tube. A faint rustling sound amongst a pile of rubbish on the dusty floor, suggested mice or much worse, rats.

John outlined his proposition. If I was prepared to convert the cellar into a viable workshop or cutting room, I would be exempt from paying him rent for a period of two years. When that date expired, a 'Cheap rent could be negotiated.'

Suddenly, John's hideous, plump wife came into the cellar. She immediately stuck two fingers, which resembled a rude gesture in front of Dave's nose and barked 'Two years renta free, you wanta.'

Dave whispered to me 'Let's get out of this dump, pronto.'

I explained to John that the cellar was totally unsuitable for my needs and would be costly to convert.

My lack of interest caused John and his wife to converse in Turkish.

This time it was my nose that was within inches of his ghastly wife's raised fingers.

'Three years renta free, not two, three years, you wanta.'

'I would not want it, if it were free for thirty years' I replied indignantly.

It took Dave and me just seconds to get out of the cellar, which had left an awful taste in our mouths.

'I told you so' remarked my friend, as we drove away in his van. 'I knew exactly what that scheming pair were up to, they wanted you to spend your money and refurbish that hovel, so that they could use it too, probably to cut their own garments, once that happen, they would have denied you access.'

I felt guilty over wasting Dave's time. That evening at the Prospect of Whitby the drinks were on me.

As the weeks went by I continued to scan the advertisement section of the Hackney Gazette. This newspaper was published twice a week. In a Friday issue I saw a 350 square foot workshop being advertised.

With my interest aroused, I visited the workshop the same day. It was situated on the first floor, above Carrington's Bakery in Pitfield Street, Shoreditch.

Cyril Godfrey, a middle-aged Jewish coat machinist, rented an adjacent workshop in the same premises; he also acted as the agent for the landlord. I could not believe my luck when Cyril explained that the rent for the workshop was just £5 a week, payable two weeks in advance. I immediately agreed to the terms.

Apart from the cheap rent and sharing the electricity bill with Cyril, there would be no cost whatsoever for heating the entire first floor during the winter as the workshops were above the bakery's ovens.

'You might get a bit hot during the summer, but you stay warm during the winter,' said Cyril, when I handed him my two weeks rent.

I was relieved to find that the L-shaped workshop had a fire exit. A wide, low window which led to a small roof garden could also be used as second fire escape.

The previous sole occupant, Fred Tournier, was a noted repairer of damaged tennis rackets. He had left the workshop in an unclean state; there were cobwebs on the ceiling and piles of detritus on the floor. I removed a huge, old crocodile skin that had been nailed to the wall and began to clean the windows and the dirty small washroom and toilet. More electricity points and fluorescent lights were needed. Once this work was completed, I attempted to build a small cutting table but my endeavours were disastrous and the table collapsed in a heap. Eventually, with assistance from David Upson, we managed, after several attempts, to construct a slightly wobbly table. The next stage was to purchase the necessary sewing machines. My shopping list was considerable.

4 Brothers sewing machines.
2 Wilcox & Gibbs 4-thread overlocking machines.
1 Reece buttonhole machine.
1 US blind-stitch felling machine.
1 Adamson button-sewer.
2 Danor steam-pressing units.
1 Eastman cutting machine.
I also purchased a small second hand van.

After the machinery was installed, I registered my trading name, Minuet Fashions, at Companies House.

David Upson gave me his full support rather than resorting to criticising my haphazard method of becoming an employer. I had a fully fitted workshop but no staff or work dockets and I had not a clue how to prepare wages or deal with the Inland Revenue.

My friend John Bradshaw, a freelance accountant's clerk, lived in Southend-on-Sea but worked in Shoreditch. On hearing of my predicament, he came to see me at the workshop to offer advice.

John explained in simple terms how to use the tax tables, how to work out employees' PAYE and how to forward their deducted tax and graduated pensions each month to the Inland Revenue. He also gave me examples of how to write invoices correctly, which would have to include the about to be introduced VAT.

I felt so confident that I was capable of managing the office side of my business that I refused John's free offer of acting as my temporary wages clerk. He had expressed concern about the possibility that I might make mistakes with my accounts during 'the early days'. Still concerned, John insisted that if I did experience any difficulties with my bookkeeping he would come to my workshop after work 'to sort out the problem.' Like a true friend, John refused payment for his assistance.

Beth Grant, a Hackney based dressmaker, was the second friend to offer me assistance. At her small factory in Columbia Road she manufactured dresses and children's' clothes. The standard of Beth's production was excellent and her reputation for producing quality garments soon attracted the attention of West End fashion houses. Several of these were eager to give her work, but Beth and her business partner Ruth steadfastly refused to accept additional dockets. They were determined to restrict their working day from 8 a.m. to 6 p.m. Monday to Friday. They knew that once they accepted additional production, it would mean expanding the business and employing more staff and, probably, working longer hours too.

One of Beth's West End contacts was Spectator Sports, an established company that manufactured squash and tennis wear. This company needed reliable sub-contractors who were in a position to offer regular production. Beth thought that as a beginner it would be wise for me to try and produce sportswear, which she considered to be uncomplicated garments. She also suggested that once I was in a position to start trading I should give her a call and she would make an appointment for me to go along and meet Mr Smith and Mr Lee, the directors of Spectator Sports. Beth stopped me at her factory door as I was about to leave. There was a smile on her face when she spoke.

'By the way, Alf, when you go for the appointment, please wear some nice clothes and get your hair cut.'

I smiled at my friend; she knew me of old.

I had now left Burns and Lux permanently and would concentrate on finding machinists who were prepared to work for me. Within a fortnight, I was employing six staff, two of them my sisters Sylvia and Mary. Since leaving school twenty years earlier, they had worked intermittently as flat machinists at various Stepney clothing factories. The next two women whom I engaged were Ada and Joan; both women were experienced special machinists who had recently left Burns and Lux. The reasons for their handing in their notice were

'Low pay and that horrible Albert.'

It did concern me that Victor Sims may have thought that I had enticed his staff to work for me, but my conscience was clear, because Ada and Joan had approached me about offering them a job.

Ada's aunt Emmy lived just a stone's throw from my workshop; she would come out of retirement and become my part time packer. The last woman to arrive was Betty, a flat machinist who lived at nearby Hackney Road.

As the proprietor of a small clothing workshop, I had to learn new skills quickly. Besides cutting the dockets and pressing, which I could do myself, in time I would have to be a proficient special machinist too. Learning how to use a four-thread overlocker, a felling machine, a buttonhole machine and a button sewer was absolutely necessary and could be put to good use if Ada and Joan who operated these special machines were ill or on holiday.

With a fully fitted workshop and ample staff ready to start work, Beth made the appointment for me to meet the directors of Spectator Sports at their showroom near Oxford Street.

I did wear clean smart clothes, but forgot to have a haircut.

The directors Reg Smith and his partner David Lee were extremely courteous. David spoke with a German accent; I learnt later that, in 1938, he had fled Vienna following Hitler's annexation of Austria.

Reg offered me a trial docket of squash skirts. The making price was not good, but there was an incentive. They agreed that they would be responsible for deliveries and collections.

I left their premises with a skirt sample, its patterns and a length of white crimplene. I would make a dozen samples, return them to the showroom for inspection and, if the standard of my work was acceptable, I could start on my first docket, a thousand skirts of the same style.

Leaving the West End, I drove directly to the headquarters of Gill. & Co. at Whitechurch Lane, Whitechapel.

Mr Singh, the wealthy owner of Gill. & Co was a wholesale warehouseman and blouse manufacturer. Occasionally, in the past, I had done some free lance cutting for him.

As soon as Singh became aware that I had planned to open a factory; he gave me a promised that once I was ready to commence production, he would supply me with a minimum of 500 cut blouses every week.

The good Sikh kept his promise; I drove away from his premises with my van stacked to the ceiling with bundles of cut blouses.

At 7.30 on the following Monday morning, my staff began to arrive. I switched on the power and turned on the radio. Ada and Joan sat down at their four-thread machines and began to put the shells of the blouses together. By 8.30

they had completed enough bundles for Mary and Betty to sew on the collars and cuffs. Meanwhile, I had cut out the 12 squash skirts. These skirts would be machined by Sylvia and pressed by me. At midday, the skirts had been made and were collected by the Spectator Sports van driver. An hour or so later, Reg Smith phoned me to say that the samples had been nicely made and he would be sending me, that very afternoon rolls of white crimplene for 1,000 skirts.

The first morning had passed by without any problems, my staff seemed at ease and I was at ease too. Minuet Fashions had all the ingredients that might make it a sustainable little enterprise: I was employing skilled staff, had plenty of dockets in the pipeline and, most importantly, my overheads were negligible.

These low running costs enabled me to pay my staff higher wages than they had received elsewhere.

It was unlikely that the business would make me a fortune, but my salary would be considerably better than I had earned in the past.

At 1 p.m. the machines were switched off, it was lunch time, but there would now be an additional daily commitment for me to undertake, a commitment that I would maintain for the next six years, making tea for my staff.

Within weeks of starting my business, I had managed to find four outdoor machinists. Two lived in Hackney, one in East Ham and an old friend of mine, Iris Lewis, who lived a little further away in Walthamstow.

I had known Iris for more than ten years; she had previously worked as an indoor machinist for Pridewear.

Iris was highly skilled; never once did I have to return her work for alteration. She was quite capable of machining approximately 40 garments every day. Visiting her home once or twice a week with bundles of blouses or skirts was always a pleasant experience. It was not necessary for me to explain to Iris how a new style had to be machined. Just a quick examination of the sample enabled her to know exactly what was required. After I finished my refreshment at Iris's house, which was usually a cup of strong tea, we would invariably chat for a few minutes before I drove back to Shoreditch.

The Lewis's Scotch collie Bruno was a very nervous and shy animal who would back away whenever visitors called at their home, but once he felt that the visitors would not harm him, he would lower his head and slowly venture up to them and sniff at their shoes; After quickly abandoning this lower area his nose would move upwards and he would attempt to sniff around the embarrassed visitor's private parts. Iris was embarrassed too. If Bruno ignored her command to stop sniffing she would give him a not too gentle slap across his long thin snout. This punishment usually sent him running into the kitchen. Bruno was absolutely terrified of fireworks. If exploding fireworks went off in the neighbouring streets he would go berserk. On Guy Fawkes' Night Iris's husband Ken would have to give their pet a sedative, enabling him to sleep throughout the celebration.

Bruno was not the only dog I got to know during my visits to outdoor machinists. Yasmin, a Turkish Cypriot machinist, lived with her husband Kemal and three teenage sons in East Ham. The family kept a little sand coloured mongrel named Freddy. Usually, I would call at Jasmin's home on a Saturday and leave her a large sack of cut skirts to machine. Although the standard of her machining was acceptable, there were occasions when her work had to be returned for alteration.

Yasmin would always insist that I stay for five minutes and have coffee. The five minutes was usually extended to about half an hour.

Kemal and Yasmin, who had many relatives living in a Greek area of southern Cyprus, were deeply concerned over the deteriorating situation on the island. Ever since Cyprus achieved independence from Britain in 1960, there had been sporadic fighting between the Greek majority and the Turkish minority.

Civil war almost occurred in 1963 when the Greeks shot down a Turkish fighter plane over Cyprus. It was said that the pilot survived the crash but was lynched by Greek villagers after he was pulled out of the wrecked plane. After that serious incident, it was inevitable and only a matter of time before the eruption of a full scale war.

Kemal dreaded the day when he would receive news that his relatives had been attacked and murdered by the Greeks. He hoped that the Turkish army would invade Cyprus and give the Greeks 'a good licking' in the process.

A year later, in July 1974, the Junta in Athens ordered their army officers in Cyprus to lead Greek Cypriot soldiers in a coup. The Turkish government, fearing for the safety of the Turks on the island, immediately sent 30,000 troops to invade northern Cyprus.

After a few weeks of intense fighting in which, much to Kemal's delight, the Greeks did indeed received a good licking a truce was declared, but not before the Turkish army partitioned the island.

There was good news for Kemal and Yasmin – their relatives survived the war; managing to flee from their village and being given sanctuary at the British army base at Akrotiri on the south coast.

Yasmin's three son's ages ranged from 13 to 15. When not at school or doing homework they rarely left the house; frolicking in the back yard seemed to be their favourite pastime.

The boys had totally different personalities. The youngest and the politest was somewhat shy; his year older, ever smiling brother seemed carefree and enjoyed wrestling with his brothers. The eldest boy, whom I did not like, had a spiteful nature; in my presence he nastily referred to his youngest brother as a 'poof,' and could be extremely cruel to Freddy.

The kitchen where I drank my coffee overlooked the back yard. Through the window I saw the eldest son continually punch and kick the dog. Just before I left, he rode his bicycle hard into the little dog's ribs. I sensed that Freddy wanted to retaliate and bite the boy, but he held back and attempted to bite the bicycle's front tyre instead. Freddy must have known that if he did bite the boy a severe beating would surely follow. Kemal who was also in the kitchen and saw me gazing out of the window, made no effort to restrain his son. Witnessing this cruelty reminded me of a conversation that I once had with a former Turkish soldier.

This man claimed that in Turkish schools, children were taught to hate not only Greeks, but dogs too.

While serving in the army, he was even shown how to kill a dog. His limited English prevented him from explaining why hating was on his schools curriculum. It was unlikely that he was telling me the truth; he may have personally hated Greeks who were his countries traditional enemies, but not for one moment did I believe that Turkish schoolchildren were taught to hate Greeks, or dogs for that matter. I suspect that because there were occasionally rabid stray dogs in Turkish towns and villages, it was a common and accepted practice for these dogs to be shot by anyone who owned a gun.

If Freddy knew I was in the kitchen, he would come running in from the yard and try and jump onto my lap, or he would sit quietly by my side and rest his chin on my knee. I knew from his sad eyes what he wanted me to do, but I could not take him away, as much as I would have liked to. Freddy was Yasmin's pet and he would remain so until the day he died.

I asked Yasmin why her son tormented Freddy; she gazed at me curiously for a moment before remarking 'He is only teasing Freddy. The problem with my boys; they get bored and never go out, if only there were some decent clubs in the area which they could attend.'

Yasmin's indifference to Freddy's suffering was deplorable. For her to describe punching and kicking a defenceless little animal as no more than teasing was clearly ignorance personified.

As I sipped my coffee, I began to reflect on my own teenage years spent in post-war Stepney. Never was I or any of my friends bored. We abandoned our back yards in favour of the parks and the surrounding bombsites. We even cleaned up a bombsite so it could be used as a pitch for football and cricket. Often joining us on the pitch was Butch, a large, handsome mongrel owned by the Holt family who lived in Mariner Street. The Holt's would allow local children to keep Butch constantly occupied.

For more than half a decade Butch was our regular companion. Despite his fearsome reputation as a cat and rat killer, he adored us children and we adored him. More human than canine, he would spend hours with us when we played happily on the bombsites. Never once did any child or adult ill treat Butch, who was a well fed, contented dog. When he passed away during the mid 1950s scores of local children soon realised that they had lost a true friend.

Manufacturing garments for two companies had advantages and disadvantages. If there was a slack period and I was receiving fewer shirt and blouse dockets from Gill & Co, it was possible to make up the loss of production by accepting more dockets from Spectator Sports, also if Spectator Sports were experiencing a slack period I might be able to increase my shirt and blouse production. However, a serious problem could arise if both companies simultaneously were offering me less work or no work at all, in which case I would have to find new suppliers. An additional disadvantage was that, because my company was small, with limited production, I was unable to meet the demands of my two suppliers, who were constantly urging me to produce more work for them. An ideal situation would have been to work for just one of these suppliers.

It soon became apparent that it was much more profitable manufacturing squash and tennis wear than skirts and blouses. The making price was always better, particularly for skirts, which were simple to make. Because they were short garments – no more than 18 inches from waist to hem – I could cut large quantities on my 12 ft table. Also these skirts were popular with my indoor and outdoor machinists, being small and light to handle, my staff never found machining the skirts strenuous, unlike heavy jackets and coats, which could place a great strain on a machinist's arms. However, I was reluctant to stop accepting shirt and blouse dockets from Singh; he had kept his word and offered me cut work from the time I had opened my factory earlier in the year.

Each week, I would manufacturer at least four different styles of squash and tennis wear, usually in white crimplene. One particular skirt that we regularly made consisted of eight identical panels with two of the side panels covered in thin white towelling. If a squash player began to perspire, she could wipe her brow with her wrist and then dry her wrist on the towelling side panel. The eight panels including the towelling were joined together on the four-threader overlocking machine.

To recruit more outdoor machinists, I placed an advertisement in a south London newspaper. The response was better than expected. Nine machinists in the Lewisham and Catford area replied; but finding out how many of them were sufficiently experienced would be a time-consuming and costly practice, and there was a strong possibility that some of these applicants might cause irreparable damage to my garments. I decided to take precautions to minimise any loss. From the cabbage of the eight panel skirt, I had cut approximately one hundred extra skirts.

It would be from my cabbage that I would test the outdoor machinist's skills. Each woman would be given a sample, a bundle of six cut skirts, a reel of cotton, zips and petersham (thick ribbed ribbon) for the waistband. Even if the skirts were ruined by the machinists, the loss would not affect my delivery docket.

Over the telephone I made arrangements with the machinists to call at their south London homes the following morning. Rather than return to Pitfield Street after completing this trip, I would remain in the Lewisham area until the afternoon, by which time all nine machinists should have completed their bundles; I would then return to their homes to inspect the standard of their work.

The first machinist I visited was Mary Hardy, a 40 year old who lived in a ground floor flat on the sprawling Pepys council estate on the banks of the Thames at Deptford.

The Pepys estate, built in the 1960s, was ugly and soulless; hundreds of maisonettes and flats were cramped together cheek by jowl. There did not seem to be any shops on the estate. Where was the bakery, the greengrocer, a laundrette, a grocery-store, an off-licence? I saw few gardens and even less window boxes.

Mary Hardy had previously worked as a machinist in several East End clothing factories. Her continual nodding as I explained how the skirts had to be machined was a strong indication that she was a very capable machinist. After I made arrangements to call back at her home later that day, I left to visit my next machinist, a Mrs Henry who lived just a ten minute drive away at Lee which was a part of Lewisham.

Lee was the complete opposite in appearance to Deptford's post war riverside, which seemed to me to be a vast ever expanding council estate. With the expansion came endless social problems. Deptford had acquired a reputation for noisiness, delinquency and drug taking and muggings were a regular occurrence. Gangs of youths could be seen lingering menacingly on street corners. I dreaded the thought of the plight of the elderly who were forced to live in the ubiquitous tower blocks on the estates; it was unlikely that they often ventured outside their homes after dark, fearing correctly that their vulnerability made them easy prey for violent street robbers.

Without question, Lee was safer for its elderly residents. Few council dwellings had been built in the borough, hence the ongoing problems that plagued Deptford were fewer.

I liked what I saw in Lee. The area was attractive and quiet, perhaps a little hilly but very green and leafy. Large well-constructed Victorian detached houses and villas with tidy lawns and pretty gardens lined both sides of tranquil roads and streets. I imagined that a hundred years previously many of these gracious houses were occupied by wealthy merchants, government officials, doctors and dentists. No doubt many of these households kept servants.

It was unlikely that during this period Lee's professional residents would have spent much time in Deptford, which was overcrowded, dirty and rife with infectious diseases. They would have had little in common with Deptford's lower classes, poor uneducated people who spent their entire working lives struggling to earn a few shillings in the local docks, factories, foundries and mills; but in 1973 both Lee and Deptford's long standing inhabitants had new neighbours – immigrants from the West Indies and Africa.

Mrs Henry, a smiling friendly Jamaican, offered me coffee when I arrived at her home. Like Mary Hardy she too was an experienced machinist, having worked for many years as a sample machinist in the West End. I left the bundle with her and felt confidant that her work would be of a high standard.

The third machinist, a Mrs Lawrence, also lived at Lee. She too was from Jamaica. Mrs Lawrence explained that she had no factory experience whatsoever and that she had always worked machining at home. I was unsure whether to leave the bundle with her. Only home machinists with factory experience interested me. Noticing my hesitation, she assured me that her work was of a top quality and added that she was quite willing to machine the skirts free of charge, just so that I could inspect her work.

Despite my doubts, I decided to leave her the bundle. If she ruined the six skirts, I was prepared to accept it. Visibly pleased, she insisted that I should stay for a few minutes and have a quick cup of tea. I thanked her and sat down on a sofa. A few moments later she emerged from the tiny kitchen with a pot of tea; as she poured me a cup, I suddenly heard the wailing of a child in an adjacent room. She looked towards the door which was slightly ajar and said

'It's my little boy,' suddenly a tall elderly woman came into the sitting room and went into the baby's bedroom. As she passed the sofa she gazed at me for a second before saying 'good morning', her Jamaican accent very pronounced. As soon as she went into the bedroom the child stopped wailing.

'That's my mother' said Mrs Lawrence 'She looks after my little boy when I am working, or have to go out shopping'

'Does your husband work' I enquired.

She placed her teacup on the low table in front of us and appeared saddened.

'Unfortunately my husband has just died.'

'Just died, how, what happened?'

'It happened just a few weeks ago, we were sitting here on the sofa watching television, when he suddenly died, He had a heart attack, and he was only thirty.'

Aware of her grief, I spoke softly 'How terrible for you and your family.' She did not answer me.

After I drank the tea and stood up to leave. Mrs Lawrence asked me to return later that afternoon to collect the finished bundle. As I walked towards the door the baby began to scream.

The remaining five machinists on my list all lived in the Lewisham area. There was no answer from two of them when I knocked on their doors. The next two machinists were Nigerian sisters who lived in the same house. Both admitted that they had little machining experience and had never worked in clothing factories. Also their sewing machines were domestic rather than industrial, which I thought would be totally unsuitable for machining the skirts. I refused to leave them any bundles which promptly annoyed them. One of them became abusive, accusing me of being a fraud and a time waster. I reminded the women that I had advertised for experienced machinists, which clearly they were not.

The final machinist, whose name I have forgotten, lived a little south near Catford. She was from St. Lucia.

A small box room at the rear of her house had been converted into a workroom, and the new Brothers industrial sewing machine installed there was a strong indication that this woman was an experienced machinist.

She carefully examined the sample before saying 'If you call back in a couple of hours the bundle will be finished.' I knew somehow that her work would be satisfactory.

When she opened the door for me to leave, two small children were about to come in. I stepped aside; they both looked at me curiously as they passed by.

'They are my children,' she said proudly.

When she spoke next, her tone was soft. 'I did have another boy, but I lost him.'

'Lost him?' I replied. 'I don't understand.'

'Yes, he was run over.'

'Run over did you say, what do you mean run over?'

'A car ran over him as he was crossing the road and he was killed.'

Relating the sad news must have been very painful for her.

Quietly I said 'I am so sorry to hear that.'

As I spoke, she glanced lovingly at her children who were removing their school blazers.

When I stepped outside, and before closing the door, the machinist asked me to return at 4pm to inspect the standard of her machining. She assured me, that I would find no fault with her work.

With a couple of hours to spare before returning to the four machinists' homes, I decided to wander around Lewisham High Street, find a café and have a sandwich.

I parked my van in one of the side roads, not to far from the famous clock tower in the centre of the high street. The clock tower, 50 foot high and built in 1897 to commemorate Queen Victoria's diamond jubilee, must have been well constructed. On the morning of Friday 18th July 1944 a German V1 (Doodlebug) landed just yards away. The missile struck the roof of an air raid shelter and destroyed several shops and two crowded buses. Tragically 59 people were killed and more than 300 injured, but the clock tower remained intact.

After leaving the café I bought fruit and a newspaper in the market and slowly walked back to my van. Sitting inside I failed miserably to complete a crossword puzzle.

It was now 4 p.m., time for me to start calling at my machinist's homes. If their work was satisfactory I would return the following day and give them each large quantities of skirts to machine. Predictably, the Catford machinist's work was acceptable.

There was no answer when I knocked on Mrs Lawrence's door. I peered through her letter box, but nobody could be seen. The faint sound of her baby whimpering in the background concerned me. A thought entered my head; surely no mother would deliberately leave a young baby alone in a house.

Perhaps the grandmother was in the bathroom or in the rear garden, or she may have been having a nap.

Again I knocked on the door, this time much louder; still there was no response, nor could I hear the baby when I pressed my ear to the letter box.

It was pointless standing at her doorstep. I would just have to return later.

Both Mary Hardy and Mrs Henry's work was excellent. Their sewing machines had been set at 12 stitches to the inch, which was the exact amount of stitches I demanded from every machinist.

Some greedy outdoor machinists would adjust their machines to eight or even less stitches to the inch. This adjustment would allow them to work at a much faster rate and earn more money, but the garments would not be securely made, the seams could easily come loose and fall apart.

Within the hour I was back at Mrs Lawrence's house. This time there was somebody at home.

The grandmother answered the door. She appeared distressed and confused when she invited me inside.

The bedroom door opposite was open; although the room was in semi darkness, I saw a movement in a cot which was pushed against the wall; suddenly the baby boy pulled himself up and stood with wobbly legs gripping the rail of the cot. When he saw me he began to cry very loud. Even I, who knew so little of babies, was aware that there was something dreadfully wrong with the boy. I asked the grandmother if her daughter was at home; she shook her head sideways before blurting 'She's gone out, she's gone out, she's gone.'

'Is the baby ill?' I asked.

In her excited state, it was difficult for me to understand her Jamaican accent which had become even more pronounced.

'Would you please speak slowly' I said firmly.

Her voice was shaky when she spoke, 'Please phone doctor, please phone doctor.'

She moved towards the sideboard which contained a phone and a notebook. While she hastily turned its pages, I went into the bedroom to have a look at the baby who had tears streaming from his eyes. When he saw me he outstretched his arms as if he wanted me to pick him up, but he fell backwards and landed on his bottom; raising himself up, he hung on to the cot rail with one hand and with his other hand he tried to hold on to my jacket sleeve. As I stood there peering down at him, I noticed a large mass on the calf of one of his legs. When I leant over the side of the cot to have a closer look, to my horror, the mass was an enormous scab that stretched from the back of his knee to his ankle. The scab seemed to be moving on a thick layer of pus and blood. Meanwhile, the grandmother had found her doctor's surgery number and was pleading with me to use the phone. With a sheet from the cot, I wrapped it around the baby, picked him up and passed him over to the grandmother to hold. I quickly dialled the number. A woman answered; she may have been the doctor's receptionist. I was in a slight excited state when I spoke.

'I am at the home of the Lawrence's family. There is a baby here whom I think has a gangrene leg, he needs urgent hospital treatment.'

The woman's voice was calm and precise. She asked me if I had a car; I replied that my van was parked outside.

When she spoke again there was an urgency in her tone.

'Right, now listen carefully, who else is with you?'

'Only the grandmother.'

'Okay, now this is what I want you to do, bring the grandmother and the baby here at once, our surgery is just two hundred yards away, we are in the same road, the grandmother knows our exact location.'

'We are leaving immediately.' I replied.

'Try to keep calm sir and please come straight away.'

I grabbed the small sack that contained my unfinished bundle and sample, and followed the grandmother outside. Thankfully, the distressed baby had stopped crying.

Within a minute we had arrived at the doctor's surgery. I waited in the van until the grandmother went inside before driving away.

What I had just experienced left me totally confused. Questions were spinning around in my mind.

How on earth could any mother neglect her child and leave it in that terrible condition?

How could she leave the child with the incapable, inadequate grandmother?

Where was the child's mother right now?

Because of these questions it became difficult concentrating on driving. Not wanting to cause an accident, I parked the van in a side street and sat still for a few moments.

Of course it was impossible to erase the shocking episode from my mind. A little later I switched on the van's engine and drove away. Driving with great care, I arrived safely back at Pitfield Street.

When I related the incident to my staff the following morning; they were appalled.

Joan thought that the baby's leg may have to be amputated.

I would never contact Mrs Lawrence again.

My trip to Deptford and Lewisham was reasonably successful. Out of ten enquiries, I had recruited three very experienced machinists. Mary Hardy and Mrs Henry would work for me for several years.

The first six months of my being in business had gone well. I had encountered no serious problems and my indoor and outdoor staff seemed happy with their wages and conditions.

In September Mr Singh the director of Gill & Co stopped giving me cut blouses; he had found another sub-contractor who was in a position to offer him much more production than I could.

Singh's decision was advantageous to me as I could now accept additional dockets from Spectator Sports. The two directors of this company had guaranteed me work for 52 weeks of the year. Although guarantees in the clothing trade are usually worthless, I was prepared to take a chance and sub-contract for Spectator Sports and no other company, but as a precaution I would make a note of established clothing companies who were advertising for sub-contractors.

By late 1973 Britain was facing a major crisis; the Yom Kippur war in October caused petrol shortages and the work to rule by the countries 270,000 coal miners led to power cuts. In an attempt to conserve energy, Edward Heath's government imposed a nationwide three day working week that began on December 13th.

London was divided into separate zones. Some were permitted to use electricity on Monday, Tuesday and Wednesday, Others were allocated the unpopular Thursday, Friday and Saturday. Most of Stepney and Poplar's three day working week would be at the beginning of the week. Shoreditch, where

I was based, could only use power during the latter part of the week. I had contingency plans in hand that would allow my business to function on a daily basis, but at a reduced capacity.

Sylvia and Mary already had sewing machines at their homes at Poplar. I would supply them with enough bundles of skirts to be machined for the three days that they were not permitted to work at Pitfield Street.

My flat at Graham Road in Hackney was situated in a Monday, Tuesday and Wednesday zone. I would install two of my four-threaders in the flat, and have Ada and Joan work there for these three days. Each morning at seven I would pick them up at Pitfield Street.

At my flat they would be given ample bundles to keep them occupied until I collected them and their finished work at 4 pm. Emmy and Betty were content to work just on Thursday and Friday.

With my ad-hoc system of working in place, my little business continued to function.

Other local clothing factory bosses also used their ingenuity to survive the crisis. Although not popular, attempts were made to persuade employees to work a 12 hour day for three days a week. Some factory owners (Usually business associates) in different zones would operate a 'transfer your worker scheme'. With their consent, employees would be transferred to another factory for three days a week when their own factory was closed. For example a Stepney factory proprietor who was forbidden to use electricity during the latter part of the week would send his staff and occasionally their sewing machines to work at a Shoreditch factory on Thursdays and Fridays. As part of the agreement, the Shoreditch factory owner would then send his staff to work at the Stepney factory on Mondays, Tuesdays and Wednesdays. Schemes like these, though only on a small scale, probably saved some businesses from going bankrupt, but several clothing factories did close down permanently as a result of the three day working week, which was to last for three months.

Some businesses just managed to survive, but at a financial loss. Jewish owned clothing factories that were only allowed to use power on Thursdays, Fridays and Saturdays were particularly vulnerable, especially if they employed devout Jews. Many of these workers were unable to work on a Saturday which was their Shabbas, (Sabbath) and they would also leave early on Friday to prepare for the following holy day.

This absenteeism, in effect left the exasperated boss opening his factory for just one and a half days a week. The production at Mr Wolf Lennard's leather goods factory in Tottenham was seriously depleted. His observant Jewish employees refused to work on Friday afternoon and on a Saturday.

Lennard, concerned that he would loose valuable export orders, wrote to the

Department of Trade and Industry requesting that he be allowed to change his three day working week from the latter part of the week to the beginning of the week. His request was refused.

Martin Ratker, the Jewish managing director of Marty Fashions based in north London, deeply regretted having to open his factory on Saturday.

'I have to consider my family, so we will just have to work on Saturday' he lamented.

To keep his workers happy he gave them tots of brandy, 'to help them through the day'.

Christian owned factories also experienced problems with Saturday working. Lesneys the matchbox toy manufacturers in Homerton employed 6,000 people, 65 per cent of them housewives and mothers with young children. Many of these women were in no position to work on a Saturday.

Mr Collins, the manager at Car & Bat, a clothing factory at Vyner Street in Bethnal Green, also lost much of his Saturday production. Saturday was the day that the majority of his women workers needed to do their weekly shopping.

With careful planning Whitbread, a letter file company in Tudor Grove, Hackney was successful in keeping its factory open five days a week. During the two days that it were unable to use electricity the company managed to find hand operating work for its staff.

S & S Goblink, who had manufactured cardboard boxes in Shackwell Lane, Dalston for nearly 80 years, were not so fortunate as Whitbread. At least half of their workforce was laid off on Thursdays and Fridays.

The production at Franklins the rubber glove makers in nearby Colverston Crescent was more secured. Being hospital suppliers, this company was granted permission to continue manufacturing five days a week, but their use of electricity was restricted to just 65 per cent.

John Williams, secretary of the Association of Clothing Contractors, was concerned that some employees, rather than have to work on a Saturdays, were leaving their firms. He wrote to Mr Peter Emery, the Under-Secretary of State for Energy, to see if clothing factories might be allowed to use electricity on Wednesdays but not on Saturdays. His request was rejected.

Peter Shore, MP for Stepney, was contacted by a group of Aldgate East shopkeepers. These traders were experiencing a huge drop in their sales due to their lighting being switched off at lunch times, which was their busiest period. Acting on their behalf, Shore wrote to the Ministry of Energy, appealing for more flexibility in special cases, but his appeal was turned down.

Some employees made use of the days when they were unable to work – holidays were brought forward, homes were decorated, old hobbies and interests revived.

Much to his delight John Smith, a Stepney photographer, experienced an unexpected surge of business during the emergency. From an average of one wedding booking a day he was receiving approximately four.

Smith believed that the 400 per cent increase was because brides-to-be who were working only three days a week were in a position to use their spare time to plan their forthcoming weddings.

During the crisis some clothing factory owners ignored the three day working week and kept their factories operating every day. If they were discovered, and some were, they found themselves appearing in the local magistrate court and being heavily fined. Many sub-contractors in the East End, especially those who were operating in illicit back street sweatshops which were established in private dwellings, continued clandestinely to ignore the three day working week. These units were operating with impunity seven days a week, often 16 hours a day. Where none were before, dark sheets, blankets and drawn blinds were permanently covering windows in the Whitechapel area.

This blatant infringement of the ban on five day working was brought to the attention of reputable clothing factory proprietors in the area, and an outraged proprietor posed urgent questions. 'Why is it that while we respect the law and comply with the three day working week, these tailoring workshops, most of which aren't registered as business premises, are allowed to function every day and why do these people who own these businesses pay no VAT or income tax and pay cash to their workers knowing that a high proportion of them receive unemployment benefit?' However, most factory owners accepted the three day working week knowing that the crisis would not last indefinitely. Their factories continued to produce garments, but at a reduced rate. Some beleaguered bosses managed to have the full co-operation of their staff during the emergency. Typical was Wally Gordon, who employed 24 machinists at his Mile End dress factory. Despite working only three days a week, his workers accepted their change of situation with a cheeriness not seen since the dark days of the blitz. No employee resigned, some extended their working hours and others were prepared to take on unskilled menial tasks in the factory when the use of electricity was banned.

Wally told a local reporter that when the three day working week began, 'doom and gloom prevailed on the factory floor, everybody was miserable and walked around with frowns on their faces,' but not for long; a spirited machinist suggested that the staff should hold a 'Crisis celebration party at lunch time, just to show the government that the three day working week can't get us down.' Unfinished garments were removed from workbenches and replaced with bottles of wine, home made sandwiches, mince pies and sausage rolls. As the wine flowed and song and laughter reverberated around the factory, Wally commented, 'if only every worker in the country could laugh like my girls, there would be no crisis'.

By the middle of March the fuel crisis in Britain was over. The Arab oil embargo had been lifted and Harold Wilson's labour government was in power after winning the general election earlier in the month and the miners who had been on strike since February 9th over a pay dispute had returned to work after accepting a 35 per cent wage increase.

Being constantly busy in the workshop did not restrict my efforts to familiarise myself with the area surrounding Pitfield Street. My immediate neighbours were shopkeepers. The pharmacy next door at number 19 was owned by Irvine a friendly, sports loving New Zealand chemist. He lived above the shop with his wife and two young children. Irvine, who was in his early thirties, was quite content to remain in Britain permanently, but his wife was not. She wanted to return to New Zealand and raise her children in the leafy suburbs of Auckland rather than the drab inner London borough of Shoreditch.

Occasionally my staff and I would purchase various items from Irvine's, but if ever I needed condoms, I would buy them at Alf Cohen's tiny hole in the wall kiosk at Cannon Street Road, Stepney. Following Alf's brutal murder in 1974 and the subsequent closure of the kiosk, my supply had to be obtained elsewhere. Obviously Irvine's pharmacy was a convenient location, but because Irvine's female counter staff knew me personally, I was too embarrassed to buy the condoms there. Fortunately, the problem was solved: the ever obliging David Upson would make the purchase for me.

A second convenient facility was J. Hirst Button Manufactures adjacent to the pharmacy.

If my stock of ladies shirt buttons became low, I would purchase a new batch from Hirst.

The business was managed by two late middle-aged partners.

While Hirst manufactured the buttons on the premises, his travelling salesman partner sold their products to outlets all over London. Although, this partner was always polite and impeccably dressed his mien was that of a shifty spiv. I would refer to him as Mr Brown. Not only did he have brown wavy hair and brown eyes he usually wore brown stripe suits.

Hirst, the effeminate partner, spoke with a charming, mid European accent; he may have been a pre-war Austrian émigré. With his fading fair hair and watery blue eyes, he looked fragile.

In the partners' frowsy basement stock room where I saw mouse droppings on the shelves, they kept a huge variety of plastic and cloth covered buttons. A delightful Hirst showed me cards which had different designed buttons fastened onto them. He handled the cards with great care like a jeweller displaying precious gems to a customer. 'Such memories, such wonderful memories,' He sighed.

Next door to Hirst's was Georgiou's Greek bakery. The bread, rolls and cakes sold in his shop always seemed fresher and tastier than those available in Carringtons bakery, which was beneath my workshop. Carringtons was also unhygienic. I had been in the preparation area at the rear of the shop and noticed ants scurrying along the floor and amongst the trays of cakes. I immediately advised my staff that under no circumstances should they buy Carringtons popular jam doughnuts again.

On the opposite side of Pitfield Street and directly facing my workshop Mrs Burges had an off-licence.

The rooms above her shop had been converted into bed-sitters and let out to several young women. The only male tenant was my friend Roger Bullock.

Roger never felt comfortable living there; he was often disturbed by the arrival of different men who were visiting the female tenants late at night and only staying for a 'short time'.

Eventually Roger would vacate his room to take up residence at my flat in Graham Road, Hackney.

Italian Giorgio was the proprietor of a café next door to Mrs Burges off-licence.

During my first year at Pitfield Street, I was a regular patron of the café, but only for morning tea and toast.

Georgio was a very bitter man who never smiled. Eventually I would boycott his usually empty café. It had become boring having to listen to his continuous tirade against everything British. He loathed the English weather. 'Not like Tuscany.' He thought British films and television programs were of a poor quality. 'Where are your Visconti's, De Sica's and Franco Zeffirelli's?'

I could have countered his remark by mentioning the gifted David Lean and Sir Carol Reed, but I chose not to. With films being one of his interests, I would have expected him to brag that De Sicas's 1948 neo-realism classic 'Ladri di biciclette', (Bicycle Thieves.) was one of the most outstanding films in the history of the cinema and if he had I would have agreed with him. This marvellous, memorable film is a particular favourite of mine.

Giogio ate only Italian food, never 'rubbish English food, like pie and chips, egg and chips or beans and chips'. But these dishes were always available on his menu.

He also believed that the local pubs were 'Rubbish places full of gangsters and drug dealers.' This criticism was unfounded. David Upson and I had visited many of the pubs in the immediate area and we found them to be respectable well managed family establishments; but most of Giogio's wrath was directed at the British government.

'Your government is rubbish, they never give financial aid and support to small businessmen like me; every few months my rent and rates go up and my takings go down.'

With several factories and offices in close proximity to his café, Giorgio's business should have been a success, but it failed dismally. Not only was he an obnoxious, unwelcoming character, the café was dirty and smelt awful. Much worse was Giogio's disgusting and filthy habit of bending down behind the counter and spitting on the floor. If I had noticed his gobbing other sharp eyed customers must have done so too. Despite his complete failure as a café proprietor, Giogio did have two loyal customers.

The Paoli brothers manufactured table lamps at their basement workshop in nearby Coronct Street.

Whenever I walked past the brother's basement, I would look through the opened escape hatch which also provided limited ventilation. The working conditions inside the workshop were absolutely shocking. I had worked in several ghastly factories over the years, but none could remotely be compared with the Paoli's premises. Thick grey dust saturated the floor, the workbenches and even the shelves, which were full of unfinished lamps. Surrounded by this dust and without face masks and protective clothing the Paoli brothers could be seen contently working their machines. I would see the older brother in Giorgio's café having an early morning coffee and a cigarette. He did not look well. Perhaps his smoking and inhaling the dust was beginning to affect his health. If, in later life, the Paoli brothers did not develop chronic respiratory diseases such as emphysema or phthisis, they were very lucky men.

Facing Hirst's on the opposite side of Pitfield Street was the longtime closed and slowly dilapidating 'Ye olde variety cinema'. It may have been a former music hall. Sadly, this building was not preserved. A decade later it was bulldozed away.

In Charles Square, just behind my workshop, an attractive 19th century mansion had been converted into offices for the National Union of Tailors and Garment Workers headquarters.

During my long career working in scores of clothing factories, I had never met a single representative, shop steward or paid-up member of this union.

If the weather was warm at lunch time, I would leave the workshop and eat my sandwiches on the grass at nearby Hoxton Square, but I usually preferred the little park in Pitfield Street which also had tennis courts.

My short stay was always enjoyable when attractive girls were playing tennis.

Directly behind the nets stands a fine old building which had been partially rebuilt and altered over the years. It was constructed in 1695 by Robert Aske, a wealthy merchant, and called the Hoxton Hospital.

The hospital was originally used as a home for 23 free men and 20 sons of freemen of the Worshipful Company of Haberdashers.

I made an acquaintance of an elderly Israeli quilter whose factory was situated at 15 Hoxton Square. I never knew his name, but I called him Sam-Sam, which was his trade name.

Sam-Sam's factory occupied the entire four floors of a tall, but not wide, ancient warehouse.

I thought that the working conditions in his factory were extremely dangerous. The well trodden floors were of old timber, as was the narrow staircase. There were no visible fire escapes, extinguishers or alarms. On each floor, large quilting machines had been installed and big rolls of fabric waiting to be quilted were stacked against the walls and piled on the floor. This lack of space inhibited the workers ability to move around safely.

It was plainly evident to me, that his factory was like a tinderbox waiting to be ignited. Just a spark could cause a fire and might trap everybody inside.

Sam-Sam, who was short, very stout and breathless, was at least 70 years old. With great difficulty he ascended the stairs. He stood still for a moment when we reached the first floor. Before continuing to the second floor, I asked him why he did not relocate his business to a ground floor premises.

'I would like to my friend,' he replied earnestly, 'but you're a businessman too, you know how expensive the rents are in this area.'

Several weeks later a distraught Sam-Sam came to see me at my workshop. He sat down on a stall, while I made him a coffee, I noticed him glancing at my fire escape and extinguishers.

There was a noticeable sadness in his voice when he spoke.

'My friend, I have some bad news, I am no longer in business.'

With watery eyes he said 'Inspectors from the Fire brigade made a surprise visit to my factory.'

He explained that the inspectors immediately ordered him to close his factory until he had fitted a fire escape.

While he sipped his coffee, I repeated the suggestion which I had made in the past that if he wanted to remain in business, he should find a ground floor factory premises, preferably one that had fire exits.

He shook his head sideways 'My friend, maybe it is time for me to retire, I am too old and tired to start again.'

Much to the relief of his concerned family Sam-Sam did retire, and his old factory, which was considered an unsafe structure, was eventually demolished.

Cyril Godfrey, who rented the workshop next to mine, was a fast, efficient coat machinist. He never seemed to be short of work. Sometimes large bundles of cut-out coats were sent to him, but usually he was responsible for collecting the bundles and delivering the finished coats.

Cyril's workshop was in a deplorable state. The windows were encrusted with dirt and the dusty floor, which seemed as if it had never been touched by a broom, was full of bread crumbs. This awful environment created a natural habitat for mice. The mice had even got inside the pocket of Cyril's well-worn overcoat which hung behind the door and devoured his cheese sandwich. He dismissed my suggestion that we should buy half a dozen mouse traps citing 'An unnecessary cost.' I was so concerned that the mice would eventually move into my workshop that I bought several traps as a precaution. Inevitably, the mice did arrive and for a short period and we were plagued by them.

When I first saw Cyril's filthy, chipped drinking mug, I was shocked. The mug's rim and inside was completely brown-stained by years of excessive tea drinking. His method of cleaning the mug after use was unhygienic; he would wet a paintbrush and give it a couple of twirls inside the mug. Thankfully he did not smoke, but his workshop was a potential fire risk. The electrical leads that connected his bench of four old Singer sewing machines were in an extremely dangerous condition. Over the years they had been clumsily repaired and extended by the use of adhesive tape. Whenever I was in his workshop, I would tread with great care and avoid standing on the leads that crossed the floor. I was convinced that if ever a fire occurred on the first floor, it would be caused by an electrical fault in Cyril's workshop.

Periodically a thin, poorly dressed, local woman of about forty would assist him to machine the coats. She never seemed to smile or speak. If Cyril was too miserly to invest in a few mouse traps, it was unlikely that the wages he paid her were adequate.

Ada was at a loss to understand how any woman could put her health at risk and work in 'That pigsty.' Within a fortnight, I too would be working in that same pigsty.

It was during Cyril's lunch break when he called me into his workshop. He had an open letter in his hand.

Before he spoke he removed his spectacles and wiped his eyes with a less than clean handkerchief. 'Carrington the landlord has put up the rent.'

This unexpected news caused me to gasp 'He has, by how much.'

He sighed heavily, 'He wants an extra six pounds a week, payable immediately.'

I felt relieved, the increase was not unreasonable. An extra six pounds would raise the weekly rent to eight pounds each, which I thought was still exceptionally low, and we also had no heating costs. Cyril replaced his spectacles and again read the letter; as he did so I could not but notice his increasingly angry expression.

His tone was acerbic. 'I am not paying more money for this place; Carrington can shove the rent up his toches.'

Cyril's reluctance to accept the rent increase gave me an idea which I thought could be mutually beneficial. I would offer to pay his share of the rent increase if he would allow me to dismantle my cutting table and re-assemble it in his workshop.

Cyril's workshop was of a similar size to mine but he only needed approximately half of the total area for his bench of four sewing machines, the remaining vacant space was wasted and used for parking two bins on wheels which were filled with moth eaten old remnants, damaged coats and probably the resident mice too.

By moving the sewing machines against the wall and placing the bins alongside, the newly created area would be sufficient for my twelve foot cutting table.

I desperately needed extra space. My workshop was cramped with ten sewing and special machines, two steam pressing units, and a cutting table, which was also used as a desk.

After Cyril read the letter a second time he tossed it aside, sat down at his sewing machine, looked up at me and said 'Carrington is a rich man, what does he want more money for?'

It was now the right moment to state my proposal.

'Listen Cyril, I have a proposition to make to you, which I believe could solve our problem.'

His eyes lit up in anticipation 'You have.'

'How would you feel, if I was prepared to pay your share of the rent increase on condition that you allowed me to re-locate my cutting table in your workshop.

I quickly added 'I would only need to use the cutting table about twice a week.'

A little smile appeared on his face; he stood up, leant across the sewing machine to shake my hand and said 'Deal done.'

Within the hour, we had moved his sewing machines and bins to the new position and I used my broom to sweep up and flatten two mice in the process.

That evening, with assistance from David Upson, we began dismantling my cutting table. By 9 p.m. we had re-assembled it in Cyril's workshop and were on our way to Dirty Dicks for a most welcome quick half.

The extra space that I had gained in my 300 square foot workshop was a blessing and the working area now seemed double its previous size. Again with valued assistance from David Upson we were able to spread out the sewing machines from their tightly fitted positions. My staff were delighted; they no longer had to work elbow to elbow. Cyril was happy too at having avoided the rent increase. I also kept to my side of the agreement; I rarely needed to spend more than two days a week in his workshop.

If ever I happen to be working at the cutting table during Cyril's lunch break, he would attempt to engage me in conversation. These interruptions could sometimes be intrusive, especially if I was using the cutting machine. I needed to concentrate as any distraction could have serious consequences: apart from the possibility that I might make a costly and irreparable mistake, I could cut my fingers. Cyril's thoughtlessness was unintentional. Because he worked approximately twelve hours a day, often alone, he must have found my presence a welcome distraction from mundane coat machining.

I explained to Cyril that I was more than happy to chat to him while I was laying the fabric or even bundling, but it would be advisable, for safety reasons, for him to refrain from speaking to me during the actual cutting process. He immediately apologized for not realising the danger.

Having his radio permanently switched on kept Cyril abreast of the news. He would have made an ideal quizmaster; for whenever the opportunity arose, especially during my non cutting sessions at the table, he seemed to enjoy asking me questions on the various news bulletins.

Typical questions were, 'what did you think were the real reasons for Harold Wilson's sudden resignation?'

'Do you believe that James Callaghan has the necessary qualities to make a prime minister?'

'Did you know that Idi Amin ate the removed livers of his executed opponents?'

'Are you aware that President Jimmy Carter was also a peanut farmer?'

'Don't you admire those brave Israeli commandos who rescued the 105 hostages from Arab terrorists at Entebbe Airport?'

Although my preferred response to these questions would have been a simple, 'no, I did not know that' or 'Really, I had no idea', I sometimes found myself being drawn into unwanted discussions. Fortunately for me, these discussions rarely lasted longer than his 15 minute lunch break

Cyril also revealed a little about his private life. He lived in North London and was married with a grown up daughter. He also mentioned that his daughter's short lived marriage had been dissolved and she was left to care for her young baby.

In due course I learnt that Cyril was of Polish Jewish descent. Fearing that his original surname Gotlieb sounded German, in the late 1930s he decided to anglicise it and Gotlieb was changed by deed poll to Godfrey. With the outbreak of the Second World War he was conscripted into the army.

'Did you experience much action?' I asked curiously.

He paused for a moment before replying 'I didn't see any action at all.'

The half grin which appeared on his face suggested to me that he was proud of the fact. Without a vestige of shame he admitted that he was given a dishonourable discharge. He chose not to reveal the reason why he was 'unsuitable'.

Continuing with our conversation, I explained that I too had been a soldier during the summer of 1960, but had bought myself out of the army after a period of 10 weeks training.

'I knew it' he said peering over the top of his spectacles. 'We have something in common.'

'We have' I replied a little surprised.

'Yes, we both avoided military service, didn't we?'

I found this remark offensive. Our army experiences were in no way comparable.

Cyril had been a conscripted soldier in wartime Britain. He should have been proud to have served his country during its hour of need but instead he was dishonourably discharged. In my case, when I volunteered to become a soldier in 1960 Britain was not at war and national service had been abolished. The British army had become a professional service made up of volunteers.

I was about to reveal my reason for being a soldier for such a short period when he remarked 'So like me, you found army life tough'.

I managed to contain my composure before saying, 'As a 19 year old in 1960, I had become very restless and needed to leave the clothing trade for a couple of months. So spending the summer at an army camp in the glorious surrey countryside and training to be a soldier seemed an ideal solution to my restlessness.'

I added, 'no I didn't find army life tough, although there was much discipline'.

Cyril removed his spectacles and began cleaning the lenses with his grubby handkerchief; as he did so he looked up at me and said 'Well we weren't meant to be soldiers were we.'

Not only did I find Cyril's remarks offensive, I was aghast, when without the blink of an eyelid; he explained his intention of joining AJEX. (Association of Jewish Ex-Servicemen & Women.)

For this cowardly man to claim he was an ex serviceman, that was beyond the pale.

I received a phone call from a Mrs Wilson, who was an outdoor machinist. She explained that she had several years experience, having previously worked in skirt and blouse factories in Stepney, but for family reasons she was now restricted to working at home.

That same afternoon I took a bundle of 12 cut squash skirts and a sample to her first floor maisonette which was situated on a council estate in Bow.

When I arrived, she introduced me to her husband, a friendly railwayman who promptly offered me a cup of coffee. Mrs Wilson explained that in between taking her two young daughters to school and doing shopping and housework, she was capable of machining approximately 100 skirts a week. Her industrial sewing machine had already been correctly adjusted to 12 stitches to the inch.

I soon appreciated the excellent quality of her work – she made sure that the zips fitted perfectly and the all important waist measurements were accurate. I was also impressed with the way she took pride in her work: the finished skirts were always neatly folded and gently tied in lots of 20.

Unfortunately for me, Mrs Wilson's next door neighbours had an aggressive mongrel that sat permanently on a coarse mat outside their front door. Getting past this dog without being bitten would become an ordeal. The pattern was always the same; the moment I appeared on the landing the dog would bark and come charging towards me. All I could do was to stand perfectly still and place my sack in front of me to act as a shield. This unfriendly hound stopped short of jumping up at me but would stand on its hind legs, place its paws on top of the sack, look me in the eye, growl viciously and attempt to snap at my hands.

The dog's owner, alerted by the barking and growling, would come rushing out of her maisonette. After grabbing her pet by the collar and pulling him off the sack she would again apologise for his 'mood swings'.

Eventually, a solution was found that would enable me to avoid being bitten. I would phone Mrs Wilson and tell her the exact time I would be calling at her home. She would then inform her neighbour the time of my arrival. The neighbour was cooperative and she would keep the dog inside for the duration of my visit. It was unlikely that the postman and the milkman had similar arrangements.

Amanda, a young designer/pattern cutter, began working at Spectator Sports. Reg Smith introduced me to her at his showroom in the West End. Within a short space of time her new range of tennis and squash wear was in production. Periodically, Amanda would bring sportswear samples to my workshop.

I liked her immediately. Not only was she thoughtful and patient, she was very pretty and had a curvaceous figure which I much appreciated, especially when I stood just a foot away as she explained the intricacies of a new sample. She was impressed with my production methods, particularly our use of four-threader overlockers. Amanda also confirmed what I was already aware of, that Reg Smith and his partner regarded Minuet Fashions as their most valued sub-contractor. She thought that because of the 'high quality' of my work the directors of Spectator Sports would be prepared to back me financially if I was interested in expanding Minuet Fashions. I explained to Amanda that if I accepted their offer

I would be duty bound to work only for Spectator Sports, a situation which I would never agree to. By remaining an independent sub-contractor, I was free to work for any supplier I so choose. Amanda responded by whispering 'I think that is a sensible decision Alfred'.

It was a Friday morning, always the busiest period of the week. Besides joining the queue at the bank, I had to prepare wages and at midday visit my outdoor machinists in east and south London. Also Amanda would be arriving later that morning with a new batch of her samples.

My time was precious; Ada had taken a week's leave. Her absence from my small work force could have caused a loss of production, but because I had learnt how to use the four-threader I was able to continue, albeit at a slow rate, to join up the skirts side seams.

By my working the four threader for the previous few days, no dockets had been cut. David Upson promptly offered his services and over the weekend we planned to cut 2,000 skirts.

Amanda duly arrived with the samples and patterns draped over her arms, she smiled when she saw me using the four-threader. I got up from the machine and Amanda and I went into Cyril's workshop where the samples, which were a mixture of skirts and shorts, were laid on the cutting table. These new designs were not difficult to make. Amanda suggested that I should make half a dozen samples of each style and deliver them at the earliest opportunity to Spectator Sports' showroom.

Noticing how busy I was, she said 'Alfred, if you need any help in your factory, I am usually free on a Saturday.'

'You are' I replied, surprised by her sudden offer.

'O yes, and I wouldn't charge you much and I can start tomorrow.'

She smiled and said, 'I am quite cheap really.'

Her smile did the trick, I accepted the hourly rate she quoted and suggested she could indeed work the following day from 8.30 a.m. until 5 p.m. with an hour for lunch.

Although it was irrelevant, I was uncertain of Amanda's motives. Did she offer to work because I was temporary short staffed and she was free on a Saturday, or did she simply wanted to earn a little extra money.

'It's probably a combination of both,' remarked David Upson when I met him in Dirty Dicks later that evening.

Dave of course was delighted that 'an English rose' would be arriving at the workshop. With a mischievous twinkle in his eye, he promised me that he would behave himself and not attempt to tease Amanda.

That twinkle, which I had become so familiar with over the years, usually meant among other things, that his promise would be discarded at the earliest opportunity.

Amanda was not as experienced with the four-threader as I had expected; she was slow too and became even slower after she had an accident.

She came into Cyril's workshop where Dave and I were laying up the fabric, stood by the door and like a little girl who had dropped and broken a new doll said quietly, 'I have had an accident'.

'An accident,' I echoed, believing that she had injured herself.

Thankfully, Amanda had not harmed her fingers on the four-threader. The accident was trivial; she had damaged two skirts, one of which was beyond repair. A look of deep disappointment showed on her face.

I told her to throw the damaged skirts in the waste bin and continue working, but she seemed a little upset at her 'carelessness'.

In an attempt to mollify her, I explained that the loss of the skirts was not a serious problem as I had always cut extra garments on every docket in case of mishaps. My explanation failed to end the matter because she insisted that I should deduct the cost of the damaged skirts from her pay.

I responded a little abruptly, 'I will do no such thing Amanda. Everybody who uses special machines has accidents from time to time. It's unavoidable and employers have to make allowances for mistakes.'

'But I might damage more skirts, what then.' She sighed sorrowfully.

Dave, now leaning on the cutting table, was listening to our conversation. It was inevitable he would intervene and say something amusing.

'Nobody is infallible Amanda. Even Alfred the Great has had more accidents with cutting machines than I have had in Daisy One, and I have had at least twenty.' (Daisy One was Dave's Reliant three wheel van.)

My friend had exaggerated his accident rate tenfold. His joke was effective. Amanda's somewhat sullen face brightened and, with her confidence restored, she returned to the four-threader.

At lunch time and after a little persuasion Amanda, still looking a little forlorn, agreed to join Dave and me at the nearby Crosby Head for a drink and a sandwich. As she collected her coat, Dave whispered in my ear 'Just leave it to me mate, I will cheer her up.'

Cheer her up he did. His original jokes soon had Amanda in fits of laughter.

For the following three consecutive Saturdays, Amanda would work for me. Every time she damaged a garment she would curse herself and immediately offer to pay for her 'carelessness'. Her offer was always refused. All I could do was repeat what I had said to her previously: that I had already made allowances for such losses.

Friday 27th February 1975 was a date that I can never forget. During the morning Amanda arrived with two new samples. She stopped for coffee and after exchanging pleasantries with Ada and Joan she left for the West End. I knew her route: a minute walk would take her to Old Street underground station where she would board a Northern line train to Bank. From there she would travel on the Central line to Oxford Street.

Later that morning there was a news bulletin on the radio. A major train crash had occurred at Moorgate Underground Station and there were many casualties. The news was chilling. Moorgate was just a half a mile away from Pitfield Street and was one of the stations on Amanda's route. I dreaded the thought that she might have been on that train and may have been one of the victims. Without thinking clearly, I immediately and foolishly alarmed my staff by remarking, 'I hope Amanda was not on that train.'

There was total silence in my workshop as I hurriedly phoned Spectator Sports, but the line was engaged. I replaced the receiver and looked out of the window. No rescue vehicles could be seen, but the continuous sound of sirens could be heard in the distance.

I phoned Spectator Sports a second time, but still their line was engaged. Was it an ominous sign?

'Keep trying Alf', said an anxious Joan whose own daughter was Amanda's age.

Eventually I got through to the showroom; Mr Price, Spectators Sports manager answered the phone.

I said just three words, 'Is Amanda safe?'

'Amanda is here' he replied, startled by the urgency of my tone.

I explained to Price that when we heard the news of the train crash, we had become concerned for her safety. As I spoke, I gave the thumbs up sign to my staff who had stopped working. A little later, Amanda phoned me to explain that she had arrived at Oxford Street shortly before the rush hour accident occurred.

Over the next few days, the country was to learn the terrible facts of the accident. It seems that the driver of the train failed to apply his breaks before crashing into the end of a blind tunnel; he was killed and tragically so were 42 of his passengers.

Emmy was horrified on hearing the news of the train crash. She had spent her entire 73 years living in Shoreditch and rarely travelled on the London tube network. Because of her nervousness of being underground she preferred the buses and walking whenever possible. She told me, that during the German blitz of London that began on 7th September 1940 she never took shelter at Liverpool Street underground station because of her fear of being trapped below ground if the station received a direct hit. Throughout the nightly blitz, she remained at home and refused to take refuge in local shelters. Emmy's decision to avoid public shelters may have saved her life.

Ada could clearly remember how scores of Shoreditch people, including whole families, were killed when a public shelter in Columbia Road market, just a short distance from where Emmy lived, was destroyed.

She also recalled that a shelter beneath the front gardens at the nearby Geffrye Museum was struck when a bomb penetrated the ground and killed everybody inside. Emmy claimed that because the shelter was so deep down in the earth. the search and rescue teams abandoned their efforts to recover the bodies of the victims. She also claimed that the gardens were eventually re-laid and a large cross of flowers was planted over the site which was recognised as a war grave. (I have never managed to verify if this tragedy did occur.)

I thought that Amanda's tenure at Spectators Sports would last for at least a couple of years, but I was wrong. After just nine months she suddenly left the company, gave up designing and became a housewife.

My friend Beth Grant, who had introduced me to Spectator Sports, contacted me. For some peculiar reason, Beth had accepted an order to make white fluffy tails to be worn by hostesses at the London Bunny Club. As Beth had no cutting facilities at her factory, she asked me if I would do her 'a favour and cut the bunny tails'.

Within the hour she had delivered the rolls of fabric and small circular patterns to my workshop. I promised Beth the tails would be cut that evening and she could collect them in the morning.

At 6 p.m. David Upson arrived at my workshop. As Dave and I began laying up the bunny tail fabric we began to reflect on the various types of garments that we had cut out in the past.

Although my friend's experience had been limited to cutting blouses, skirts and dresses, which was my main speciality too, I had cut a variety of other garments, including ladies and gent's coats, jackets and slacks. I could also recall cutting shirts, waistcoats, shorts, aprons, pinafores, socks and culottes, and even dresses to be worn by transvestites.

'And now bunny tails too.' chuckled Dave.

After I finished cutting out the tails, Dave jokingly suggested that I should ask Beth if we could deliver the finished tails to the Bunny club.

'Who knows,' he remarked hopefully, 'We might be present when the bunny girls attach them onto their bottoms.'

The next morning Beth collected the cut bunny tails and paid me my agreed fee. She also invited me to a party to be held at her Hackney flat the following Saturday evening.

'George Davis is innocent okay'

As I drove around the East End to and from my outdoor machinists, I noticed the words 'George Davis is innocent, okay' had been daubed on several railway bridges and brick walls.

I had no idea who George Davis was and neither had my staff, but within weeks of the white graffiti appearing George Davis, who was languishing in prison, would be known, not only to vast numbers of people in East London, but to increasing numbers of people throughout the British Isles.

It seems that Davis, a Stepney mini-cab driver, had been convicted with three other men of taking part in an armed robbery at the London Electricity Board Accounts office at Ley Street, Ilford.

The gang had entered the offices and stole £7,615.

While the robbery was in progress a police patrol car had arrived and was parked in Ley Street adjacent to the L.E.B offices. When the robbers fled from the building they were chased by the police from the patrol car. The robbers managed to escape, but not before shooting and wounding PC Brian Grove, one of the pursuing police officers. Meanwhile, another police officer who happened to have a camera with him managed to take several photos of the masked robbers as they hurriedly left the scene of the crime.

Eventually, Davis and three of his associates were arrested and charged with robbing the bank and wounding a police officer.

At the subsequent trial at the Old Bailey in March 1975, two of the accused men were found not guilty and acquitted. The jury was unable to reach a verdict in the case of a third man and he was remanded in custody pending a re-trial. However, George Davis, the fourth man, was found guilty.

The prosecution's use of identification evidence without any substantial corroborative evidence resulted in Davis receiving a prison sentence of 17 years for the armed robbery and three years for wounding PC Brian Grove, but 'Davis is innocent' protested his family and friends. So determined were they to prove that Davis was a victim of mistaken identity and, worse, that in order to get a conviction the police had lied at the trial, they began a prolonged direct action campaign of publicising the George Davis case.

Peter Chappel, Colin Dean and Davis's wife Rose were the principle activists involved.

Chappel, the most vocal and articulate of the group, argued that it was not possible for Davis (who was a friend of his) to have been involved in the robbery, because at the exact time of the robbery he had seen him going into the mini-cab office where he was based.

The 'George Davis is innocent' campaign began peacefully at first. Rose Davis and Peter Chappel visited New Scotland Yard in an attempt to air their grievances, but the police refused to see them. The couple then tried to persuade the editors of several leading London newspapers to take an interest in their case, but they were unwilling or unable to assist them, citing various legal reasons.

Chappel and Rose Davis led a march of several hundred people to 10 Downing Street where they handed in a 3,500 signature petition. Frustrated by having received no assistance from the press and being ostracized by the police, the campaigners decided to adopt a plan of direct action which would publicise their case. Peter Chappel, with ruthless efficiently, put the plan into practice.

Just weeks after Davis was sent to prison, Chappel drove his van down Fleet Street and crashed into the windows of the Daily Express. Reversing the van, he then rammed it into the revolving doors of the Daily Telegraph, followed by similar crashes at the entrances of the Daily Mirror and the Evening Standard. With police cars following him, he raced down Fleet Street and along the Mall before ploughing into the gates at Buckingham Palace, where he was arrested. Miraculously, nobody was injured during his reckless and dangerous escapade.

Chappel appeared in the dock at Bow Street where he faced five charges of criminal damage to property totalling £2,000, and three additional charges of driving a vehicle while under the influence of alcohol. He was remanded on £250 bail. Later he would receive a six month suspended jail sentence.

Other acts of deliberate unlawfulness followed. Bricks were hurled at the office windows of the serious crime squad in Stepney. Peter Chappel threw a stone through a window at the British embassy in Paris. Rose Davis and Chappel chained themselves together in Fleet Street and laid down in the road. Colin Dean and his brother James found themselves in the dock at the old Bailey and being charged with criminal damage after they broke a padlock on a door that led to the roof of St. Paul's Cathedral. Before climbing up the dome they released balloons and fastened a 'Justice for Davis' banner on the railings. The duo pleaded guilty and were each fined £20. Colin Dean also danced naked and climbed up trees on the little island in the lake at Victoria Park before being arrested by the police and being charged with committing a public nuisance and contravening public propriety and decency. For this misdemeanour Dean was again fined £20. The ever active Peter Chappel received another six month suspended sentence for plunging the lit up Christmas tree in Trafalgar Square into darkness by tampering with the fuses. Coupled with this direct action, peaceful demonstrations and marches were taking place in London and Paris.

Rose Davis wrote to the Queen about her husband's situation and also embarked on all night vigils outside the Home Office and the residence of Roy Jenkins the Home Secretary. With two friends, Rose appeared at the top of the London Monument where they threw hundreds of leaflets into the wind. Before chaining themselves to the railings they opened two canisters of thick orange smoke. For this episode they were each remanded on £20 bail.

Gradually the press and the general public were taking a greater interest in the 'George Davis is innocent' campaign. Questions were now being asked.

'Could there have been a miscarriage of Justice?'

'Might Davis have been a victim of mistaken identity?'

'How safe was a conviction which relies on identification evidence without any corroborative evidence?'

Lord Longford was so convinced that Davis was innocent that he wrote a formal complaint to Sir Robert Mark, the Metropolitan Police Commissioner. Even the MP Michel Foot, Leader of the House of Commons and shortly to become Deputy Leader of the Labour Party, suggested that there may have been a miscarriage of justice.

During August 1975, Peter Chappel, Colin Dean, Richard Ramsay and Geraldine Hughes left London and headed north to Leeds. Their plan was to obtain maximum publicity by disrupting the last day of the third test match between England and Australia that was being played at Headingly.

Ignoring the fact that cricket is loved by millions of people and England were in a strong position and might have won the match, Chappel and his friends waited until darkness before breaking into the ground. They dug up the batting area, poured oil on the pitch and left their now customary slogans daubed on the fences. The damage they inflicted was so severe that the match had to be abandoned. Having done the deed the culprits gave themselves up to the police and were remanded in custody.

At Birkenhead Crown Court 'The Headingly four' pleaded guilty to causing criminal damage to the cricket ground. Dean was sentenced to nine months prison suspended for two years. Ramsay and Hughes each received six months prison also suspended for two years. However, in Chappel's case the judge would show no leniency. He considered Chappel, to be an unrepentant and persistent offender and the leading activist behind the campaign.

Passing sentence the judge took into account two of Chappel's previous unlawful acts committed during the campaign, for which he had received suspended six months prison sentences. The activities of the energetic Peter Chappel would now be curtailed, he was sent to prison for 18 months.

The Justice for Davis campaigners also received support from a Bow minister. The Rev, David Moore speaking from his pulpit at a Remembrance Day service compared the Davis supporters, 'who were fighting for justice,' to that of serviceman killed in the Great War.

The Reverend also erected a huge white painted sign outside his mission in Bow Road.

'To punish the innocent is not ok. Proverbs 17:26.'

The sign was removed after a few days following complaints from local people.

I mentioned the Reverend Moore's involvement with the Davis campaign to David Upson while we drank in Dirty Dicks. Dave, as an ex-serviceman who had seen action in the Far East, was aghast at the Reverend's remarks.

'How dare that prat of a priest compare protesters to our brave soldiers who were killed on active service.'

'Perhaps he had consumed too much altar wine which had affected his better judgment,' I remarked sarcastically.

Dave had taken a keen interest in the George Davis case. He believed that as Davis had associates who were known gangsters, there was a strong possibility that he might have willingly or even unwillingly allowed himself to be drawn into their criminal activities. He later said, 'the fact remains, people do judge you by the company you keep, which of course is wrong, but I have a niggling feeling that Davis was probably involved in that robbery.'

I asked my friend, 'But what of Davis's supporters, you cannot deny that they genuinely believe in Davis's innocence.'

Dave gave a thoughtful answer.

'I am not denying the fact that the Davis's campaigners seem utterly convinced that there has been a miscarriage of justice, but Alf, you have to look at it two ways, Davis might be a good liar who is able to convince his family and friends that he is innocent. Alternatively, the supporters might be cheats, who believe that by continuing with their forceful campaign of civil disobedience they can eventually persuade the authorities to release him.'

More support for the Free Davis campaign, came from an unexpected source.

On October 10th 1975 a play entitled 'George Davis is innocent ok,' written by the Irish playwright Shane Connaughton opened at the tiny Half Moon Theatre at Alie Street near Aldgate East.

The theatre, converted from a former old synagogue, was in a very poor condition. Although, the Half Moon received limited financial assistance from the Arts Council and from the London borough of Tower Hamlets, there were no spare funds available to repair the rapidly dilapidating building. It was amazing how the company that administrated the Half Moon managed to survive on a shoestring.

Because the theatre was so tiny and without a stage, productions were put on in the centre of the floor.

During one play which I saw there, buckets were placed on the floor amidst the performing actors to catch the rainwater that dripped continuously from the leaky roof. Whilst sitting on a near collapsing chair just feet from the cast, a droplet of water landed on the back of my neck.

'Why weren't you wearing a sou'wester?' joked David Upson.

Connaughton's play, which relied on transcriptions of the George Davis trial and interviews with his supporters, was an immediate success. Throughout its four week run, every performance was sold out.

As the George Davis campaign gathered momentum, the jailing of Davis and the activities of his supporters began to arouse much interest in the East End. Opinions varied; discussions and arguments concerning the Davis saga were taking place in homes, factories, offices and pubs. I can recall two adjacent stallholders at Petticoat Lane market momentarily ignoring their somewhat bemused customers, while they argued passionately whether Davis was innocent or guilty, and on another occasion, whilst drinking with David Upson in Charley Brown's pub at Limehouse, two regular drinkers actually came to blows because of their opposing views of the Davis trial.

In my workshop, we may not have argued passionately whenever George Davis's name was mentioned, but we did discuss the case on several occasions.

Ada was unequivocal in her belief that Davis was guilty as charged. She remarked cynically, 'crooks like him should stay behind bars forever.'

Joan believed the opposite, 'Of course Davis is innocent and he should be released.'

She lowered her voice to almost a whisper 'The police have obviously set him up.'

My sisters Sylvia and Mary had no strong opinions whether Davis was innocent or guilty and Emmy and Betty expressed minimum interest in the case.

I found the George Davis campaign totally perplexing. Without question, I was mightily impressed with the single-mindedness of the three principle activists especially Peter Chappel, who seemed totally sincere, dedicated and utterly convinced that his friend was innocent. Yet I could not accept the accusation that members of the police robbery squad had deliberately connived and colluded to send an innocent man to prison, knowing that the real bank robber was still at liberty and might well take part in future armed robberies.

Because of the incessant marches, demonstrations, all-night vigils and well publicised unlawful acts by the George Davis supporters, Mr Colin Woods, the deputy commissioner of the Metropolitan Police, was pressurised into allowing Chief Superintendent Jack Moulder of the Hertfordshire Constabulary to begin an enquiry into the whole of the George Davis affair and try to establish if there might have been a miscarriage of justice. Included in Mr Moulder's team were officers from Scotland Yard's A10 branch, whose role it was to investigate serious complaints against the police.

Even though, after several months, Chief Superintendent Moulder had not completed his enquiry, an interim report of his findings was delivered to the Home Secretary.

The report stated that the detectives had found no fault with the serious robbery squad, who had investigated the Ilford robbery, and the subsequent arrest of George Davis, but there was a possibility that Davis may not have been involved with the robbery.

During the afternoon, on Tuesday May 12th 1976; the Home Secretary, Roy Jenkins, announced to members of the House of Commons that 'my conclusions about the shift in the balance of evidence in the case are such that it would not be right for Mr Davis to remain in prison.' He concluded by saying that 'because there was insufficient evidence of Davis's innocent, I am unable to grant a full pardon.'

Following this announcement and Davis's immediate release from Albany prison on the Isle of Wight, there was jubilation in the East End.

Peter Chappel heard the groundbreaking news in his cell at Walton prison, Liverpool.

Shortly after Peter Chappel's discharge from prison on February 17th 1977, and his campaigning days finally over, he became an East End social worker based at the Bow mission. He also assisted the Bow Triangle association with their fundraising. This association was keen to convert a derelict bombsite into a small farm and park for the benefit of local people.

Chappel must have sensed that the Australian cricket team bore him no permanent ill will for disrupting their test match with England two years earlier. He contacted the Australian captain Greg Chappel (no relation) who was in London and explained to him the plans of the Bow Triangle Association.

Greg Chappel listened sympathetically. After the captain and the rest of the Australian team penned their signatures on a cricket bat, it was handed to Chappel to be auctioned, with the proceeds going to the association.

Now that Davis was a free man, one would have thought that he would have been eternally grateful and indebted to his loyal family and friends who had campaigned so vigorously and unremittingly to secure his freedom, but unfortunately this was not the case.

In September 1977, just 16 months after Davis was released from prison, the police robbery squad received information that a gang was about to rob the Bank of Cyprus in Holloway, North London.

Armed police officers hid inside a furniture van parked near the bank. During the actual robbery a few shots were fired but neither police nor bank robbers were injured.

The police ambush was successful and they managed to arrest the gang intact. A little later, a police photo taken at the scene of the robbery was released to the press. The photo of one of the bank robbers clutching a sawn of shotgun and being pinned down on the ground by the police was none other than George Davis.

'I told you so' said an elated Ada, 'That crook was guilty all along.'

Joan, who two years earlier was convinced that Davis was innocent and had been 'set up' by the police, made no comment.

The Serious Robbery Squad, who had originally arrested George Davis for his alleged role in the Ilford robbery and were later accused by Davis's supporters of being corrupt and liars, must have felt totally 'over the moon' as David Upson remarked. My friend, who still retained his 'niggling' feeling that Davis was probably guilty, continued with his appraisal.

'For the past three years the George Davis supporters have with impunity vilified the police. In their eyes, it's the police who are the criminals not Davis and his associates. At least the police, who were never given an opportunity to answer their critics, must now feel that they have been thoroughly exonerated.'

I felt deeply sorry for Rose Davis, Peter Chappel and Colin Dean; the news of Davis's arrest must have been devastating for them. They had given so much time and effort into freeing George Davis. Both Chappel and Dean had to endure periods in jail for continually breaking the law during the campaign and now they were to witness their friend again being charged with armed robbery.

This time Davis's guilt was never in doubt and he received a long prison sentence.

Rose Davis would eventually divorce her husband.

George Davis would not remain a bachelor indefinitely. Ironically, a few years after he was released from prison, he married a policeman's daughter.

It has been suggested that because of the massive publicity over the George Davis case, coupled with the increasing concern of jurists who were unhappy with the acceptability of identification evidence in courts to obtain a conviction; the Home Secretary, on May 1st 1975, appointed Lord Devlin to review the whole issue of identification evidence.

Lord Devlin's report, which was published on the 26th April 1976 and just two weeks prior to Davis's release, was a landmark in the British justice system. The report's main recommendation was that in future, if identification evidence was to be used in criminal cases it must be supported with corroborative evidence.

Even today, more than 30 years after the slogan 'George Davis is innocent okay' first appeared on bridges and walls in Tower Hamlets, local people on occasions still discuss the Ilford robbery. There are those who believe that Davis was innocent. Others argue, sometimes vociferously that he was 'guilty as sin'.

Of course, there are many people, and I am one of them, who still remain a little baffled by the whole affair.

As the months went by I had become extremely busy in the workshop. Besides cutting garments, pressing, and spending periods using the felling and button sewing machines, I was constantly driving around East and South London delivering and collecting work from my outdoor machinists. Preparing wages every Friday morning was also time consuming.

Finding additional staff to relieve this ever increasing workload would be the answer.

My unemployed close friend Victor Clarke was keen to find a temporary job. For the previous 15 years, ever since leaving school, he had been a machinist for his recently retired father, who owned a small trouser-making workshop in Whitechapel. Vic's father was proud that he had once made trousers for Sir Winston Churchill.

Vic had no desire to return to machining, but he was quite willing to work for me as a presser.

We sat in the pub and discussed conditions and wages. I also agreed with his request that he could start work the next day.

When Vic and I became friends in 1965 I was 24 and he was 21. It was surprising how much we had in common. Neither of us had any formal education, we were of working class stock, lived in the East End of London and had spent our working lives in the clothing trade. Our interests were similar too: girls, pubs and opera.

After the pub closed and while walking home to Poplar (I had sold my flat in Hackney and was now living in my father's maisonette) I began to wonder if I had not made a mistake in offering Vic a job. Although I had no doubt that he was hardworking and conscientious, I did have some reservations about his ability to prevent himself from expounding his uncompromising right wing views to my staff. Also I was not happy with him having to smoke in the workshop.

For the first few weeks as my presser, Vic behaved impeccably; he worked diligently and hardly spoke, but this self discipline was short lived and he began to dominate the conversation during the lunch and tea breaks. My staff soon realised that Vic was fiercely patriotic and proud of his 'English yeomanry ancestry'. He also bragged that he had many solutions to the country's ongoing problems. His agenda was radical.

'Britain should return to its traditional role of being a major exporting country, we should produce all of our own food, coal and oil and never rely on foreign imports, and overseas aid should be linked to investment. Capital punishment and national service should be reinstated and unrestricted third world Immigration into Britain was wrong. These foreigners are milking us dry, repatriation is the only answer.'

Although Ada enthusiastically supported Vic's views, especially on repatriation, she could not agree with him the moment he began to criticise the Jews.

Vic was in no doubt that the holocaust was 'wartime propaganda designed to justify the takeover of Palestine'.

Ada protested, 'Victor how you can say those poor Jews weren't gassed is beyond me, I have seen the newsreels of piles of dead bodies being bulldozed into pits.'

Vic tried to explain to an increasingly agitated Ada that the vast majority of the victims who perished in German concentration camps died as a result of epidemics.

'A fact confirmed by onsite investigations carried out by the wartime International Red Cross.'

His explanation had no effect; Ada, was not convinced.

'Be honest Victor, you just don't like the Jews, do you?' she remarked acidly.

Vic raised his voice a little 'I can assure you Ada I have no argument with Jewish people whatsoever. They have been hoodwinked into believing that a holocaust did occur, just like the rest of us.'

My friend also claimed that the diary of Anne Frank was fraudulent.

I asked him where the evidence of fraud was. His answer seemed to be well prepared.

'Anne Frank died in Belsen in 1945 after contracting typhus, yet parts of the diary are known to have been written in a ball point pen; and Biro pens were not invented until 1951.'

'Then who wrote the diary?' I replied,

He answered confidently 'Most revisionist historians believe that much of the diary was probably written by Otto Frank, Anne's father.'

Ada may have thought that Vic disliked Jews, but I disagreed. Not for one moment did I believe that Vic bore any personal animosity towards Jewish people.

David Upson, also a close friend of Vic's, shared my view, though he was convinced our mutual friend was without question 'an anti-Zionist'.

Vic defended his criticism of 'Racist Israel' by reminding Dave and me that the United Nations General Assembly had recently adopted a resolution declaring

Zionism 'a form of racism and racial discrimination'.

Because our discussions during the lunch and tea breaks never became heated, I allowed them to continue, but one incident in the cutting room involving Vic and Cyril caused me to caution my friend.

Vic disliked Cyril intensely. I was probably the cause of this resentment as I had casually mentioned to him that Cyril had been dishonourably discharged from the army during the Second World War.

This disclosure was a mistake. I should have remembered that Vic loathed those who failed in their duty to defend their country, particularly conscientious objectors, whom he regarded as cowards. He singled out Harold Wilson as a 'prime example'.

I thought Vic's criticism of conscientious objectors was somewhat harsh, not all of these men were cowards. Some who became ambulance drivers and stretcher bearers were decorated for displaying great courage in battle situations. Vic was also highly critical of civilians of military age who, in an attempt to avoid being called up for war service had enlisted in the Auxiliary Fire Service, which had been expanded just before the outbreak of the Second World War.

'They thought that they had found an escape route from the line of fire, but they were wrong, for when the German blitz on London began these AFS men found themselves on the streets trying to put out fires while the bombs and incendiaries were still falling all around them and of course they suffered many casualties.'

After the Israeli Labour Government defeat in the general election of May 1977, Menachem Begin, the hawkish leader of the Likud Party, became Premier of the newly formed coalition.

Vic was dismayed when he heard the news of Begin's success.

'Now that butcher is prime minister, there will never be peace with the Palestinians,' he said gloomily.

I knew little of Begin or his right-wing Likud party, but I did read somewhere that Begin was a former terrorist. Vic soon gave me details of Begin's career, which I found disturbing.

'Begin was born in Poland. After he deserted from the Polish army during the Second World War he sneaked into Palestine. Shortly afterwards, he joined the ranks of the Irgun, which was a ruthless terrorist organisation dedicated to ending the British mandate and to expel the Palestinian Arabs who made up the bulk of the population. Once these objectives were achieved, the terrorists plan was to create an all Jewish state.' Even David Upson, an ardent admirer and vocal supporter of Israel, admitted to me that the very name Jewish State could be interpreted has having 'racist undertones'.

I was appalled when Vic listed the terrible atrocities that the Irgun, which

Begin led from 1943 to 1948, and the more sinister group the Stern gang had committed. At least 250 British servicemen and policeman were murdered and countless numbers of innocent Palestinian men woman and children were brutally killed.

I was laying up fabric with Vic when Cyril arrived for work. Before he began machining the coats, he made a mug of tea, switched on his radio, sat comfortably in his chair and glanced at Vic and me as we worked. Suddenly and much to my disappointment, Vic raised his voice and barked at Cyril.

'I see your Israel has elected a butcher to be prime minister.'

Vic's provocative remark startled Cyril who almost slid off of his seat.

I was distracted from reprimanding Vic by Cyril's instant reaction; he stood up, leant over his sewing machine and shouted at my friend, 'and you have Enoch Powell, haven't you.'

Cyril had the good sense to remain behind his sewing machine, had he stepped towards the cutting table. Vic who was tall, well-built and impulsive, would not have hesitated in flooring him.

I quietly warned Vic, who was still glaring menacingly at Cyril, that unwanted confrontations like this could affect my business. My warning had an immediate effect, he turned his head away from Cyril who had now sat down and was calmly drinking his tea.

From that day Vic and Cyril would never utter a single word to each other, a situation which I welcomed.

Because I did not adhere to Vic's entrenched right-wing views, he regarded me as a 'typical liberal'.

'You're not a liberal,' said David Upson, 'You're a centre-right conservative.'

I found it odd that my friends' opinions of me were at variance with each other.

During the mid 1970s I did not consider myself to have had any strong political leanings. I rarely voted, had never been affiliated with any political party and, like increasing numbers of people, I distrusted politicians. I thought most of them were careerists who wanted your vote but not your opinion.

Dave also had little faith in politicians.

He was convinced that politicians often 'avoid telling the truth, which was tantamount to lying'.

He once quoted words that he attributed to General De Gaulle.

'Since a politician never believes what he says, he is quite surprised to be taken at his word.'

Several weeks after his clash with Vic, Cyril became involved in another confrontation.

Cyril had begun machining coats and jackets for Bronit, a local garment manufacturer.

Bronit was an obnoxious character who was always impatient and rude. He had a habit of bursting into Cyril's workshop, scooping up the machined coats and remonstrating quite loudly with Cyril for his continued failure to complete his orders on time. Bronit was not prepared to listen to Cyril's 'Excuses for late deliveries.'

It was just after seven in the morning when Bronit marched into my workshop. He demanded that I unlock Cyril's workshop immediately so he could collect any finished coats that Cyril had completed the previous evening. I explained that without Cyril's authority, I was unable to let him have access and that he should return latter when Cyril arrived. Frustrated at my refusal, he attempted to force the door of the workshop and as he did so Cyril came up the stairs.

After the two men went inside a furious argument occurred. Shortly afterwards a red faced and snarling Bronit, carrying a few finished coats came out of the workshop and slammed the door behind him. A little later, I asked a tired looking Cyril how on earth could he work for such a meshuggeneh.

He replied wearily 'You are right, he is a meshuggeneh, but what can I do, the putz (Jerk) pays good money.'

Unknown to me Cyril, who did not have a phone in his workshop, gave Bronit my telephone number. Bronit began to take full advantage of this free facility. I found it time consuming having to stop work and answer the telephone and pass on messages from Bronit to Cyril.

'Tell Cyril that the collars are not centre enough.'
'Tell Cyril that there is too much fullness in the back seam.'
'Tell Cyril that the left side pocket flap seems puckered.'
'Tell Cyril to have the coats ready at lunchtime.'

As expected, Bronit was incapable of saying please or thank you.

After several weeks of 'Tell Cyril' I ordered Bronit to stop dialling my number and suggested that he should persuade Cyril to install a telephone. The meshuggeneh reacted with typical asperity, promptly accusing me of being uncooperative before slamming down the telephone.

It was during a mid morning and I was busy making a marker when suddenly Bronit charged in to the workshop.

He loomed over Cyril, who was seated at his sewing machine, and raised his voice.

'Where is he Cyril, where is my nephew, I know your hiding him?'

Apparently Bronit employed his teenage nephew as a factory general help.

The nephew, who always seemed totally dispirited, would sometimes collect Cyril's finished coats

According to Cyril, because the lad loathed Bronit and the menial tasks he was asked to do he would disappear from the factory for long periods whenever the opportunity arose.

Again Bronit accused Cyril of hiding his nephew somewhere in the workshop. Cyril explained that the last time he had seen the nephew was the previous day, but Bronit did not reply, he was to busy searching the workshop for the elusive lad. I watched with amusement as he hastily looked inside a cupboard and under Cyril's bench of four sewing machines, he even crouched down to peer under the cutting table to see if the lad had concealed himself amongst the rolls of fabric. I thought that Bronit was quite mad. Satisfied that his nephew was not hiding in the workshop, he quickly left. Cyril and I looked out of the window and just managed to catch a glimpse of Bronit hurrying around a corner.

By the late 1970s, I had lost all interest in remaining in business. By coincidence, during this period, my staff were either retiring or planning to find employment elsewhere. Change was coming, which I welcomed.

Having to work 70 hours every week had become increasingly tiresome. Ever since leaving school in 1956 I had continually worked six and often a seven day week. Friend's descriptions of me were apt.

'Alf the worker.' 'Alf lives to work.' 'He's made the factory his home.'

I was envious of these friends, none of whom worked more than 40 hours a week.

Friday 1st June 1979 was an ideal date to discontinue Minuet Fashions.

From March of that year I allowed the production to decrease each week. As my staff left they were not replaced. Joan was the first to go. She accepted a position as an office filing clerk, and Emmy and Betty had retired. Ada was to fulfil her dream and settle in Somerset and Vic had been offered a vacancy as a chauffeur. My sisters Sylvia and Mary were leaving to get married and would move out of the East End.

Iris Lewis, my most consistent and skilful machinist, was deeply sorry that I would no longer be able to supply her with work. For the past six years she had come to depend on her regular weekly wage. Alleviating her fears of loss of earnings was easy. I contacted Victor Simms of Burns and Lux.

At my request, Victor was able to offer a grateful Iris as much machining as she could cope with.

Mary Hardy, another of my talented outdoor machinists, suddenly stopped working the previous February. Her husband Bill, who worked as a night porter at Guy's Hospital, phoned me and insisted that I should call at his flat as soon as possible to collect Mary's finished and unfinished skirts. I asked him if Mary was unwell; to which he replied, 'Mary is no longer living here'. He refused to disclose any further details.

As I drove to the Hardy's flat, I began to make a mental list of the various reasons why Mary was no longer living at the family home none seemed plausible. She seemed to be in good health and happily married, or so I presumed, and she had two likeable, well-behaved teenage children, a boy and a girl.

The day before, I had delivered bundles of tennis skirts for Mary to machine; as usual I stopped by for coffee. Sprawled out on a sofa in the lounge and smoking one of his rolled up cigarettes was the now familiar sight of 'Slim' the indolent, jobless boyfriend of Mary's 15-year-old daughter Carol.

I thought Slim an odd character. His brown eyes, dark curly hair and propensity for wearing coloured neck scarfs suggested that he was of gypsy stock. In the past I had attempted to exchange a few words with him but he showed no interest in responding. He also avoided eye contact, which left me wondering if he had something to hide.

Carol was alone in the flat when I arrived. She led me to one of the bedrooms where her mother's sewing machine was in front of a window. I put the unopened bundles at the bottom of my sack and the twenty or so finished skirts on top. Carol refused to accept payment.

Although, I was curious to know what caused her mothers' sudden departure, I did not want to embarrass her and ask uncomfortable questions, so I chose a different route, which I thought would give me an answer.

As I swung the sack on to my back I said 'And how is your boyfriend keeping?'

'I have packed him up' she replied phlegmatically 'He was a two-timer.'

It seemed plain to me that Slim was two-timing with her own mother.

I said goodbye to Carol, left the flat and drove back to Pitfield Street.

The Devil's Disciple

*'The worst sin towards our fellow creatures is not to hate them, but to be
indifferent to them: that's the essence of inhumanity.'*
(The Devil's Disciple by George Bernard Shaw act 2)

With my production decreasing by the week, I was able to spend less time in
the workshop and more time socialising. Apart from womanising, partying and
drinking with David Upson, which became my regular routine I saw several
operas at Covent Garden and a number of productions at the Half Moon
Theatre at Aldgate East and the Theatre Royal, Stratford.

I took Susanne, a girlfriend of mine, to see a play at the Half Moon.

Susanne, a fervent Tory, was deeply saddened on hearing that the Shadow
Northern Ireland Secretary, Airey Neave, had been assassinated a few days
earlier on 30th March.

It seems that during a shocking lapse of security, terrorists managed to gain
entry into the underground car park at the House of Commons where they
attached a bomb under Airey Neave's car. As the MP drove up the exit ramp the
bomb was detonated and he was fatally injured. The Irish National Liberation
Army, who claimed responsibility for the atrocity, issued a statement.

'Neave was targeted because he was engaged in rabid militarist calls for more
repression against the Irish people.'

The Half Moon had a capacity audience. Latecomers who were unable to
obtain a seat were allowed to stand at the rear. Because Susanne and I had
arrived early, we managed to secure excellent seats with unrestricted views.
When the lights dimmed the actor Andrew de la Tour, who was to appear in
a forthcoming production of Dario Fo's 'Accidental Death of An Anarchist',
rose from his seat, stood in the centre of the floor and faced the audience. After
making a brief announcement about the evening's performance he suddenly
said 'Poor old Aiery Neave, he managed to jump out of Colditz Castle but he
couldn't jump out of that car-ramp.'

The reaction from the audience was immediate, some people laughed, others
hissed. With his head held high, De la Tour went back to his seat.

I was baffled. How on earth could any person be so heartless?

Possibly De la Tour was a paid up member of the Socialist Workers' Party or some other militant left wing organisation and on hearing the news of Airey Neave's death had seized the opportunity to express his hatred of the Conservative Party.

I whispered in Susanne's ear 'I hope when De la Tour is an old man and has some sense, he remembers this evening.'

She replied bitterly 'Revolting people like him, who tell cruel jokes, never change.'

De la Tour did indeed remember that night.

In a reply to a letter which I sent to him in June 2007, he stated that although he had taken no 'active pleasure' in the assassination of Aiery Neave he certainly had 'never regretted making the remark'. He also said that 'Aiery Neave, as Thatcher's mentor, bore some moral responsibility for the suffering and death of scores of Northern Ireland's Catholic community. It was not I who was heartless; the word better describes Thatcher's response to the death of the Republican hunger strikers who demanded nothing more than the recognition that they were prisoners-of-war-a status that Neave himself of course was readily afforded by the Nazis.'

If De la Tour can claim that he took no active pleasure in the brutal killing of Aiery Neave, he must be an extraordinary gifted actor, because he certainly convinced me and many other people in the Half Moon audience that for him the death of the MP was a joyous occasion. I am sure most civilised people would agree that to have no regrets whatsoever after telling a cruel and unnecessary joke is a vile trait of human nature.

I knew a clothing factory mechanic who was interested in buying my sewing machines and the Eastman cloth cutter. Contrary to my expectations, the price we agreed was much better than I had hoped for.

My two pressing units, which I had bought from Norris a steam engineer six years earlier, were sold back to him. Norris was in a generous mood when he came to inspect the units. His excellent offer was immediately accepted.

Cyril feared, correctly, that with my departure his rent would increase to eight pounds a week. I had no sympathy for him whatsoever, but I did manage to find a tenant to occupy my workshop. The new tenant who had a lucrative business repairing burglar alarms, was quite willing to continue subsidizing Cyril's rent.

After vacating my workshop, I decided that a short break would be necessary before I started looking for work in earnest. Because David Upson was unemployed too, it would be an ideal opportunity to see more of my best friend before the pubs opened.

Each morning I would accompany Dave when he knocked on clothing factory doors enquiring about vacancies.

Starting early, Dave and I would head for the Aldgate East and Whitechapel area where several clothing factories were located. Some factory proprietors were considerate, they took Dave's phone number, assuring him that if a stock cutting vacancy became available they would contact him. Others thought that my friend had insufficient cutting and marker making experience, a few were downright rude and slammed their doors in our faces, One sympathetic coat manufacturer did offer Dave a job 'but you must be willing to help the other cutters unload the cloth from the van'. When Dave and I saw the enormous rolls of heavy fabric under the cutting table, our jaws dropped. Dave, who was in constant but mild pain from a hernia, which may have been caused by carrying fabric in the past, wisely refused the offer.

At lunch times a quick half in a Whitechapel pub was usually called for before resuming our search for work. We also visited the Aldgate East Star Agency but our visit proved fruitless. The agency had no current vacancies for stock cutters.

Dave hated not being able to work. Even when he was fully employed and was forced to take a break when his company closed their factory for a two week summer holiday, he would look for any employment to keep himself occupied. Sometimes he would return to his former trade, handbag framing. There were still a few handbag manufacturers in the East End who were willing to engage him temporarily. Derisory as the wages were, my friend never complained. Dave was well aware that if he was not working during these unwanted breaks he would inevitably spend much of his free time in the pubs and squander his hard earned savings 'on drink and loose women'.

When Ronnie Radlett heard that Dave and I were unemployed he came to see us at the Prospect of Whitby.

In 1975 Ronnie had become disillusioned with the clothing industry and joined the Post Office Railway.

The POR operated small driverless trains carrying trolleys full of heavy sacks of mail on an underground network that called at seven stations from Paddington to Whitechapel.

Ronnie suggested that Dave and I should 'get out of the clothing trade, once and for all' and become Post Office Railwaymen.

Dave was enthusiastic about working on the railway and I, though I did not share his enthusiasm, would in due course also become a railwayman.

Dave loved his new job and stayed for 13 years until he retired at 65. I managed to survive for nine months working below ground and loathed every minute of it, as I described in more detail in 'An East End Story'.

Finding suitable long-term full or part-time employment after leaving the railway proved difficult. As in the old days, answering advertisements for stock cutters and knocking on clothing factory doors became my daily routine. I also contacted the GCCMA to see if they had any vacancies on their books. The association had several vacancies, mostly located at Holloway and Haringey, but to reach these areas would involve much travelling. My preference would be to work further south, particularly in Stepney or Bethnal Green. These two boroughs were within walking distance or a short bus ride of my home in Poplar. However, there was one vacancy that the GCCMA recommended which seemed interesting; it was for part time dress cutting; just two days a week and £4 an hour, but there was a disadvantage: the factory was situated near the Archway in north London. Although I had reservations about the distance, I still decided to go for an interview. Travelling to Archway for two days a week might just be tolerable. There was also a possibility that I could eliminate the journey from Poplar to Archway by staying for two days with Suzanne, who lived opposite Highbury Fields. The bus from Highbury to Archway would have taken only ten minutes. Hopefully if the interview went well, I could start work the same morning.

The owner of the Archway dress factory was Demetrius, a young Greek Cypriot. His small factory was situated in a courtyard at the rear of a much larger factory. The interview took place on his doorstep and as he spoke he closed the machining room door behind him in an attempt to dull the noise of the vibrating sewing machines and the bouzouki music. Closing the door had the desired effect; we could now hear each other speak. Demetrius spoke perfect English.

After confirming that I was Alfred the top cutter and answering a few questions about my experience and capabilities, he invited me to view the cutting room. We crossed the tiny courtyard and went inside a small building. Although the cutting room was on the first floor there did not seem to be a staircase.

To gain access to the cutting room meant climbing a very thin aluminium ladder which was placed up against a trapdoor in the ceiling. Also in the ceiling was an opening which seemed to be about four foot square.

On reaching the top of the ladder Demetrius used his head to lift the trapdoor and I followed him through, emerging in the cutting room. Without a staircase or a lift, it was impossible to see how rolls of fabric could be brought to the cutting room. Carrying heavy fabric up a ladder was impractical and extremely dangerous. Perhaps sensing my concern, Demetrius mentioned that he would shortly be installing a small lift. I gazed around the cutting room. It had ample fluorescent lighting with extra light from the large windows. The cutting table, approximately 20 feet long, was well constructed, and the Eastman cutting machine seemed to be in a pristine condition. An absence of rolls of fabric under the cutting table and no dress samples or patterns on the rails was a clear indication this was a new cutting room which had never been used.

Demetrius explained that because he did not have cutting facilities in the past he could only accept poorly priced cut work from suppliers, but now having a cutting table he was in a position to accept more lucrative CMT dockets. His plan was to cut about a thousand dresses a week, then gradually over a period of time decrease cut work production and at the same time increase CMT production. Eventually he would dispense with cut work altogether. Suddenly we were interrupted by the trapdoor being raised; a woman's head appeared and she spoke to Demetrius in Greek. Facing me, he said 'Would you excuse me for a moment Alfred.' After he climbed down the ladder, I leant on the cutting table and began to twiddle my thumbs. Several minutes later, he still had not returned and rather than continue staring at the floor I thought it might be more interesting to stare out of the window instead. As I went behind the end of the cutting table, I nearly fell through the opening which I noticed earlier just prior to climbing the ladder. The opening was probably where the lift was going to be installed. Demetrius was careless; he should have covered it with wooden sheeting or roped off the area.

I soon became totally bored standing by the window and began to wonder if Demetrius had forgotten about me. It was now obvious that my wanting to start work that morning was premature and my travelling up to the Archway had been a wasted effort. This Greek was only interviewing prospective cutters. My time was too precious to spend waiting around in an empty cutting room. After a few more moments had past and still no sight or sound of Demetrius, I climbed down the ladder and left the building.

I met my friend Frank in a Whitechapel café, he too was unemployed. Frank had been cutting garments for over twenty years, but recently had been made redundant. He preferred to work for Jewish factory owners rather than Greeks or Turks, but that preference was no longer an option. The Jewish involvement in the East End clothing industry was declining fast.

Several of Frank's cutter friends had strongly advised him to avoid seeking employment at a Cypriot owned clothing factory. These same friends had similar stories to tell. They had all lost wages and holiday pay when their Greek and Turkish employers had deliberately made themselves bankrupt.

Frank was interested to know if I had ever worked for foreign employers. I explained that I had, adding, although it was well known in the trade that many Greek and Turkish Cypriot clothing manufacturers were dishonest, it would be wrong for me to stereotype the entire community as being incorrigible cheats.

My advice to Frank was that if he was unable to find work in a Jewish owned factory and was offered a stock cutting position by a Cypriot manufacturer and the wages and conditions were acceptable, he should seriously consider working there, but also be aware that at some stage in the future his employer might suddenly become bankrupt and he could find himself out of a job, minus any outstanding wages that were due.

Although, Frank seemed to be interested in my advice, I felt that he was still reluctant to work for non Jewish employers, but I was wrong.

About a fortnight later, I noticed Frank in the same café. When he spotted me queuing at the counter, he grinned and gave me a thumbs up sign, which I interpreted to mean that he had found suitable employment. I sat down at his table. He waited for a moment before saying 'I did take your advice Alf and worked for a foreigner.'

'And how was it?' I replied.

'Well for the five consecutive days that I worked it was reasonably straight forward, just cutting skirts and slacks, but' he suddenly stopped in mid flow, he was interrupted by our mutual friend Jock who came into the café and sat next to us.

No sooner was Jock, a freelance garment cutter, sitting comfortably, Frank continued.

'Let me start from the beginning; I saw an advertisement for a stock cutter in Forest Gate. The governor who interviewed me in his office was a whisky guzzling, bearded Punjabi. He was knocking back the stuff like it was going out of fashion and when I told him that I had more than twenty years cutting experience he said "excellent, you're just the man I need." Having said that he put his hand in his trouser pocket and pulled out a thick wad of £10 notes; he then began to peel the notes off one by one and slowly placed them in a straight line along the desk. After each note was placed, he would look up at me, it was as if he was trying to read my mind, trying to asses how much I would be prepared to accept. When twelve £10 notes were on the desk, he poured himself another large whisky, tapped his fingers continually on his chest and said "The scotch keeps my lungs warm."

As Frank was about to relate the next episode Jock suddenly intervened 'That Punjabi was a moron, if you were an opportunist, you could have grabbed the cash and ran.'

Frank chuckled before answering him, 'Believe me, if I had known what a snide he was, I would have snatched the money and done a runner.'

Still chuckling, Frank continued 'The governor asked me, what was the total amount on the desk; when I said £120 he gathered up the money and said "That is the wage I am offering you for forty five hours a week. If you are interested you can start work immediately."

I tried to visualise myself or Jock being in Frank's position sitting in that office. The moment the Punjabi started playing his money games I would have wished him good morning and left. Jock, who was over six foot tall, powerfully built and possessing an uncontrollable temper, would probably have left his mark on the Punjabi's bearded chin.

Frank explained that he accepted the offer and began work that same morning. He described the cutting area, which was in a corner of a large machining room, as spacious and clean and cutting the skirts and slacks was a 'piece of cake.' The staff were predominantly Asian and there was little contact with them.

The only criticism Frank had of his five days spent in that factory was having to listen to the incessant 'Tuneless' Indian music which was relayed across the factory floor throughout the day.

'And now for the crunch.' said Frank who took a deep breath before speaking.

'When I was given my wages on the Friday evening, I found that there was only two thirds of my agreed salary inside. Obviously a mistake had been made so I spoke to the governor in his office, but do you know what the blighter said, while drinking his whisky; he had the audacity to say; it wasn't an error at all, he had simply forgotten to mention that when he interviewed me for the job, he would only pay me two thirds of my wages, the remaining third, I would receive when I sign on at the Social Security office. Well I was bloody furious. Why should I have to sign on and be a cheat? I have never signed on in my life, never needed to.'

'I hope you shoved your fist down his gullet,' said Jock clenching his fist.

'It wasn't necessary' replied Frank.

'When I threatened to call the police, he nearly choked on his whisky.'

It seems that the threat worked. The governor immediately dipped into his pocket, gave Frank £40 and quickly escorted him off the premises.

Frank's unfortunate episode seemed to have affected him permanently. Unable to find a suitable Jewish employer and convinced that all foreign factory owners were 'crooks,' he decided to give up stock cutting and become a London mini-cab driver.

I too had applied for a stock cutting vacancy at an Asian owned factory in Forest Gate.

Mr Singh, the bespectacled proprietor, interviewed me in the cutting room where two turbaned youths were laying up fabric. At another table an elderly Asian man, long past retirement age, was struggling to cut out a huge lay. The cutting room was unusually warm; most cutting rooms that I worked at had little or no heating. I undid my coat buttons.

Leaning on one of the disused cutting tables and stroking his beard, Singh asked me how long had I been in the trade.

I replied in a self assured tone. 'About 25 years, ever since I left school.'

Seemingly impressed with my answer, he stopped stroking his beard, straightened himself up and said, '25 years' experience, that's a very good record.'

Before continuing, he glared disapprovingly at the two youths who were quietly chatting as they worked. The order which he shouted at them in Punjabi had an immediate effect, they became silent.

Singh explained that he was an outworker who manufactured cheap dresses for fashion warehouses in the Whitechapel area.

In Jock's dictionary and now mine, cheap dresses meant cheap wages. Any interest I might have had in working for Singh promptly disappeared. Out of politeness, I decided to give him just a few minutes more of my time before making a hasty departure.

He guided me past the cutting tables; we stopped outside the open door of the machining room where I peered inside. There may have been about thirty Asian workers. The flat and special machinists were all women, and the pressers, numbering about four, were men.

With hands on hips, Singh stood by the door for a moment and gazed momentarily around the machining room. After removing his thick-rimmed glasses; he turned to face me and said 'We are a family business; my wife, my sisters, my father and mother-in-law all work here. I am also planning to open a factory in India, as you know in India we have a stable labour market and production costs are low.'

His business aspirations meant little to me. We walked across the cutting room where Singh again leant on one of the cutting tables. I looked at my watch a second time and calculated that if I left immediately, it would take me about thirty minutes to reach the Star Agency at Aldgate East. Periodically I would visit the agency to see if they had any interesting stock cutting vacancies on their books.

I would have thought that my nonchalant expression and the fastening of my coat buttons and the repeated glances at my watch were obvious signs that I had no intention of working for him, but I was wrong, because he offered me the job.

'I expect my cutters to work from 8 a.m. to 6 p.m. Monday to Friday and on Saturday from 8 a.m. to 1 p.m. You will make the markers for your own dockets, and also markers for the other cutters too; and I would like you to continually check their work. I cannot afford to have mistakes made in the cutting room, and don't be afraid to tell the boys to be quiet if they do start talking. The salary for the position is £90 per week, which I can assure you is comparable to what other cutters receive in Katherine Road. Also I expect you to work two weeks in hand.'

I began to feel extremely angry listening to him. £90 a week was the salary which I was earning a decade earlier. Only a cutter in dire straights would have been interested in accepting his ludicrous, insulting offer. Rather than react in a rude or abusive manner, I decided to be sarcastic instead.

'You are too generous Mr Singh. I would have been quite prepared to have worked not just two but six weeks in hand and £90 is a very good wage for only five and a half days work and being in charge of your cutting room. In fact Mr Singh, I have to be honest and admit I am not worth £90 a week. If you had offered me £75 and not £90, which in my case would be a fair wage for my capabilities, I would have gladly accepted the vacancy. So, Mr Singh, I really don't want to take advantage of your generosity, goodbye.'

My sarcasm left him speechless. Having said my piece and impatient to leave, I turned my back on him and walked towards the exit. The two turbaned youths must have been eavesdropping. To stop themselves laughing, their hands were clasped over their mouths.

In the nearby Romford Road, I boarded the number 25 bus to Aldgate East.

Jock had similar encounters with ghastly employers. Although he preferred working for the Turks, 'they always pay a fair wage,' he had a strong aversion to working for Greek Cypriots.

'Never let the bubble and squeaks, retain your wages for more than one day Alf, always insist that you are paid at the end of each working day.'

One of Jock's memorable encounters occurred at a Hackney dress factory. He had been promised three weeks work, but at the end of the first week he was told by his boss, a Nicosia born Greek, that as the standard of his cutting was unsatisfactory he need not complete the remaining two weeks.

Jock, a highly skilled and methodical cutter, instantly demanded to know why his work was unsatisfactory. The answer he received was astonishing, he was accused of cutting a sleeve 1 inch short on its length.

'That is impossible,' retorted Jock. 'If a mistake has occurred, it must have been caused by one of your other cutters.'

The boss refused to listen and attempted to guide him towards the exit, but Jock refused to move until he had checked the cash inside his paper thin wage packet.

Sensing Jock's growing anger and fearing being physically attacked, the Greek beckoned to his son who was also a stock cutter. The son hurried to his father's side.

Opening the wage packet, Jock was shocked to discover that he had only been paid for three days work and not five. With the greatest of difficulty he managed to contain his rage. Speaking calmly, he insisted that he would remain by the cutting table until he was shown proof of his mistake, and furthermore why had he only been paid for three days work.

Realising that Jock wanted answers, the Greek cautiously said "It is impossible to show you proof of your mistake, as new sleeves have already been cut, and the garments are now in production; regarding the two days loss of pay; the deducted money had to be used to purchase fabric to recut new sleeves."

Jock demanded to know why he had not been informed when the mistake was first discovered.

The Greek's son who, like his father, spoke faultless English, explained "Because that particular style had been cut by several of our cutters, it was difficult at first to ascertain who had cut the sleeve 1 inch shorter, but by a process of elimination, we were able to confirm that it was your work."

Jock finally snapped. 'Process of elimination my arse. I will prove to you two bubble and squeaks that I did not make a mistake and after that, I want an apology, and my two days wages which you owe me.'

Unknown to the father and son, Jock had a trump card. Like many conscientious cutters he always recorded his work for future reference. After cutting out a lay of garments, he would keep the paper patterns from the markers, roll them up, sign and date them and then store them under the cutting table. This simple but effective measure was essential. If a problem arose during the machining of the garments, for example if important nips were missing or had been cut to deep, or parts of the garments were cut badly, a cutter could check his stored paper patterns to see if his cutting was the cause of the ill fitting garments.

With a bewildered father and his now slightly nervous son standing next to him, Jock bent down and pulled out from under the cutting table the rolled up paper patterns, he quickly unwound the paper and removed the sleeve patterns.

'Now see for yourselves' snarled Jock.

With the evidence displayed in front of them, the Greeks carefully examined the sleeve patterns. It took them less than a minute to establish that none of the sleeves had been cut 1 inch shorter.

Moving a little distance away from the cutting table the two men began to converse in Greek. Suddenly the father became visibly annoyed and began to raise his voice. After giving his son a protracted stare, he stretched out his arm and with his finger pointed towards the office. Lowering his head, the son obeyed his father and went inside the office and closed the door.

The boss came over to Jock and instantly apologised for the 'inconvenience'.

For my friend's inconvenience, he was given £100, which was more than sufficient for the deducted two days pay.

As Jock walked towards the exit he noticed the now grim faced boss snatch a wooden yardstick from the cutting table before going into the office.

Still analysing the unpleasant situation which had given him much grief, Jock thought that it was possible it may have been the son who had accidentally cut one of the sleeves 1 inch shorter and, fearing punishment from his father had attempted to blame him.

'Perhaps a good smack with that yardstick taught the son a lesson' remarked Jock with a grin.

It was Jock who, a decade earlier, had advised me to record my work whenever possible. This sound advice had proved invaluable. There had been a few occasions over the years when I would have to refer to my saved paper patterns to settle disputes.

'Irish Mick' was a talented freelance cutter and pattern grader. Mick had no qualms about working for Cypriots. In fact he rather enjoyed working for them. Whenever he needed work he would make his way to the offices of 'Verma', a Greek weekly newspaper which was situated in Kingsland Road, Dalston. He knew that if he visited the Verma premises on the evening before the newspaper's latest edition was distributed to their outlets a copy of this edition would be freely available to be read by the public in the Verma's reception area.

Mick understood a little Greek, just sufficient to scan the advertisement page to see what clothing companies were seeking stock cutters. Having access to the latest vacancies, he was able to contact prospective employers in advance before other out-of-work cutters.

Mick used his ingenuity in another way, which I thought wrong. If he was working in the Whitechapel area and wanted a cheap meal, he would pose as a patient's relative and visit the London Hospital's restaurant. This subsidised restaurant was for hospital staff and visiting family and friends of patients, certainly not for members of the public. Mick tried to persuade me to accompany him to the restaurant but I politely refused. My excuse was that I had already bought onion bhajis at Shalamar's, the local Asian take-away.

Zandos the Greek

I had known 60-year-old Zandos, a Greek Cypriot dressmaker, ever since he began sub-contracting for Pridewear, in the late 1960s. As Pridewear's cutting room manager, I was responsible for allocating dockets to about twelve Greek and Turkish sub-contractors.

Zandos was a forceful character, forever impatient and incredibly rude. Whenever he came into the cutting room he would expect immediate attention, even if I was speaking on the telephone he would stand next to me and continually tut-tut; he would also attempt to jump the queue. Ignoring other sub-contractors who were waiting patiently to collect their dockets and fabric, he would insist on being given priority.

Because the quality of his production was acceptable and he was a reliable manufacturer, I had to tolerate his bad manners.

During my last few final weeks at Pridewear I had the prescience to give my phone number to all of the sub-contractors, with a suggestion that if they ever needed some occasional part-time cutting done, they could contact me. A few did take up my offer and one of them was Zandos.

It was quite early on a Monday morning when I received an urgent phone call from him. He explained that his regular cutter was ill and could I please come at once and help out at his factory. He offered me five days work at £5. per hour. He agreed, (though I sensed reluctantly) to my requirement that I would receive my wages at the end of each working day. With some trepidation, I took the underground to Camden where Zandos's factory was situated.

Camden was some distance from Tower Hamlets, which was my preferred working area, but for one week only I was willing to make the daily journey to North London.

Zandos's factory was formerly a shop. Its ground floor cutting room seemed to be in a good condition; the walls were whitewashed, the floor was well swept and there was adequate lighting and no mousey smell, but the 15 foot long wooden cutting table was old and had extremely rough edges which could cause irritating splinters. The machining room situated on the first floor was previously two rooms which had been extended by removing the dividing wall.

Throughout the 1960s and 70s there may have been scores of Cypriot dressmaking sub-contractors in north London, but following the decline in garment manufacturing in Britain the majority of these small companies went out of business.

As Zandos had limited knowledge of garment manufacturing, the production was left to his efficient wife. The only tasks that Zandos undertook in the factory were assisting the cutter to lay wide fabric and helping to remove the cotton ends of the newly pressed dresses.

During the day he was often out of the factory making deliveries of finished garments to his suppliers and visiting his outdoor machinists, and most likely bookmakers and gambling dens too.

At the Zandos's factory the staff consisted of a small team of flat and special machinists and a single presser. The outdoor machinists were Greek and Turkish Cypriots. Many of these home workers were virtually slaves in their own homes. Given no opportunity to learn English they were required by their husbands to machine garments throughout the day and late into the evenings seven days a week. Despite having to work long hours, they still had to find the time to care for their children and do the housework.

I once visited a Turkish Cypriot family living in Walthamstow. It was about 9 p.m. While Haniffa sat at the sewing machine, her husband was sprawled out on a sofa leisurely smoking a cigarette. The moment I entered the living room, Haniffa looked up at me and smiled. Noticing her stopping work for just a second, the husband instantly snapped his fingers. The poor woman, who was in her mid sixties, immediately looked down and continued to machine the garment.

I arrived at Zandos's factory at 8 a.m. He was in a desperate situation, a docket of 500 dresses needed to be cut quickly 'because my machinists need work at once'.

When I began to examine the dress sample and its patterns to see if no parts were missing, he became impatient and began to pressurise me to start making the marker.

I explained to Zandos, that it was absolutely essential he allowed me just five minutes to familiarise myself with the sample and patterns. He reacted by tut-tuting before going up the stairs to the machining room.

With Zandos out of the way, I began making a marker for three dresses. The fabric was 60 inches wide.

I spent approximately an hour to make the marker; I also achieved a tight costin, which was much less than the costin allowed by Zandos's supplier. It took me just a few minutes to calculate that my costin would give Zandos about 100 yards of extra fabric.

Just as I expected, I received no acknowledgment from Zandos when I told him about the saving on the costin. Instead he urged me to start laying the fabric immediately, adding that he would be my assistant. Short, rotund, slow and clumsy, he soon proved to be a hindrance rather than a help. Periodically, his face would become a little distorted and he would stand still for a moment and rub his shoulder; I suspected that he suffered from angina.

As we layed up the fabric, he began reminiscing about his upbringing in 1930s Cyprus.

During the Second World War he served in the British army, but soon found himself behind bars after being involved in a knife fight with a fellow soldier.

Zandos allowed me a 15 minute lunch break, which was just sufficient time to consume my feta cheese sandwich, kindly supplied by his wife.

During the break and while Zandos had momentarily left the cutting room, his wife told me that she was deeply concerned about her husbands health. The previous year he had suffered a slight coronary thrombosis. He would never listen to her and refused to accept that his health was failing. She had tried unsuccessfully to persuade him to loose weight, stop smoking and think seriously about retiring and resettling in Cyprus.

After lunch, Zandos implored me to stay late and cut and bundle the dresses, so that his staff would have work the following morning.

In my haste to cut out the lay, I nipped the top of my finger. The cut was not deep or painful, but it caused a trickle of blood. I asked Zandos if he had a plaster.

He quickly examined my finger and remarked 'It's only a scratch, just carry on.'

'It might only be a scratch' I explained, 'But if the blood drops on the lay and marks the dresses, I won't be held responsible.' My warning was effective, he went into the machining room where the first aid cabinet was kept and returned with his wife who placed a small plaster over the cut.

Once they left the cutting room, I quickly used a steel T pin to remove a sharp wooden splinter from my thumb. Splinters from the rough edged cutting table must have caused many a cutter in the past to yelp in pain.

At 8 p.m. I finally stopped working. The day had gone well. With a great deal of effort I had managed to cut out the lay and had divided the parts into bundles of approximately ten dresses. Zandos helped me to carry the bundles into the machining room where we placed them into the overlockers work bins.

Excluding the 15 minute lunch break, I had worked continually for nearly 12 hours. A simple calculation told me that I had earned about £60. With this figure in mind, I went over to Zandos to collect my money, but this money was not forthcoming when I asked him to 'Settle up.'

'Payday is usually on a Friday, not Monday,' he snapped.

I reminded him that we had an agreement, which he must honour.

'What agreement?' he replied slyly.

I answered him firmly, 'you agreed with my prior condition, that I would receive wages on a daily basis.'

He responded by deliberately lying. 'There seems to be a misunderstanding, I actually said, if I had some spare cash I would pay you daily, but at the moment I don't have any spare cash, and I was too busy today to draw cash from the bank. Can't you wait until Friday?'

As a Cypriot clothing manufacturer Zandos was no exception. The ability and readiness of these people to be devious was legendary, although his excuse for not going to the bank was probably genuine. For much of the day he had remained in the factory, but I knew for certain he had sufficient cash in his wallet to pay my fee. Earlier in the day I saw Monty, a well known cabbage buyer, come into the cutting room. Cabbage buyers always pay cash for their purchase. Shortly afterwards Monty left with dozens of Zandos's cabbage.

Zandos suddenly decided that our conversation must end. He put on his jacket and hat and quickly removed keys from his pocket. I waited while he locked the factory. Outside in the street, his departing words were 'be here at eight in the morning'.

As I headed towards Camden underground, I tried to determine why Zandos had not kept his word. There were several possible reasons, but the most likely was that he had become concerned that if he had paid me the £60 and realising how hard I had worked, I would neither have the energy or enthusiasm to come back the next day. By withholding payment I would be compelled to continue working for the remaining four days.

Zandos was extremely lucky that he wasn't dealing with a cutter like Jock. My Scottish friend would never have left the premises if he had found himself in a similar predicament. Had Zandos attempted to forcibly evict him, Jock would have gone berserk.

The following Tuesday and Wednesday, which I spent at Zandos's factory, were less arduous than Monday's heavy work load. During these two days Zandos spent long periods away from the cutting room. His absence was welcome as it enabled me to cut the dresses at a slower and safer rate, unlike the previous Monday when I was working at a fast and dangerous pace.

If Zandos was unable to assist me to lay the fabric, I was assigned an obese, sweaty cotton cleaner who spoke limited English. Despite her size, she was sprightly on her feet. Thankfully, she had to work at the opposite side of the wide cutting table, thus sparing me the ordeal of having to inhale her garlicky body odour and awful halitosis.

On the Wednesday I managed to leave Zandos's factory earlier than my usual

8 p.m.

At Camden underground, I boarded a northern line train to Liverpool Street where David Upson would be waiting for me at Dirty Dick's.

During the late 1960s when Dave had worked with me at Pridewear he often had to carry heavy rolls of fabric from the cutting room to Zandos's van parked outside the factory.

Dave disliked the Greek, whom he described as 'arrogant and discourteous'.

Unlike Zandos, the majority of the other sub-contractors carried their own fabric or sacks of cut bundles.

If Dave did assist them with their humping, they were always grateful and sometimes my friend would receive a small gratuity for his efforts. Never once did Zandos say thanks to Dave for his assistance.

In between drinking my cool beer I explained to Dave how Zandos had welshed on me. Moreover, I was becoming concerned that the unsavoury Greek might attempt to withhold my fee, which I was hoping to receive the following Friday.

Dave raised his eyebrows and shook his head.

'I am afraid Alf, there is a possibility he might just do that.'

Aware that I had a 'short fuse,' he added, 'if Zandos does try to defer payment, be assertive and polite and insist that he must pay you your money, but do not threaten or whack him. If you do use those tactics, ultimately you might not receive a penny.' Sound advice of course, but in my case, Dave's words of wisdom may not be adhered to. Suddenly my personal problems were put aside; a party of Scandinavian tourist entered the bar. A group of them, which included several good looking females sat down at our long table. Dave immediately engaged them in a conversation.

As I approached Zandos's factory the following morning, I noticed him walking towards his van with a stranger. The two men seemed to be in high spirits. When Zandos spotted me a little distance away, the grin disappeared from his face. He waved his hand at me dismissively and shouted 'Not today, come back tomorrow.' I had no chance to reply; he quickly got into the van with the stranger and drove off. Once the van went around the corner I changed direction and headed towards Camden underground station.

As I walked along the busy main road, I began to feel extremely annoyed with the thoughtless Zandos. If he did not require my services that day he should have notified me the previous evening. My losing a days work meant little to Zandos. During the afternoon I managed to speak to him on the telephone; he hurriedly explained that because his regular cutter had made a recovery and was now back at work, my assistance was not required. As expected there was no apology for wasting my time; no offer of a refund for the cost of travelling to and from Camden and no mention of when I would receive my wages. With the greatest of effort, I managed to suppress my anger, but only just. I spoke calmly

'And when can I collect my wages?'

There was a pause before he answered me.

'Give me a call, sometime next week.'

His answer infuriated me and I deliberately enunciated my words in a slight threatening tone.

'Listen mate, I am coming to your factory right now and I want my money when I arrive.'

I did not wait for Zandos's response; instead, I replaced the receiver.

Within the hour I rang Zandos's factory doorbell.

A thin, gaunt Greek man in his mid thirties opened the door. The small apron around his waist indicated he was a cutter.

His English was perfect and he spoke politely 'Mr Zandos is out at the moment, can I help you?'

I brushed past him uttering in the process 'I am prepared to wait.'

The cutter made no attempt to persuade me to leave the cutting room. Instead he pointed to a stool and said

'You better sit there.'

Mrs Zandos came into the cutting room; she seemed genuinely surprised when she saw me.

'We did not expect to see you today Alfred, is there something wrong?'

Although, I would have preferred not to have mentioned my grievances to her, I was unable to control my frustration, ignoring the Greek cutter and the cotton cleaner assistant who was helping him to lay the fabric, I spoke in a forceful tone.

'Yes Mrs Zandos, there is something wrong here, your husband has not been fair with me and I really do not want to list my complaints, all I want is my three days money.'

She seemed confused. 'I thought my husband had paid you.'

I answered her irritably. 'No he has not and I have every reason to believe he is in no hurry to pay me.'

She cast her eyes downwards, which suggested to me that witnessing angry workers who were upset over her husband's actions, was not a new experience.

Collecting her thoughts she said 'Unfortunately, my husband is away until the afternoon, but I can contact him on the telephone.'

I sighed deeply before saying 'Would you please do that at once'.

She went up the stairs to the machining room, presumably to make the call. The cotton cleaner who had just finished assisting the cutter followed her.

Immediately after the two women left the cutting room, the cutter leant on the table, lit up a cigarette and said 'Zandos often keeps me waiting for my money too, I am sure he goes to the casino'.

'Why do you stay here?' I replied. 'There are other Cypriot factories in the area.'

He looked towards the stairs before whispering 'I know there are, but I can't leave until Zandos pays me all what I am owed. He is smart, by retaining your previous week's wages; you're committed to work for him.'

Our conversation suddenly ended; footsteps could be heard coming down the stairs. The cutter quickly switched on the Eastman cutting machine. Mrs Zandos came into the cutting room and asked me to speak to her husband on the telephone.

Inside the noisy machining room I picked up the receiver.

Zandos's tone was sharp. 'I thought I told you to come next week for your money.'

My tone was even sharper. 'And I told you, I am coming today to collect my three days pay, where is it.'

'Let me speak to my wife.' He demanded.

I handed the receiver to his anxious wife who immediately began to argue with Zandos.

After several minutes, she placed her hand over the mouthpiece; turning to face me, she said 'My husband wants to know would you accept a cheque.'

My reply was absolute, 'No, I want cash, as agreed.'

She relayed my answer; but this time the conversation was brief.

After replacing the receiver and without saying a word to me, she dipped her hand into a work box adjacent to her overlocking machine and brought out a handbag concealed at the bottom.

'My husband has told me to pay you your money Alfred, how much is it?' She looked and spoke wearily.

I handed her a note which listed the daily hours I had worked. The total was 32 hours at £5.per hour.

She began to calculate my figures.

'Its £160, is that correct Alfred?'

'Yes that is correct Mrs Zandos, thank you.'

She sat down at her overlooking machine and removed some cash from her handbag.

After counting the notes she looked up at me and said 'Alfred, I only seem to have £150, would you mind accepting this amount and when you come next time my husband will give you the £10.'

Having no intention of ever working for Zandos again, I was prepared to forfeit the £10.

I took the money from her and quickly left the machining room.

As I passed through the cutting room, I gave the thumbs up sign to the cutter.

A few days later and to my utter astonishment, I received a frantic phone call from Zandos.

'Alfie, listen my friend, you must come at once; my useless cutter is ill again and my machinists need cut work now, please come Alfie, you are my friend.'

On reflection, my response to his appeal was unnecessary cruel, though at the time it gave me some satisfaction. I told him to 'fuck off and don't ever phone me again'.

Within seconds of my replacing the telephone he phoned back. Seemingly oblivious to my abusive language, he pleaded 'Alfie, Alfie, please don't let me down, come now.'

I bluntly explained to him that under no circumstances would I ever step inside his factory again and that my decision was final.

Resigning himself to the fact that I was uncooperative, he asked me if I knew of another cutter whom I could recommend. I knew several very experienced cutters, but it would have been irresponsible of me to have given him their telephone numbers. All I could do was to suggest to Zandos that he should contact the Greek-Cypriot Clothing Manufacturers Association to see if they had any stock cutters available.

Without saying thank you for my suggestion, he slammed his receiver down.

I soon found part-time work cutting ladies trouser suits at a Turkish factory at Shore Road, Hackney.

The company employed about 30 workers, most of whom were Turkish. My job entailed laying fabric, stock cutting and bundling. I was exempted from making markers because the company had their own marker maker. This was good news, full time marker makers usually produced excellent markers, but I would still follow my standard practise of carefully checking markers not made by myself. Even the most skilful marker maker was not infallible.

Much to my surprise, there was a small mistake on my very first marker; a single shaped pocket flap did not pair. Tactfulness had to be applied when pointing out the error to Omar the marker maker. I had no idea how he would react. Hopefully he would be grateful that I had spotted the mistake, but he could respond in a tart way, (as some marker-makers had done in the past) suggesting that I should just rectify the error myself and not disturb him. I took the marker over to Omar's table and spoke politely; 'I am afraid Omar there is a small mistake with your marker.'

Omar, who was in his early twenties, was surprised and pleased that I had taken the time to examine his marker and to inform him about the mistake. Within seconds he reversed the flap. Thereafter he would call me 'Agabey.' (pronounced Arbi) I thought Agabey was Turkish for Alfie, but Faisal, who assisted me to lay the fabric and spoke perfect English, explained that Agabey was a term of respect for an older person.

Amongst the staff I noticed two Jewish workers. Both men were in their early sixties, short and thick set.

One of them, Joe, seemed to be a technical adviser. Carrying a tape measure he would spend much of the day walking around the factory floor constantly examining the machinists work. Unlike Joe, who was bald, Bernie had thick grey wavy hair. He was a very experienced machinist and sometimes other machinists working at the same bench would lean across to him and ask for his advice.

Faisal told me that Bernie and Joe did not like each other. He related a recent incident. Bernie had passed out at his sewing machine and other staff attempted to revive him. Joe, alerted by the commotion went to investigate. Looming over the collapsed Bernie he remarked coldly, 'Is he dead?'

Far from being dead Bernie opened his eyes, looked up at Joe and replied angrily 'Not yet, you shmuck.' (Vulgar Yiddish word, meaning stupid ass, prick)

I tried to hazard a guess as to what had caused this mutual animosity. Could it be that prior to working for the Turks the two men were former businessmen. It was certainly possible that Joe the technical adviser and Bernie a very experienced machinist may have been clothing factory proprietors. Perhaps they were rivals; they may have even been in partnership together and had fallen out.

Bernie spoke to me during a lunch break. He wanted to know if I was Jewish; when I replied that I was a gentile, he immediately asked me if I had ever worked for Jewish people. I explained that after I left school in 1956, I spent four happy and beneficial years working for the Jewish brothers Alfie and Barney Hyams at their Bethnal Green factory and that it was Barney who taught me how to cut garments and make markers. I also mentioned that even though 20 years had passed since I left their employ, I was still in contact with them.

Satisfied that I liked Jewish people, Bernie wanted to continue with our conversation. Being of a diminutive statue, he grabbed a small stool, which he stood on and lifted himself up onto the cutting table and sat next to me. For a brief moment, he glanced menacingly at Joe who was seated eating a sandwich by the pressing units. I wondered what truculent thoughts were circulating inside Bernie's brain.

After Faisal, who was also sitting next to us on the cutting table, finished eating a kebab, he lit up a cigarette and went over to the coffee machine where his workmates were smoking and chatting.

Faisal's departure was welcomed by Bernie, who could now freely air his grievances. His tone was caustic.

'I hate working here for these Turks, they came to this country without a penny to their name, or a pot to piss in, but in next to no time they have their own factory; they have undercut my people and pushed us out of the trade. Give these Turks a job; I wouldn't let them clean my toilet.'

Defending the Turks, I suggested to Bernie it was the same scenario in every country where poor immigrants had settled; certain sections of the indigenous population would always accuse immigrants of job stealing. Bernie dismissed my suggestion.

'You're totally wrong Alfred, we Jews never stole work from anybody, and we always created jobs in every country we migrated to.'

Before continuing, Bernie crossed his legs, clasped his hands around his knee and discreetly pointed his thumb at Joe who was still sitting by the pressing units.

'Take that shtoonk (Stinker) all he does is suck up to the Turks; he should be ashamed of himself.'

With just minutes left before the lunch break was over, I managed to ask Bernie just one question; it was probably the only question that could be asked in such circumstances.

'If you are not happy working for the Turks, why not find a job elsewhere?'

Bernie uncrossed his legs. Before gently lowered himself from the cutting table he said 'Where can I go. All the Jewish factories are closing down, I will just have to carry on in this karsy for a year or two before I retire; then I am away from Hackney for good. My wife and I want to move to Bournemouth.'

I thought Bernie was an embittered man who was incapable of being reasonable. He was ready to accuse the enterprising and energetic Turks of forcing the Jews out of the clothing trade, but failed to realise that a hundred years previously English factory workers in London's East End had accused the recently arrived Jewish immigrants of forcing them out of their jobs by accepting lower wages.

Besides being embittered, Bernie was a hypocrite. He despised the Turks, yet he was quite willing to work for them. He should have considered himself lucky that he had a job, which I assumed he could remain at until retirement, providing of course his employers did not follow the usual pattern of their countrymen of deliberately declaring themselves insolvent. No doubt the wages he was receiving were reasonably satisfactory. He also lived nearby, which enabled him to walk to work and not rely on public transport, but most importantly, he should have tried to suppress his internal rage. Maybe it was the same rage that had caused him to collapse at his sewing machine.

Joe would eventually speak to me too, but not at the factory. We met in Well Street one morning, on our way to work.

Whereas Bernie was intense and agitated, Joe was the opposite; throughout the day he always seemed relaxed as he worked.

As we approached the factory, Joe explained that as he lived locally, the job was 'handy'. He then surprised me by mentioning Bernie's name.

'I saw you the other day talking to that grumpy old shneider Bernie. (Shneider is Yiddish for tailor.) Do you know, I have known that man for years and he has never said a kind word about anybody in his life? I bet he criticised me too.'

It made sense for me to remain impartial, but I did say 'I can assure you Joe, whatever Bernie disclosed to me, it went in one ear and out of the other.'

I immediately changed the subject 'Tell me Joe how long have you worked at the factory?'

After a momentarily pause he said 'Probably about 18 months, I used to have my own smutter business, but it didn't pay any more'.

I asked him how he felt working for the Turks.

He replied cheerfully 'I have no complaints whatsoever. Hopefully, if I remain fit, I can stay on until I retire.' He also said, 'Because I have a lot of experience in the trade, they pay me a good salary, and they leave me alone to get on with the job, which I appreciate. I suppose the only problem that I do have is that not all of the Turks speak good English, but they are an incredibly hardworking, uncomplaining people, they just want to work all the time. It's not 8.30 to 5.30 Monday to Friday for these people, they want to work seven days a week, every one of those machinist would stay until midnight if they could.'

He sighed before continuing; 'If only I had Turkish staff when I had my factory, I would have been a millionaire today. Instead of having a two week annual holiday at Westcliffe-on-Sea I could have had my beach apartment in Florida.'

I totally agreed with Joe that the Turks were an exceptionally hard working people.

I could not recall a single instance when Turkish workmates expressed any complaints whatsoever about poor working conditions or the low wages which they sometimes received.

However, the Turks were not totally immune from complaining. They did have one deep-rooted complaint which seemed to be widespread among their community.

Because they were rarely employed in Turkey, they were never subjected to paying income tax, but now in London and working, income tax was being deducted from their wages. A further grievance was that they had no say in the matter.

Time and time again over the years, I had witnessed Turks expressing their abhorrence of the taxman.

Even the Turkish workers Jock spoke to seem to have felt the same way. Their wages was sacrosanct; nobody had the right to deduct any tax from their earnings. Yet, almost to a man, their attitude to valued added tax was the opposite to their loathing of personal income tax.

My Turkish workmates all seemed to agree that even if the VAT rate was 20, 30 or 50 per cent on goods purchased they would not object. I did from time to time, attempt to explain to the Turks that with out income tax there would be insufficient funds for schools, hospitals, social services and the armed forces, but they were not prepared to listen; their argument was that funds for government spending should be raised only by VAT and that tax deducted from wages should be abolished.

A remark by Salem a young Turkish presser was typical; 'If our wages were tax free, then we will have more money to spend on goods, surely that makes sense.'

After my short tenure at the Turkish factory was over, I found temporary freelance work at several Cypriot factories in the Hackney area. Each engagement lasted between two and five days. My fees were never in excess of £5 an hour.

In one of these factories at Dalston Junction I met Nic, who was born in London of Greek Cypriot parents.

Nic was the production manager and besides being an experienced presser he could operate every one of the special sewing machines with ease – but his knowledge of stock cutting was limited. He seemed to be a capable mechanic too. If a machinist's sewing machine had ceased up, Nic would be summoned to repair it.

I thought it inevitable that Nic, who was about 30 years of age, would eventually have his own business. He was competent, self assured and had vast knowledge of clothing production.

Periodically, he would glance at me as I worked. Why he did so, I was unsure.

It was a Friday morning and my last day at the factory. Nic came over to the cutting table during the tea break. He wanted to know where I went for food at lunch time.

'At Tanzi's Italian café.' I replied.

He smiled as he spoke. 'Not today Alf, I am going to buy you a meal at the pub.'

I grinned and replied 'You are.'

'Yes, at 1p.m. sharp.'

Before I had a chance to ask him why he wanted to buy me a meal, he turned around and walked away.

Nic's invitation left me intrigued; I was not his friend or even an acquaintance but a temporary stock cutter who he would probably have no further contact with after my short assignment at the factory was over. Obviously, he had a separate motive in inviting me to lunch. Not for one moment did I believe he was just in a generous mood.

At 1 p.m. Nic and I left the factory together. He suggested that we visit the nearby Crown & Castle in Dalston Lane.

For the past hour I had felt exceptionally hungry. Usually a couple of ham or cheese rolls at Tanzi's café would be an adequate lunch, but the thought of a hot wholesome meal at the pub had increased my hunger pangs.

The mixed grill was superb and Nic also bought our drinks. As I would be cutting that afternoon, fruit drinks were preferable to beer.

Sitting quite relaxed and smoking a cigarette, Nic remarked 'Alf, I like the way you carefully handle the cloth when you lay up.'

'Well its my long arms' I joked.

Nic went on to say that several of his machinists had told him that the new cutter's work was very clean and they had had no problems whatsoever with the nips.

I replied appreciatively, 'That's very kind of them.'

He explained that ever since he had become production manager at the dress factory, a succession of inexperienced stock cutters had given him a continuous 'headache'. Although there had been numerous 'cock ups' in the cutting room, some of which were serious, it was the badly nipped bodices that had created havoc with the garments measurements.

Nic looked at his watch. He was now ready to explain the reason why he had invited me to lunch. Although, I was virtually a stranger to him, he spoke candidly.

'During your week with us Alf, I suppose I gave you the impression that I was satisfied with my job. Well I can tell you, I am not. The boss has got me on the cheap and he has not kept his word. I never received the wage increase or the bonus he promised and I am concerned that he might suddenly shut down the factory and leave me and the staff without any wages.'

He smiled and said 'Don't worry Alf; I will make sure that you get your fee tonight, even if I have to pay you out of my own pocket.'

His frankness impressed me. I felt that he was a man who would keep his word.

Suddenly two Greek looking men sat on an adjacent table. Their presence seemed to concern Nic, so we finished our drinks and left the pub.

As we walked down Kingsland Road towards the factory he revealed his future plans.

'Alf what I am telling you next is confidential, just between you and me; unknown to the boss, I am at the moment in the process of renting a fully fitted dress factory in Richmond Road. My brothers will be working for me too; one of them is a presser and the other a special machinist and I know dozens of indoor and outdoor flat machinists I should be able to persuade to work for me, but most importantly, I need an experienced, conscientious stock cutter who I can rely on, somebody who would cut accurately and not give me a headache. Alf I believe that person is you; would you be prepared to work for me part time at first and once I am established full time?'

I replied immediately 'Of course.'

'By the way Alf' he added 'I promise to pay you top wages.'

At 5.30 p.m., Nic gave me my wage packet. After he wrote down my phone number, I received an assurance from him that he would give me a call 'within a fortnight'. I did not doubt his sincerity, but I knew from past experience that offers of well paid jobs for top cutters should always be considered with some reservation.

Within a fortnight I received a call from Nic. He asked me to start part-time work at his factory in Star House, 3 Richmond Road, Dalston.

Star House, was an old factory premises situated on a narrow bend in Richmond Road. The front part of the house may have been a pre-Second World War residence. After the war the structure, which was connected to an ancient foundry at its rear, was converted into industrial use. In 1948 the Clevelend Coat Manufacturing Company was the first clothing business to be established at Star House.

Nic's factory was in the basement, adjacent to a railway track. A machining and pressing unit was set up in one of the rooms; another room, oblong in shape was for cutting. This room was in a terrible condition; it had insufficient lighting, no heating and, because of the fractured window frames and holes in the wooden sliding door, which overlooked the railway track, it was extremely draughty. Half of this room was taken up by the cutting table; the remaining space was a dumping area for discarded old remnants and unusable moth eaten rolls of fabric. This massive pile of putrescent detritus was about four foot high. From the moment I entered the basement, I knew that rats or mice were in residence. The smell was awful; having worked in some appalling malodorous factories and workshops ever since leaving school, I had become acutely aware of what I called the mousy smell.

It was late in the afternoon when the rats first appeared. At least half a dozen of them emerged from gaps beneath the detritus. When the rats began to venture close to the cutting table; I raised an aluminium yardstick high above my head and with great force struck the cutting table. The deafening sound sent the rats scurrying back to the detritus, where they darted into the gaps.

I complained to Nic and his brothers about the rats. One brother responded light heartedly. He suggested that as I worked alone in the cutting room, the rats were good company for me. Nic assured me that he would soon remove all of the rubbish and improve the conditions in the cutting room, but he was unable to give me an exact date as his top priority was to find more suppliers who could send him adequate dockets and also to engage extra staff, particularly flat machinists.

I felt disappointed that at the end of my fifth and final day working at Nic's factory, the detritus had not been removed or a pest controller notified. If one of those rarest of creatures a factory inspector had made a surprise visit to the cutting room, he would have instantly ordered Nic to put padlocks on its door.

Nic confirmed that he would phone me in a day or two 'to cut more dockets next week'.

I hoped he would not contact me, as I had already decided never to work in that cutting room again; the conditions were totally unacceptable.

Nic did phone me, but only after several weeks. He was not offering me work, but to explain that his cousin Christos was now his full time cutter and that my services for the time being, were not needed.

Whilst working in the Dalston area, I would sometimes stroll down Ridley Road market at lunch time.

It was during one of these excursions, that I heard my name being called. There standing on the opposite side of the road and grinning was Lui, an old cutting colleague I had not seen since 1970. We walked towards each other, met in the middle of the road and shook hands warmly. A few minutes later we made our way to Tanzi's café in nearby Kingsland High Street.

Opposite Tanzi's, the old Pridewear factory above the Jands Modes shop was still being used for clothing production.

Drinking coffee in the café and reflecting on the past with Lui was an enjoyable experience. Lui was no longer skinny with slightly sunken cheeks. The passing years had been kind to him; he had put on weight, his face was fuller and the pencil thin moustache had enhanced his dark Latin looks. As we chatted, I felt a little envious of him; he seemed to have aged handsomely.

On hearing that I was still a stock cutter, Lui gazed at me in disbelief. Then with sudden intensity he said 'Why do you stay in that lousy, crummy trade Alf, the job is not worth a dime. In the 60s when I was a cutter I was forever broke and always having to borrow money to get by.'

I was occasionally broke too in the early 60s, but rather than borrow money from David Upson, I relied on the pawn shop in Crisp Street market at Poplar.

Lui explained that after leaving the clothing trade a decade before, he had acquired a new skill, roof tiling.

'Since I became a self-employed tiler, life has been swell; I own a nice terrace house, have a decent car and, best of all, I am living with a smashing girl.'

He proceeded to tell me how he had met his smashing girl. His story did seem somewhat incredible, but like David Upson, Lui could be relied on to always tell the truth.

Apparently, he was replacing some broken tiles on the roof of a house of multiple occupation in Islington. All of the bedsitters were let to young females.

'I was careless I thought that the small area I was tiling would support my weight, so I didn't bother to use boards. All of a sudden I slid and fell through the hole which had rotting battens and landed in the loft. Luckily I wasn't hurt to bad, but the racket I made disturbed the girl in the bedsitter directly beneath the loft. as I sat there rubbing my shin, the hatch was raised and the most beautiful face appeared. The girl was Irish, she asked me if I was injured, I said I was okay, but could she give me a glass of water as my mouth was full of dust.'

He chuckled before continuing 'And that's how I met my girl.'

Lui may have been disillusioned with the clothing trade but I remained optimistic that one day I would find a suitable well paid job. Although, at times it could be difficult remaining optimistic; especially after unsuccessfully trudging the streets in the rain and knocking on factory doors enquiring about possible vacancies.

One seemingly paranoid factory proprietor eyed me suspiciously when he answered the door.

'Do you have any vacancies for experienced stock cutters?' I enquired.

Rather than answer my question, he promptly accused me of being 'up to no good'.

'What do you mean up to no good?' I replied angrily.

'You know exactly what I mean up to no good' he snapped.

'Why did you ring my bell and waste my time, have I got a sign up for a cutter, no, did I advertise for a cutter in the Hackney Gazette, no, did the Labour Exchange or the Star Agency send you here, no, so why are you ringing my bell, pretending to look for work are you. I know your type, once you're inside my factory, you start thieving, bugger off.'

I did bugger off, but not before giving him a well directed punch in the mouth.

As I hurried away from the factory, a brief thought flashed through my mind; maybe I should leave the clothing trade and become a roof tiler.

That same evening, I called at David Upson's flat.

With his uncanny instinct, he knew that I had been involved in an incident.

Rather than relate the episode with the factory proprietor in the presence of his mother and sister Barbara, I suggested that we visit his local pub, The Black Prince.

Sitting inside the pub, Dave shook his head.

'It's not like you Alf to resort to violence.'

I admitted to my friend that I had no regrets about giving the factory proprietor a bloody mouth and would do so again, if a similar situation occurred.

Dave concluded by recommending that in future I should only enquire at those factories that were advertising for stock cutters.

During the summer of 1980, I began working at Wearwell Ltd, a clothing company situated in Commercial Road, Stepney.

Wearwell operated from three factories in the road. Two of them manufactured dresses and the third leather garments.

Asil Nadir, the ambitious Turkish Cypriot owner of Wearwell, had recently become the major shareholder of Polly Peck Ltd, a respectable, long-established gown manufacturing company which had fallen on hard times.

Whilst at Wearwell, I became quite pally with Chris, a young Asian cutter. Chris explained that once a year Nadir would invite several of his cutters to spend a couple of months working at a Wearwell owned clothing factory at Famagusta in Cyprus. Chris, who had taken up the offer in the past, advised me not to go.

'They put you up in a little hotel and then you are sent each day to the factory and are expected to work very long hours, money-wise you are no better off than if you had stayed in London.'

Chris may have advised me not to work in Famagusta, but he enthusiastically urged me to buy some Polly Peck shares, 'They are worth about a pound each at the moment, but everybody expects them to soar.' Initially I was tempted to invest £500. but my knowledge of the stock market was limited.

'Buy penny shares instead,' advised David Upson.

'If you do decide to invest in some Polly Peck shares, its possible that you might see your investment rise in value and you could make a lot of money, equally the shares could nosedive, if that happens you will be out of pocket. If you do have any spare cash Alf, I would still recommend that you buy some penny shares.'

I never bought Polly Peck shares or penny shares either. Eighteen months later Polly Peck shares had risen from £1 to an incredible £35. This rapid increase was due to Asil Nadir expanding Polly Peck Holdings into non-textile enterprises in Northern Cyprus and Turkey.

Chris informed me that each week about 30 thousand cut garments were loaded onto a large lorry at the Wearwell factory and delivered overland to Cyprus where they were made up by scores of home machinists in the villages near Famagusta. According to Chris, the wages that these machinists received was 'chicken feed.' The lorry would return to London with the previous week's production. In charge of the Cyprus enterprise was Asil's father Irfan.

Twenty years previously Irfan had left Cyprus and settled in London where he opened a ladies' separates factory. Five years later Asil also became a proprietor of a clothing factory. With boundless energy the youthful Asil rapidly expanded his business. Within a decade Wearwell had become one of the most successful clothing companies in Stepney, with a huge weekly turnover of cheaply made garments mainly due to low production costs in Cyprus.

To increase the cutting production at the Wearwell factory, stock cutters were not allowed to make markers or bundle their cut garments; these tasks were done by other staff.

At first, I found cutting Wearwell's garments reasonably tolerable, but inevitably the daily routine of just laying fabric and cutting had become repetitious and mundane. After about three weeks at the factory I had become so bored that I handed in my notice and left the company.

Throughout the 1980s, Polly Peck/Wearwell were often in the news. Besides clothing manufacture, Asil Nadir was creating new industries in Cyprus and Turkey. In Cyprus a cardboard box making and packaging plant was set up to export citrus fruits. On mainland Turkey electronic goods, including colour televisions, were manufactured and mineral water was being exported to Arab countries. Grandiose plans for car making under licence from Daihatsu were in the pipeline, but Nadir had overreached himself. These enterprises were not well managed and the envisaged profits were not forthcoming. Their viability was also deeply affected by the ever diminishing value of the Turkish Lira. As the shares in Polly Peck began to slide inexorably downwards, major corporate and private investors decided to 'cut and run' and sell their shares in the company.

In 1989 Polly Peck went into liquidation and rather than face his critics and accusations of dishonesty Nadir abandoned London and slipped away clandestinely in the night. Shortly afterwards he emerged in Northern Cyprus where he remained until 2010. That same year Nadir returned to London and is currently awaiting trial.

I met a buoyant Jock at a bus stop near Dalston Junction. He had just finished a lucrative five day stint at a Turkish Cypriot owned dress factory. '300 quid, free kebabs and coffee, not bad Alf, not bad at all.'

I could only gasp at his good fortune. Jock estimated that he had cut approximately 4.000 garments at the Cypriot factory, which was slightly more than I had cut at a neighbouring factory, but the wage I received was a paltry £125. and I had to pay for my own refreshments.

Not only was Jock buoyant he was in a generous mood. He suggested that we meet later that evening at Stratford Broadway and visit the local pubs 'Of course Alf, the booze and the Chinese nosh will be on me.'

Jock's offer was politely refused. I had already arranged to meet Suzanne at her Highbury flatlet.

Jock and I caught the 277 bus which would take us back to the East End. He thought it unlikely that the Turks would recall him in the foreseeable future as their regular cutter had resumed work. Apparently the cutter had sliced his forefinger whilst using the unpopular and sometimes lethal round knife cutting machine. I always tried to avoid this type of cutting machine, nicknamed the 'bacon slicer', but there were occasions when I had to use it. Over the years I did have some minor but painful accidents involving cuts to my fingers but none which required hospital visits. My friend Ronnie Radlett narrowly escaped a serious accident when he was using an Eastman round knife. As he began cutting out a lay of garments the round blade which had a circumference of about 24 inches suddenly came loose and broke off, missing his stomach by inches as it flew across the cutting room and imbedded itself in a wooden door.

Jock thought that the Turkish factory which he had just left was unusual. There were few machining and pressing staff on the premises. It seems that every docket which he had cut and bundled was instantly removed from the factory to be machined elsewhere. 'Possibly Cyprus or Turkey.' At the factory, he also saw quantities of well made ladies and gent's jackets and slacks which had been imported from Istanbul. These garments were immediately collected by Turks with 'gold rings on every finger and driving expensive Mercedes'.

As the bus travelled down Mare Street, Jock suddenly lowered his voice even though no other passengers were sitting close by.

'Alf did you ever see the film The French Connection?'

I replied 'no, but I was aware that the critics had rated it as an excellent thriller.'

Jock proceeded to relate the film's plot, which apparently was based on a true incident.

Drugs were being smuggled into New York via Marseille, hence the French connection.

Ruthless crooks in Marseille had ingeniously concealed heroin inside the bumpers of cars which were being exported to New York. It was not that difficult to detect what was on Jock's mind; he probably felt that those Turks with gold rings were involved in importing drugs into Britain. With an ever increasing number of garments being sent from London to Turkey to be machined, it was an ideal opportunity for narcotics to be hidden amongst the finished garments that were being delivered back to London.

Jock's suspicion may not have been unfounded. The police were well aware of the Turkish connection, and their well planned operations to catch the criminals involved in the racket resulted in a significant number of London based Turkish gangsters being sent to prison, either for drug smuggling, possessing or supplying drugs.

Just before Jock got off the bus at Mile End he said 'Alf, you and me are two of a kind, every week we find ourselves working in different factories and we suspect that some of these enterprises might well be fronts for illegal activities, but we have to earn a living and all we can do is get on with the job and mind our own business.'

The following Monday lunch time, I met Jock in Tanzi's café. His drinking session in the pubs around the Stratford Broadway on the previous Friday had been a disaster; not only did he drink too much whisky and beer, he had eaten a 'dodgy Chinese meal' which caused him to be sick in the gutter.

For much of the Saturday he had suffered a painful hangover which had become even more painful when he realised that in his drunken state somebody had dipped into his pocket and stolen most of his £300 wages.

'I never learn do I Alf,' he remarked woefully.

To help my friend through the week I loaned him £10.

Kingsland Road is a mile and a half long straight road. It begins at Shoreditch in the south and ends at Dalston Junction in the north.

In 1982 there were approximately 30 clothing factories in the road and at least 25 businesses associated with the footwear trade, which included wholesalers, importers and shoemakers. The majority of these clothing and footwear businesses were located on the eastern side of the road.

If I was unemployed and in the Shoreditch area, I would pay a visit to the Department of Employment centre which was situated at the southern end of Kingsland Road, but most of the stock cutting vacancies which were being advertised on their boards were poorly paid.

Adjacent to the employment centre were the offices of HM Inspector of Factories. In 43 years of cutting garments in scores of East and North London factories and workshops, many of which were in a dreadful, unhygienic, rat infested condition, I never saw a single factory or fire prevention officer pay a visit. Perhaps these officers were not entirely to blame for their absence. Many of these unregistered clothing businesses were operating illegally in cellars and rooms of old houses or in rundown workshops in back yards. With no employer's insurance liability, fire escapes or extinguishers, these businesses continued with impunity, but once their presence was detected by the local authorities, the premises would be quickly vacated and the staff and machinery removed to another secret workshop, usually in the same area.

I may have not seen any inspectors, but Jock had. He claimed that he had been present in a number of factories when inspectors had made unannounced visits to inspect the premises safety facilities. He could recall when a few years earlier a combined team of factory and fire service inspectors had raided several hundred clothing factories and workshops in the East End to see how safe the steam boilers were. In nearly a third of the factories the inspectors discovered that there was a danger of faulty boilers exploding. Warnings were instantly given to the factory owners that their boilers must be repaired or replaced.

When the inspectors returned unannounced at a later date to see if their recommendations had been carried out, they noticed that in several of the premises the defective boilers were still in use.

For their irresponsibility the factory owners were summoned to court and heavily fined.

It was unlikely that the dress factory which I worked at in the Kingsland Road was registered.

The factory was inside a large four story house and the cutting room was situated on the top floor. There was no fire exit available.

Having to work in these unsafe old factories, I always preferred the cutting rooms to be above ground level rather than in basements and cellars. Ever since I managed to put out the fire in the Wills dress factory several years previously, I had become acutely aware of the possibility of again being trapped in a cellar cutting room fire. At least by working on the upper floors the windows might be used as a means of escape.

Whenever I found myself working in these above ground level cutting rooms, I was reminded of Hans Christian Andersen.

I had read that Andersen had a perennial fear of perishing in a fire. As he travelled around Europe he often stayed in cheap hotels and less than desirable rooms in ancient houses. It seems that Andersen always kept a large strong rope by his side so that, if a fire did occur on the premises, he could attach the rope to the bed and lower his six foot, six inch frame out of the window. I was not prepared to take a long strong rope with me whenever I worked in cutting rooms which were situated on the upper floors of old houses, All I could do, if there was a fire inside the premises and I was unable to use the stairs to escape would be to use a roll of fabric as a substitute for a rope.

There were probably two dozen staff at the dress factory. The majority were Turks, but there were a few Kurds too.

The Turkish Cypriot proprietor not only spoke perfect English he was also fluent in Greek. I had noticed in the past that many middle-aged Turkish

Cypriots spoke Greek, but Turkish speaking Greeks of a similar age were a rarity. I had also known Turks who could converse in Greek, English and also German. There was usually a pattern why these Cypriots were multi lingual; they had been taught some English at school, and by living in those Cyprus villages which had Turkish and Greek residents they had an opportunity to grasp the Greek language at an early age. Another factor many Turks had worked in post-war Germany when the country suffered a chronic labour shortage.

A young, articulate Kurd named Mustafa ably assisted me to lay fabric.

During the morning break Mustafa and I sat on the cutting table and drank coffee. He explained that ever since the disintegration of the Ottoman Empire following the First World War, millions of Kurdish people who live in the mountains of eastern Turkey, Iran and western Iraq have aspired for an Independent Kurdistan.

Mustafa insisted that he had no quarrel with Turkish people, 'only that fascist government in Ankara'.

There was bitterness in his tone when he continued, 'the Turkish government hate us Kurds and are determined to suppress forever our national aspirations. They even refuse to recognise us as Kurds, they refer to us as Turkish mountain people; they forget that we have our own language, culture and traditions, which is as ancient as their own. The government even want to stop the Kurdish language being taught in schools, but we are not going to be subjugated any longer, we want and need an independent Kurdistan and we want it now.'

Mustafa planned eventually to return to Diyarbakir in eastern Turkey and join the militant Kurdish Workers Party (PKK) and if necessary he would become 'a freedom fighter, for our independence'.

At this point I interrupted him. 'Surely Mustafa, military action should be the very last resort and only if all channels of negotiation have failed.'

He nodded before replying, 'of course you are quite right my friend, but you must understand that the Turkish government will never agree to our aspirations, so we are left with no alternative but to take up arms.' He predicted and deeply regretted that many Kurdish and Turkish lives will be lost during the struggle, but the loss of life had to be accepted if his people were to achieve their independence.

In 1983 the Turkish parliament further outraged the Kurds by introducing an unpopular law which made it illegal for Kurdish to be taught in schools and the country's six million Kurds were forbidden to speak their own language. I suspect that when this law came into effect an outraged Mustafa probably left London and returned to Diyarbaker to support the PKK.

Many lives were indeed lost as Mustafa predicted. During the following 15 years PKK insurgents and the Turkish army were involved in endless, fierce gun battles which resulted in the deaths of more than 30,000 Kurds and Turks.

'New Image'

During the summer of 1983, I was to learn that Ellis Bridal Wear Ltd of Copperfield Road, Bow was advertising for a stock cutter, I made an appointment with the manager for an interview.

Ellis's was one of the countries leading wedding dress manufacturers. Because their designs were immensely popular; much of their production was exported to more than thirty countries. In 1980 the firm was awarded the Queen's medal for industry. (In reality, it is not an award that is bestowed by the Queen but an award that a company can apply for, if more than 50 per cent of its production is exported overseas.)

From a small shop in Stepney's Commercial Road in 1912, the Ellis family began making bridal wear to order and by the mid 1980s it was known all over the world for its high quality designs. The management boasted that for the previous twenty years they had, within twenty four hours, produced an exact copy of every royal wedding dress from the moment it was first seen by the public.

Princess Anne accepted an invitation to visit the Ellis factory in October 1987 where she was warmly received. The Ellis staff had collected £200 for Save the Children, the princess's favourite charity. Besides the cheque she was presented with an electric blue cocktail suit.

As I walked down Copperfield Road for my appointment with Ellis's production manager, childhood memories returned. In 1947, when I was six years old and living with my family in nearby Carr Street buildings, I played with other local children on the massive bombsite on the south-eastern corner of Copperfield Road.

During the Second World War German prisoners of war were billeted in Nissen huts on the site. With the cessation of hostilities in 1945 the POWs were repatriated and the huts dismantled. Within a short space of time dozens of abandoned lorries and cars were scattered all over the bush covered site. The entire area, though potentially dangerous, was an exciting and popular playground for children.

In 1952 the rusty vehicles were removed and the following year, a park and playing field was created on the site. Named the King Edward V Playing Fields, the park was officially opened by the Duke of Edinburgh in 1953.

The mid Victorian warehouses and more recent industrial factories on the west side of Copperfield Road backed onto the tow-path of the Regent Canal. Fortunately for posterity the Victorian warehouses survived the blitz.

The warehouses at number 46-50, adjacent to the iron Victory Bridge built in 1907, was once a ragged day school established by Dr Barnardo in 1877. The school offered free basic education to poor local children and equally importantly hot meals during the winter months. It was possible that my grandparents on both my mother and father's side, who were born and grew up in the slums of nearby Limehouse Fields, may have been beneficiaries of the good doctor's charity. (Limehouse Fields was known as Donkey Row because of the large numbers of horses, carts and stables which were kept there.)

Since the Ragged Schools' closure in 1915, various industrial companies occupied the old warehouses.

In 1983 Radley & Co., manufactures of motor cycle clothing, were at number 48 to 50. There were also six neighbouring clothing companies producing skirts, slacks, dresses and menswear. Other businesses in the road included a furrier, the Learay Trading Co., who were wholesale chemists; Cohen Bros Oils Ltd and Courthouse Ltd, linen suppliers.

The Ellis factory occupied the first floor at the Falcon Works at the northern end of Copperfield Road.

On the floor above, the 'New Image' dressmaking company were also advertising for a cutter.

My interview with Ellis's impatient manager was almost over before it began. He asked me two or three questions about my experience, wrote my telephone number in his notepad, and then quickly guided me to the exit; 'You will be hearing from us' were his departing words.

Past experience had taught me that 'You will be hearing from us' usually meant your name would be placed at the bottom of a list of prospective applicants.

I rang New Image's doorbell. An obese, cheerful man in his mid-thirties answered the door. When I enquired about the stock cutting vacancy he politely asked me to step inside.

The two directors, Bill Cooper and Nic Koutsoudes, interviewed me in their office. I explained that I had been cutting various types of garments since 1956. They seemed impressed when I mentioned that I was also a former cutting room manager. The two men were keen to know what my duties were when I was in charge of Pridewear's busy cutting room.

During the interview, a slim, effeminate youth wearing a bow tie came into the office and placed some unopened letters on the desk. When the youth turned around to leave he gave me an extended stare; Bill also noticed him staring at me and sighed irritably.

Bill waited until the youth left the office before describing my duties.

'Just simple marker making, stock cutting and bundling.' He also added 'There isn't much overtime at the moment, only the occasional Saturday morning.'

He emphasised that I would sometimes have to help with the loading and unloading of the van.

This additional duty did not please me. As Bill was speaking, he was interrupted by a second appearance of the youth. Bill annoyed with this intrusion snapped at him, 'What do you want Ian?'

The youth handed Nic a document, turned around and left the office, but not before giving me another extended stare. Bill still visibly riled, groaned and said to Nic 'I don't know what's going on in Ian's mind, do you?' There was a half grin on Nic's face when he replied, 'haven't got a clue'. I did not believe them, both men knew exactly what was going on in Ian's mind; he had come into the office on a pretence to look me over.

The wage that Bill and Nic offered was £120 per week, slightly lower than I could have earned elsewhere, but the hours worked were acceptable, 8.30 a.m. to 5.30 p.m. I also liked the location of the factory: it overlooked the Regent's Canal with access to the towpath which was just a few yards away and it would only take me twenty minutes to walk to work from my home in Cordelia Street. My interview with Bill and Nic ended the moment I agreed to start work the next day.

During my walk home down the Bow Common Lane, I began to reflect on the interview. I thought that I had conducted myself well and created a good impression and I had no concerns about cutting New Image's medium priced dresses. No doubt the work would be routine and probably a little tedious, but my tenure at the factory would only be temporary until I found a more suitable job with better prospects.

Bill and Nic seemed to be archetypical East End clothing factory partners. Usually one partner is responsible for the production side of the business and works on the factory floor. The other partner, though he often has some production experience, looks after the office side of the business, including accounts, wages preparation and dispatch. I imagined this was Bill's role; Nic was probably the production manager.

Though my short interview lasted less than ten minutes I had tried to analyse the partners' characters to see if I would be comfortable working for them. I thought that I could work well with Nic, I found him to be polite and affable, but I had reservations about Bill, who seemed to me to be a person who did not suffer fools gladly. I felt that he could be unnecessarily rude, especially after witnessing his brusqueness with Ian. I also noticed he would not look me in the eye and it seemed strange that his eyes were focused sideways whenever he spoke.

The cutting room at the New Image's factory was quite spacious; there were two long cutting tables that stretched from the entrance to the windows that overlooked the Regents Canal.

Paul Readon, an efficient stock cutter, operated the automatic cloth laying up machine and would be responsible for cutting bulk work. My role would be to cut smaller dockets. If I needed help in laying wide fabric Gary, a nineteen year-old trainee cutter, would assist me.

Each morning Bill would come into the cutting room and give me a docket and its dress patterns; I would make the relevant marker, commence with the laying of the fabric and cut and bundle the dresses.

I had to be exceptionally careful when listening to Bill's instructions. He did not like to repeat himself and there were a few occasions when I thought that he had given me insufficient information or that I had misheard or misunderstood him. If I politely asked him to repeat his instruction, he was prone to utter sneering remarks like 'I have already explained that' or 'don't you understand me.'

As a rule, I would never accept this curtness from employers, but somehow, with great effort, I managed to maintain my equanimity and tolerate his bad manners. I would have preferred Nic to have given me my dockets as he was always courteous and patient, but unfortunately, because he rarely left the machining room next door, my contact with him was minimal.

Being summer time, Paul and I would sometimes stand by the windows during our tea breaks. We would watch with interest as bargemen scooped up flotsam and jetsam from the water. Paul may have been one of the last witnesses to the canals commercial use; he could recall earlier in the year seeing a motorised barge carrying what he believed to be bales of copper wire.

On the opposite side of the canal the Ocean Canoeing Children's Club had its boat shed. Throughout the summer months dozens of local children were to be seen canoeing or swimming in the canal. Although the children were well supervised, I could not understand how young toddlers were allowed to swim in the often smelly water, especially with so many rats about. I had seen the rats swimming in the canal and running along the towpath. A local man had cut his finger, after foolishly dipping his finger in the same canal to wash away the blood; he contracted Weil's disease and became seriously ill. He may have died.

In July, the dangerous waters of the Regent's Canal would claim another victim. 21 year old Raymond Human was swimming in the lock by Victoria Park. Apparently sluice from the floodgate dragged him beneath the swirling waters, where he was trapped against an iron grill. Several brave rescuers dived into the lock in an attempt to save him. Eventually the unconscious man was brought to the surface, but tragically he later died in hospital.

At lunch time, I would leave the factory and join other workers for ball games in the park at Copperfield Road. At other times I would stroll along the towpath and chat to strangers fishing from the bank near Johnson's lock. The area was a pleasant alternative to some of the ghastly locations that I had worked at in the East End.

Not long after I started working at the New Image factory Gary, the trainee cutter, surprised me by saying, 'did you know that Bill and Nic are gay and they live together?'

I had absolutely no idea that the two men were gay. Bill was at least 50 years old, he was about 5ft 10 inches tall, slim with blue eyes and grey wavy hair; despite having one lung, throughout the day he smoked expensive cigars. Nic, 15 years his junior, was born in Cyprus. His Greek parents brought him and his sister Lulu to London when they were infants; short, dark skinned, muscular and a non smoker, he kept himself extremely fit by exercising and weightlifting.

I explained to Gary that, with the exception of the obnoxious Bill Cooper, the dozens of homosexuals I had known over the years were usually kind and tolerant people, and that their sexuality was of no interest to me. Although I did find it highly amusing when Gary revealed that Nic had attended a fancy dress night in a tough Roman Road pub dressed as a sugar plum fairy complete with a silver wand. I wondered if his partner Bill was dressed as one of Cinderella's ugly sisters, which I thought would have been appropriate, but Gary had no information on how Bill was attired.

Bill, Nic and Ian the 'dogsbody' and Bill's nephew, also called Bill, but known as Billy (it was he who asked me to step inside the factory when I first enquired about the stock cutting vacancy) usually visited a local pub during the evenings after work. They must have looked a slightly odd group with their various shapes and sizes drinking at the bar.

I liked Billy; not only was he New Image's driver, he was also responsible for opening up the factory during the mornings – jovial, garrulous and unmarried, he lived with his sister, who was a London policewoman.

Paul, Gary and I were ordered to assist Billy unload rolls of fabric from the van. While we took a short break from the heavy unloading and were loitering on the pavement, Billy pointed to one of the industrial buildings just a few yards away. 'It happened a few years ago when the Watford Chemical Company had their plant there. The poor fellow didn't stand a chance.' He then proceeded to explain how Alfred Pratt, who was the company's fire officer, was killed when he became trapped by an explosion which caused a fire on the premises.

Tragically, Billy was soon to die. Being vastly overweight must have put an enormous strain on his heart.

Billy failed to arrive at the factory to unlock the premises and a grief-stricken Bill and Nic appeared shortly afterwards and told us the sad news that Billy had collapsed and died.

As the weeks went by, I noticed with increased frequency whenever Bill came into the cutting room he spoke to me and ignored Paul. If he wanted to know when certain dockets would be cut out, if more new dockets were required or if Gary the trainee cutter was being fully occupied or whether there was sufficient fabric in stock, he would asked me rather than Paul. At first I was mystified as to why he was directing so many questions at me, but I soon realised Bill's motives. He was furtively manoeuvring me into a position of being in charge of the cutting room, but still paying me stock cutters wages. It was a devious trick; he had employed me as a stock cutter, not as a foreman. If he wanted somebody to manage the cutting room the obvious choice should have been Paul, who was a very experienced cutter and had worked for the partners for some time. Perhaps Paul had been offered the position, but had refused it. My workmate seemed quite content remaining as a stock cutter.

I was not happy with this new situation. If Bill and Nic wanted me to be the cutting room manager, they should have first discussed the matter with me. It was possible that I might have considered being promoted, but only on the condition that my wages would have to be increased substantially. If they could find the vast sums to build their new hotel in southern Cyprus, they could quite easily have found the few extra pounds a week to increase my wages.

Bill's deviousness worked, albeit temporarily. Reluctantly and uncomplaining I accepted my new role as the foreman cutter without being offered an increment, but I would leave at the earliest opportunity.

My departure came more quickly than expected.

Bill was in a bad mood. I could now detect what mood he was in by the way he focused his eyes. If his eyes were focused sideways, either to the left or the right, thus avoiding eye contact, he was in a reasonably contented mood, but if he was directly facing me, eye to eye, he was often in an angry mood.

On this occasion he was facing me. Earlier he had instructed me to cut some urgent samples, but he kept changing his mind about the fabric to be used. It did not occur to me to write down his final instruction, it was not necessary as I had made an exact mental note of what fabric was to be used for each sample.

Bill spoke rudely; he accused me of not listening to him which resulted in my cutting the wrong fabric for his samples. I tried to explain in a calm manner that I was absolutely sure I had followed his instructions correctly and had cut the relevant fabric. My explanation had no affect; he banged his wrist hard on the cutting table and again accused me of not paying enough attention to his orders. At this stage I became extremely annoyed with Bill. 'Are you so infallible?' I retorted.

'Just use the correct fabric next time,' he growled.

I followed him into the corridor that led to the machining room; he stopped walking when he heard my footsteps close behind, turning around, he removed the cigar from his mouth and said 'yes?' I spoke just five words: 'I am leaving this Friday'. Without waiting for his reply, I quickly turned around and went back into the cutting room.

Hassan, a Turk, was a New Image presser who worked at a piece rate. Another presser, a turbaned little Sikh, also a pieceworker, worked alongside him. The system in place was that each presser would take one dress at a time to press, thus ensuring fairness, but whenever it came towards the end of the day the greedy Sikh would grab the last of the garments waiting to be pressed thus refusing Hassan access.

Hassan, normally a mild mannered man, had become so incensed at this continuous greedy behaviour that he attacked the Sikh and sent him to the floor with a split nose and a ripped off turban.

Somebody in the factory had told Hassan that I had handed in my notice. He came into the cutting room during the tea break. Speaking quietly, he advised me to visit the Cannon Street Road area of Stepney, where several Turkish clothing factories were located.

'They are always looking for experienced cutters and they pay nice wages.'

I thanked Hassan for his concern and assured him I would follow his advice.

My last three days at the New Image factory were surprisingly enjoyable; I worked at a leisurely pace. Thankfully, Bill had decided to distance himself from me, he spoke only to Paul or Gary. Nic was not so aloof, but I did notice our conversation was always brief.

After collecting my wages and P45 from a reticent Bill on the Friday evening, I dashed to Cannon Street Road just over a mile away to check out any vacancies.

Hassan was correct. Several Turkish factories were situated in Cannon Street Road and there were also a number of Asian clothing manufactures in the surrounding area, especially in Turner Street and New Road.

Not all of the clothing manufactures located around the Cannon Street Road had vacancy signs outside. The lack of signs did not necessary mean there were no vacancies available; they might be recruiting staff by advertising in the local press, making use of the employment exchange or they could be taking on staff who, like me, would apply in person. Alternatively, some manufacturers might be deliberately avoiding advertising their businesses because they were unregistered and operating secretly, ready to disappear in the night, lock, stock and barrel before irate creditors came banging on their door.

The first clothing factory I enquired at occupied the second floor in a large modern industrial building.

Within seconds of ringing the bell, a thick set man who I assumed to be Turkish opened the door. He did not seem to understand me when I said 'I am a cutter' Fortunately, I had remembered a few Turkish words, tapping my chest; I remarked 'Mi kesici.' (Cutter) he responded by saying 'Okay.'

I followed him inside where he led me to a small wooden framed office close by. As he did so, I glanced around the factory floor; there were about 30 male and female workers; most seemed Turkish, but there were also a couple of Chinese machinists.

Hussein, the Turkish managing director, spoke good English. He invited me to sit down in his untidy office which reeked of tobacco. I noticed an opened bottle of Turkish raki (Aniseed flavoured spirit.) on his desk.

Hussein, who may have been about fifty, placed his cigar end in an ashtray and asked me the same question that I had been asked so many times in the past.

'Can you grade dress patterns and make markers?'

I answered him in my well-practiced manner. 'Yes, I can make economical markers and do simple grading.'

'Em, that's very good.' He remarked.

To my surprise, there were no further questions, instead he began tapping his fingers on the desk and for a moment gazed up at the ceiling. I gained the impression he was juggling figures.

Leaning foreword with his clasped hands resting on the desk, he said 'Actually my son-in-law Fasa is the regular cutter here. He is away at the moment, but if you're interested in working for me, I can offer you three pounds an hour, which I believe is reasonable. I have to mention that my factory is very busy at the moment, we are open from 8am until 10pm and also there is no time and a half rate for overtime. I only pay the hourly rate which applies to weekend working.'

I realised at once that if I agreed to work there, it would mean having to work much longer than an eight hour day and it was unlikely that I would receive holiday or sick pay. These benefits, as Jock confirmed a few years previously, were rarely offered in a Turkish or Greek factory. You simply got paid for the hours worked, be it ten hours or 100 hours a week.

Being denied benefits did not really concern me. I was rarely ill and as I had no plans for a holiday, the wages and long hours was acceptable, though the loud Turkish music being relayed from a loudspeaker might prove to be an irritant.

Hussein, who was now smoking a cigar, seemed to have taken it for granted that I was willing to work for him. He asked me if I had any questions about the job.

I hesitated for a second then said 'There is only one.'

'Only one?' He echoed with a half smile.

Fearing he might be offended, I chose my words carefully.

'Yes, there is only one question; can you possibly deduct my income tax and national insurance contributions from my wages? '

'No problem there.' He assured me.

Again I was reminded of Jock's words of wisdom.

'Promises and assurances are meaningless in the rag trade.'

As he poured himself a raki he said 'And when would you like to start work?

I mustered a little enthusiasm 'Preferably in the morning, if it's possible.'

With a quick gulp, he swallowed the remaining raki in his glass, stood up to shake my hand and said 'In the morning will be fine'.

I left the office with Hussein, and we stood in the middle of the factory floor. He pointed his finger at two middle-aged Turkish looking men who, with great speed, were laying up fabric by the open windows which overlooked the street. I could tell immediately by their clumsy body movements and the way they were handling the fabric that they were not very experienced.

Hussein assured me that when I arrived in the morning, 'Bari and Sabri will have finished that lay, which will be ready for you to cut out.'

The huge lay of dresses was indeed finished when I arrived at eight the following morning.

Bari and Sabri were nowhere to be seen. Hussein explained that the two men had worked until the early hours of the morning and were 'now sleeping', but what Hussein failed to tell me was that the two men were sleeping under the cutting table.

When I switched on the cutting machine, I was startled by Bari and Sabri emerging sleepy eyed from under the table. They scratched their heads and said 'Gunaydin.' (Good morning) to me, before staggering across the factory floor to the hot drinks vending machine located by the exit.

The marker, which I carefully checked, was drawn part in pencil and part in ball-point pen. It was for five short sleeve dresses and was not well made; some of the back bodices were slightly off grain and, much worse, a single sleeve had not been paired. As the fabric had been layed right side up, this unpaired sleeve was a major error. Had I not noticed the error and had gone ahead and cut out the lay 200 dresses, one sixth of the total lay, would have had their sleeves not pairing. I called Hussein to the cutting table and explained that I was unable to start the cutting until I had rectified the marker. He was furious over the delay. Apparently it was his son-in-law Faza who had made the marker. Clenching his fist, he struck the cutting table and said, 'My son-in-law calls himself an experienced kecici, but he is a lazy, useless kasap'.

Of course I was familiar with the term kesici, but not kasap. I was to learn later it was Turkish for butcher.

Hussein spoke quietly; 'My friend, please correct the marker immediately and thank you for spotting the mistake.'

Having access to the dress patterns, it took me only a few minutes to alter the marker.

Two hours later I had cut out the lay. The stayflex fusible lining for the 1,000 dresses had already been cut, presumably by Faza.

Hussein refused to allow me to bundle the dresses.

'As a top cutter.' he said patronisingly, 'Your time is too valuable to spend bundling and laying fabric. Just concentrate on the cutting and making markers for the dresses and stayflex; all other tasks must be given to Bari and Sabri, your assistants.'

I began making a multiple marker for six sleeveless dresses. When the marker was completed I invited Sabri and Bari, who were cousins, to examine the marker. They glanced at each other with bewildered expressions. With the greatest of difficulty I explained that if they had only spent a few moments checking the marker of the 1,000 dresses which I had cut out, they would have noticed the unpaired sleeve and the back bodices, which were not marked in perfectly straight.

Although both men spoke limited English, they were intelligent enough to know that I was not attempting to humiliate them; moreover they seemed pleased that I had involved them in my work.

'New lesson, learn us.' said a grinning Bari.

I stood alongside Sabri and Bari as they attempted to examine my long marker for possible mistakes. As we moved along the cutting table, I explained how important it was for them to agree that all patterns paired.

A few moments later, Sabri who spoke slightly better English than Bari, confirmed that the 'marker, very excellent, good'.

While the cousins were preparing to lay the fabric, which would be for approximately 150 runs, I began making a 36 inch wide stayflex marker. Shortly afterwards Hussein came over to the cutting table and explained that as he urgently needed Bari to work elsewhere, I must lay the fabric with Sabri. I thought Hussein might be suffering from short memory loss, only a couple of hours earlier, he insisted that my time was too valuable to lay fabric. But I had no cause to complain, I welcomed the opportunity to lay the fabric.

Sabri was a reliable assistant, though a little overweight, he was quite agile. Despite having large, rough hands, he had a light touch, which was ideal for laying fabric, and he never once tugged at his selvedge edge.

During the course of working with Sabri, I attempted to make conversation with him, which proved somewhat frustrating for both of us, but with great effort he managed to explain that he and Bari had been living in London for about nine months. When they first arrived neither he nor his cousin could speak a single word of English. Hussein, who had been their friend since schooldays in Istanbul, had invited them to work at his factory.

Sabri and Bari were carpenters by trade; not only had they built the very cutting table which we were working at, they had also constructed Hussein's wood panelled office.

Struggling with his English, Sabri explained that a few days earlier the recently married Faza had left London to spend a 'sweet' (which I interpreted to mean honeymoon) with his wife in Bodrum, and would be returning in three weeks to continue as Hussein's kesici.

I assumed that when Faza returned, Hussein would probably ask me to leave.

The thought of leaving did not concern me too much because I knew that other local jobs were available. There was, of course, the possibility that Hussein might decide to retain my services, perhaps on a part time basis.

The following Friday was payday. During the early afternoon, I was distracted from cutting the stayflex by a commotion on the factory floor. Staff who a moment before were busy machining and pressing the dresses suddenly ran out of the fire exit. This was odd. If there was a fire, why had the alarms not gone off and where was Hussein to organise the evacuation. I tried to analyse what was happening; if it was not a fire, what on earth was in progress. Could it be that the whole building was about to collapse, might gangsters be on the premises intending to steal workers' pay packets. The situation seemed even more bizarre; Bari and Sabri decided to abandon the laying of the fabric and clamber under the cutting table, where they kept perfectly still.

I was now totally confused because at least a third of Hussein's staff were still at their work benches. Suddenly the entrance bell began to ring continuously and only stopped ringing when the elusive Hussein came out of his office and opened the door. As he did so, two police officers and about a dozen officials, each carrying a briefcase swept passed him. Hussein immediately began remonstrating with these unexpected visitors. As he did so one of the police officers told him in a commanding voice to 'just calm down'. Having calmed down, a grim faced Hussein went into his office with the same policeman and two officials. Meanwhile other officials were sitting amongst Hussein's remaining staff and were asking them questions. One of the officials came over to the cutting table, rudely ordered me to switch off the cutting machine, and even more rudely demanded to know my name. Having a lifelong aversion of rude people, I instantly retaliated, 'hold your horses mate, lets start from the beginning shall we, just take a few steps back, then move forward and politely state your business.'

The man made no attempt to step backwards, but my robust reply did have an effect, when he opened his briefcase and took out a notebook his tone was modified.

'My associates and I are from several agencies which include the Inland Revenue, the Department of Health and Social Security and the Immigration Service. For various reasons for which I cannot disclose, we are currently visiting clothing factories in this area.'

Still peeved I said, 'Surely, if you are questioning me, I have the right to know why'.

Reluctantly he explained. 'The main reason for our visit is to make sure British law is not being abused; so would you now give me your name and address and can you tell me how long have you worked at this factory.'

I answered cordially and gave him the information he required.

After he wrote down my answers in his notebook, I thought this interrogation would now end but I was wrong. He continued, 'can you prove to me that you began working at this factory just a few days ago'.

'Of course,' I replied impatiently.

'I gave the boss Mr Hussein my P45 the day I started working here. If you need to inspect it, I suggest that you speak to him.'

Deciding that I had given him adequate information, I switched the Eastman machine back on and resumed cutting the stayflex.

The man replaced the notebook in his briefcase and promptly marched into Hussein's office.

The officials remained in the factory for at least an hour. Throughout that time, not a sound came from under the cutting table. I was tempted to crouch down and see how Sabri and Bari were coping.

It was now evident to me why this raid had taken place. The officials were trying to catch illegal immigrants and culprits who were working and claiming unemployment benefit.

I suspected that someone must have informed Hussein's staff of the impending raid; by doing so it gave time to those workers who were breaking the law to escape. Obviously, those who remained at their workbenches had nothing to fear and were working legitimately.

It did not seem to me to be a well planned raid. The police should have first sealed off the entire building before going inside. Had they done so, the two thirds of Hussein's workforce who fled down the fire escape would have been apprehended.

Hussein came over to the cutting table and shouted 'Sabri, Bari.' On hearing their names being called, the cousins came out from under the cutting table and to the sound of their bones creaking, stretched themselves before proceeding to lay the fabric.

With tongue in cheek Hussein turned to me and said, 'my friend these government inspectors are always harassing us, they seem to think every Turkish businessman is operating outside the law and cheating the state.'

Throughout the afternoon the majority of Hussein's workers who had made a hasty departure from the factory began to return. Apparently, the team of investigative officials were more successful when they visited the three other clothing factories in the building; they caught and questioned many illegal workers.

Over the next decade, in various local factories, I would witness several raids by inspectors, particularly from the Department of Health and Social Security. On one memorable occasion in a Whitechapel factory Azzis, a Bangladeshi presser who had been working while receiving unemployment benefit, was so terrified of being caught that he managed to run out of the factory just seconds before the inspectors paid a visit.

Azzis must have kept running until he reached London Airport, because twenty-four hours later he had arrived in Dacca.

However, other illegal workers in the factory left it too late to escape; policemen were posted outside the front entrance and the fire exits. With the inspectors from the DHSS banging on the door, there was pandemonium as workers hastily tried to hide inside the factory. Beneath the cutting table was always a favourite sanctuary, but not this time, there was no space available as dozens of rolls of fabric had been stored there

It was amusing to watch two young Kurds with the speed of monkeys climb on top of the wooden partitioned office and cover themselves with remnants. Another man hid in a metal rack where bundles of cut garments were placed on his body and a woman machinist slid into an open-topped container where unpressed dresses were kept.

When the door was opened a team of inspectors quickly filed past the protesting Turkish managing director. The procedure was always the same; every worker was thoroughly questioned by the inspectors. I was questioned by a polite and pretty woman from the Inland Revenue. As she spoke, a noise could be heard from inside a nearby large cardboard box. Fortunately for whoever was hiding inside, I was able to convince the investigator that the noise was mice.

'Mice' she shrieked as she moved closer to me for protection. When the inspectors finally left the factory 'Little Kim,' a diminutive Chinese overlocker who had overstayed the duration of her work permit, popped smilingly out of the box.

A couple of weeks after I began working for Hussein a sudden and unexpected slack period occurred and I was given hardly any dockets to cut. Hussein took immediate steps to keep his business functioning. The factory would be closed on Saturday and Sunday and during the weekdays the sewing machines switched off at 6 p.m. The workers were disappointed at being forced to work just 40 hours a week and, with the arrival of Faza who was reinstated as the firm's kesici, it was inevitable that I would be asked to leave.

Hussein called me into his office, where he offered me a glass of raki. He seemed a little remorseful when he explained, 'regretfully my friend, with Faza now working here and not having many dockets at the moment, I have to ask you to find another job.'

He turned a new page in his diary and said 'Would you mind if I made a note of your phone number, Alfred, just in case I need to call you some time.'

As Hussein wrote down my number he sighed heavily, 'You know us Turks, its family loyalties; I only wish that useless kasap Faza would have stayed in Turkey.'

To show his gratitude for my 'short but good service' an extra £20 was added to my final pay packet.

When I left Hussein's factory for the last time, rather than leave the building I thought it would be worth enquiring at the three other clothing factories on the upper floors, to see if there were any vacancies for stock cutters. But I had left it too late; two of the factories were closed for the evening although the third factory, situated on the top floor, was still open.

I went inside and was greeted by an acquaintance I had known several years previously. Uddin, the Pakistani director, was originally a hardworking and ambitious machinist who was determined to own his own clothing business. It may have taken Uddin a decade to achieve his goal.

As soon as we were seated in his office he said 'Of course Arthur, (Many Asian people whom I had come into contact with in the clothing trade would call me Arthur) I would like you to work for me, how does £4. an hour sound? ' It sounded fine, but his offer was refused. I should have realised from the moment that I stepped inside his factory and could smell the Hoffman pressing machines that Uddin manufactured ladies coats and jackets and not dresses and separates, which was my speciality.

Somewhat disappointed Uddin asked me if I knew of any other qualified cutters who might consider working for him.

The only skilled coat cutter who I thought might be interested, if the wages were satisfactory, was Jock. I gave Uddin my friend's phone number and suggested that he contact Jock. He assured me he would that very evening.

After leaving Uddin's factory, I needed to visit the W.C. on the landing. I opened the door and was confronted by an objectionable scene. Six Asian men, whom I presumed to be Uddin's employees, were furiously scrubbing their feet in the hand wash basins; perhaps they were preparing themselves for Friday night prayers. Apart from the awful prevailing smell and the entire floor being covered by the splash water, a disgusting sound of loud gobbing was coming from one of the cubicles. I instantly changed my mind about using the convenience. Within minutes, I was out of the building and walking home to Poplar.

As I walked along the Commercial Road, disturbing thoughts entered my head and I began to feel that I had made an awful mistake in suggesting to Uddin that he should contact Jock and offer him the vacancy.

If it had been Jock and not me who had witnessed that ghastly scene in the W.C., he would not have hesitated in verbally abusing those employees who had their feet in the hand wash basins. Had any of the men dared to retaliate, it would not only have been their feet which were being washed but their bloodied noses and mouths too, the result of Jock's well aimed fists.

On arriving home, I immediately phoned Jock who was about to leave for his regular drinking session at Stratford Broadway. I explained to my friend, that if he did receive a call from Uddin offering him a job, it would be in his interest to ignore it. Jock assured me that he had sufficient work to keep himself occupied for the coming months.

The Hypocrites

The next morning at eight I was back in the Commercial Road and walking west towards Aldgate East.

As Saturday was usually a working day for many employees in the East End clothing industry, I knew that the majority of factories located around the Cannon Street Road area would be open. In nearby New Road, a factory above a dress showroom was advertising for a stock cutter. The entire building had originally been a dwelling, as were the adjacent showrooms.

The managing directors of the factory and showroom, Haroon and his brother Tariq, were polite Indian Moslems. They invited me to inspect the oblong shaped cutting room on the first floor. As expected there was no fire escape, but there were fire extinguishers.

Haroon explained that he desperately needed an experienced cutter who was able to cut small quantities of garments. The £3. an hour which he offered me was inadequate, but as the brothers were amiable and easy to talk to and my duties seemed to be non-pressurised, I decided to work for them, albeit temporarily.

Because Haroon and Tariq were constantly busy dealing with customers in their showroom, I was left on my own to work independently. I enjoyed the solitude. The only time other staff members came into the cutting room was if I needed an assistant to help me to lay wide fabric.

Although Tariq was a director, he sometimes felt the need to 'escape for an hour' from the busyness of the showroom and assist me in the cutting room. In between inhaling his cigarettes he liked to chat as we worked. He explained that his family, originally from India, had settled in London when he and Haroon were young children. They both left school at 15 and became junior salesmen in various Whitechapel clothing showrooms.

'That's where we learnt the business of selling,' he said with a grin.

Reflecting on those past days he added, 'for nearly 20 years, we worked long hours and the pay was always bad. Then one day we made a decision. We decided that it was about time we stopped helping other people get rich and start making ourselves rich. So Haroon and I pooled our savings and opened this showroom a couple of years ago. So far we haven't done to bad, but as you know Arthur, there is a lot of competition in Whitechapel.'

Tariq was determined to give up smoking. He claimed that he smoked at least 30 cigarettes a day.

'For years I have been trying to kick the habit, but it is so hard to stop. I do try Arthur, I really do. Haroon has never smoked, he hates me smoking, I know that if I don't stop smoking, then one day I might have to face the consequences.'

His predicament of wanting to 'to kick the habit' but being incapable of doing so reminded me of the similar situation of my friends David Upson and Victor Clarke. Both men were chronic smokers' who, unfortunately, lacked the necessary will power to permanently abstain. Sadly, in time their smoking would have a devastating and irreversible effect on their health.

Dave had read somewhere that the craving for cigarettes may be caused by irritable nerve endings which had been severed by nicotine. I explained this hypothesis to Tariq who listened with interest. Looking up to the ceiling he sighed and said, 'God willing, I won't be dependant on the fags for much longer, I don't want to follow in my father's footsteps; he was a heavy smoker too and was not 50 before he died of lung cancer'.

A painfully thin packer named Anwar was assigned to help me in the cutting room. Just after we began laying the fabric, he suddenly felt the need to inform me that he was a 'Good Moslem' who prayed five times a day and regularly worshiped at the huge Whitechapel mosque. I had to restrain myself from asking why the necessity to pray five times a day.

At 10 a.m. we stopped working for a short break and sat next to each other on the cutting table and drank tea. During the course of our conversation Anwar told me that for the past year he had a weekend occupation teaching Moslem children the Koran. 'I earn £5 an hour,' he bragged.

'That's almost double my hourly earnings' I remarked enviously.

He began to stroked his bead before answering.

'Ah but your in the wrong profession Arthur.'

Testing his honesty I said 'But surely Anwar that £5 would be much less after you paid tax.'

He responded by muttering 'What are you talking about Arthur, why should I pay tax.'

'Why not' I remarked. 'Because it's the law, every one must pay tax on their earnings.'

'I refuse to declare it' he replied defiantly.

It was pointless continuing the conversation with this hypocrite. I could not understand how he could claim that he was a 'Good Moslem' who practised a code of ethics as taught in the Koran and in the same breath admit to me with impunity that he was cheating the Inland Revenue.

The next day Anwar was again sent to the cutting room.

During the 1p.m. lunch break, I sat by the window to eat my sandwiches while Anwar knelt down behind the cutting table and began to pray. After he finished praying he left the factory to buy food.

Within ten minutes he returned with samosas and sat on a stool next to me.

While reading my newspaper I glance at Anwar as he consumed his food. He was ravenous and the samosas were devoured very quickly, as was the fizzy drink. Unfortunately for me, Anwar remained seated on the stool. After he had finished eating, I knew exactly what was going to happen next, he would want to talk to me and as expected the subject would be religion.

'Arthur, are you a Christian?' he asked inquisitively.

Working in clothing factories alongside workers of so many different faiths and nationalities it was inevitable I would be asked what my religion was. Often it was the Moslems who were the most curious.

I folded my newspaper before answering Anwar.

'I was baptised a Christian, but now days I am a committed atheist, or what you Moslems call an infidel.'

'Arthur, you don't believe in God' he gasped.

'No, I certainly do not,' I replied adamantly. 'I consider myself to be far to intelligent to believe that a virgin can give birth to a baby who Christians claim is the son of the creator of the universe; equally, I can never accept the Moslems belief that Mohammed is the messenger of that same creator whom you call Allah.'

Emphasizing with his hands, he stated 'but the proof is there for you to see, Allah's words are written in the Koran.'

I responded by saying 'This book which you call the Koran, has it ever been scientifically examined to see if it is genuine?'

He thought carefully before answering me. 'It is only possible to examine a copy of the Koran, because the original Koran is in paradise placed alongside Allah's throne.'

Anwa's explanation was unsatisfactory and totally unconvincing.

I thought that this tax cheat who claims to be a devout Moslem might be somewhat offended by my next question, but I did not care.

'Do you really expect me to believe that your Allah sits on a throne in heaven and has a book by his side that contains his instruction on how to be a god fearing Moslem?'

Surprisingly, Anwar was not offended; he smiled and said 'Of course Arthur, it's true.'

I continued with my criticism 'Well you might believe it, but I certainly don't. According to your beliefs Allah has a human form. Surely Allah would have no human characteristics?'

Anwar did make an attempt to explain how he visualized Allah, but I found his interpretation of Allah being 'the most beneficent, and merciful' inane.

During this unwanted lunch-time discussion, I was reminded of what Albert Einstein was reputed as saying,

'I cannot conceive of a God who rewards and punishes his creatures, or has a will of the kind that we experience in ourselves.'

The second of my assistants was Miah.

Like Anwar, Miah too would hurry to the Whitechapel Mosque every Friday lunchtime.

Miah was absolutely 'Fed up' with working in a fashion showroom. He planned to hand in his notice and join his family's property acquisition business.

Miah's father, an accountant, was the financial director of the company and his two older brothers were responsible for the purchase and restoration of semi-dilapidated houses, mainly in the Forest Gate and Plaistow area.

'Our property portfolio is increasing by the month' he said proudly.

'O really,' I remarked.

As Miah seemed willing to talk about his family's business, I was quite content to listen.

'After we refurbish these old houses, my father decides whether to sell them at a profit, or let them on a short term. If that happens, we only let to students or young working people.'

Eager to learn more I said, 'why students and young people?'

'Its good business acumen,' he enthused.

'Because these young people are always transient they are no threat to us and they are happy to rent from us for just a year. After they vacate the house we get a valuation done, if the house has increased considerably in value, our father might sell, but if there is no noticeable increase, he lets it out for a further year.'

'So you never let your properties to families?' I asked in a matter of fact way.

Shaking his head he said, 'families are taboo, especially if they have young children. If we let our houses to families there is a danger that they might apply to a rent tribunal for security of tenure and having their rent assessed and possibly fixed. If that happens we would never be able to evict them.'

Feigning empathy, I continued with my soft probing.

'And have you ever had any problems with awkward sitting tenants?'

'We have had some,' he admitted. 'A few months ago, we bought a house cheaply at auction which was divided into two flats and both occupied. We wanted to sell it on, but we could only make a good profit if the house was empty. We managed to persuade the man on the first floor to give up his tenancy by offering him money, but the old lady who occupies the garden flat won't budge, no matter how many times we offer her money we can't get rid of her.'

Getting rid of tenants was redolent of Rachmanism.

(Note: Peter Rachman was a notorious Polish-born slum landlord who owned approximately eighty houses in West London. When Rachman's tenants could no longer afford to pay the exorbitant rents he charged or he wanted them to vacate his properties, he resorted to hiring thugs with Alsatian dogs to terrorise them into moving out. Rachman first came to public prominence when he was linked to Mandy Rice Davies, a key player in the Profumo scandal that damaged the Conservative Government in 1963.)

It was unlikely that Miah's family would make use of Alsatian dogs to terrorise the old lady into giving up her tenancy, but I did feel that as their offer of money had been refused, it was possible that they might attempt to use alternative persuasive measures. I had once read an account of an unscrupulous landlord who had installed a paid agent provocateur into one of his houses of multiple occupation. The hireling was instructed by the landlord to make life so unpleasant for the tenants that they would vacate their flatlets. After taking up residence, the hireling began having regular, noisy, well attended late night parties.

The harassment worked, one by one the tenants found accommodation elsewhere. When the last tenant had left, the delighted landlord paid his hireling the pre-arranged fee and promptly sold the empty property making a huge profit.

Parvis, whose sobriquet was 'Speedy' was another of my assistant layer-uppers. 'Speedy' had a reputation for never paying his petrol bill. After filling up at service station and with lightning speed he would drive off the forecourt and be gone before he was noticed by the sales staff. I asked Parvis, if he was ever worried that one day he might be apprehended and have to face the consequences.'There is nothing to worry about' he replied smugly.

I responded by saying 'And what if somebody made a note of your car registration number?'

With a self-satisfied grin he said 'Not if you have a false number plate.'

I held back from questioning Parvis further, I had remembered a conversation that I once had with David Upson, who was concerned over my 'perennial habit' of asking personal questions.

'Alf, you are fortunate in having an inquisitive mind, which is healthy, but you should always avoid asking a stranger too many personal questions, I repeat personal questions, because you just don't know how they might react.'

Every Friday at lunch time, an amplified, wailing voice from the top of the minaret at the Whitechapel Mosque summoned the faithful for prayers. The showroom and factory would become near empty as Haroon, Tariq, Anwa, Miah, Parvis and other members of staff answered the call.

There was no doubt in my mind that Haroon and Tariq were devout Moslems, but I had strong reservations about my three assistant layer-uppers.

I could not see how a tax evader, a petrol thief and somebody who had no qualms whatsoever about evicting an elderly woman from her home were Allah fearing Moslems who practised a code of ethics as instructed in their Koran.

Sitting in the pub with David Upson, he listened with interest when I relayed the various conversations I had with Anwa, Miah and Parvis. Dave agreed with my assessment that these supposedly sons of Mecca were no more than classic hypocrites.

I was surprised by what my friend said next.

'Alf, I know that you are blessed with a knack of being able to create some sort of rapport with people who assist you in the cutting room.'

'Do you think so?' I replied with raised eyebrows. I was not aware that I possessed the knack, although I often found that my cutting room helpers who usually came from a variety of countries which included Africa and the middle and Far East, seem to show a willingness to chat to me, especially about their country of origin.

My friend continued, 'You see Alf, you don't come across as being a supercilious Englishman, but just another fellow worker, who, like them are trying to earn a living, I am sure these people feel completely at ease with you.'

Spending so much time working in East End clothing factories which were predominantly staffed by foreigners, I was often surprised to learn that many of my assistant layer-uppers were highly educated with university degrees. Besides working alongside former farm labourers from Bangladesh, some of my Kurdish helpers were scientists and medical doctors who for various reasons were unable to practise their profession in Britain. It would also be fair to say that many of them were bogus asylum seekers.

A cutter friend told me that the Turkish directors of Good Gear Ltd, based in Cannon Street Road needed a dress cutter, I visited their factory, which was on the fourth floor of a modern industrial building; although there were lifts, I used the stairs.

Situated on each floor there were toilets and wash rooms. I peered inside one of the wash rooms; it was spotlessly clean.

When I reached the fourth floor, I could hear loud shouting inside the Good Gear factory. Suddenly the door opened and out stepped a burly Turkish man in his mid twenties. He seemed upset and brushing past me he dashed down the stairs. As he did so an agitated middle-aged couple, also Turkish, came out of the factory and began calling out to him, 'Akut, Akut, Akut'.

There was no response from the man, who I presumed had now left the building.

I waited until the couple had gone back inside before ringing the doorbell. Almost immediately, a smartly dressed, bespectacled man in his early thirties opened the door. He was obviously Turkish.

He spoke politely 'Can I help you.'

'Do you need an experienced kesici'

He chuckled, 'You speak Turkish.'

I explained that I knew just a few Turkish words.

The man invited me into his office which was adjacent to the factory entrance.

A huge see-through mirror stretched across one wall giving a clear view of the entire workforce busy at their machines.

Somehow I sensed, correctly, that the various holes in the hardboard walls of the office were caused by the fists of the burly young Turk who had just ran down the stairs.

The man said that his name was Sedat and that he and his partner Akut (pronounced 'icoot') were subcontractors for mainly West End fashion houses and that their production was approximately three thousand dresses a week.

He went on to say that he employed Carl, a Jamaican cutter, but the man was totally unreliable.

'He comes one day and the next day he does not.'

I was asked two questions: can I accept three pounds an hour and could I start work straight away. Although the hourly rate was less than what I expected, I answered yes to both questions.

Sedat assured me that he would deduct my national insurance contributions. As expected there would be no sick or holiday pay.

Within five minutes of arriving at the factory. I began cutting a multiple lay of dresses.

I suspected the fabric had been layed up by the absentee Carl.

Some two hours later I had cut out the lay and was promptly given a cup of coffee by a slim dark-haired girl in her early twenties. I had noticed her earlier trimming the cotton ends of newly pressed dresses.

As she handed me the cup she said 'Hello, my name is Fisun and I am a Turkish Cypriot.'

I responded by saying 'Hello, benim adum Alf' (My name is Alf.)

Her pretty face lit up and she said 'I see you know some Turkish'.

Fisun explained that Sadet and Akut, who were originally from Istanbul, rarely spent more than three or four hours at the factory and that they usually remained in the office for most of that period rather than helping in the factory.

'Then who is in charge of production?' I enquired.

'Akut's parents, Salih and Nejla,' she replied, pointing to a middle-aged man and a woman who were eating sandwiches at a work-bench by the factory door. They were the same couple who had called out to Akut as he dashed down the stairs.

After the coffee break was over, I began to separate the cut lay into bundles. The first of the completed bundles were instantly collected by the overlockers, who had been sitting patiently at their machines.

I soon got to know the three overlockers. The youngest, an Asian girl, was called 'Sweetie'. For somebody who had a dour character, never smiled and only spoke occasionally, I thought the sobriquet was inappropriate. The second overlocker, Pat, was a local woman in her mid-thirties. The words love and hate were tattooed on her fingers. Finally there was ever smiling, chain smoking Connie.

Maltese born Connie seemed past retirement age. She had moved to Croydon after spending more than thirty years living at Stepney. By coincidence she was a former next door neighbour of my friends the Lomiglio family.

Towards the end of my first week at the factory, Carl the absentee cutter arrived for work. Fisun had already informed me that 'Carl was not a nice man.' I gained the impression by the tone of her voice that she might be a little afraid of him.

Fisun's description of Carl was accurate; he was most certainly not a nice man and he took umbrage when he noticed me glancing at his hastily made marker.

'Why are you looking at my marker?' he asked.

I hesitated before replying 'I thought that as the fabric for the lay is 60 inches wide, perhaps you should have made the marker 59 inches and not 60 inches.'

'And why should I have done that?' he snarled.

I explained that if some of the rolls of fabric were not quite 60 inches wide we might have to alter the marker and make it narrower.

Before rudely turning his back on me, he muttered 'You do your work and I will do mine.'

I was more than happy to comply.

The next day, which was a Friday, Carl failed to come in to work, which pleased me. However, the next day he arrived at 11am; there was no response when I wished him 'good morning'.

Just as Carl was about to begin making a marker, Sadet came over to the cutting table and explained to Carl that as he did not come into work the previous day and that the new cutter (Me) was reliable and very experienced, he should find work elsewhere. Carl sighed with disappointment. Striding towards the exit, he glared at me menacingly. His departure brought an instant smile on

Fisun's face.

Sweetie, in one of her rare loquacious moods, told me that for several weeks Carl, unknown to Sadet or Akut had been in the process of opening a small clothing workshop and that whenever he was short of funds he would arrive at the factory and expect to be allowed to work.

Because the fabric for the dockets was 60 inches wide, I was in constant need of an assistant layer-upper. Usually my helper would be one of the pressers, but whenever the pressers were busy Salih would volunteer. If he was unavailable then as a last resort a reluctant Sadet or Akut would be forced to assist me.

At times Salih could be a little heavy handed with the fabric, but overall his occasional tugging of the selvedge edge was easily rectified. During the laying up process we often chatted; he spoke good English, unlike his wife Nejla, whose English was very limited.

Salih mentioned how he and Nejla and their two children 14-year-old Akut and his younger sister left Turkey in 1975 and settled in London's East End. Nejla, a skilled sample machinist, had been invited by Irfan Nadir to work at his Stepney Wearwell dress factory. Salih was also offered work at the same factory.

When Akut was not attending the Robert Montefiore School in nearby Vallance Road, especially during the school holidays, he would earn pocket money by doing odd jobs at the Wearwell factory. After leaving school at 16 he began working full time at the same factory, where he learnt to be a special machinist. Two years later he went to Istanbul to complete his national service. After basic training he was posted to northern Cyprus where he joined an infantry battalion. When he completed his national service, he returned to his family in Stepney. Shortly after his return he became friends with Sadet and in due course the two men formed a partnership and opened up the Good Gear manufacturing company, they also persuaded Salih and Nejla to leave Wearwell and manage their factory.

I enjoyed working with quietly spoken Salih. He was intelligent and well read – one of his favourite authors was Charles Dickens – and he was fond of the cinema too. Like me he adored Vittorio De Sica's neo-realism film 'The Bicycle Thieves'.

Salih often reminisced about his homeland and each summer he and Nejla would spend two months holiday at their seaside apartment near Istanbul.

It was from Salih that I first learnt about the revered Turkish statesman and soldier Mustafa Kemal Pasha (1881-1938) otherwise known as Ataturk, Head of the Turks. Salih explained that in 1915 Ataturk, as a military commander, successfully defended the Dardanelles against the British and ANZAC forces. In 1921 Ataturk's troops drove the Greek occupying army out of Turkey's Asia

Minor. Following the military success over the Greeks and the collapse of the Ottoman Empire, Ataturk was made first president of the newly formed Turkish republic.

The next day Salih again assisted me to lay fabric; I was glad because it would be another opportunity to familiarise myself with Turkish history. Salih explained that at Ataturk's insistence, his People's Party immediately embarked on a radical policy of westernising the republic. Polygamy was outlawed, and Islam was no longer to be the state's religion and a new legal system based on European models was introduced. Salih also told me that the Turkish army had always held real power in Turkey. It was wholly independent and its loyalty was first and foremost to the ideals and aspirations of Ataturk. The army would never allow an extreme left-wing, communist or Islamist party to govern Turkey. Salih quoted an example of the army's intervention in state affairs. In 1960 the then unpopular Turkish premier Adnan Menderes of the ruling Democratic Party attempted to abolish the opposition party and ban the freedom of the press; the army soon intervened and arrested Menderes and members of his cabinet.

'And what happened next?' I enquired.

He quietly replied, 'Menderes was hanged.'

Salih was highly critical of the Kurdish Workers Party (PKK), who were engaged in a violent struggle with the Turkish Army. He could not understand why his country's Kurdish minority wanted to create an independent Kurdistan in eastern Turkey when they were already fully integrated into Turkish society.

'Some Kurds are government ministers; others hold senior positions in industry and the universities. Yes, they should have a greater autonomy, but not full independence.'

He was convinced that the Kurds ongoing military campaign was disastrous for both the Turks and the Kurds.

His tone was ominous when he continued. 'No matter how many thousands of lives are lost, the Turkish government and particularly the army would never allow the Kurds to fulfil their ambitions.'

During my first month at the factory both Akut and Sadet would also help me to lay the fabric.

Sadet was a superb assistant; he possessed a gentle touch and never once did he tug at the fabric. He also had cutting experience which had proved invaluable whenever the unreliable Carl had not arrived for work.

When Sadet noticed I never wore a watch, he immediately removed his own watch and offered it to me as a gift. Not to offend him, I told a little lie. I was unable to accept his kind offer as my own watch was being repaired.

Sadet, a married man with two young children, was always impeccably dressed in expensive suits and silk shirts. He enthusiastically disclosed his future plans to me. As well as clothing manufacturing, he and Akut wanted to expand into other businesses, notably imports and exports.

At a later date, when Sadet assisted me to lay the fabric, he seemed keen to inform me about his ever abiding problem. He was an addicted gambler who frequented casinos and he admitted that his addiction might seriously inhibit his business plans.

'I had never been inside a casino' I casually remarked.

He replied in a serious tone, 'My friend, never go to the casino, stay away. Since coming to London three years ago, I have lost over £100,000 in the casinos.'

Unfortunately for Sadet, his compulsive gambling would eventually cause his ruination. His wife divorced him and his partnership with Akut came to an end.

Akut was not a capable assistant layer upper; he was clumsy and continually pulled at his selvedge edge, which made it difficult and time consuming for me to keep my edge perfectly straight. But despite his clumsiness I enjoyed working with him. Akut was unmarried. He had moved out of his parents Stepney council flat and had bought a large three bedroom house in Ilford. I often wondered how he and Sadet's partnership survived; their characters were so different. Sadet was calm, softly spoken and never raised his voice, even when there were serious problems with the production. Akut was the opposite; he was unable to control his temper and constantly shouted. His fury was never directed at Sadet or the staff, but always at his parents, whom he blamed for every major or minor mishap which occurred in the factory. He would go berserk if an important telephone message was not passed on to him or if Salih had been unable to have a docket of dresses ready in time for delivery.

Akut's excessive tantrums were followed by his fists or powerful hands breaking up various objects and furniture in the office. While Akut was in a destructive mood, Sadet would look the other way or leave the office. I once accidentally bumped into the muscular Akut during one of his rages; it felt as if I had collided with an oak tree. When in a relaxed mood, usually during the lunch breaks, Akut would come out of the office and challenge any of his male employees to an arm wrestle. It was an unfair duel; no opponent could ever beat Akut, who had Herculean strength. He enjoyed being referred to as Rambo, but resented being called Tarzan.

Despite his regular tantrums in the factory, which often distracted the staff from their work, nobody disliked Akut; in fact he was very popular in the factory. When not shouting, he was amiable and very friendly to his staff and his immense strength proved useful.

An elderly woman was being molested outside the factory by an intoxicated Somalian.

When Akut heard her cries, he raced down the stairs and into the street. I looked out of the window and saw Akut grab the Somalian by the throat and lift him high against the wall. After the woman hurried away, Akut released his grip on the man's throat who instantly slid to the ground in a heap.

Unlike Sadet, who preferred a suit and tie, Akut always wore trendy casual clothes. Avoiding casinos, his evenings were spent at the Stringfellows West End discothèque where his good looks attracted a constant array of international girls. He had a penchant for fast cars too, which he regularly wrecked. Unquestionably a demon driver who seemed to received weekly speeding tickets, he never understood the need for speed limits. Getting from point A to point B in the shortest possible time was an absolute necessity for Akut.

He invited me to join him for lunch at a well known Turkish restaurant near Oxford Street.

Sitting in his Transom car I clung to my seat throughout the journey. His reckless driving resulted in two minor accidents and although he had caused the mishaps, he still blamed the other drivers.

My accompanying him was well worth it, the Turkish food was superb, dish after dish was brought to our table, and each dish was more delicious and larger than the previous one. I had never eaten so much exotic food in my life.

After an hour of continually eating I felt as if I was about to burst, but not Akut, who had an enormous appetite. He ate and ate and ate. His insatiable appetite was legendary. He once invited his two close friends Jumblut and Abdul for dinner at his home, where he had cooked a large joint of beef. While his impatient and hungry guests sat at the table, Akut set about cutting the beef. Instead of cutting it evenly three ways as they expected, Jumblut and Abdul were each given a thin slice of the beef no more than half an inch thick. The remaining joint the size of a small loaf of bread was plonked onto Akut's plate. The vegetables were dispensed in a similar manner.

With amusement, Jumblut related to me an episode which involved him and Akut.

They had met two American girls at the Stringfellows discotheque.

Just before returning to California, the girls invited Akut and Jumblet to spend a holiday with them at their Malibu apartment.

The invitation was too good to ignore; both girls were blonde, blue-eyed beauties.

Whist in California the foursome spent a great deal of time on the beach or relaxing around the apartment's swimming pool.

It was during the afternoon when Akut left the beach alone and returned to the apartment. Feeling hungry he opened the fridge and devoured every item of food inside, including the entire stock of fruit drinks and beer. After leaving the kitchen he staggered sleepily to a bedroom and collapsed onto the bed.

A few hours later, Jumblut and the girls returned to the apartment. They went into the kitchen to get some refreshment. The girls, but not Jumblut, were shocked to discover the fridge was completely empty. They thought that burglars had entered the apartment and had raided the fridge. Jumblut managed to persuade the girls not to contact the police. Suddenly the sound of loud snoring could be heard coming from one of the bedrooms. Akut was spread-eagled on the bed and the girls knew by the size of Akut's enormous stomach why the fridge was bare. From that moment, Akut and the guiltless Jumblut were persona non grata. The next day the two Turks returned to London. There would be no further contact with the girls.

Akut's lifestyle of discotheques, dating girls and fast cars was frowned upon by his mother. She was desperate for him to get married and raise a family. Finding a bride for her son became her top priority and friends in Istanbul were asked to find a respectable applicant. Eventually such a girl was found.

To appease his mother Akut agreed to meet the girl, but he had no real intentions to get married. Rather than fly to Istanbul, he decided to go overland by car. Somewhere along the route he spotted an attractive girl hitchhiking; he stopped the car alongside her and she got inside. As they drove away the girl placed her hand on his knee; Akut immediately responded by driving into a quite lane. Sitting in the back seat he was shocked to discover the girl had male genitals. Besides having male genitals the transvestite would now have a bruised bottom which was caused by Akut's trainers when he booted her out of the car.

Akut duly arrived in Istanbul where he met the intended one. After failing to seduce her, he jumped into his car and embarked on the long journey back to London.

His mother was dismayed but not totally disappointed when he explained that he did not think that the Turkish girl would have made a suitable wife and that she (his mother) could continue to search for a prospective bride. That same evening he made his way to Stringfellows.

During the lunch breaks, it was an opportunity for me to wander around the factory floor and try and get to know the employees, who seemed to be from all over the world. There were Turks from Istanbul and Cyprus, Turkish Kurds, Greek Cypriots, Sikhs, Pakistanis, Bangladeshis, Maltese, Macedonians, Africans and two or three English people.

Joseph, a Nigerian presser, believed that one day he would be able to correctly forecast the six winning national lottery numbers. He was absolutely convinced that the numbers were not randomly picked but were the result of a pre-arranged fixture which had a set pattern.

From the day the national lottery was introduced in Britain he made a weekly note of the winning numbers. By comparing these numbers past and present he thought he would eventually 'crack the code'. He showed me his long list of the previous jackpot numbers.

'Now you see the number 6 is followed by number 17, well in two weeks time the number 7 should be followed by number 18 and you see number 23 is followed by 31, in three weeks time number 32 will follow number 19.'

I felt extremely sorry for Joseph. It seemed obvious to me that he was living in a fool's paradise. Throughout the tea and lunch breaks he would sit quietly by the pressing machine and study his formula. He probably spent much of his time at home repeating the same exercise.

To put is theory into practice, he needed to spend a minimum of £80 each week buying lottery tickets, but by his own admission he rarely won more than £10.

Forever optimistic he explained, 'I haven't quite got it right yet, but I know I am on the right track.'

Sadly for Joseph, he was never on the right track, after spending thousands of pounds on the National Lottery and no big wins, he finally conceded defeat. I advised him to buy premium bonds instead.

'At least your money is safe and there is always the chance that you might win the monthly £1,000,000.'

Not to make him look foolish, I declined to mention that, like the National Lottery, premium bond numbers are picked randomly.

Tariqe, also a Good Gear presser was born in East Ham of Pakistani parents; he spoke with a cockney accent.

When Tariqe reached 21, his mother insisted that it was time for him to get married. Unwilling to upset her he agreed to give up his partying, drinking and womanising and marry the girl his mother had chosen for him;, but there was a problem. He had never met the girl, who was living in Lahore, or had even seen a photo of her. However, the girl was brought over from Pakistan and the marriage was quickly arranged and would be held in an East London mosque. Sadet and Akut were invited to the wedding.

Sadet who was standing alongside Tariqe in the mosque pointed to a group of girls and whispered in his ear 'Tariqe which one of those girls is the bride?'

He answered insouciantly 'Don't ask me, I haven't got a clue.'

Shortly after the wedding Tariqe was back at work and I asked him if he thought his marriage would survive. His answer was a resounding 'No'.

'Then why did you get married?' I asked.

He smiled 'Just to pacify my parents.'

Tariqe's mother would not remain pacified for long. She became outraged when Tariqe left his pregnant wife and promptly returned to his hedonistic lifestyle. Divorce followed soon afterwards.

Another presser, Satnam Singh, was originally from New Dehli. In due course Satnam and I became good friends. Not only was he a hard working presser, he also had experience of garment cutting and was a first class assistant layer-upper. he was also quite capable of doing minor repairs to the factory's sewing machines. Moreover, he would on occasion be Good Gear's driver. Because of his versatility and willingness to work long hours he was promoted to foreman.

Like many Sikhs, Satnam had a fondness for alcohol. Sitting in the pub after work he explained to me that he had had an arranged marriage in the Sikh tradition. He admitted that he would have much preferred a 'love marriage'. I suspected from his slightly maudlin state that he had an unhappy home life. My suspicion soon proved correct. His wife ordered him out of the family home in Croydon, denied him access to their young son and began divorce proceedings.

Being single again, my friend hoped that in time he would meet other woman, but if he married again, it would be for love.

Meeting woman proved difficult for Satnam, he blamed his lack of success on his rapidly receding hair line which he thought woman found unattractive.

'How can I stop going bald Alf? ' he remarked plaintively.

Because baldness is a delicate subject, being tactful was essential when I gave him my answer.

'Unfortunately Satnam, I don't know if there is a reliable remedy that can prevent hair loss, your pattern of growth is probably inherited from either side of your parents; perhaps hair transplants might help, but from what little I know, transplants cost a fortune.'

My answer caused him to frown.

The next day and to my astonishment, he had shaven his hair and was completely bald. He came over to the cutting table during the morning tea break and was in an elated mood.

'Alf, last night, I was given some professional advice how to grow new hair.'

'You were?' I replied, totally mystified.

'Yes, I was told that if I shave of all of my hair, the baldness will stimulate new growth.'

I thought whoever had given him that advice was an imbecile.

A few weeks later when Satnam realised that no new hair was appearing where none was before, he became very disappointed. I tried to console him by suggesting that if he meets the right woman she would be unconcerned about his receding hair line, alternatively he should try and find the money and have a hair transplant.

He spoke glumly 'Where can I find the money, my wife has taken the lot.'

After his divorce, Satnam rented a room in a sparse Whitechapel council flat. The tenant was a Sikh friend named Rangit.

Rangit no longer slept on the premises. Every morning from Monday to Sunday he would arrive at the flat.

At 9 p.m. he would leave the flat and return by bus to his freehold house in Plaistow, East London which he shared with his wife and two teenage children.

Although it was illegal for council tenants like Rangit to sub-let and also to own a freehold house which he lived in, the rule did not deter Rangit from owning, besides his house in Plaistow, one or two other houses which he let out.

From the rents received from his properties, Rangit had sufficient funds to give up work and laze around all day drinking Scotch whisky at the Whitechapel flat.

According to Satnam, Rangit was an alcoholic who consumed at least two bottles of whisky every day. My friend also told me that Rangit's wife had long ago accepted her husband's alcoholism, but refused to allow him to drink at the family home, insisting that if he had to drink, he should do so at Whitechapel.

I met Rangit when Satnam invited me to the flat for an Indian meal which he had cooked.

Rangit, who was in a dishevelled state, declined to sample the curry and rice, instead he preferred to sit in an armchair and continually drink neat whisky. I soon noticed that he was a chronic hay-fever sufferer; several times he almost spilt his whisky when he was seized by an attack of loud and uncontrollable sneezing.

With so many germs from Rangit's nose heading towards the dining table, Satnam's carefully prepared meal was less appealing. I ate just a morsel before leaving the flat and going home.

At work the next day Satnam apologised for Rangit's thoughtlessness.

Sedat was involved in a serious argument with two Vietnamese outdoor machinists, both of whom demanded to be paid for their badly machined dresses. Sedat refused and insisted that they must alter and repair the garments before they received payment. When the men began to remonstrate, Sedat attempted to push them out of the factory. The men responded by punching him. Sedat retaliated by punching them back. The Vietnamese who were short and slightly built were injured by Sadet's ferocious blows; picking themselves up from the floor they scampered out of the factory.

For Sadet, this incident was only the beginning; the Vietnamese wanted revenge.

Within the hour the two men returned with at least a dozen of their associates, each man was armed with a stick.

Salih tried to prevent the outraged mob from entering the factory. Had Akut been on the premises, he would have taken on the mob single-handed. Sedat who was in the adjacent office and had heard the fracas, quickly darted out of the office and ran down the fire escape at the rear of the factory floor. Instead of leaving the area, he unwisely went inside one of the little Asian cafes opposite the factory.

When the Vietnamese realised that Sadet had managed to escape they left.

From the windows the Vietnamese could be seen loitering on the pavement. Suddenly a finger was pointed at the cafe where Sadet had taken refuge, he had been spotted. Shouting and waving their sticks the Vietnamese charged into the café and began to beat Sadet viciously around his head and arms.

The assault lasted just seconds. Having satisfied themselves that Sadet had received sufficient retribution, the Vietnamese got into their cars, which were parked nearby, and quickly drove away. Meanwhile, the café proprietor had phoned for an ambulance. Sadet was taken to the nearby London Hospital at Whitechapel, where a brain scan revelled no damaged had been done, but as a precaution he was kept in the hospital overnight for observation.

Like the Turks, the Vietnamese were a hardworking people. A few of the more enterprising Vietnamese opened clothing factories, but the majority preferred being outdoor machinists where they could work long hours, seven days a week. However, machining at home, especially if they lived in council accommodation, created problems with their neighbours, who would complain about the incessant noise from the sewing machines. I knew of an extended Vietnamese family who had installed six industrial sewing machines in their top floor flat of a Hackney skyscraper. The African residents in the flat below complained about the sewing machines continuous vibrations. The Vietnamese's response was to offer them £50 a week compensation if they would tolerate the disturbance. The bribe was accepted.

To cut the required 3,000 plus dresses each week at the Good Gear factory, I needed to work a minimum of 70 hours from Monday to Sunday. After working 80 consecutive days, my friend David Upson managed to persuade me to have a Sunday off because 'Barbara (his sister) has cooked us a pilchard curry.'

I devised a new cutting system that would take the pressure off me at work and also speed up the cutting process. My usual work pattern was to cut a docket of dresses first and then cut the stayflex fusible lining for the dress's neck and armhole facings later. Rather than cut twice, I would combine the fabric and the stayflex into one cut. The old method was time consuming and costly; each facing had to be manually layed singly onto its stayflex and when it was approximately 30 pieces high it was steam pressed.

My new method was relatively simple and would eliminate the need to lay the facings onto the stayflex.

I would incorporate a mini-marker in the lower left corner of the dress marker. This mini-marker would be 36 inches wide, which is the same width as a roll of stayflex and would contain all of the dress markers facings. After each run of 60 inch wide fabric was layed, a run of stayflex would be layed.

The combined fabric and stayflex could be up to 250 runs high. As I cut each facing it would be kept intact by small ties. At the pressing stand Salih would steam press multiple layers of them. By the time I had cut the rest of the lay, the pressed facings would be ready for me when I did the bundling.

Akut and Sadet were so appreciative of my time saving new procedure that I was given a small pay rise.

When the bundles were overlocked they were placed in big racks and collected by the machinists, who were piece-rate workers. Each machinist would take one bundle at a time as required by Nejla, but when there were just a few bundles remaining, some machinist would ignore Nejla's ruling and grab two or three bundles. This greed provoked acrimony amongst the machinists.

Two machinists, Nicki and Chris, were Greek Cypriot sisters. Both sisters sat opposite the racks and were prone to snatch the last of the bundles.

Nicki had a terrible cough as a result of her life-long smoking. She also had an uncontrollably nasty temper which caused her to argue and occasionally strike other machinists, particularly her two enemies Joyce and Vida, whom she referred to as 'snakes'.

Nicki's always made careful note of the bundles in the racks. Usually, if there was just one bundle left, she made sure it was hers. I peered over the top of the cutting machine with amusement as Nicki quickly got up from her sewing machine and almost ran towards the racks. She had spotted a Vietnamese male machinist about to pick up the last bundle of 25 dresses. Both Nicki and the Vietnamese had their hands on the bundle and a tug-of-war ensued. Nicki won and carried the bundle away; in the process she told the Vietnamese to 'fuck off'.

After I had worked at the factory for about six months, the inevitable happened – Good Gear Ltd went bankrupt. The bankruptcy did not affect the workforce, we just continued working. Overnight a new company had been formed.

Akut bought dozens of rolls of floral cotton fabric from a man who claimed he was a travelling salesman.

I thought that Akut had acted foolish buying the fabric, which looked dated and totally unsuitable for any of the current styles which we had in production.

As I was very busy cutting dockets for our regular suppliers, it would be several weeks before I could cut the cotton fabric; even then it was unlikely that we could find an appropriate style.

I raised my concern with Akut and advised him to return the fabric and be refunded.

'But Alf, I bought the cloth cheap' he emphasized cheap.

The day after Akut had made the unwise purchase, four men who were obvious plain-clothes policeman came into the factory; Sadet and Akut had yet to arrive. While two of the policemen stood by the entrance the other two, followed by Salih and Nejla strode towards the cutting table, I immediately switched off the cutting machine. Without a word being said to me, one of the policemen looked under the table and pulled out a roll of the cotton fabric. He turned to the other policeman, whom I assumed was in charge of the raid and said 'it's here guv'.

The sergeant, a giant of a man, towered over Nejla, who was standing close by with folded arms.

Pointing his finger at her, he spoke sternly 'Your son is very naughty'.

Although Nejla had no idea what the word 'naughty' meant; she answered him by nodding her head and saying 'yes naughty, naughty'.

Her answer caused me and both policemen to giggle.

In between giggling, I explained to the sergeant that Nejla did not understand what he was saying.

'I know that,' he replied sympathetically.

When a shocked Akut arrived shortly afterwards, the policemen were removing the rolls of cotton fabric from under the table and were carrying them out of the factory.

Luckily for Akut, the police accepted his explanation that he thought that he had bought the fabric legitimately and he had no knowledge that it had been stolen. He also assured the police that in future he would only buy fabric from established cloth merchants.

For Akut the episode had been costly. He would never recover the money spent on purchasing the fabric.

In the mid 1980s my father suddenly became ill. The doctor who examined him diagnosed Bell's Palsy, but after further tests it was discovered that he had suffered a mild stroke.

Akut never complained when I had to take my father for his hospital appointments, he even offered to drive us to the London hospital. Unfortunately, co-operation was not forthcoming from Sadet who, much to my surprise and regret, objected to my leaving the factory for a few hours. He stopped me at the door and insisted that I must stay and finish cutting a lay of dresses. I explained that I would only be away for a short period and perhaps Satnam could cut the lay in my absence. Sadet was not prepared to listen and he again demanded that I return at once to the cutting table.

'Return at once to the cutting table?' I replied angrily.

'How dare you tell me what I can and can't do, my father's health is much more important than this job.'

I did not wait for Sadet's response and quickly left the factory in an agitated state.

During the ten minute drive to Poplar to collect my father for his hospital appointment, I decided that instead of returning to the factory after the appointment I would seek employment elsewhere.

Later that afternoon, I phoned Akut and explained that because of Sadet's heartlessness, I could no longer work at his factory. Akut immediately apologised for Sadet being 'out of order'. Following the apology he said, 'please don't leave us Alf, you're one of the family, and we can't manage without you.'

As much as I was fond of Akut and his parents, I felt that I had made the right decision and told him so. There was sadness in his voice when he asked me to come to his office and collect my wages and P45.

The next day when I returned to the factory, I was prepared for a verbal or even a physical confrontation with Sadet, but he was not in the office when Akut handed me my wages.

Before leaving the office, I explained to Akut that I had absolutely no quarrel with him and if ever his partnership with Sedat came to an end, I would be willing to work for him again.

'Thanks a lot Alf' he replied with a gratifying smile.

For the next six months I worked at several clothing factories in the Whitechapel area. During this period Akut would phone me constantly. His questions were always the same.

'How is your father's health? '

'Where are you working? '

'Do you earn good wages? '

It was a late evening when a slightly excited Akut phoned me.

'Alf, Alf, Sadet is no longer my partner, he is gone forever; I know you will keep your promise Alf. My Mum and Dad miss you too. Alf you must come to the factory so we can talk.'

On entering Akut's factory at 1 p.m. the following day, the workers were about to take their lunch break.

Akut was not in the office but I soon spotted him at the far end of the factory by the cutting table.

As I walked across the factory floor, I was greeted by a smiling Salih and Nejla and loud cheering from the entire workforce; it was a touching and memorable scene.

At the cutting table, a beaming Akut with his vice like grip shook my hand. He made no mention of why he and Sadet had ended their partnership. Although I had a strong suspicion that it may have been as a result of Sadet's occasional borrowing the staff wages to pay off his gambling debts. He also revealed that his company now had a new name, which did not surprise me at all.

Akut explained that since I had left his employ six months earlier he had been unable to find a suitable cutter and subsequently the production had been reduced and because there was less bundles of cut garments available for his machinists, who were on piece work, he had been forced to ration the bundles, which in turn had created arguments and friction amongst the workers. He pointed to scores of rolls of fabric which were stacked under the cutting table and spoke frustratedly.

'I have plenty of dockets, dresses, blouses and slacks, but I can't get them cut; that's why I need you, Alf.'

He went on to say that he could not always spare Satnam to do the cutting as he had other duties which kept him occupied. However, he currently employed Nina, an Australian cutter, but she had insufficient experience.

I made just one demand, which Akut promptly agreed to: I would have total control of the cutting section and I would be allowed to dismiss any cutter or assistant cutter that I thought was unsuitable. Suddenly Akut was called to the office to answer the telephone. Whilst he was away, Fisun came over to the cutting table and told me of an incident that involved Nina the day before.

Apparently Nina, who had only been working at the factory for just a few weeks, had not been forewarned that the factory's fire alarm would be tested. The sudden loud ringing of the bell had caused her to panic and grabbing her coat and bag she ran out of the factory in tears and had yet to return.

The next day I arrived for work at 7.30 a.m. It felt good to be back, knowing that I would be surrounded by old friends. Nejla gave me a cup of coffee and said 'Alf, lunch time, I give food. nice you like.'

I certainly liked Turkish food. Ever since I began working for Akut three years before, his kind mother regularly gave me plates of scrumptious Turkish dishes to enjoy.

After I drank the coffee and at great speed I set about making a multiple shirt-blouse marker.

While I was making the marker, a thought entered my mind; if Nina did arrive for work that morning and had limited cutting experience, as Akut claimed, would she be capable of cutting accurately the all important blouse collar stands? If she did ruin a stand, we could be in deep trouble. As a precaution to avoid that possibility, I decided to allow space in the marker for two additional collar stands.

An hour or so later Nina arrived. She was about 25, slim and at least 5 foot 7 inches tall. I wished her good morning and introduced myself. What happened next surprised me; she blew her nose into a tissue, but instead of placing the used tissue into a nearby rubbish sack it was thrown to the floor. There was no noticeable reaction to my look of surprise.

With the marker almost completed, Nina began dragging out the relevant rolls of fabric for the lay from under the cutting table. Despite her slender frame she seemed quite strong.

A moment later she blew her nose a second time and as before the used tissue landed on the floor.

Working with a female cutter for the first time might be a challenge and I hoped that she would not be uncooperative but my hopes were dashed that very morning.

After I had finished the marker, I suggested to her that before we begin laying the fabric, perhaps she would like to carefully examine the marker to see if I had made any errors.

Her blank expression was a clue; checking markers was as alien to her as using the rubbish sack for her discarded tissues.

Apart from her disgusting habit, Nina proved to be a competent layer-upper and we worked at a fast pace.

It took us about four hours to lay the fabric and during that time at least half a dozen more of her tissues were scattered on the floor.

When we began cutting the lay, her lack of experience soon became evident. She was pushing the Eastman cutting machine hard into the fabric and the inevitable happened – her forcefulness almost caused the machine to tip over. Fearing that she might cut her fingers, I immediately stopped her working and politely advised her not to push the machine, but to allow it to cut into the fabric at its own speed

'I know all that' she replied irritably.

Her rude rebuff startled me. My first reaction was to ask her to leave the factory and not to come back but then I thought she should have another chance and at the end of the day I would make a decision whether she should stay or go. My warning did have had an effect because when she resumed her cutting, she no longer pushed the cutting machine into the lay.

A little later, I watched with concern as Nina began to cut a delicate collar stand. Her method was completely wrong. She was trying to cut the stand in a continuous cut rather than several cuts, which was the tried and tested way. Consequently the finished stand was badly shaped: one end was rounded and the other went to a point. As I observed her working, I could not but wonder why Akut engaged somebody who was so inexperienced.

I stopped Nina working a second time and explained that because the collar stand which she had cut was unusable, she must concentrate on cutting the more easy bodices and sleeves.

'Does that mean that you are going to cut out the remaining collar stands?' she snapped.

I immediately snapped back 'Yes I am.'

She had an available answer.

'So far, not one machinist has criticized my work, not even Nicki.'

Her argument was probably fair. Since she began working at the factory she had only cut simple dress dockets, where mistakes were less likely to occur, but now she was cutting a shirt-blouse docket, which included the extremely difficult collar stands.

I had made the right decision to allow space in the marker for re-cutting any damaged collar stands. Nina glared at me when I threw her useless collar stand into the waste cuttings sack and marked the new stand in the marker

During the afternoon ten minute break, Nina took her cup of tea and sat amongst the overlockers. While she was away Akut came up to the cutting table and asked me if I was satisfied with Nina's work.

I was certainly not satisfied with her work. Had I had told him so, he would have instantly dismissed her.

Somehow, I felt it was premature to give him a definite answer, but I did say 'It's too early to say at the moment.' I hoped that in the coming few days the standard of Nina's work would improve and that she would refrain from being rude to me, if there was no improvement, then I would ask Akut to replace her. There was indeed a noticeable improvement, which began that very next day. She adopted a polite tone when speaking to me and she seemed to show some interest when I explained the correct way to cut collar stands.

Over the next two weeks we cut approximately six to seven thousand dresses and blouses. Akut was very pleased with the figures, but there was a setback. Nina began making some serious mistakes when she did the bundling.

A furious Nicki and Chris complained to Nina that her bundles of blouses had the wrong size labels inside. Nina refused to accept blame, but showed a willingness to rectify the error. By denying responsibility she was indicating to Nicki that I might have mixed up the labels. This scenario reminded me of the pathetic Lionel's failed attempt to blame me for a similar mistake when I worked at Marco Gowns in 1961, but since working for Akut I no longer initialled the back of the labels, it was not necessary. Over the years, I had developed an almost infallible method of eliminating bundling mistakes. Nina's refusal to admit responsibility could have been adequate grounds for her dismissal, but because she began to replace the correct labels in the bundles, I made no comment.

A week or so later Nina made another bundling mistake which was more serious than the previous one. She had accidentally put size 16 blouse bodices in size 12 bundles. Fortunately, Connie noticed the mishap when she was about to overlock one of the bundles. This early detection enabled Nina and me to rectify the bundles. After we had finished, I appealed to Nina to pay a greater attention when she did bundling.

My appeal was not well received. She barked at me 'Why are you always picking on me? '

I was quite shocked by her unwarranted riposte.

'But I am not picking on you,' I explained. 'It's essential that we co-operate with each other in order to keep ahead with the cutting, surely that makes sense.'

She answered spitefully, 'I can never co-operate with you, and you're just a know-it-all.'

Ignoring her asperity, I said 'Trust me Nina, I have been cutting garments for 30 years, don't you think you should be grateful that you are benefiting from my experience?'

My appeal was ignored. After cussing and calling me a 'bloody big head' she put on her coat, picked up her bag and hastily left the factory.

As I began to sweep up Nina's used tissues from the floor, Connie got up from her overlocking machine and came over to me and said 'Where is Nina going?'

'Hopefully, back to Australia,' I remarked.

Akut did not employ another cutter after Nina's sudden departure and consequently my work load was increased considerably. To lessen the burden I began to work extra hours. By doing so, I was able to cut Akut's weekly minimum requirement of 3,000 garments. Also my friend Satnam was beginning to spend more time at the cutting table. Although Satnam was unable to make markers or do simple pattern grading, the quality of his cutting was excellent and he rarely made mistakes during the bundling process.

Although at times it could be arduous working six and seven days every week, I rarely experienced tiredness, but tiredness did occur when I began working through the night.

David Upson gave me a stark warning.

'Alf you're crazy, you work all day, then through the night and then continue cutting the next day, you will be sorry mate, mark my words, if you don't work less hours you will have an accident with that cutting machine.'

I explained to Dave that if you work at a Turkish factory you must be prepared to work long hours.

Dave's prediction soon came true; I did indeed have an accident. Just for a second or two I dozed off whilst cutting out a lay of dresses. The result was painful: I sliced the top of my finger and blood cascaded onto the cutting table.

Within ten minutes I had arrived at the casualty department at the London Hospital. Half an hour later, and with five stitches in my finger, I walked back to the factory and finished cutting out the lay.

Earlier in the day, Maria, a diminutive Maltese button sewer, also had an accident. The button sewing machine's three inch needle went through her finger and was protruding out of the other side. The needle with Maria's finger still attached was unscrewed from the machine. While I held Maria's finger taught, Akut using pliers, pulled out the needle. A few moments later, Maria was back sitting at her button sewing machine and continued with her work as if nothing had happened.

I would have thought that as Akut's business was now flourishing he would have mellowed somewhat and ceased shouting at his long suffering parents, but it was not to be. He continued to shout at them with ever increasing intensity.

I knew that at times Akut suffered from excruciating pain from an old hip injury. He often walked with a slight limp. He claimed that the injury was the result of him jumping awkwardly out of a military helicopter whilst serving as a soldier in Northern Cyprus. Perhaps he needed a scapegoat to help him cope with the pain. If that were the case, who better than his ever compliant parents.

Akut eventually had two operations on his damaged hip. When he was discharged from hospital he was loaned a walking stick. After hobbling around the factory for several weeks, he no longer needed the stick; rather than return it to the hospital, he threw it out of the window during one of his verbal outbursts.

Akut's daily tantrums began to concern me. It was during the late morning when there was a terrific altercation taking place in the office and objects were being smashed. Suddenly, Akut and Salih came out of the office and began remonstrating in full view of the workforce. Nejla tried to stop them arguing but she was ignored. The next moment Akut was lying on the floor, his face contorted and he was shrieking like a spoilt child. Satnam and I and a few of the concerned pressers left our work places and gathered around Akut who was still on the floor. Meanwhile Salih, who decided that he had had enough of his troublesome son for one day, put on his jacket and left the factory. No sooner had Salih gone; Aycut stood up and ran towards an open window where he tried to climb out. Satnam and I and now joined by two pressers and Chris the machinist tried desperately to hang on to him as he was half dangling out of the window. Had we released him he would have fallen four floors to his death. After we managed with great effort to haul him back inside, we took him into the office where he remained in a quiet state for some time. When Salih returned several hours later, he refused to speak to his son.

Connie, commenting on Akut's real or phoney attempt at suicide, joked 'you should have let Akut fall.'

In due course there was another serious incident at the factory which alarmed the staff.

Hussein, a short, stocky cotton cleaner, had inadvertently upset Joseph the presser.

During the lunch break Hussein had tried to speak to Joseph while he was studying lottery numbers.

Joseph, annoyed with this interruption, slapped Hussein across the face. Hussein walked away and returned with a knife. Joseph, fearing for his safety, began to run around the factory followed by Hussein with the knife raised above his head. Akut and Salih were not in the factory and Nejla was too frightened to become involved, so it was left to Satnam and me to try and stop possible bloodshed.

Satnam, with the assistance of Khan, a tall presser, managed to hold on to Hussein, but he broke free and continued to chase Joseph. As Hussein was about to pass me, I stuck out my foot and tripped him up. Satnam, Khan and I quickly held Hussein onto the floor, but we were unable to persuade him to give up the knife.

After some twenty minutes Hussein agreed to release the knife. Still on the floor and looking up at me he said 'You my friend Arthur, me good Moslem and keep promise to you and no kill him.'

Hussein kept his promise and avoided all contact with Joseph.

Nejla's 18 year-old nephew Recept (pronounced Regep) was sent over from Istanbul. He would live with Nejla and Salih and work at the factory as my permanent assistant.

Akut had earlier asked me if I would teach Recept stock cutting, marker making and bundling. I had no complaints about having an assistant and if Recept was keen to learn the trade, I was quite willing to teach him.

Recept, a handsome young man, spoke very good English. He soon proved to be a capable assistant layer-upper and bundler, but he showed no interest whatsoever in learning to cut garments or make markers. These two aspects of the trade required much concentration, which he was unable to give. Other matters occupied his mind, particularly girls. He had become very impressed by his cousin Akut's ongoing success with the girls and wanted to follow suit. I fully understood how he felt, when I was 18, meeting girls was high on my list of priorities.

Recept soon began visiting clubs and discotheques; he bragged to me that whenever he walked into a club, girls would gaze longingly at him, 'they think I am Tom Cruise'.

I warned him, that 'Being promiscuous might be fun but' he interrupted me before I could finish what I wanted to say.

'What is promiscuous? '

'Having regular sex with different girls.' My explanation brought a grin on his face.

Still grinning, he stretched his arms backwards and said 'So what is wrong with that, I am enjoying my life.'

I suggested that if he wanted to continue enjoying his life, he should take precautions and use condoms.

'I will never use them' he replied nonchalantly.

Again I warned him 'You will be sorry.'

I also said, 'If you're not careful, you might contract a sexually transmitted disease.'

To emphasise my concern, I explained that because I was irresponsibly in the past, I had to be treated twice for non specific urethritis, and luckily for me it was not the more serious gonorrhoea and syphilis.

Recept would ignore my warning.

He came grim-faced into the factory one morning and spoke quietly to me at the cutting table.

'Alf I have a personal problem and I need your advice.'

I knew exactly what the problem was, which Recept soon confirmed. He had contracted a venereal disease.

Because he seemed a little worried, I offered to take him during the lunch break to the nearby VD Clinic at the London Hospital. I explained what the procedure was.

'At the reception desk, the clerk will not require your name and address, instead you will be given a small piece of paper with a number on it; then you will be asked to sit in a waiting area. When your number is called, you will be sent to a treatment room to be examined by a doctor; you must be prepared to give blood and urine samples, and also have a long thin wire with a small circle on the end threaded down your willy and twisted.'

'Twisted' He shuddered 'What is that for.'

'That's to teach you a lesson' I joked.

Not to make him to anxious, I explained that the implement would remove a small specimen of bodily fluid for analysis and would not be painful 'But might sting a bit.'

After I accompanied Recept to the clinic and left him at the receptionist desk I returned to the factory.

Recept was diagnosed with non-specific urethritis.

Like Akut, Recept drove cars fast and recklessly. As he sped down the

Whitechapel Road, he crashed into the back of a car which was about to stop at traffic lights. Rather than accept blame for the crash, he appealed to me to be a false witness.

'Alf, just say you were walking down the Whitechapel Road and that you saw the other car suddenly stop at the traffic lights even though they were green and that I could not stop in time.'

I refused to cooperate and was annoyed that he had the audacity to ask me to lie and break the law. From that moment I began to distance myself from him. Eventually that distance was extended further when Recept was switched from being my assistant and given other work to do in the factory, and my contact with him became less, but whenever we spoke it was always cordial.

Akut's business went bankrupt yet again, a new company was formed and Recept was installed as the company director. Being a director of a London registered company did not prevent him breaking English law. When he returned from a brief holiday in Turkey, he foolishly attempted to smuggle hundreds of small attractive birds in a big case through London Airport. He hoped that he could sell the birds through a contact in Hackney and make a large profit.

Recept's little enterprise failed. Custom officers at the airport heard faint chirping coming from inside the case; when the officers ordered Recept to open the case, they found many of the birds had expired.

The hapless Recept was promptly arrested, put on trial, found guilty and sentenced to three months in prison.

Recept's trial was reported in a leading newspaper.

Reading the headlines 'Company director gets the bird.' caused me to burst out laughing.

(Getting bird is gangsters slang for going to prison.)

Being a well-behaved prisoner, his sentence was reduced and when he was released from prison he returned to work. Having learnt his lesson, he became a law abiding citizen.

Recept was thrilled to learn that his mother and father would be coming to London for a working holiday and that they would be staying at Nejla's flat and help out at the factory.

Neither his parents could speak a word of English. Their stay in London lasted for about six weeks. Shortly after they returned to Istanbul, tragedy struck. Recept's mother, who was just 40 years old, suffered a heart attack and died. Recept was inconsolable when he heard the devastating news.

Several weeks after his mother's funeral I asked Recept if other members of his family had heart problems.

'Only my father' he replied. 'But that's because he is a heavy smoker.'

Even though he was aware of the dangers of smoking it did not prevent Recept taking up the habit.

In early July 1990 an appalling accident occurred in Saudi Arabia. Over 1.5 million pilgrims had gathered in the country and were visiting Mecca and Medina to celebrate the annual Eid-ul-Adha festival (festival of sacrifice). Although the purpose built foot tunnel which led from the holy Kaaba shrine in the grounds of Mecca's Great Mosque to nearby Mount Arafat had a capacity for a 1000 pedestrians; poor supervision had allowed 5000 pilgrims to cram inside. This decision had tragic consequences: the air conditioner had broken down and with soaring temperatures the pilgrims became trapped. Crushed against each other, they began to suffocate and other pilgrims were trampled to death during the struggle to escape.

When the rescue services retrieved the victims from the tunnel, the body count was 1,500.

In Cannon Street Road, several Bangladeshi men with collection boxes were appealing for money to be sent to the victim's families. When one of the collectors came into the factory the Moslem workers gave generously. One of those who donated money was Ali, a 40-year-old presser.

Ali was an old acquaintance of mine whom I had known from working in other factories in the area. He was originally from Bangladesh and had been living in Stepney for the previously two decades. Prior to settling in the area, he had worked briefly in a Lancashire mill.

In the old days Ali, who had a likeable and temperate personality, enjoyed a lively bachelor life style in the Whitechapel area. He wore snappy clothes, drank regularly in the pubs and dated local girls. However, since his arranged marriage and having children, he had changed completely. His neglected faith had been restored; he attended a local Mosque, grew a long beard and wore a Moslem white patterned cap.

On hearing that Ali had been on Hajj, his fellow workmates referred to him as Hajjis. (Hajj is a pilgrimage to Mecca and Medina that all Moslems are encouraged to undertake once in their lifetime.)

It was lunch time at the factory. With a sandwich in hand, I left the cutting table and wandered across the machining floor to where the pressing units were located.

Ali and a few other pressers were sitting in a group eating food. After they had finished their meal, I raised the subject of the tragedy involving the pilgrims in the Mecca tunnel.

'Wasn't it terrible Alf' sighed Ali.

The other Moslem pressers made comments too.

One man remarked 'Allah has called them.'

Another presser said to me 'Allah, for reasons we Moslems never question, allowed them to enter paradise.'

What Ali said next brought fierce looks of disapproval from his colleagues.

'Allah could and should have saved those Hajjis.'

'So what are you saying Ali.' I spoke seriously, 'Your Allah is capable of divine intervention.'

'I don't understand you Alf,' he replied 'What is divine intervention?'

After I gave my interpretation of what divine intervention meant, he remarked, 'Of course Alf, don't you think so too?'

I smiled at my old friend before saying 'Ali you should not direct that question to somebody like me who is a non-believer'.

Another presser spoke quietly, 'We Moslems accept what happened in that tunnel as Allah's will'.

I disagreed and remarked 'I am afraid, I do not see it like that at all, as far as I am concerned, it was an accident which could have been prevented. If the numbers of pedestrians were strictly controlled and the air conditioning was functioning properly, the tragedy would never have occurred.'

The same man became acerbic.

'You're a Christian, what do you know of Islam and the prophet Mohammed?'

I retaliated 'No, you are wrong, I may have been baptised a Christian, but I am not a Christian, I do not believe in God because I have never seen any proof that God exists. Therefore without proof, the existence of God must remain a theory and I cannot accept a theory as being a fact.'

'You're just a kuffi' (Non believer) he snapped.

I took up the challenge.

'It's irrelevant that I am a kuffi. Those 1,500 pilgrims' men and woman did not want to die in that tunnel, they wanted to live. If Allah exists and had the power to prevent their deaths, why did he not do so? Surely that is proof enough there is no God.'

'Allah does exist" he retorted; 'He is the beneficent, the merciful and you should be ashamed of yourself for criticising Islam.'

I was not ashamed one iota and I wanted to continue with the discussion, but a signal from Ali suggested that I should end the conversation. I left the pressers and walked back across the factory floor towards the cutting table.

In 1991 Akut announced to his staff that he would be relocating his business to another factory premises at nearby New Road. A new company would be formed and called Quick Active Fashions.

The new factory was situated in a yard at the rear of a clothing showroom. Not only was the factory small and dirty, it smelt of mice. There was also a scattering of old rat droppings under the cutting table. The mice soon made their presence known, but I saw no rats. Hopefully they had migrated elsewhere.

Whilst working at the factory, I made a serious mistake. It was my worse mistake since ruining 200 dresses at the Prideware factory 30 years previously.

This mistake also involved dresses. I had made a treble dress marker and had mistakenly used the sleeve patterns from a different style. I failed to spot my error and went ahead and layed and cut the fabric. It was only when I began to bundle the cut lay that I discovered the wrong sleeves. Realising what I had done sent me into an immediate state of utter despondency.

Salih must have noticed my anguished expression because he came over to the cutting table followed by Nejla. I asked Nejla if she would summon Akut from the office.

I was about to experience every cutter's fear, having to inform his employer of a major blunder.

With Akut and his parents now standing next to me, I explained that I had carelessly cut the wrong sleeves for over 500 dresses and there was no more fabric in stock to re-cut the sleeves.

Having admitted my carelessness, I sighed deeply and momentarily lowered my head in shame.

'It's alright, it's alright Alf' Whispered Salih who placed his hand on my shoulder.

'Not worry Alf, not worry' said Nejla kindly.

Looking up at Akut, I apologised for causing the costly setback and offered to buy new fabric to re-cut the correct sleeves.

'O no you won't' replied Akut. 'It's not a problem Alf. You never make mistakes and I don't want you to worry about it; I can deal with it.'

Their empathy and kindness affected me and with the greatest of difficulty I managed to prevent a tear trickling down onto my cheek.

Within hours, Akut managed to obtain matching fabric, which enabled me to cut the appropriate sleeves.

After trading for a couple of years, Akut decided to look for a more suitable factory. 5,000 square feet became available on the third floor at Universal House, which was at the junction of Wentworth Street and Brick Lane, Whitechapel. With the factory came a new name 'Prolex.'

The factory floor was in an excellent condition; it was spacious and had ample light. The cutting table was of a sound construction and at least 25 foot long. There was only one drawback; although the factory seemed clean, it was infested with mice and cockroaches.

Nejla had a shock. As she attempted to remove some remnants from under the cutting table, she disturbed a mouse nest. Her cry was piercing, 'fareler, fareler' (mice, mice). The nest which was made of chewed up paper contained about a dozen wriggling baby mice; pink in colour and hairless; they were probably just a day old. Scooping them up with an ash pan, I had no choice but to flush them down the toilet.

Recept soon spotted a large fat mouse by the cutting table. The mouse was probably searching for its young to milk feed them. It too was shown no mercy. Using a cardboard pole, Recept crushed it to death.

I suggested to Salih that he should get a kedi (cat) to deal with the mice, but he was not interested, instead he bought several traps, which in time reduced the mouse numbers.

Working in Turkish, Greek and Asian clothing factories, I had become accustomed to their respective music which was constantly relayed over the tannoy. I enjoyed the lively and tuneful Greek music and could tolerate the often mournful Turkish songs and rhythms, but I loathed Asian music.

'My people always sing of lost love and broken relationships,' said Turkish Arcan, my assistant layer-upper.

Because Akut employed many Asian workers he allowed their music tapes to be played throughout the day.

Arcan, who had a Turkish university degree, disliked this concession. Like me, he thought that Asian music was bland, repetitious and unmelodic.

'These Indian women singers sound like cats meowing,' he remarked sarcastically.

Arcan was not the only fellow worker who used this analogy when describing Asian music.

Forster, an African doctor of medicine, claimed to be an asylum seeker and because of his status he was unable to practise his profession in Britain.

For several weeks Forster had been working casually as a general help at the factory. I welcomed his assistance at the cutting table. As Forster and I were laying the fabric and with loud Asian music and songs being played in the background, he suddenly said 'Alfred, don't you detect a common factor with these Indian female singers?'

'I am not sure what you mean'

'Well, the singers all seem to me to produce a child-like whining sound which, dare I say it, at times is just like cats meowing.'

I was in a mischievous mood. Amongst my record collection, I had a 1967 live recording of Elisabeth Schwarzkopf and Victoria De Los Angeles singing Rossini's comic duet 'Due Gatti' (Two cats) with Gerald Moore at the piano.

Schwarzkopf and De Los Angeles do not actually sing any lyrics, but imitate two cats meowing.

Discreetly, I would borrow one of the Indian cassette tapes from the office; keep the tape over night and return it the following morning. My plan was to superimpose the 'Due gatti' duet five minutes into the tape.

The next morning, and again discreetly, I placed the altered tape into the tape recorder. I knew that when the staff arrived the music would be switched on.

Arcan was bundling at the cutting table.

When he heard the Indian music, he looked over at me and remarked 'Not that kedy music again.'

After five minutes the music stopped just for a second and the 'Due gatti' duet continued.

Unnoticed by Arcan, I gazed around the factory floor to see if there was any reaction from the workers. I was hoping that my prank would have induced laughter or smiles from the staff.

Although the tape was quite loud, no machinists raised their heads; neither did any of the pressers.

I was amazed at the staff's oblivious reaction, but it was not an entirely disappointing effort. Arcan stopped bundling and came over to me. He glanced up at the tanoy and said 'Listen Alf, if those singers aren't reincarnations of cats, then I am Genghis Khan.'

When I confessed my little prank, Arcan was unable to prevent himself from laughing. His intermittent bursts of laughter continued throughout the day.

For the next few years we were quite busy at the factory but in 1996 Akut, who was now trading as Cat Woman Ltd., found that he was receiving less dockets from his regular suppliers. The reason soon became apparent: his suppliers were increasingly outsourcing their dockets abroad.

To make up for this loss of production, Akut contacted several West End fashion houses in an attempt to obtain dockets. However, there was a problem. Akut had always manufactured cheap garments for suppliers who were more interested in quantity than quality, but these new fashion houses that he contacted, produced expensive middle-range dresses and separates where quality was essential.

It was inevitable that Akut's workforce would not be able to achieve the high standard of production which was required. I began to sense that Akut's career as a clothing factory proprietor would soon come to an end.

We were given trial dockets by the new suppliers. When these dockets were in production, their quality controllers visited the factory to inspect our work. Akut hated their visits and he soon began arguing with the controllers whenever they found fault with the garments machining, measurements and pressing. He seemed to believe that their ongoing fault finding was a personal attack on him. He also began to adopt a threatening attitude towards the QCs which caused two of them to flee from the factory.

It was obvious to me what Akut's tactics were. He thought that by scaring off the 'troublemakers', he would be able to deliver the finished garments to the showrooms without them first being checked by the QCs, but they simply examined the deliveries at the showroom.

In many cases the garments were rejected and returned to the factory for alteration or repressing.

With Cat Woman's production at a minimum, the business was no longer viable.

After a few months of struggling to find the weekly wage bill, Akut decided to close the factory indefinitely.

I had worked for Akut for almost 14 years and throughout that period never once did I or any other worker receive holiday or sick pay. Of course, there would be no redundancy pay on offer. It was unlikely that the words 'redundancy pay' was part of the Turkish vocabulary. But despite this lack of benefits, not for a single moment did I ever regret working for Akut Eral.

Akut, like so many of his Turkish friends who were former East End clothing manufacturers, would change direction. In due course he became a mini-cab driver and within a decade he had been married three times.

Salih and Nejla would retire, spending the summer in Stepney and winter at their seaside flat in Turkey. Satnum moved away from Whitechapel and became a security guard at London Airport.

Recept found a job as a nightclub doorman. After being married and divorced twice and at the young age of 36 he tragically died as a result of a heart attack.

End of an Era

Just days after the closure of Akut's factory, I began working for Uniforms Unlimited. This company manufactured garments for the ambulance service, airlines and security staff.

Although the company had its headquarters and showroom near Canary Wharf, the factory was situated on the Elisabeth Industrial Estate at Deptford south London.

Reaching the factory from my home on the Isle of Dogs was easy. I would park my car at the southern tip of the island and walk through the Greenwich foot tunnel and, emerging by the Cutty Sark, I would continue to walk to Deptford. The journey took me 45 minutes. It was a pleasant walk, especially when I reached Deptford creek. As I crossed the bridge, I would often spend a few moments watching the Prior boats discharge their cargo at the adjacent little dock. (The Prior Shipping Company based at Fingringhoe near Colchester in Essex owned a small fleet of vessels which carried sand and gravel to a number of Thames-side wharves. Each vessel is named after a member of the Prior family; Mark Prior, Brenda Prior etc.)

Some of the factories on the Elisabeth Industrial Estate were built during the late Victorian era, but the Uniforms Unlimited factory was probably erected in the 1950s.

Because the factory occupied about 5,000 square foot. I thought that there would be dozens of workers employed there, but to my surprise there were just seven men and two women employees.

As in previous factories, I was keen to obtain a little information about my new co-workers.

In charge of production was middle-aged Remsi Akbus, a hard drinking, heavy smoking Turk from Istanbul.

Remsi's perspiring red face, alarming cough and bulging stomach which overlapped his trouser belt, was the end result of years of abusing his body. Much of his time was spent, not on the factory floor, but seated in the office where he drank huge quantities of whisky and beer. Whenever his stock of alcohol and cigarettes were low, he would send one of the workers to the local off-licence to buy new supplies. These errands were a daily occurrence.

Prior to managing the factory, Remsi owned a succession of coat manufacturing companies in North London. It came to no surprise for me to learn that he had been made bankrupt on numerous occasions.

The room next to Remsi's office was occupied by Caroline, a diminutive, dark-haired designer and pattern maker who preferred to have little contact with the staff.

The other cutter, Etam, was an affable Turkish Cypriot who spoke near faultless English.

Etam, short and thickset, would cut the jackets and I would cut the slacks and skirts. We worked at the same table and soon developed an excellent working relationship. When Etam noticed that I was suffering pain from my hernia, he immediately insisted that it would be he and not me who would be responsible for lifting the heavy rolls of fabric on to the cutting table. His act of kindness was much appreciated.

Rashid from Morocco spoke perfect English and French. Although educated, he was employed at the factory as a cotton cleaner and sweeper-upper. During the lunch breaks, Rashid who had a pleasant nature often chatted with me. He was candid about his private life. For the previous twenty years he had been living in South London. Shortly after arriving in the city he had met and married a young woman from Newcastle. Within months of their daughter being born, the marriage experienced a bad period and his wife returned to Newcastle with her baby daughter. In later years Rashid's' daughter would spend several weeks during her school holidays staying at his Catford council flat. I was amazed to learn that even before she was a teenager the girl would travel down to London unaccompanied. Her mother would place her on a coach in Newcastle and Rashid would be waiting to collect her at the coach station in London.

Rashid, like so many Moslems I had spoken to in various factories, had fixed views on the ever abiding Israeli / Palestinian conflict. He firmly believed that the Israeli's had stolen the Palestinians land and that 'the Israeli aggressors' would only be evicted from Palestine by force or the threat of force. He defended the right of Iran and possibly Egypt to possess nuclear weapons. 'If the Israelis' have atom bombs, they can't complain if the Arab states have them too.'

'But surely Rashid' I argued 'You don't honestly believe that Israel would dare drop atom bombs on its Arab neighbours?'

Rashid did not agree, he thought that in the event of Israel losing a conventional war the Knesset would not hesitate in ordering its nuclear strike force to attack her enemies. He also believed it was inevitable that Iran would be the first Islamic country in the Middle East to have a nuclear capability. He quickly added, 'but Iran would never use atomic weapons on Israel because not only would the Jews be wiped out, so would Israel's large Palestinian community.'

I questioned him further. 'If Iran would never attack Israel with atom bombs what would be the purpose of developing the bomb in the first place?'

Rashid had an available answer. 'To scare the Israelis into leaving Palestine. Once the Jews know that a hostile Iran had nuclear bombs, they would migrate abroad en mass and after their departure the country would again be occupied by its rightful owners – the Palestinian people.'

I did not accept Rashid's analysis, although I did agree with him on one important point. There was no doubt in my mind that Iran would in the future possess atom bombs.

'Of course,' said Rashid, 'the situation could change overnight. If the Americans and the world community managed to persuade the Israelis to remove their atomic arsenal then the Iranians would have no option but to abandon their nuclear plans too.'

Rashid proved he was a good listener when I suggested what I had always considered to be the best solution to solve the Israeli/Palestinian crisis. I explained that Israel and Palestine should merge and become one country. By joint ownership the two communities could administer the new nation as partners not as rivals. Jewish immigration should be restricted until all of the Palestinians who are languishing in refuge camps scattered around the Middle East are allowed to return.

Unlike David Upson, who dismissed my plan as 'unworkable', Rashid thought it was an excellent idea.

Rashid was also an admirer of the maverick Scottish MP George Galloway, who he thought understood Arab politics and the situation in the Middle East far better than any other British MP or government minister.

'Because Galloway speaks the truth he is ostracised,' exclaimed my friend. 'If there was only a dozen other MPs who held similar views to Galloway, they could oppose the influence of the Conservative and Labour friends of Israel in parliament.'

Besides the perennial crisis in the Middle East which seemed to occupy much of Rashid's thoughts, he often mentioned a personal problem that concerned him deeply. He felt embarrassed by the shape of his nose. Two or three times he asked me the same question.

'Don't you think my nose is to fat, Alf? '

Each time I gave him the same answer 'No, not at all.'

He responded wistfully. 'I wish I had a little pointed nose.'

I explained that if he was really concerned about its shape, there was a simple remedy which would give him peace of mind. 'Your suggesting a nose job aren't you Alf? '

'Well, em, yes I am actually.'

Rashid said that he had made some enquires about having a new nose, but he could not have the operation done under the national health service because it was considered to be a cosmetic operation. But he had been told by a friend that there were clinics in Poland where the operation could be done quite cheaply.

'For the sake of a few hundred pounds I can have a little pointed nose which I have always wanted.'

Sadly for Rashid his dream would never be fulfilled.

Another employee I enjoyed chatting to during the lunch breaks was Mauritian-born Bertie Latchman, who was responsible for stayflexing the jacket facings.

Bertie looked about sixty. He had spent twenty years in the Royal Navy as an electrician. After leaving the navy he joined the maintenance staff at the BBC's headquarters in London's Langham Place. Taking early retirement from the BBC, he devoted much of his spare time tending his large garden. He originally had no plans to ever work again, but he was persuaded by his brother-in-law Fermi, who was a Hoffman presser at Uniforms, to accept a vacancy as a stayflex presser.

Bertie, a kind and happy man, constantly giggled and was well-liked by the staff. Although he had left Mauritius forty years previously, he still retained a pleasant soft French accent. Always generous, he insisted on sharing his home-grown vegetables or 'greens' as he called them, with us fellow workers.

Fermi, a Christian Armenian who spoke Turkish, looked a very sick man. He was overweight and hunchback and walking seemed arduous for him. Throughout the day, he chain-smoked and kept several cans of beer on a bench by his Hoffman pressing machine.

It was customary for Remsi, as he passed the Hoffman to snatch the can which the accommodating Fermi was drinking from and have a quick swig. I once counted the time it took Remsi to stop at the Hoffman, grab the can, swallow the beer and be on his way; it was five seconds.

When I mentioned Remsi's behaviour to Barbara Upson, she uttered just one word – 'dipsomania'.

The second female staff member was tall, blonde Christine who worked the special machines. She was born in Poland during the early 1950s and married to an Englishman. Christine was a fading beauty; although middle-aged she had a trim and upright figure.

Without question, Christine was the bibulous Remsi's favourite worker and he granted her concessions which were denied to the other workers. Her extended tea and lunch breaks were always spent in his office where she was a willing partaker of the ever available alcohol. She was also allowed mini breaks during the day.

A not too discreet signal from Remsi would cause Christine to switch off her buttonhole machine, pick up her cigarettes and, with head bowed, walk quickly past the other workers and disappear into Remsi's office.

I did not find the two other workers, Nelson, a Nigerian presser, and Abdul, a Bangladeshi machinist, particularly friendly. Several times I attempted to make conversation with both men, but failed.

Nelson did not trust British police. He was adamant that the police were not interested in bringing the killers of Stephen Lawrence to justice.

'And why is that?' I asked, knowing full well what his answer would be.

'Because Lawrence was black,' he replied indignantly.

Not trusting and even despising British police seemed to me to be a common factor amongst the many Nigerians whom I had known in clothing factories. Their prejudice probably had its origin in Nigeria, where the police force had a reputation for being extremely corrupt.

Abdul, a Moslem, may have resented me because I accidentally disturbed him while he was praying. I was not informed that Remsi had allowed him to use a small fabric stock room as a prayer area. When I entered the poorly lit stock room for the first time I almost tripped over his kneeling body.

Besides being a machinist, Abdul would visit car auctions during the evenings and buy second-hand vehicles which he later sold to Bangladeshis living in Tower Hamlets.

I put a question to Abdul. 'Do you give your customers guarantees?'

'Of course not' he snapped. 'All my customers know what they are buying from me, if the cars break down, so what.'

I enjoyed working at the Uniforms Unlimited factory. Not only was it a congenial and relaxing atmosphere, it was exceptionally quiet. The music from the tannoy was not loud and with so few noisy sewing machines in operation the vibrations were at a minimum. Another agreeable factor was Remsi, who preferred the staff to work on their own initiative and only contact him if it was absolutely necessary. Each morning, Remsi would give Etam and me our work dockets before quickly retreating to his office and the comforts of alcohol and cigarettes.

Although the staff members were allowed to chat as we worked, most of us chose not to. We also worked at a slow pace and never once did Remsi encourage us to increase the production.

I was content to remain at Uniforms for the foreseeable future, but it was not to be. Two years after I began to work at the factory, the owner of the company sold the business to his marketing director.

The new owner retained the showroom but closed the factory. Shortly after the sale I was the first of the employees to be told that my services 'were no longer required.'

I was not eligible for redundancy pay, but the rest of the workforce, who had been employed at the factory for several years were offered small amounts of money as compensation.

Because of the friendships I had formed with Rashid, Bertie and Etam, I remained in contact with them after they were made redundant, but within two to three years, illness and death was cruelly inflicted on my former workmates. Bertie contracted prostate cancer and soon died. Fermi, who was in his mid forties, passed away in his sleep and, following Etam's separation from his wife, pemphigus, a distressing skin disease, was diagnosed.

Rashid was not spared either; he became ill with colon cancer, the same illness that killed his mother. Etam and I went to see Rashid at his sparse Catford council flat where his teenage daughter had arrived from Newcastle to look after him.

It was upsetting to see Rashid, a once fit and sprightly man lying on a sofa covered by a blanket. A small coffee table by his side was full of various tablets and medicines. Although he was an extremely sick man, he seemed to be in good spirits.

Eventually, Rashid's daughter was unable to cope with his deteriorating condition and he was admitted to St. Francis's Hospice at Sydenam South London. When Etam and I went to visit Rashid at the hospice, I was given sad news by one of the staff. The wonderful Dame Cicely Saunders, who was instrumental in establishing St. Francis's in the 1950s, was also a terminally ill patient at the hospice.

With just days to live, Rashid appeared calm and at peace. Our conversation was light-hearted, but we also reminisced about our time at Uniforms Unlimited. After Rashid became sleepy, Etam and I decided to leave. I glanced back at our mutual friend as we quietly left the ward. Rashid's eyes were closed and his arms were folded across his chest. In one hand he was holding the Koran.

My attempts to find a cutting vacancy after I was laid off at Uniforms Unlimited proved difficult. There were so few clothing factories left in the East End and those which were still in business had adequate staff.

As I passed factory premises near Limehouse Station, I could hear the familiar vibrations of sewing machines in operation. On impulse, I rang the factory bell.

A Sikh opened the door and politely said 'I am Mr Singh the managing director, can I help you.'

I explained that I was an experienced stock cutter and was looking for full or part time work.

'How strange' he replied. 'I happen to need a temporary cutter while my regular cutter is ill.'

I followed him up the stairs to the first floor where we went into a large noisy production area. The entire workforce, numbering approximately twenty, was Asian.

As we walked towards the cutting table, I asked Singh how long the temporary position would last.

He replied assuringly 'I can guarantee you a minimum five days work.'

Standing by the cutting table, I asked about the wages on offer.

His reply was instant. 'Five pounds an hour, payable at the end of each working day.'

Because the hourly rate was reasonable I accepted it.

The solid built cutting table which seemed to be about 25 foot long was parallel with the windows; a stack of 60 inch wide fabric was close by.

After Singh gave me a dress sample and its patterns, he pointed to the fabric and said, 'those rolls of cloth are for your docket'.

He outlined my work plan. I would cut a thousand dresses; the sizes would be 10,12,14 and 16 and the cutting ratio 1, 2,1,1.

Once I had made the marker I would be allocated an assistant to help me to lay the fabric. I hoped this assistant could speak adequate English.

Making the marker would be simple and the arithmetic involved even simpler. I needed to make a marker for five dresses, and 200 lays of fabric would be sufficient for the required 1,000 dresses.

After I had completed the marker and was ready to lay the fabric Singh assigned a young English speaking Punjabi woman as my assistant layer-upper.

The woman, whose name was Indira, wore a sari ,and around her neck dangled a long chiffon scarf.

I had always felt that the customary habit of Asian women wearing scarfs in clothing factories was a risk factor. I had known of incidents where some women had nearly been asphyxiated when their scarfs had become entangled in the revolving belts of sewing machines.

Indira handled the fabric confidently; she explained that besides her main job in the factory which was cotton cleaning she often had to help the cutter to lay wide fabric.

By the early evening Indira and I had finished laying the fabric. When my assistant returned to her cotton cleaning duties Singh came over to the cutting table. His contented expression was an indication that he was satisfied with my work. Standing alongside me he took a wallet from his pocket, gave me 40 pounds and said

'That's for eight hours work, Arthur.'

In fact, I had done nine hours work, but I was not prepared to demand the five pounds which he should have paid me. I was grateful that Singh had offered me five days work. Over the years, I had occasionally been cheated by devious factory proprietors; usually it was for small amounts of money, so I rarely complained.

As I buttoned up my coat, I asked Singh what time would he want me to start work the following morning.

His contented expression suddenly changed. He glanced downwards and hesitated before answering.

'Unfortunately Arthur, there is a change of plans; my cutter has just phoned me to say that he has recovered and is eager to return to work.'

Still glancing downwards he added 'So I am afraid I don't need you anymore.'

I was not surprised that Singh had changed his plans; past experience had taught me that the role of a part time or freelance cutter was precarious. At the end of a working day, you were never sure if you would be layed off.

Jock, my freelance cutter friend, was prone to react truculently to employers if he was ever given the 'high jump' at short notice.

Listening to Singh giving me the high jump, I began to feel that it was now within my rights to demand the five pounds which he owed me.

My tone was polite but business like.

'Regarding my wages Mr Singh, I should mention that there is a discrepancy, you only paid me for eight hours work when I actually worked nine hours.'

'You did' he said with a phoney expression of surprise.

I replied firmly 'Yes I did.'

Singh probably realised that I would not move away from the cutting table unless he gave me the five pounds and fearing an unwanted dispute, he immediately gave me five one pound coins.

After I put the money in my pocket he said, 'I must apologise for my mistake Arthur'.

Instead of replying, I glared at him before heading towards the exit. Suddenly Singh called out to me. 'Arthur, would you leave me your phone number, just in case I need to contact you for future work.'

Reluctantly, I came back to the cutting table and gave him my phone number, which he wrote down on one of the dress patterns. Moments later, I was out of the factory and walking eastwards along the busy and noisy Commercial Road.

I spent the next few days visiting East End job centres. During one of these visits I was offered a rare stock cutting vacancy.

The factory was situated in an old industrial building in Pixley Street, Stepney and when I arrived the manager, a Mr O'Conner, interviewed me by the cutting table. He explained that the vacancy was not permanent and probably would last for no more than a fortnight. He also wanted to know how long I had been cutting dresses.

When I said more than forty years, he looked aghast and remarked 'My god, you must have seen some changes during that period.'

I was not particularly interested in talking about the history of the clothing industry, but I did say that when I came into the trade in March 1956 it was a flourishing and still expanding manufacturing industry and now, forty years later, I was witnessing its demise.

O'Conner sighed deeply before remarking 'You are of course right, we are witnessing the demise.'

Collecting his thoughts, he introduced me to Jim, one of the other cutters.

'Alfred, you and Jim can work together for the next fortnight.'

Although the production floor was spacious and the cutting tables well constructed, the antiquated gents WCs which were located in a cellar were extremely unhygienic. Water leakage was everywhere.

Jim told me that 'periodically the water dries out but it always comes back'. He thought that the putrid leakage had somehow seeped into the cellar via the adjacent Limehouse cut.

Fortunately, there was an iron rail which you could hang on to when you trod on the slimy wet stairs which led to the cellar. Much of the floor by the urinals was covered by an inch of water and the malodorous cubicles were absolutely disgusting, I had seen cleaner pigsties at the Mudchute Farm on the Isle of Dogs.

Jim explained that he and other male employees had complained to the management about the leakage, but to no avail. He assumed that the management were uninterested in modernising the WCs because they did not have any spare funds. He had also heard through the 'grapevine' that the business would probably go into receivership later in the year.

'I am not worried at all,' he remarked. 'I have had enough of this bleeding trade anyway.'

Jim had 'contingency plans in hand' if he was made redundant; one option would be to become a refuse collector. He suggested that because the 'rag trade was on its last legs' I should become a refuse collector too 'for the job security'.

I appreciated Jim's thoughtfulness, but after spending 42 years in the clothing trade and carrying thousands of rolls of fabric on my shoulders, I had no desire to embark on a new career humping dustbins.

Mr O'Conner was correct, my tenure at the factory lasted just two weeks.

Several years later I met Jim in the street. He could barely remember me, but he did confirm that the factory had indeed gone into liquidation and that he was now working as a refuse collector.

After leaving the Pixley Street factory, I continued to look for work, but I was disappointed, not a single stock cutting vacancy was being advertised in job centres or the local press and when I took the bus to Aldgate East, which was once the centre of the East End clothing trade, I was further disappointed. The Star Agency, which only recruited garment workers, had closed down and the few remaining clothing factories in the area had removed their vacancy boards.

I soon got over my disappointment and would just have to adapt, like so many of my cutter friends, and find alternative work, but the jobs I was offered were unappealing. I just could not imagine myself being a security guard, a supermarket shelf stacker or a mini-cab driver.

A friend who knew that I was unemployed told me that the principle of a college in East Ham was looking for somebody who could teach part-time trouser cutting. I made enquires about the post, but the college principle failed to acknowledge my letter.

As the weeks went by, the thought of returning to work seemed less appealing, especially after my partner Linda suggested that I should devote my spare time to writing a book about my 37-year friendship with David Upson.

I liked her suggestion, but was a little unsure if I was capable of writing a book.

Eventually, after further encouragement from Linda, I began writing the book in earnest. The book would be entitled 'An East End Story, a tale of friendship'.

Even before the manuscript was finished, I was already planning to write another book which would be a chronicle of my long career as a cutter in the East End clothing trade. Included in the book would be numerous photos of the factories that I had worked at since 1956.

With camera in hand I wandered around the East End.

It was unlikely that the excursion would be very successful; many of the factories and ghastly workshops had either been demolished or converted into offices and dwellings.

It was pointless visiting Blythe Street at Bethnal Green where the A&B Hyams factory was originally located; the street had been demolished 30 years previously.

I soon made my way to Poplar High Street. The industrial building where T& J Blake had their factory was still there, but the three storey building only had one tenant: a firm of stationary suppliers occupying the ground floor. The upper floors were empty.

The ancient Wills dress factory which was situated on the corner of Commercial Road and Albert Gardens had been bulldozed away in the 1970s. Ugly council flats now occupied the site. Even today, when I pass this location I can vividly recall the occasion when I was almost trapped by a fire in the basement cutting room.

In Cavell Street, the C&H Fashions factory at number 52 had been demolished in the 1980s and was now replaced by a dismal tiny park. The well constructed factory at number 54 where David Upson framed bags for D&W handbags had been converted into 12 apartments.

At Copperfield Road in Bow, change had also taken place. Although there were still a few businesses located at the southern end of the road adjacent to the Ragged School Museum, none were clothing manufacturers.

The post-war factories at the northern end of the road had been demolished. Where these factories once stood, luxury apartments had been built and more were in the process of being erected.

The Falcon Works factory building that originally housed six clothing manufacturers, including New Image, had already been converted into dwellings.

During the late 1980s Bill and Nick, the directors of New Image, ceased trading as dress sub-contractors and began manufacturing children's clothes under their own label, mainly for the Middle East market.

In 1997 New Image went bankrupt and their 30 employees lost their jobs. Apparently crooked importers in Saudi Arabia and Kuwait withheld large sums of money that was owed to Bill and Nick. Shortly afterwards this odd couple settled in the Greek section of Cyprus to manage their hotel.

Ellis, the noted bridal wear makers, also vacated Falcon Works in the late 1990s and moved their business to Wood Green in North London. They also ceased manufacturing wedding dresses in Britain. It seems sad to me that Ellis's, who once employed a highly competent workforce, producing first class garments which were exported to over 20 countries, now prefer to out source their production to China.

One cannot but wonder how many former skilled machinists who were made redundant during the decline of the East End clothing industry are now working as low-paid, part time checkout staff in various East London supermarkets.

The large factory building in Cannon Street Road where Akut's company Good Gear Ltd was situated had a change of use. After the four other clothing companies in the building had ceased production during the 1990s, St. Paul's College of Further Education became the only occupant of the entire building.

Sclare & Lee's factory in adjacent Rampart Street remained, but it had been converted into apartments.

The three former Wearwell Factories in the nearby Commercial Road were now offices.

At the eastern end of Ali Street the huge vacant industrial building seemed abandoned. Several of the windows were broken or cracked and those which remained were in an unclean state. In 1972 I worked briefly as a relief dress cutter for one of the firms on the second floor. Other clothing firms on the premises manufactured skirts, trousers, knitwear and anoraks.

The old Marshall Walker factory in the centre of Ali Street had been demolished and was replaced by a characterless office block. Fagin's rat infested workshop in nearby Leman Street and Lui's café next door had been obliterated several years previously.

Ten minutes later I was in Spitalfields. The eighteen century house in Artillery Lane which was occupied by Greycloth Limited, a rayon dress manufacturer in 1961 and where I pushed Carter the nasty manager to the floor, looked exactly like it did all those years ago. I was unable to determine if the house was now a dwelling or an office. Just two hundred yards away in Fashion Street, the old Myers dress factory remained intact. But the factory had been transformed into offices. A company called First Conference Ltd who promote and market business through conferences, had their headquarters in the building..

A cloth merchant was now operating from the former B&S Katz's workshop at no 52 Brick Lane.

Universal House on the corner of Brick Lane and Wentworth Street was empty. In 1996, besides Akut, who was trading on the top floor as Cat Woman, there were two coat manufactures on the lower floors.

With my photographic record completed, I walked home to the Isle of Dogs.

Although not a single clothing factory or workshop remained at Whitechapel, where there were once dozens, the area still retained a thriving link with the fashion trade. Many wholesale clothing warehouses, mostly stocked with foreign made garments, were centred around the western end of Commercial Road.

As Britain is now a major importer of cheap clothes, it seems to me that these wholesale clothing warehouses will be in business for the foreseeable future.

Besides clothing manufacturing in the East End other local and traditional industries have also disappeared. Following the closure of the five London Docks that began in 1967, many small companies that serviced the docks, which included ships towage, warfingers, transport contractors, ship stores suppliers, engineering firms, shipwrights, coppersmiths and foundries, went out of business.

In 1959 there were four major breweries in Stepney, but less than 30 years later there were none.

The first brewery to close was Taylor Walker's Barley Mow Brewery at Limehouse in 1960. 15 years later Charrington's Anchor Brewery in the Mile End Road also ceased production.

Mann, Crossman and Paulin's Albion Brewery, which was situated in the Whitechapel Road, closed in 1979.

As I walked down Brady Street each morning on my way to work at Bethnal Green during the late 1950s, I would be pleasantly engulfed by the all pervading aroma of the brewing process which emitted from the sprawling nearby Albion Brewery. My friend Peter Reece Edwards, who had spent most of his working life in West London breweries, explained that what I could smell were the hops, yeast, barley and malt being boiled in giant kettles.

In 1988 the famous Ben Truman's Brewery which had been established in Brick Lane at Spitalfields since 1666 finally closed its doors. It seems that Ben Truman had gone out of business because it had become extremely difficult for their big lorries to negotiate the old narrow streets surrounding the brewery.

During recent years, scores of minor but long-established manufacturing companies in the East End had either moved their production out of the area, gone into liquidation or had their factories seized through the council's compulsory purchase policy. Where these businesses premises were originally situated huge council housing estates now occupy the space.

In 1968 a Bow Common Lane road haulier, who was forced to give up his transport depot under the terms of a compulsory purchase order, predicted that other local companies would soon have to vacate their premises 'as Tower Hamlets Council wants the land to build a vast dormitory'.

With hundreds of industrial buildings demolished, it is unlikely that there will ever be significant engineering companies, furniture manufacturers, food processors, furriers, handbag and hat makers in Tower Hamlets again.

It saddens me deeply to think that so many skilled jobs have gone and others felt the same way.

At Frank's café near the eastern end of Commercial Road while enjoying one of Frank's noted ham-off-the-bone sandwiches, I began to eavesdrop on a querulous octogenarian's conversation with two elderly ex-dockers.

'The effing country has gone down the pan and it's the effing welfare state that's caused it. If we didn't have an effing welfare state, you wouldn't have millions of free loaders from the third world living here.'

'Your so right Nobby' lamented Sam, who was shaking his head.

Nobby continued, 'would you believe it, every effing electrical appliance in our flat is made in the Far East: washing machine, television, wireless, kettle even my old woman's hair dryer, don't we effing make stuff anymore?' Sam reinforced Nobby's argument by stating 'My reading light is made in China.'

The third docker mentioned that all of the toys which he had bought for his grandchildren at Christmas had been produced in China too.

Before the three men changed their conversation to horse and greyhound racing, Nobby had the final say, 'we should only import effing stuff which we can't produce ourselves'.

The ex-dockers conversation was typical of what I have listened to in recent years, especially in the local pubs and cafes. Should Britain only import goods which we can not manufacture ourselves? Nobby thought so, but for somebody like me, who had witnessed the collapse of the once mighty and well established East End clothing industry, his suggestion must remain a pipe dream.